AUSTRALIAN CONSTITUTIONAL VALUES

Vigorous debate exists among constitutional scholars as to the appropriate 'modalities' of constitutional argument, and their relative weight. Many scholars, however, argue that one important modality of constitutional argument involves attention to underlying constitutional purposes or 'values'. In Australia, this kind of values-oriented approach has been advocated by leading constitutional scholars, and also finds support in the judgments of the High Court at various times, particularly during the Mason Court era. Much of the scholarly debate on constitutional values to date, however, focuses on whether the Court should in fact look to constitutional values in this way, not the kinds of values the Court should consider, given such an approach.

This book responds to this gap in the existing scholarly literature, by inviting a range of leading Australian constitutional lawyers and scholars to address the relevance and scope of various substantive constitutional values, and how they might affect the Court's approach to constitutional interpretation in various contexts. It is essential reading for anyone seeking a deeper understanding of Australia's constitutional system.

Volume 21 in the series Hart Studies in Comparative Public Law

Hart Studies in Comparative Public Law

Recent titles in this series:

The Scope and Intensity of Substantive Review
Traversing Taggart's Rainbow
Edited by Hanna Wilberg and Mark Elliott

Entick v Carrington
250 Years of the Rule of Law
Edited by Adam Tomkins and Paul Scott

Administrative Law and Judicial Deference
Matthew Lewans

Soft Law and Public Authorities
Remedies and Reform
Greg Weeks

Legitimate Expectations in the Common Law World
Edited by Matthew Groves and Greg Weeks

The Dynamics of Exclusionary Constitutionalism
Mazen Masri

Constitutional Courts, Gay Rights and Sexual Orientation Equality
Angioletta Sperti

Principled Reasoning in Human Rights Adjudication
Se-Shauna Wheatle

Human Rights and Judicial Review in Australia and Canada
Janina Boughey

The Foundations and Traditions of Constitutional Amendment
Edited by Richard Albert, Xenophon Contiades and Alkmene Fotiadou

The Federal Idea
Public Law Between Governance and Political Life
Edited by Amnon Lev

Comparative Federalism
Constitutional Arrangements and Case Law
Francesco Palermo and Karl Kössler

Governance by Numbers
The Making of a Legal Model of Allegiance
Alain Supiot

Australian Constitutional Values

Edited by
Rosalind Dixon

•HART•
OXFORD • LONDON • NEW YORK • NEW DELHI • SYDNEY

HART PUBLISHING

Bloomsbury Publishing Plc

Kemp House, Chawley Park, Cumnor Hill, Oxford, OX2 9PH, UK

HART PUBLISHING, the Hart/Stag logo, BLOOMSBURY and the Diana logo are trademarks of Bloomsbury Publishing Plc

First published in Great Britain 2018

A catalogue record for this book is available from the British Library.

Library of Congress Cataloging-in-Publication data

Names: Dixon, Rosalind, editor.

Title: Australian constitutional values / edited by Rosalind Dixon.

Description: Oxford [UK] ; Portland, Oregon : Hart Publishing, 2018. | Series: Hart studies in comparative public law ; volume 21 | Includes bibliographical references and index.

Identifiers: LCCN 2017050987 (print) | LCCN 2017050500 (ebook) | ISBN 9781509918416 (Epub) | ISBN 9781509918409 (hardback)

Subjects: LCSH: Constitutional law—Australia. | Australia—Politics and government.

Classification: LCC KU1750 (print) | LCC KU1750 .A933 2018 (ebook) | DDC 342.94—dc23

LC record available at https://lccn.loc.gov/2017050987

ISBN: HB: 978-1-50991-840-9
ePDF: 978-1-50991-842-3
ePub: 978-1-50991-841-6

Typeset by Compuscript Ltd, Shannon

Foreword

This interesting collection of stimulating essays contributes to the debate on functionalist constitutional interpretation in Australia by identifying distinctive Australian constitutional values—values that find support in the text, history and structure of the Australian Constitution. The essays focus on values which are not wholly co-extensive with, or protected by, independent constitutional guarantees—such as the implied freedom of political communication and the requirement that all acquisition of property by the Commonwealth for its purposes shall be on just terms. The reason for this focus is that the contributors are looking for non-controlling values which may be relevant, even influential, in the consideration of questions of constitutional interpretation or construction.

Functionalist interpretation, as Professor Dixon points out in chapter one of this collection, is a close relation of realism and pragmatism. It is an interpretive approach inviting consideration of policy factors and practical consequences of judicial decisions, as well as questions of political morality. For present purposes, the importance of functionalism is that it argues the High Court should engage with values which are sourced in the text, history and structure of the Constitution and, also, prior constitutional precedents.

Although these essays focus on the use of values in constitutional interpretation, constitutional values—once identified—will unquestionably have an impact not only on statute law but also on the development of the common law, except in so far as the value itself is grounded in the common law. Just what that impact will be, will depend on the specific issues which arise for consideration, and just as the value will be non-controlling in the context of constitutional interpretation, it will also be generally non-controlling in the development of the common law.

Values tend to be abstract and general. For this reason, apart from any other, they tend to be non-controlling and to constitute one of a number of factors to be taken into account—whether the issue under consideration is one of interpretation or of common law. The non-controlling aspect of a value is significant because it is important to avoid—as far as it is legitimate to do so—constitutionally colonising aspects of the common law. Constitutionalisation of the common law impairs the freedom of legislatures to legislate on the relevant subject.

A critical question is whether constitutional values are values from the 1900s or contemporary ones. In my view, the relevant constitutional values are contemporary after taking into account history and precedents as well as text and structure. The Constitution speaks not only to the generation in which it was adopted but also to future generations. Therefore, its interpretation is necessarily linked to contemporary conditions and circumstances, and, even more relevantly, to values as they have developed over the life of the Constitution.

Because the Australian Constitution is in its essence a framework of government for a federation, it is concerned with the powers of government and limitations upon those powers, rather than with the rights of individuals. The Constitution contains no Charter or Bill of Rights, and it has little to say about the relationship between government and citizen. So, in terms of express values, the constitutional cupboard is relatively bare; and, so far, the High Court has done relatively little to distil values from the provisions of the Constitution which can play a part in constitutional interpretation or construction, accepting the distinction between the two made by Professor Goldsworthy in his chapter in this collection.

This feature of Australian constitutional jurisprudence is a consequence of the legalism which has been a central element in Australian constitutional interpretation. Legalism focuses on the text and structure of the provisions of the Constitution; so much so, that there are statements that it is not permissible to look to values located outside the text and structure of the Constitution as factors relevant to constitutional interpretation.[1] This approach would seem to exclude values derived from constitutional history, traditions and assumptions on which the Constitution was based, such as the rule of law, to which Sir Owen Dixon resorted to in *Australian Communist Party v Commonwealth*.[2] The shortcomings of the limited text and structure approach to values have been exposed by Professor Adrienne Stone.[3]

The suggested exclusion of considerations not found in the text and structure of the Constitution is driven by concerns about legitimacy, arising from the constitutional separation of legislative, executive and judicial powers as well as the limited scope of judicial power. To desert the text and structure of the Constitution might attract criticism that the Court is taking into account non-constitutional values, even the personal values of the Justices themselves. After all, the main advantage of legalism as an interpretive approach has been that it gives the appearance of an exclusive engagement with the words and structure of the Constitution itself, however illusory this may be.

The contributors, though broadly supportive of functional constitutional interpretation, point in varying degrees to problems in identifying and using particular values sought to be derived from the Australian Constitution. By way of a preliminary caution, we need to recollect that the *Engineers Case*[4] affirmed responsible government is the central principle of democratic government under the Australian Constitution. Associated with this is another major principle, that of parliamentary supremacy, as enunciated by Professor AV Dicey, significantly qualified nevertheless by limitations arising from the Constitution itself. More importantly, the legislative powers granted have always been regarded as plenary, subject again to such

[1] See *McGinty v Western Australia* (1996) 186 CLR 140, 182–83 (Dawson J), 231, 233–34 (McHugh J); *Lange v Australian Broadcasting Corporation* (1997) 189 CLR 520, 567 (Brennan CJ, Dawson, Toohey, Gaudron, McHugh, Gummow and Kirby JJ).

[2] (1951) 83 CLR 1, 193 (*Communist Party Case*).

[3] See 'The Limits of Constitutional Text and Structure: Standards of Review and the Freedom of Political Communication' [1999] 23 *Melbourne University Law Review* 668; 'The Limits of Constitutional Text and Structure Revisited' (2005) 28(3) *UNSW Law Journal* 842.

[4] *Amalgamated Society of Engineers v Adelaide Steamship Co Ltd* (1920) 28 CLR 129.

limitations as are to be found in the Constitution itself. Hence, the primacy of the political process under the Constitution. Questions of policy and politics, including protection of individual rights, are left predominantly to legislative choice and judgment.[5]

It is therefore difficult, indeed impossible, to distil constitutional values which are at variance with these constitutional characteristics. This difficulty explains why most constitutional implications found in the Australian Constitution have been located in Ch III dealing with the Judicature. Nonetheless, the chapters in this collection discuss possible constitutional values which stand, at least in part, outside Ch III—such as government accountability, democratic delineation, political equality, equal treatment and non-discrimination and liberty. Other values discussed, for example the rule of law and impartial justice, are more closely related to Ch III.

Of all the values discussed in this collection, the rule of law has the strongest case for recognition, if only by reason of its *imprimatur* by Sir Owen Dixon in the *Communist Party Case*.[6] In his judgment in this case, he remarked that the Constitution was framed in accordance with many traditional conceptions—to some of which it gives effect, others are simply assumed—and that the rule of law forms such an assumption. He then proceeded to state why a law which depended for its validity on a legislative recital of the law's connection with the power relied upon, the incidental power, could not be sustained, having regard to the rule of law.

As Lisa Burton Crawford notes in chapter five of this collection, the rule of law has many facets, some of which may well be incorporated in the Constitution itself rather than constitute values which inform its interpretation or values on which it is based. One such facet or element of the rule of law is access to justice which would seem to be the essential foundation of much of the High Court's rhetoric (an expression which I do not use in a pejorative or critical sense) about the important role of section 75(v) of the Constitution in enabling the High Court to keep the Executive within the limits of the law.

Indeed, the High Court could make use of this element of the rule of law. The Supreme Court of the United Kingdom has recently described access to justice as a central element of the rule of law and as a constitutional right.[7] Even if, in the Australian constitutional context, this might be a step too far, there is a strong case for arguing that it is a constitutional value.

Crawford rightly points out that section 75(v) of the Constitution secures a basic element of the rule of law, namely ensuring the means by which the executive branch of government does not trespass beyond the functions and powers assigned to it by law. Likewise, the separation of powers has influenced, if not defined, the scope of judicial interpretation of statutes. On the other hand, Crawford identifies some aspects said to be inherent in the rule of law, which are not enshrined in the Constitution. The consequence is that the Constitution does incorporate some rule

[5] See S Gageler, 'Beyond the Text: A Vision of the Structure and Function of the Constitution' (2009) 32 *Australian Bar Review* 138, especially at 151–52.

[6] *Communist Party Case* (1951) 83 CLR 1, 193.

[7] *R (UNISON) v Lord Chancellor* [2017] UKSC 51.

of law values which can be availed of in constitutional interpretation, even if the occasion for resorting to them may be limited.

A similar comment may be made about Sarah Murray's chapter, 'Impartial Justice'. The very object of judicial independence, which the Constitution is so concerned to secure by its provisions in Ch III, is to promote impartial judicial decision-making. The value of judicial independence and judicial impartiality as a characteristic of the constitutional conception of a 'court' has been a driving force in the High Court's refinement of the *Kable* principle.

Murray makes the interesting suggestion that judicial impartiality can be linked to procedural fairness, thereby enabling that concept to be called in aid as a constitutional value. Another suggestion is that recognition of judicial impartiality as a constitutional value could possibly lead to a reformation of the *Boilermakers* principle that prohibits a Ch lll court from exercising non-judicial functions.

In his chapter on liberty, James Stellios identifies a variety of potential sources of support for liberty as a constitutional value in the text and structure of the Constitution. It can, of course, be said of liberty that—text and structure apart—it is so strongly embedded in the common law that it forms part of not only our history but, more importantly, of our fundamental and traditional legal conceptions and in this way is a relevant constitutional value.[8] We can make the same comment about other strong common law values—such as freedom of expression, which was called in aid in *Davis v Commonwealth*[9]—to justify the conclusion that certain prohibitions on the use of various expressions associated with the bi-centenary of Australia were disproportionate, and therefore outside the scope of the implied incidental power.

I conclude by observing that the values relevant to constitutional interpretation are more likely to be found in the traditions which influence our Constitution, than in the text and structure of the Constitution itself, and that, following Sir Owen Dixon, it may be more appropriate to refer to traditional conceptions rather than to history,[10] acknowledging of course that history enables us to identify what these conceptions are.

Sir Anthony Mason
Former Chief Justice of Australia

[8] See *M68/2015 v Minister for Immigration and Border Protection* (2016) 257 CLR 42, 99 [138]–[139], 103–05 [155]–[159] (Gageler J); P Gerangelos, 'Section 61 of the Commonwealth Constitution and an "Historical Constitutional Approach": An Excursus on Justice Gageler's Reasoning in the M68 Case' (2017) forthcoming *University of Western Australia Law Review*.

[9] (1988) 166 CLR 79.

[10] *Communist Party Case* (1951) 83 CLR 1, 193.

Table of Contents

Notes on Contributors

Rebecca Ananian-Welsh is a Lecturer at the University of Queensland TC Beirne School of Law.

Gabrielle Appleby is Associate Professor and Co-Director, The Judiciary Project, Gilbert + Tobin Centre of Public Law, UNSW.

Nicholas Aroney is Professor of Constitutional Law at the University of Queensland.

Janina Boughey is a Senior Lecturer at UNSW Law School.

Lisa Burton Crawford is a Lecturer at the UNSW Law School.

Jonathan Crowe is Professor of Law at Bond University.

Rosalind Dixon is Professor of Law at UNSW Sydney, director of the Gilbert + Tobin Centre of Public Law Comparative Constitutional Project and co-president elect of the International Society of Public Law.

Jeffrey Goldsworthy is Emeritus Professor of Law at Monash University and Adjunct Professor of Law, University of Adelaide.

Brendan Lim is a Barrister, New South Wales Bar and Fellow, Gilbert + Tobin Centre of Public Law, UNSW.

Dylan Lino is a Lecturer at the University of Western Australia Law School.

Nicola McGarrity is a Senior Lecturer at UNSW Law School.

Sarah Murray is Associate Professor at the University of Western Australia Law School.

Amelia Simpson is Associate Professor at ANU Law School.

James Stellios is Professor at the ANU Law School and a Barrister, New South Wales Bar.

Scott Stephenson is a Senior Lecturer at Melbourne Law School.

Joo-Cheong Tham is Professor at Melbourne Law School.

Professor Gonzalo Villalta Puig is Head of the School of Law and Politics and Professor of Law at the University of Hull. He is the inaugural holder of the University of Hull Chair in the Law of Economic Integration.

Greg Weeks is Asociate Professor at ANU Law School.

Part I

Introduction: Constitutional Values and Interpretation

1

Functionalism and Australian Constitutional Values

ROSALIND DIXON

IN MANY COUNTRIES worldwide, the practice of judicial review involves open and consistent engagement with 'constitutional values'. In Canada, for example, the Supreme Court of Canada regularly looks to values both explicit and implicit in the 1982 Charter of Rights and Freedoms as a guide to determining the requirements of 'fundamental justice' or a 'free and democratic society' under sections 7 and 1 of the Charter.[1] In South Africa, section 1 of the 1996 Constitution lists human dignity, human rights and freedoms, non-racialism and non-sexism, the rule of law and democracy as 'founding values', and the Constitutional Court has suggested that attention to these values is essential to repudiating the past legacy of 'arid formalism' under apartheid, and moving towards a new more meaningful democratic constitutional jurisprudence.[2] And in Latin America, Manuel Cepeda J links this to a turn on the part of many courts in the region towards a form of 'new constitutionalism'.[3]

Australia, in contrast, lacks any express statement of constitutional values: the Constitution of the Commonwealth of Australia (Australian Constitution) from the outset adopted a 'thin' approach to defining constitutional values.[4] Subsequent attempts to amend the Constitution to expand these values, including attempts to incorporate a new preamble or comprehensive national bill of rights, have also

[1] See, eg, *R v Keegstra* [1990] 3 SCR 697; *Reference Re BC Motor Vehicle Act* [1985] 2 SCR 486.

[2] See A Chaskalson, 'Law in a Changing Society: The Past Ten Years: A Balance Sheet and Some Indicators for the Future' (1989) 5 *South African Journal on Human Rights* 293; A Sachs, 'Towards a Bill of Rights for South Africa (1991) 35 *Journal of African Law* 21; D Moseneke, 'A Jurisprudential Journey from Apartheid to Democratic Constitutionalism' (speech delivered at the 62nd Annual Meeting of American College of Trial Lawyers, New York City, 19 October 2012); D Moseneke, 'Courage of Principle' (speech delivered at the Ruth First Memorial Colloquium, Johannesburg, 17 August 2012); J van der Westhuizen, 'A Few Reflections on the Role of Courts, Government, the Legal Profession, Universities, the Media and Civil Society in a Constitutional Democracy' (2008) 8 *African Human Rights Law Journal* 251; Zakeria Mohammed Yacoob, 'South Africa: The Road to Democracy' (speech delivered at Francis King Carey School of Law, University of Maryland, 16 October 2012).

[3] MJ Cepeda Espinosa, 'The Judicialization of Politics in Colombia: The Old and the New' in R Sieder, L Schjolden and A Angell (eds), *The Judicialization of Politics in Latin America* (New York, Palgrave Macmillan, 2005) 67.

[4] E Arcioni and A Stone, 'The Small Brown Bird: Values and Aspirations in the Australian Constitution' (2016) 14 *International Journal of Constitutional Law* 60.

consistently failed. Indeed, since the adoption of the Constitution in 1901 there has been no revolutionary constitutional break in Australia.[5] The closest to such a 'revolution' occurred with the adoption of the *Australia Act 1986* (Cth), and the severing of formal legal ties to the UK. This revolution, however, was limited in scope: it arguably gave new meaning and force to popular sovereignty, as a value underpinning the Australian constitutional system. But it otherwise had a largely procedural rather than substantive effect. Other possible candidates for constitutional 'revolutionary moments', such as the 1967 constitutional referendum expanding the scope of the race power, had similarly muted values-based dimensions.[6]

This does not mean, however, that there is no role for values in Australian constitutional law or discourse. Whether explicitly or not, Australian courts routinely consider a range of political and moral values in making constitutional decisions—the question is simply when and how openly they do so, and on what sources they rely in giving content to relevant values.

I. THE ROLE OF VALUES IN AUSTRALIAN CONSTITUTIONAL LAW

Processes of constitutional decision-making in Australia, as elsewhere, involve processes of both 'interpretation' and 'construction' by the High Court.[7] As Jeffrey Goldsworthy usefully explains in his chapter, 'interpretation refers to revealing and clarifying the pre-existing linguistic or communicative content of a constitutional provision', whereas 'construction is a more creative process which must be resorted to when clarification is unable to resolve an interpretive difficulty, and [a] constitution's communicative content or meaning is relevantly indeterminate'.[8] Values-based considerations will also inevitably play a role in processes of construction of this kind. They may even play a role in helping resolve ambiguity in the process of interpretation in certain contexts.

Take the marriage power in section 51 of the Constitution: the word 'marriage' could potentially be understood to refer only to opposite-sex marriage or both opposite *and* same-sex marriage. Which interpretation one prefers depends on the level of generality at which the concept of marriage is understood—ie, the union for life of a man and woman to the exclusion of all others,[9] or any officially sanctioned lifelong union between two consenting adults.[10] Even moderate originalists, such as Lawrence Solum and Goldsworthy, suggest that the choice between these understandings may legitimately be guided by the purposes or values embedded in the Constitution—or values such as uniformity and effective national government, in

[5] This has led leading scholars such as Geoffrey Sawer to describe Australia as the 'frozen continent', see: G Sawer, *Australian Federalism in the Courts* (Melbourne University Press, 1967) 208.

[6] R Dixon, 'Amending Constitutional Identity' (2012) 33 *Cardozo Law Review* 1847.

[7] L Solum, 'The Interpretation/Construction Distinction' (2010) 27 *Constitutional Commentary* 95.

[8] See ch 3 by Jeffrey Goldsworthy in this collection, p 51.

[9] See, eg, the traditional view of marriage expounded in *Hyde v Hyde* (1866) LR 1 P & D 130.

[10] See, eg, *Minister of Home Affairs and Another v Fourie and Another* [2005] ZACC 19; *Fourie and Another v Minister of Home Affairs and Another* [2004] ZASCA 132.

the face of truly national problems such as divorce and child custody (in all family forms).[11]

The application of the marriage power may also call for the Court to engage in additional forms of constructional choice: in the 2013 *Same-Sex Marriage Case*, for example, the High Court was required to determine the relationship between Commonwealth and territory marriage law.[12] This also required the Court to make an important form of constructional choice as to how broadly or narrowly to approach the concept of an implied intention on the part of the Commonwealth to cover the field of marriage for the purposes of section 28 of the ACT *Self-Government Act (1988)* (Cth), which in the circumstances the Court held had a relevantly similar operation to section 109 of the Constitution.[13] Statutory (or constitutional) constructional choices of this kind are also inevitably informed by broader values-based considerations—or attitudes to federalism, and same-sex marriage itself.

Values-based considerations also inevitably play a role in the application of 'savings' tests, such as tests of reasonable proportionality. The idea of proportionality in a constitutional context is generally understood to encompass four broad requirements—ie, the requirements that: (i) the government shows a legitimate purpose for enacting a particular law; (ii) there be a 'rational connection' between the legislature's stated purpose and the means it selects to pursue that objective ('suitability'); (iii) a law be 'narrowly tailored' to its purpose ('reasonable necessity); and (iv) truly proportionate, in the sense that it achieves greater benefits in terms of this objective, than it does equivalent costs on other constitutional values or commitments (true proportionality, or proportionality *stricto sensu*).[14]

Both the third and fourth stages of this analysis also invite attention to substantive constitutional values. In making judgments about necessity, for example, the Court must first identify a substantive set of norms against which such judgements are to be made: the notion of 'minimal impairment' is that a law minimally impairs certain constitutionally privileged norms or values. Sometimes, these norms may take the form of independent constitutional protections—such as an implied freedom of political communication. In others, however, they may simply be constitutional values that inform the scope and application of other provisions.

In the *Communist Party Case*, for example, Dixon J found that the Commonwealth law dissolving the Communist Party was not reasonably necessary for the defence of the Commonwealth. One of his reasons for reaching this conclusion was also that the law in question went further than necessary in impairing common law

[11] Goldsworthy largely bases this on his theory of rectification: see ch 3 by Jeffrey Goldsworthy in this collection, pp 54–55; see further J Goldsworthy, 'Implications in Language, Law and the Constitution' in G Lindell (ed), *Future Directions in Australian Constitutional Law: Essays in Honour of Professor Leslie Zines* (Sydney, Federation Press, 1994) 183. See also J Goldsworthy, 'Interpreting the Constitution in Its Second Century' (2000) 24 *Melbourne University Law Review* 677, 699–700; Solum, above n 7.

[12] *Commonwealth v Australian Capital Territory* (2013) 250 CLR 441 (*Same-Sex Marriage Case*).

[13] (2013) 250 CLR 441, 465–66 [50]–[53], 468–69 [58]–[61].

[14] M Cohen-Eliya and I Porat, *Proportionality and Constitutional Culture* (Cambridge University Press, 2013); VC Jackson, 'Constitutional Law in an Age of Proportionality' (2015) 12 *Yale Law Journal* 3094; A Stone Sweet and J Mathews, 'Proportionality Balancing and Global Constitutionalism' (2008) 46 *Columbia Journal of Transnational Law* 72; DM Beatty, *The Ultimate Rule of Law* (Oxford, Oxford University Press, 2005).

rights, such as the right to property, and broader constitutional *values*, such as the rule of law.[15] Similarly, in *Nationwide News*, three justices found that the law in question went further than was necessary to protect the institutional integrity of the Industrial Relations Commission, in part because it did not minimally impair the freedom of political communication.[16] To apply a test of necessity, therefore, the Court must inevitably consider the values a constitution recognises as deserving of respect or protection. The question is simply whether it does openly, or in a more curtailed and elliptical way.

Similarly, in weighing the true costs and benefits of a law, it will often be necessary to consider how those costs and benefits are connected to broader constitutional values: one of the criticisms of balancing is that it often seeks to compare incommensurables.[17] One of the responses, in turn, is that a focus on values can often provide a mediating principle that provides a more meaningful basis for making such comparisons.[18]

The language of proportionality is also playing an increasingly central role in Australian constitutional discourse. Some form of proportionality test has been endorsed by members of the Court as a basis for determining whether a law: is properly understood as 'implementing' an international treaty to which Australia is party;[19] can properly be characterised as imposing a fine or penalty, or rather effects a compulsory acquisition of property other than on just terms;[20] or provides for a scheme of preventative detention, or rather a form of punitive detention that can only be authorised as an incident of the exercise of Commonwealth judicial power.[21]

More recently, the Court has held that in determining whether laws that burdened interstate commerce offended section 92 of the Constitution, it was necessary to determine whether the laws were proportionate, in the sense of being 'not disproportionate'[22] or 'reasonably necessary' to achieving a non-protectionist

[15] *Australian Communist Party v Commonwealth* (1951) 83 CLR 1, 180–01, 193, 200–02 (*Communist Party Case*).

[16] *Nationwide News Pty Ltd v Wills* (1992) 177 CLR 1, 50–53 (Brennan J), 79–80 (Deane and Toohey JJ) (*Nationwide News*).

[17] See, eg, *Bendix Autolite Corp v Midwesco Enters, Inc*, 486 US 888, 897 (1988) (Scalia J); RA Epstein, 'Are Values Incommensurable, or is Utility the Ruler of the World?' (1995) *Utah Law Review* 683; D Luban, 'Incommensurable Values, Rational Choice, and Moral Absolutes' (1990) 38 *Cleveland State Law Review* 65; V Afonso da Silva, 'Comparing the Incommensurable: Constitutional Principles, Balancing and Rational Decision' (2011) 31 *Oxford Journal of Legal Studies* 273.

[18] See, eg, *McCloy v New South Wales* (2015) 257 CLR 178, 283–84 (Gordon J) (*McCloy*); WH Moore, *The Constitution of the Commonwealth of Australia* (London, John Murray, 1902) 328–29, as discussed by Joo-Cheong Tham, ch 9 in this collection, pp 164–65. See further R Dixon and MC Nussbaum, 'Abortion, Dignity and a Capabilities Approach' in B Baines, D Barak-Erez and T Kahana (eds), *Feminist Constitutionalism* (New York, Cambridge University Press, 2011).

[19] *Victoria v Commonwealth* (1996) 187 CLR 416 (*Industrial Relations Act Case*).

[20] *Attorney-General (NT) v Emmerson* (2014) 253 CLR 393, 449 (Gageler J).

[21] See, eg, discussion in *Re Woolley; Ex parte M276/2003* (2004) 225 CLR 1, 33–34 (McHugh J).

[22] *Castlemaine Tooheys Ltd v South Australia* (1990) 169 CLR 436, 473–74 (Mason CJ, Brennan, Deane, Dawson and Toohey JJ).

purpose.[23] Similarly, in *McCloy*,[24] in determining whether a law effectively burdening freedom of political communication was consistent with the Constitution, the High Court recently refined the prior test for validity it developed in *Lange*[25] and *Coleman*,[26] to ask whether the law in question was *reasonably proportionate* to achieving a legitimate government purpose, in a manner compatible with the constitutionally prescribed system of representative and responsible government in Australia.[27] In doing so, the Court also explicitly adopted the structured approach to proportionality analysis set out above.[28]

In recent cases such as *Murphy*, a majority of the Court cast some doubt on the idea that proportionality would continue to spread to apply to all areas of constitutional doctrine in Australia.[29] Indeed, a majority of the Court rejected the usefulness of notions of proportionality in assessing the compatibility of restrictions on access to the franchise with the constitutionally prescribed system of representative and responsible government. Gageler J also repeated the criticism, made earlier by his Honour in *McCloy*, of proportionality as too uniform an approach to assessing constitutional validity, which is insufficiently sensitive to differences in context, including most notably the degree to which legislative processes are functioning in an adequate and appropriate way.[30]

There is, however, reason to believe that these reservations will be just that, and insufficient to halt the progressive turn towards a test that, logically at least, invites more open engagement by the High Court with constitutional values.[31] Proportionality can be adapted to different contexts, including potential defects in the political process, or process-based concerns. The Supreme Court of Canada, for example, has progressively 'nuanced' its version of proportionality (the *Oakes* test) to create flexibility, but also greater sensitivity to a variety of contextual factors.[32] In an

[23] *Betfair Pty Ltd v Western Australia* (2008) 234 CLR 418, 477 [99]–[104] (Gleeson CJ, Gummow, Kirby, Hayne, Crennan and Kiefel JJ) (suggesting that the language of 'not disproportionate' should be understood as equivalent in this context to a test of 'reasonable necessity'). See also *Betfair Pty Ltd v Racing New South Wales* (2012) 249 CLR 217, 269 (French CJ, Gummow, Hayne, Crennan and Bell JJ); *Sportsbet Pty Ltd v New South Wales* (2012) 249 CLR 298, 324 (French CJ, Gummow, Hayne, Crennan, Kiefel and Bell JJ).

[24] *McCloy* (2015) 257 CLR 178.

[25] *Lange v Australian Broadcasting Commission* (1997) 189 CLR 520 (*Lange*).

[26] *Coleman v Power* (2004) 220 CLR 1 (*Coleman*).

[27] *McCloy* (2015) 257 CLR 178, 194, 206–08 (French CJ, Kiefel, Bell and Keane JJ).

[28] ibid 194–95, 215–16 (French CJ, Kiefel, Bell and Keane JJ).

[29] *Murphy v Electoral Commissioner* (2016) 90 ALJR 1027 (*Murphy*); see also S Chordia, 'Structured Proportionality after McCloy and Murphy' (paper presented at the Australian Association of Constitutional Law, Federal Court of Australia, Sydney, 17 May 2017); J Griffiths, 'Keynote Address: Judicial Review of Administrative Action in Australia' (speech delivered at Public Law Weekend, Museum of Australia, Canberra, 28 October 2016) 11–12: <law.anu.edu.au/sites/all/files/media/documents/events/keynote_address_judicial_review_of_administrative_action_in_australia_-_griffiths.pdf>.

[30] *McCloy* (2015) 257 CLR 178, 235 [141]–[143].

[31] In light of the recent decision in *Brown v Tasmania* [2017] HCA 43, there is reason to believe that these reservations will be just that, and insufficient to halt the progressive turn towards a text that, logically at least, invites more open engagement by the High Court with constitutional values.

[32] See, eg, the discussion by Sopinka J in *R v Hebert* [1990] 2 SCR 151, [41] regarding the limiting effects on rights prescribed by law. Contrast with Anne Twomey's concern that the 'more rigid and mechanical the test becomes, with different layers of considerations and different factors applied at

Australian context, Shipra Chordia has likewise proposed one way in which the Court could potentially nuance its application of proportionality, so as to apply more or less demanding notions of the 'minimal impairment' requirement based on the perceived degree of threat to the constitutionally prescribed system of representative and responsible government in various contexts.[33]

In either event, constitutional values will also continue to play an important role in guiding the Court's application of relevant 'savings' tests: in other areas of Australian constitutional law, while the Court does not use the language of proportionality, it asks whether a law can be considered 'reasonably appropriate and adapted' to a particular purpose.[34] While this does not require a court to engage in a form of ultimate balancing of legislative costs and benefits,[35] it does require a court to consider whether a law is narrowly tailored to a particular legislative objective.[36] The Court, as part of this process, will also inevitably be required to consider how a law impacts on other constitutional norms or commitments, including potentially substantive constitutional *values* as a baseline for judgements about reasonable necessity.

II. CONTINUED FORMALISM AND THE CALL FOR A FUNCTIONALIST TURN

Despite these developments, however, Australia remains a jurisdiction in which, in comparative terms, a great deal of constitutional argument remains firmly centred on questions of constitutional form, and where there is often little attention both by parties and members of the High Court to substantive questions of substantive constitutional justice.

This also has implications for the democratic legitimacy or desirability of judicial review. It affects the degree to which judicial review represents a meaningful attempt to resolve the actual political controversies at stake, in various settings; the degree to which the constitutional jurisprudence of the High Court is understandable to elected representatives, and citizens; and the degree to which it provides a sound and predictable basis on which citizens can order their lives.[37] It is thus one reason why, in recent work, I have called on both constitutional litigants and the

different stages, there is a real risk that we cease to see the woods for the trees' in '*McCloy* and the Revised Test of Proportionality' (speech delivered at the ALRC Freedoms Symposium, Federal Court of Australia, Sydney, 9 October 2015).

[33] See Chordia, above n 29.

[34] See, eg, *Nationwide News* (1992) 177 CLR 1. cp also *Communist Party Case* (1951) 83 CLR 1.

[35] This is one reason some scholars and commentators prefer this test to one of true proportionality: see, eg, Twomey, above n 31; M Wesson (Comment), 'Crafting a Concept of Deference for the Implied Freedom of Political Communication' (2016) 27(2) *Public Law Review* 101, 102–03; Sir Anthony Mason, 'The Use of Proportionality in Australian Constitutional Law' (2016) 27(2) *Public Law Review* 109, 121–23.

[36] See, eg, A Stone, 'Proportionality: Between Substance and Method' (paper presented at Comparative Constitutional Law Conference Round-Table, UNSW Law School, 7 August 2017) 5–6; S Evans and A Stone, 'Balancing and Proportionality: A Distinctive Ethic?' (2017) (unpublished, copy on file with author).

[37] J Waldron, 'The Core of the Case Against Judicial Review' (2006) 115 *Yale Law Journal* 1346; R Dixon, 'The Functional Constitution: Re-reading the 2014 High Court Constitutional Term' (2015) 43 *Federal Law Review* 455.

High Court itself to adopt a more overtly 'functionalist', values-oriented approach to constitutional argument and reasoning.[38]

Functionalism, as I note in the *Federal Law Review*, is a close relative of *realist* approaches to constitutional interpretation, which emphasise the role of individual judges' moral and political outlooks as an influence on constitutional interpretation, and often call for more open engagement by judges with questions of political morality. It is also related to various forms of pragmatic, policy-oriented approaches to constitutional interpretation, which invite judges to pay explicit attention to questions of policy and practical impact, or the practical consequences of judicial decisions, as part of the process of constitutional construction. Indeed, as Jeffrey Goldsworthy notes in his chapter, in many cases functionalism will lead to results quite close to those produced by a realist or pragmatic approach.[39]

Functionalism, however, also carries with it an explicit commitment to legal form, as well as substance. It suggests that any reliance by a court on 'values'-based argument should first depend on serious engagement with the text, history and structure of a constitution, as well as prior precedent. The text, history and structure of the Constitution may lend itself to different values-based understandings. But there is also important value from both a democratic and rule of law perspective to courts attempting to ground ethical or moral-political argumentation in formal legal materials or 'modalities'[40]—ie, in the Australian context, the text, history and structure of the Australian Constitution, or prior precedent.[41]

The Constitution, as Sir Anthony Mason has noted, is 'itself a source of rights and values which can be used in the development of general principles of law'.[42] To the maximum extent possible, members of the Court should thus attempt to rely on values in some way sourced in the Constitution—and not simply their own values, or those of the community—in engaging in processes of constitutional interpretation or construction.[43]

Constitutional values could equally be regarded as constitutional 'principles' or purposes in an objective sense: as Allsop CJ notes in his illuminating discussion of 'Values in Public Law', values lie on a continuum with other norms, principles and rules: 'the[y] are not clearly identifiable separate vehicles, but expressions along a gradation of particularity'.[44] But equally, as values or functions, they do not have the status of independent constitutional guarantees or norms equivalent to

[38] Dixon, 'The Functional Constitution', above n 37.

[39] See ch 3 by Jeffrey Goldsworthy in this collection, p 52.

[40] See P Bobbitt, *Constitutional Fate: Theory of the Constitution* (New York, Oxford University Press, 1982).

[41] See ch 3 by Jeffrey Goldsworthy in this collection; J Goldsworthy, 'The Case for Originalism' in G Huscroft and BW Miller (eds), *The Challenge of Originalism: Theories of Constitutional Interpretation* (New York, Cambridge University Press, 2011); LB Solum, 'What is Originalism? The Evolution of Contemporary Originalist Theory' in G Huscroft and BW Miller (eds), *The Challenge of Originalism: Theories of Constitutional Interpretation* (New York, Cambridge University Press, 2011).

[42] Sir Anthony Mason, 'Rights, Values and Legal Institutions: Reshaping Australian Institutions' (1997) *Australian International Law Journal* 1, 11.

[43] ibid. In some cases, as I note in 'The Functional Constitution', above n 37, it may be impossible to avoid ultimate reliance on personal or community values, but this should occur only after open and serious engagement with constitutional values.

[44] J Allsop, 'Values in Public Law' (2017) 91 *Australian Law Journal* 118, 121.

constitutional implications. As Appleby and Lim note in their chapter, constitutional norms cease to be (I would add *solely*) values, and instead become constitutional 'rules [or] standards', when they gain a sufficiently determinate and mandatory content.[45] But, short of this content, they may still be ethical commitments that find an important form of support in the text, history and structure of the Constitution, as well as prior constitutional case law.

III. THE CONTENT OF THE FUNCTIONALIST CONSTITUTION

A key question this raises, however, is how to define the specific *content* of the functional Constitution for Australia.[46] Disagreement about Australian constitutional values can come from a variety of different directions. How one answers questions of this kind will depend, in part, on one's theory of constitutional interpretation: the more strictly textual or originalist one's approach to constitutional meaning, the more difficult it will be to see how the text and structure of the Constitution provide support for a broad range of values; whereas the 'looser', or more hybrid one's approach to interpretation of the text, the more scope there will be to find indirect sources of support for a variety of constitutional values.

There is also legitimate room for disagreement as to how constitutional values may, or may not, evolve over time. Under more originalist theories of interpretation, for instance, the text of the Constitution will have a relatively settled meaning or connotation; and so too one might argue, the content or connotation of various values will remain relatively unchanged. Under more 'living' or evolving approaches to constitutional construction, in contrast, both the connotation and denotation of various textual guarantees *and* values may be more open to change. As Goldsworthy notes in his chapter, this also raises complex questions about the ability of a functionalist as opposed to more pragmatic approach to interpretation.

Finally, there at least two possible understandings of what it means for the text and structure of the Constitution to provide support for various values in this context: one 'stronger' understanding, which focuses on the idea of *affirmative* support for various values, and another 'weaker' understanding, which requires only that certain values are consistent with the text and structure of the Constitution. When the High Court identifies a freestanding implication under the Constitution,[47] the current interpretive consensus in Australia is generally that it must show textual and structural support of a stronger, more affirmative kind.[48] But where values are relied

[45] I disagree with Appleby and Lim here as to the appropriate classification of 'principles'.

[46] B Lim, 'The Convergence of Form and Function: Commentary on Dixon' (2015) 43 *Federal Law Review* 505.

[47] I use the term 'implication' here in its most widely understood sense, though I note the point made by Jeffrey Goldsworthy that many of the implications in this context are actually 'fabricated' rather than 'genuine' from the perspective of the original communicative meaning of the text of the Constitution. See, eg, J Goldsworthy, 'Constitutional Implications Revisited' (2011) 30 *University of Queensland Law Journal* 9, 18–22.

[48] See, eg, *Lange* (1997) 189 CLR 520; cp *Australian Capital Television Pty Ltd v Commonwealth* (1992) 177 CLR 106. See also A Stone, 'Australia's Constitutional Rights and the Problem of Interpretive Disagreement' (2005) 27 *Sydney Law Review* 29; A Stone, 'The Limits of Constitutional Text and

on only as a source of additional guidance to the Court in interpreting and enforcing some other capital 'C' constitutional norm, it seems plausible to apply either a strong or weak notion of textual and structural support.

These are all important and difficult questions for any scholar, judge—or indeed any legislator or government officer—interested in the application of a functionalist approach to constitutional interpretation.[49] The aim of this collection is thus to contribute to debates over functionalist interpretation in Australia, and elsewhere, by inviting some of Australia's leading constitutional scholars to reflect on these questions.

It takes as its starting point a list of values that could that be regarded as in some way connected to broadly recognised *structural* commitments under the Constitution, such as the commitment to representative and responsible government, federalism and an entrenched separation of judicial and non-judicial power.[50] It also invites authors to consider the *ultimate* values-based commitments that may be relevant to or implicated in these commitments. The Constitution, for example, clearly enshrines a clear structural commitment to 'representative and responsible government'.[51] At the same time, there remains controversy as to what this entails at the level of basic constitutional values, such as the idea of individual freedom or political equality among citizens,[52] or notions of government or accountability. Similarly, in a comparative context, federalism is often understood to promote a range of different political values, including (a) government accountability; (b) democratic experimentalism; (c) the accommodation of diversity or pluralism, across states; and (c) government closer to the people. Which of these values embodied in the Australian federal system, however, remains an important open question.[53] It is likewise well settled that the Constitution recognises a separation of judicial and non-judicial power, and creates a similar, if somewhat weaker guarantee at a State level of the 'institutional integrity and independence' of State courts (the so-called

Structure: Standards of Review and the Freedom of Political Communication' (1999) 23 *Melbourne University Law Review* 668; A Stone, 'The Limits of Constitutional Text and Structure Revisited' (2005) 28 *UNSW Law Journal* 842; T Roux, 'Re-Interpreting "The Mason Court Revolution": An Historical Institutionalist Account of Judge-Driven Constitutional Transformation in Australia' (2015) 43 *Federal Law Review* 1; R Dixon and G Appleby, 'Constitutional Implications in Australia: A Tale of Acceptance and Resistance' (2016) (unpublished manuscript, copy on file with author).

[49] On the relevance of these questions to a non-judicial audience, see, eg, G Appleby, *The Role of the Solicitor-General: Negotiating Law, Politics and the Public Interest* (Oxford, Hart Publishing, 2016) 139–43.

[50] See C Saunders, 'Constitutional Structure and Australian Federalism' in P Cane (ed), *Centenary Essays for the High Court of Australia* (LexisNexis Butterworths, 2004); A Lynch and G Williams, 'Beyond a Federal Structure: Is a Constitutional Commitment to a Federal Relationship Possible?' (2008) 31 *UNSW Law Journal* 395; J Finnis, 'Separation of Powers in the Australian Constitution' (1968) 3 *Adelaide Law Review* 159; J McMillan, 'Re-Thinking the Separation of Powers' (2010) 38 *Federal Law Review* 423; C Parker, 'Protection of Judicial Process as an Implied Constitutional Principle' (1994) 16 *Adelaide Law Review* 341. But contrast F Wheeler, 'The Doctrine of Separation of Powers and Constitutionally Entrenched Due Process in Australia' (1997) 23 *Monash University Law Review* 248, questioning the firmness of the separation of powers commitment.

[51] Constitution ss 7, 24. See discussion in *Lange* (1997) 189 CLR 520.

[52] See, eg, *McGinty v Western Australia* (1996) 186 CLR 140; *Roach v Electoral Commissioner* (2007) 233 CLR 162.

[53] For an important attempt to begin to address this question, see P Kildea, A Lynch and G Williams (eds), *Tomorrow's Federation: Reforming Australian Government* (Sydney, Federation Press, 2012).

Kable principle). Yet there is ongoing debate over the ultimate values served by these structural principles: are they important, for example, for ensuring *impartial* justice, a substantive commitment to individual liberty and the rule of law, or all these values?

The complex relationship between the Constitution and the common law in Australia means that the common law itself arguably provides an additional source of support for certain values as small 'c' constitutional in nature.[54] Sir Anthony Mason, for example, identifies personal liberty, freedom of expression, no imprisonment without trial, inviolability of the person, and procedural fairness as values long recognised by the common law.[55] Allsop CJ likewise identifies the values of 'fairness, reasonableness and justice in the framing of legal rules and in the exercise of power in a free society' as core public law values.[56] His Honour further notes that the criminal law has long recognised 'fairness and equality' as values;[57] equity values of fairness and protection of the vulnerable;[58] and common law administrative doctrines rule of law values such as certainty, and non-arbitrary government.[59] Broader common law doctrines (including tort and property law) also provide a rich source of support for various values, including values such as individual freedom of speech, movement, bodily integrity, privacy and protection for private property, and the rule of law.[60] Allsop even suggests that the common law supports the idea of individual 'humanity and dignity', as well as autonomy, as core public law values.[61]

The key focus of the collection, however, is ultimately on values that might be considered distinctive *Australian* constitutional values. Values of this kind inevitably overlap with and are complemented in an Australian context by a range of more 'generic' public law values, common to the Anglo-American world. But others have already done impressive work exploring the content of these more general, public law values derived from the common law tradition.[62] The focus of the collection is

[54] Mason, 'Rights, Values and Legal Institutions', above n 42, 11. On the Constitution and the common law, see, eg, A Stone, 'Choice of Law Rules, the Constitution and the Common Law' (2001) 12 *Public Law Review* 9; A Stone, 'Rights, Personal Rights and Freedoms: The Nature of the Freedom of Political Communication' (2001) 25 *Melbourne University Law Review* 374; G Taylor, 'Why the Common Law Be Only Indirectly Affected by Constitutional Guarantees: A Comment on Stone' (2002) 26 *Melbourne University Law Review* 623. On the notion of small 'c' constitutional cp, eg, R Dixon and G Williams, *The High Court, the Constitution and Australian Politics* (Melbourne, Cambridge University Press, 2015).

[55] Mason, 'Rights, Values and Legal Institutions', above n 42, 8–11.

[56] Allsop, above n 44, 119. *cf* Griffiths' discussion of public law values in judicial review, procedural unfairness and good administration: above n 29, 18–23.

[57] Allsop, above n 44, 131.

[58] ibid 126–27, 131.

[59] ibid 127–28.

[60] See, eg, *Coco v The Queen* (1994) 179 CLR 427; *Australian Broadcasting Corporation v Lenah Game Meats Pty Ltd* (2001) 208 CLR 199; *Roberts v Bass* (2002) 212 CLR 1; *Communist Party Case* (1951) 83 CLR 1.

[61] Allsop, above n 44, 121.

[62] See, eg, P Cane, 'Theory and Values in Public Law' in P Craig and R Rawlings (eds), *Law and Administration in Europe: Essays in Honour of Carol Harlow* (Oxford, Oxford University Press, 2003); M Aronson, 'Public Law Values in the Common Law' in M Elliott and D Feldman (eds), *The Cambridge Companion to Public Law* (New York, Cambridge University Press, 2015) 134; D Davis, A Richter and C Saunders (eds), *An Inquiry into the Existence of Global Values: Through the Lens of Comparative Constitutional Law* (Oxford, Hart Publishing, 2015).

therefore largely on values that can potentially find support in the text, history and structure of the Australian Constitution.

In addition, the focus of the collection is on values that are not wholly co-extensive with—or protected by—independent constitutional guarantees, such as the guarantee of freedom of political communication, or protection of individual property from acquisition by the Commonwealth other than on just terms. Freedom of political expression, and some form of protection for private property, are arguably important values under our system of representative and responsible government, but they will generally be protected by independent limitations on Commonwealth legislative power, rather than interstitial judgments informed by values-based arguments. There is thus less utility, at this stage of the functionalist project, in attempting to clarify the values-based dimension to these constitutional principles, and commit to other principles that lack any independent institutionalisation.[63]

Finally, the collection attempts to promote critical engagement with the idea of functionalist interpretation or construction, by inviting attention to certain more controversial—and potentially less normatively attractive—values. National security, for instance, is a value that commands broad public support, but also opposition from civil rights and liberties organisations as a basis for limiting individual rights and liberties.

Even with these caveats, however, there is clearly a much longer list of values that could potentially find at least some degree of weak support in the text and structure of the Australian Constitution—including values of individual dignity, pluralism, and social inclusion and protection. TRS Allan, for example, argues that in UK public law the commitment to the rule of law implicitly entails a further set of values-based commitments, including a commitment to human dignity: 'the equal dignity of citizens', he argues, 'is the basic premise of liberal constitutionalism, and accordingly the ultimate meaning of the rule of law'.[64] Important common law decisions of the High Court, such as *Marion's Case*,[65] arguably give important support to dignity as a fundamental small 'c' constitutional value in Australia. And one could argue that the constitutionally prescribed system of representative and responsible government, in sections 7 and 24, provides additional support, as does, over time, the external affairs power, which recognises Australia's place in a global legal order now firmly committed to human dignity as a foundational principle.[66]

[63] The chapter that comes closest to this is Gonzalo Villalta Puig's on free trade in this collection, but here again there is an attempt to consider the relevance of such a value beyond the context of a provision such as s 92 of the Constitution.

[64] TRS Allan, *Constitutional Justice: A Liberal Theory of the Rule of Law* (Oxford, Oxford University Press, 2001) 2.

[65] *Secretary, Department of Health and Community Services v JWB and SMB* (1992) 175 CLR 218 (*Marion's Case*).

[66] On the role of human dignity as a foundational principle of international human rights law, see, eg, MS McDougal, 'Perspectives for an International Law of Human Dignity' (1959) 53 *Proceedings of the American Society for International Law* 107; AH Henkin (ed), *Human Dignity: The Internationalization of Human Rights* (New York, Aspen Insitute for Humanistic Studies, 1978) and more recently C McCrudden, 'Human Dignity and Judicial Interpretation of Human Rights' (2008) 19 *European Journal of International Law* 655.

The Constitution likewise could be seen to provide at least some weak support for commitments to social welfare. The benefits clause, for example, could arguably be understood not just as a formal source of legislative power, but an implicit recognition of a broader commitment in Australia to an active role for government in guaranteeing minimum social protection for all citizens, in circumstances of vulnerability. There are undoubtedly also many other values, some more or less normatively attractive in nature, which could be attributed to the Australian constitutional order. Some, for example, might suggest that the Australian Constitution goes beyond simply entrenching Indigenous non-recognition as a value. By failing to acknowledge Australia's First Peoples, and their traditional ownership of land, and potentially allowing for various racially discriminatory laws under the race power, it in fact affirmatively entrenches a form of institutionalised racism.

IV. THE COLLECTION AND THE FUNCTIONALIST CONSTITUTION

The remainder of the collection is divided into six parts. Part I of the collection focuses on various methodological questions, including the relationship between theories of constitutional interpretation and the scope and content of various constitutional values.

Nicholas Aroney, in his chapter on the justification of judicial review, explores the foundations for the exercise of judicial review in Australia in the text and structure of the Constitution. He further suggests that the institution of judicial review can be understood to serve a range of values or purposes explored in later chapters, including federalism, accountability and free trade.[67] But equally, he suggests that these textual and structural sources do not tell us how the power should be exercised: this is a question that can only be answered by appropriate attention to a range of different modalities of constitutional argument in dialogue with each other, including the constitutional text, structure, history and ethical principles and empirical consequences.

Jeffrey Goldsworthy, in his chapter on constitutional functions, purposes and values, provides a helpful restatement of the idea of functionalism, and its relationship to notions of constitutional interpretation and construction. At the same time, he poses a challenge to the stability of functionalism as a distinctive approach: he argues that if values are used by the Court to resolve true ambiguities in constitutional meaning, reliance on values will simply involve a form of 'purposive formalism'.[68] The 'function of a constitutional provision', according to Goldsworthy, 'is to achieve a purpose, which is an intention to achieve something believed to be of value'.[69] Further, 'the purposes of constitutional provisions are often crucial

[67] See ch 12 by Gabrielle Appleby and Brendan Lim; ch 6 by Janina Boughey and Greg Weeks; and ch 15 by Gonzalo Villalta Puig in this collection.

[68] See ch 3 by Jeffrey Goldsworthy in this collection, pp 43, 50.

[69] ibid, p 59.

to clarifying their meanings', and hence 'sensible formalists who strive to clarify meanings of constitutional provisions must ... be purposive formalists'.[70]

Conversely, if values are used to resolve vagueness in constitutional meaning—ie, to aid in processes of construction, or what Goldsworthy calls supplementation—they will rarely be sufficient to resolve relevant controversies. Goldsworthy references my notion of 'intermediate' and 'ultimate values', and generalises this idea by developing the idea of a 'chain of linked purposes and values', which could be either progressively more concrete or abstract in nature.[71] But even the most concrete, ultimate values, Goldsworthy argues, will often be quite abstract in nature. Values may also conflict in ways that create new forms of indeterminacy. In both cases there will thus be the need to supplement constitutional values with other extra-constitutional values, in ways that closely resemble ordinary forms of pragmatic or realist approaches to constitutional interpretation. Indeed, Goldsworthy suggests that pragmatism may be defensible in these circumstances, even for a moderate originalist such as himself, 'because it is much less vulnerable to the originalist objection that it amounts to amending the constitution contrary to the prescribed amendment procedure'.[72]

Goldsworthy also usefully draws attention to one studied ambiguity, and another question left open by my own prior work on functionalism: the ambiguity, explored above, relates to the degree of support (ie, strong or weak support) required for a value to count as 'sourced' in the text, history and structure of the Constitution. The second question, which I address more directly but leave open in the 'Functional Constitution' relates to the degree to which values may be understood in a more or less intentionalist, or what I call 'backward' versus 'forward' looking way. As Australia's leading originalist scholar, Goldsworthy also goes on to defend at least a partially backward-looking approach to defining relevant values, suggesting that the purposes of constitutions are primarily the purposes of those responsible for creating or amending them, or that 'true purposivism is inherently originalist'.[73]

Jonathan Crowe, in his chapter on functions, context and constitutional values, takes up this distinction between more or less backward-looking approaches to defining constitutional purposes or values, or what he calls an 'intentionalist' and 'contextualist' approach to defining the content of constitutional values. An intentionalist approach, Crowe suggests, means that constitutional values 'should have some basis in the intentions of the framers of the constitutional document', whereas a contextualist approach means that we should focus on the functions or purposes of constitutional provisions and structures from a more contemporary perspective, or by reference to 'contemporary beliefs and attitudes'.[74] This approach, Crowe argues, provides greater guidance in giving concrete content to constitutional values 'when its meaning is in dispute', and an account of how to resolve conflicts between law's

[70] ibid.
[71] ibid, p 44.
[72] ibid, pp 59–60.
[73] ibid, p 59.
[74] See ch 4 by Jonathan Crowe in this collection, p 73.

'intended and socially accepted functions'.[75] In this way, he, like Goldsworthy, offers a distinctive—and distinctly more fleshed out—functionalist account than I offered in my earlier work on this question.

Parts II–VI of the collection focus on various substantive values that might be considered candidates for recognition as 'constitutional' in Australia. It invites contributors to consider three core questions—ie, the degree to which (1) the text of the Australian Constitution provides support for such a value as 'constitutional' in nature; (2) various constitutional structures provide support for such a value as constitutional; and (3) existing decisions of the High Court explicitly or implicitly endorsed the relevance of such a value to constitutional interpretation in Australia.

Contributors were also invited to reflect on the degree to which, if such values *were* clearly recognised as constitutional in nature, this might reshape existing constitutional discourse in Australia. A functionalist approach does not simply seek to describe existing constitutional practice in Australia. It also seeks to critique and reorient that practice. The collection thus invites contributors to reflect on how, if certain values were in fact recognised by the Court as constitutional in nature, greater attention to such values could change existing approaches to interpretation or construction across two to three different areas of Australian constitutional law.

As one would expect, contributors to the collection reach a range of quite different answers to these questions. Lisa Burton Crawford, in her chapter on the rule of law, suggests that the Constitution *as a whole* supports the rule of law as a constitutional value. The idea of the rule of law denotes the existence of a legal system, she suggests, and 'the Constitution brought such a system into being'. More importantly, the system created by the Constitution is one in which all government power is limited by law—found in the Constitution itself or statutes validly enacted thereunder—which is enforced by an independent judiciary. She further points to specific textual provisions, such as sections 51, 52, 71 and 75, and the *Communist Party Case*[76] as providing additional support for the rule of law as a *constitutional* value in Australia.

Such a value, Crawford argues, can also usefully inform the Court's approach to statutory and constitutional interpretation in a range of areas. Yet she cautions against too broad, or uncritical, an application of the rule of law idea in this context: unlike TRS Allan, who sees a commitment to government under law as a paramount value, to be applied consistently in all public law cases,[77] Crawford argues that the Australian Constitution supports a narrower, more historically contingent understanding of the rule of law, which emphasises the primacy of the text and structure of the Australian Constitution, and the importance of the distribution of powers that it effects. For example, the rule of law is understood to impose limitations on the power of the executive, but also on the power of courts to supervise execution action. Crawford demonstrates this by discussing the treatment of no-invalidity clauses in federal legislation. She argues that, while Parliament can define the scope

[75] ibid.
[76] *Communist Party Case* (1951) 83 CLR 1.
[77] Allan, above n 64.

of executive power, it cannot assert its validity. Thus, properly understood the rule of law supports the view that Parliament has some—but not unbridled—power to use these devices to constrain judicial review.

Janina Boughey and Greg Weeks, in their chapter on government accountability, suggest that accountability should be understood broadly as 'the basic idea that the executive branch and its delegates must be answerable, and as a general principle justify their actions, to the public, the Parliament, the courts or any administrative agency'.[78] On this basis, they also go on to identify several sources of support for 'government accountability' as a constitutional value in Australia: section 75(v) of the Constitution, and its guarantee of legal accountability; and sections 49 and 64 and their guarantee of responsible government, and thus a system of political accountability. They also note some support, albeit limited, for this understanding in judgments of the High Court such as *NEAT*,[79] *Jia*[80] and *Patterson*.[81]

This form of accountability, Boughey and Weeks argue, is necessarily shaped by its source in the text and structure of the Constitution, or the basis of its entrenchment. It does not, for example, extend to providing a complete form of legal accountability, or encompassing perhaps the most important modern form of accountability—ie, administrative accountability. But within these bounds, it may still be useful in resolving potential areas of uncertainty or ambiguity in construing various provisions of the Constitution, such as the scope for the Commonwealth Parliament to compel the production of documents by the Commonwealth executive, the ambit of the term 'government' for the purposes of sections 75(iii) and 75(v), and the scope for Parliament to impose invalidity clauses.

Sarah Murray, in her chapter on impartial justice, notes the degree to which such a value intersects with, but is also distinct from, the concept of independent justice. Impartial justice, she argues, 'refers to whether a decision-maker remains open-minded', whereas judicial independence 'is concerned with whether a decision is made without interference'.[82] She also suggests that impartiality may in some cases have a broader reach or 'wider berth'.[83] Having defined the relevant value in this way, Murray also goes on to identify support for this value in various provisions in Chapter III of the Constitution, such as sections 71 and 72, broader provisions—including sections 99 and 102 of the Constitution, as well as the High Court's Chapter III case law.

More direct engagement with the idea of impartial justice, Murray further argues, could usefully guide the Court in the application of principles such as the open court principle, and the *Boilermakers* principle.[84] In *Hogan v Hinch*,[85] for example, Murray suggests that the application of this principle was guided by a focus on the

[78] See ch 6 by Janina Boughey and Greg Weeks in this collection, p 103.
[79] *NEAT Domestic Trading Pty Ltd v AWB Ltd* (2003) 216 CLR 277 (*NEAT*).
[80] *Minister for Immigration and Multicultural Affairs v Jia* (2001) 205 CLR 507 (*Jia*).
[81] *Re Patterson; Ex parte Taylor* (2001) 207 CLR 391 (*Patterson*).
[82] See ch 7 by Sarah Murray in this collection, p 122.
[83] ibid.
[84] *R v Kirby; Ex parte Boilermakers' Society of Australia* (1956) 94 CLR 254 (*Boilermakers*).
[85] *Hogan v Hinch* (2011) 243 CLR 506.

impact of relevant procedures on impartial and independent justice as the ultimate value, or touchstone. Similarly, she argues that a focus on these values could provide the basis for a reorientation of both Chapter III and *Kable* jurisprudence towards a more flexible approach, which focuses on notions of 'contextual incompatibility'.[86] She also points to the potential relevance of such a value to the application of the rule against bias. At the same time, she notes dangers or limitations in any such exercise: if over-stretched to include too many other decision-making contexts, the value could lose 'its utility as a precise constitutional value'.[87] It is also a value that invites difficult questions about the ultimate values served by the Constitution—the kind of 'chain logic' Goldsworthy notes in his chapter. It could be, Murray argues, that in fact impartial justice is better understood as serving a range of ultimate or 'primary' values, including fairness, accountability, justice, dignity and welfare of the person.

Scott Stephenson, in his chapter on democratic deliberation, argues that the text and structure of the Constitution provide clear support for deliberation as a constitutional value: provisions such as sections 7, 24, 49, 51, 53, 64 and 109 clearly enshrine a commitment to institutions such as federalism, responsible government, bicameralism, and representative democracy, and these institutions, he suggests, all 'require mediation through discourse', and in most cases, 'discourse that is of a deliberative standard'.[88] While in most cases the Constitution contemplates that Parliament, and/or the people, will be responsible for promoting deliberation of this kind, there are also limited areas where the High Court could legitimately consider deliberation as a value. For instance, in giving effect to the notion of indirect inconsistency under section 109 of the Constitution, the Court could 'allow[] more scope for complementary State legislation, which would help protect deliberation between the Commonwealth and the States'.[89] In interpreting section 61, it could consider the value of deliberation within Parliament, and in the broader public sphere, in determining the scope of the executive government's power to spend and contract. And in construing section 71, and the scope of the Commonwealth's judicial power, the Court could rely on notions of democratic deliberation to favour a more flexible view of the scope of Commonwealth judicial power (or I might add, at least powers incidental to it).[90]

Joo-Cheong Tham, in his chapter on political equality, effectively adopts a strong notion of what it means for the text and structure of the Constitution to support the identification of relevant constitutional values: despite its invocation by the High Court in *McCloy*, he argues that political equality does not find sufficient support in the text, history and structure of the Constitution to count as a true *constitutional* value or principle. Indeed, he cites provisions such as sections 25, 41 and 128 of the Constitution, and historical sources (such as statements by Harrison Moore), as negativing the existence of such a constitutional principle. Even if it does find

[86] See ch 7 by Sarah Murray in this collection, pp 126–27.
[87] ibid, p 129.
[88] See ch 8 by Scott Stephenson in this collection, p 136.
[89] ibid, p 134.
[90] See, eg, *Momcilovic v The Queen* (2011) 245 CLR 1, 223 [589] (Crennan and Kiefel JJ).

some support at an abstract level, Tham further suggests, its internal complexity means that as a value it provides limited guidance in deciding concrete constitutional controversies: to whom, for example, does such a principle extend? Does it imply a formal or substantive understanding of equality of arms in the political process? How we answer these questions will clearly lead to quite different conclusions about the validity of campaign finance and other forms of electoral regulation under the implied freedom of political communication.

James Stellios, in his chapter on liberty, traces a wide variety of potential textual and structural sources of support for liberty as a constitutional value. The constitutionally prescribed system of representative and responsible government, and federalism, are both important guarantors of individual liberty in the positive sense, of a right to participate in processes of self-government. They also serve to protect negative liberty, or the freedom of the individual from arbitrary interference with their person, possessions, or bodily movement. This, Stellios argues, is also true both generally and for specific provisions such as sections 61 and 109 of the Constitution, which respectively require legislative authorisation for Commonwealth executive action, and protect individuals from certain kinds of state action. The Constitution's provision for a system of separated powers may likewise be understood as an important guarantee of both positive and negative liberty: the separation of judicial and non-judicial power is arguably the most important protection for liberty in this context, but limitations on delegation imposed by the separation of legislative and executive power may also play a role. Additional protections for negative liberty, or freedom from arbitrary interference by the state, can arguably be found in the entrenchment of judicial review over executive action (ie, section 75(iii) and (v)), and various rights-based protections or limitations, including section 51(xxxi) and the just terms requirement, and section 80 and the guarantee of trial by jury. But other provisions such as sections 116 and 117, which seem rights-inflected, may ultimately be better understood as designed to promote values of federalism.[91] Stellios further notes the overlap between common law protections of liberty and the potential constitutional value, as well as support in the common law for such a value. The most notable example is, of course, the reasoning of Dixon CJ in the *Communist Party Case*,[92] but Stellios draws attention to the more recent reasoning of Gageler J in *Magaming* in this context.[93]

At the same time, Stellios notes the potential ambiguity and complexity behind the idea of liberty as a constitutional value. Liberty, as already noted, can be understood as having both negative and positive connotations, and each has different sources of support in and relationships to constitutional text, structure and construction. It can also be understood in more or less substantive terms (as is evidenced by the High Court's approach to section 80 of the Constitution). Stellios further argues that the text and structure of the Constitution point to the Commonwealth

[91] For my own arguments along similar lines about other rights-based provisions, see R Dixon, 'An Australian (Partial) Bill of Rights' (2016) 14 *International Journal of Constitutional Law* 80.

[92] (1951) 83 CLR 1.

[93] *Magaming v The Queen* (2013) 252 CLR 381, 400, 401 (*Magaming*).

Parliament, rather than the High Court, as the prime institutional guarantor of liberty. For a constitutional notion of 'liberty' to play a useful role in processes of judicial decision-making, Stellios argues therefore, it must ultimately be combined with or underpinned by a more fully developed account of the judicial role—that is also consistent with the text, structure and history of the Constitution.

Amelia Simpson, in her chapter on equal treatment and non-discrimination, notes the variety of different sources of support for a norm of non-discrimination in the text of the Constitution, including sections 7, 51(ii), 51(iii), 88, 92, 99, 102 and 117, and broader structural provisions of representative and responsive government, and federalism. At the same time, she identifies four different potential understandings of equality or non-discrimination as a constitutional value: formal and substantive equality of persons; and formal and substantive equality of units within the federal system. Individual equality values, she argues, are also quite distinct from federal equality values. They find different sources of support in the text and structure of the Constitution, and imply quite different approaches to constructional choice.

There is also utility, she argues, to distinguishing more clearly between individual equality and federalism values in different areas of constitutional discourse. The Court, Simpson suggests, often seems to search for a unified approach to questions of discrimination under the Constitution, when the quite different values served by different provisions in fact point towards the desirability of a much more varied, context-dependent approach. For instance, in *Cole v Whitfield*,[94] Simpson suggests that the Court quite properly relied on federalism-based values (rather than individuals' equality values) to inform the interpretation of the words 'absolutely free' under section 92 of the Constitution. In *Street*,[95] Simpson argues that the Court could usefully have relied on federalism values to inform, and clarify, its interpretation of section 117 and its guarantee of freedom of movement across State lines. And in *Fortescue*,[96] and like cases involving the relationship between section 51(ii) and section 99, Simpson argues that a focus on substantive federal equality could usefully have guided the Court in reconciling these provisions. Indeed, she notes that in *Fortescue*, in adopting a three-pronged approach to the question of 'discriminatory' taxation, French CJ seems to have adopted just this kind of functionalist (ie, federalism values-based) approach.

This, Simpson argues, is ultimately one of the benefits of a values-based approach: it helps support the development of an appropriately varied, as well as unified, constitutional jurisprudence across different contexts. To serve this function, however, Simpson argues that values must ultimately be understood in a sufficiently concrete way: if equality is understood too abstractly (as it arguably was in *Street*), she suggests, it may tend to obscure more than to clarify, or justify what is far from justifiable.[97]

[94] *Cole v Whitfield* (1988) 165 CLR 360.
[95] *Street v Queensland Bar Association* (1989) 168 CLR 461 (*Street*).
[96] *Fortescue Metals Group Limited v Commonwealth* (2013) 250 CLR 548 (*Fortescue*).
[97] See ch 11 by Amelia Simpson in this collection, p 208.

Gabrielle Appleby and Brendan Lim, in their chapter on democratic experimentalism, provide an illuminating treatment of the idea of democratic experimentalism, drawing on the ideas of early twentieth-century American philosopher John Dewey. Experimentalism as Dewey understood it, they suggest, involves the idea of democracy as 'provisional, dynamic and self-correcting',[98] and as attuned to evidence of actual consequences. There is also ample scope for experimentalism of this kind under the system of political constitutionalism created by the Constitution in various contexts, as well as under the federal structure it creates. Neither structure *requires* experimentalism of this kind, but both allow scope for it. Federalism in particular can enable experimentalism in two important ways—by lowering the cost of particular experiments (by allowing them to occur in smaller sub-units, or States as 'laboratories of democracy') and by creating 'multiple decision-making centres',[99] which can generate multiple, overlapping experiments. In this sense, the structure of the Constitution may also be seen to provide some support for the idea of democratic experimentalism as a value, at least in the weak sense of being consistent with it. There is also some support for it as a value, in the drafting of the Constitution, and subsequent case law: while the framers of the Constitution were not directly influenced by Dewey, or his ideas, they were influenced by figures such as James Bryce, who was himself an influence on Dewey. More recent case law, and particular certain dissenting opinions of members of the Court, also endorse experimentation as a contemporary value of the federal system.[100]

Appleby and Lim further note two areas in which, as a potential candidate constitutional value, democratic experimentalism could bear on questions of constitutional construction by the Court: section 99, where a focus on experimentalism might favour a narrower view of the scope of the guarantee, as permitting greater scope for the Commonwealth to engage in localised forms of experimentation, and section 109, where it could point towards a narrower view of indirect inconsistency (or the circumstances in which a Commonwealth law should be interpreted as impliedly covering the field). In the political domain, they further note ways in which fiscal federalism could be adapted to promote greater experimentalism—eg, through targeted grants, which require recipients to engage in experimentalist forms of information-sharing.[101] At the same time, in these contexts as in others, they note that an emphasis on democratic experimentalism may come at the expense of other—potentially preferred—constitutional values. They thus do not necessarily endorse these approaches. Rather, consistent with the broader functionalist project, they suggest that there is benefit to the Court consciously engaging with 'democratic

[98] See ch 12 by Gabrielle Appleby and Brendan Lim in this collection, p 222.

[99] ibid, p 230.

[100] See, eg, *New South Wales v Commonwealth* (2006) 229 CLR 1, 222 [534] (Kirby J); *South Australia v Totani* (2010) 242 CLR 1, 96 [246] (Heydon J); *Public Service Association and Professional Officers' Association Amalgamated of NSW v Director of Public Employment* (2012) 250 CLR 343, 369 [61] (Heydon J).

[101] See ch 12 by Gabrielle Appleby and Brendan Lim in this collection, p 239. cp also modern notions of the key features of modern experimentalist governance discussed in MC Dorf and CF Sabel, 'A Constitution of Democratic Experimentalism' (1998) 98 *Columbia Law Review* 267.

experimentalism—together with all other relevant constitutional values'[102] in these and other relevant areas of constitutional discourse.

The final three chapters focus on values that might be regarded as more contestable, or indeed more problematic for the idea of a functionalist approach to constitutional construction. Dylan Lino, in his chapter on Indigenous recognition, notes the variety of ways in which Indigenous recognition could be understood as a value: in symbolic terms; in terms that focus on achieving a more inclusive and non-discriminatory settlement for Aboriginal and Torres Strait Islander peoples; and in terms that focus on 'collective Indigenous empowerment'.[103] Overlaid with these three broad understandings is also the idea of 'recognition' involving legal and political acknowledgement of past historical injustices against Aboriginal and Torres Strait Islander peoples. 'While the visions of recognition are varied', he suggests, 'the underlying value is about achieving respect for Indigenous identity'.[104]

He further notes the degree to which the Constitution provides only limited textual and structural support for *any* of these different understandings of recognition as a value. Indeed, he argues, where First Nations have been concerned, the dominant purpose or function of the Constitution has been 'consolidating Indigenous dispossession through the service of foreign forms of government, society and economy ... suppos[ed to] serve the values of progress and civilization'.[105] This is embedded in a variety of mundane constitutional provisions that helped to advance the 'project of settler expansion'.[106] For the Constitution to support the value of Indigenous recognition, either symbolically or at the level of political empowerment, it thus clearly requires a process of formal constitutional change, not simply functionalist reinterpretation.

Yet Lino also offers a reading of the text, history and structure of the Constitution that emphasises its potential to support a more normatively attractive functionalist approach—ie, one that emphasises values of recognition over dispossession. Like Simpson, Lino notes the support in the text and structure of the Constitution for equality as a general constitutional value. He also notes the 'egalitarian values' embedded in the 1967 amendment to the race power. Either or both these values, he further argues, could be relied on to support a construction of the race power that limited its scope to positive forms of discrimination. Similarly, it could be relied on to support a construction of the term 'race' in the race power that gave First Nations 'communal control over Indigenous community membership',[107] itself a critical aspect of self-determination and thus recognition as a people.

Rebecca Ananian-Welsh and Nicola McGarrity, in their chapter on natural security, note the degree to which national security is itself a contested and protean concept. They follow Peter Hanks in suggesting that, at a minimum, it involves the

[102] See ch 12 by Gabrielle Appleby and Brendan Lim in this collection, p 242.
[103] See ch 13 by Dylan Lino in this collection, p 252.
[104] ibid, p 254.
[105] ibid, p 246.
[106] ibid.
[107] ibid, p 259.

idea of a collective attempt to 'counter threats to the state', but note the inherent ambiguities even in this quite thin, minimalist understanding.[108] They nonetheless identify a range of sources of textual support for national security as a potential Australian constitutional value: the defence power in section 51(vi) and related powers in relation to property, railways, immigration and taxation (section 51(ii), (xxxi), (xxvii) and (xxxviii). They also note a strong degree of historical support for this as a value, including in the Convention debates.

Reliance by the Court on national security as a value, they suggest however, is usually more dangerous than it is helpful. Like notions of 'law and order', appeals to national security tend to have a dominant, if not overriding—ie, 'hegemonic'—force in constitutional discourse: examples that they point to include the role of security-based arguments in limiting the implied freedom of political communication, and modifying the application of prohibitions against administrative detention, and the content of procedural fairness and open justice principles. The challenge, they suggest therefore, is not so much to find adequate textual and historical support for national security as a value, but rather, to identify appropriate doctrinal and institutional means of *cabining* its role in constitutional construction. McGarrity and Ananian-Welsh further explore three potential restraints of this kind: the idea of treating national security as a preferred value only up to a certain threshold; linking it to other, ultimate values such as liberty and security *of the person*; or weighing it against liberty of the person, and the rule of law, as equally—if not preferred—constitutional values. None of these restraints are likely to be wholly stable, they suggest however. For both authors, this also calls into question the normative attractiveness of a functionalist approach.

Gonzalo Villalta Puig, in his chapter on free trade, identifies important support for free trade as a value in the text of the Constitution, including provisions such as sections 92, 99, 117 and arguably section 51(ii) as interpreted by the High Court in *Fortescue*, as well as broader structural provisions found in Part IV. Like Goldsworthy in his introductory chapter, Puig notes the importance of this value as a guide to resolving the ambiguity in the language of 'absolutely free' in section 92 of the Constitution. He further argues that it could legitimately inform the construction of other provisions, including section 51(i) of the Constitution. Yet he suggests that, to be legitimate, any reliance by the Court on free trade as a value must account for the conflict between free trade and other competing values, which itself is recognised in the text and structure of the Constitution (as, for example, in section 92).

V. LIMITS TO THE COLLECTION AND FUNCTIONALISM

These diverse conclusions, however, are ultimately entirely consistent with the aim and spirit of the collection. The aim of the collection is certainly *not* to 'fix' once and for all the content and scope of values under the Australian Constitution.

[108] See ch 14 by Rebecca Ananian-Welsh and Nicola McGarrity in this collection, p 268.

Indeed, if that were its aim, the collection would seem extremely ill-conceived: as already noted, the collection is far from comprehensive in the range of values it purports to explore. Constitutional values are often expressed in extremely broad and general terms, in ways that call for a great deal of further working out in various cases. The concrete scope or denotation of various values may change with time, along with changing social circumstances and understandings. The application of different values may vary, depending on a judge's broader theory of constitutional interpretation.[109] And constitutional values may conflict in various concrete cases, in ways that raise distinct and difficult questions about how best to balance or reconcile competing values and commitments.[110]

Some public law scholars, writing about values in administrative law, sometimes suggest that certain values carry with them a predetermined weighting, or lexical priority: Paul Daly, for example, suggests that various administrative law values—such as the rule of law, good administration, democracy, and the separation of powers—have varying 'weight', which can guide the resolution of values-based conflicts.[111]

I am, however, more sceptical of this possibility in the Australian constitutional context. It seems to overstate the determinacy of the formal constitutional modalities, such as constitutional text, structure and precedent, and further to understate the importance of conceptions of the judicial role in determining the ultimate weight to be given to various values in different contexts. Like Allsop CJ, I believe that values can inform and guide processes of constitutional construction, but are unlikely to be 'dispositive': 'they are part of the legal framework against which law is construed and moulded', rather than 'providing the content for hard rules of law'.[112] Lim and Appleby make the point beautifully when they suggest, in their chapter, that values-based arguments are best understood as helping 'inform' rather than control choices about constitutional construction under the Constitution.[113]

Goldsworthy also makes this point lucidly in his chapter, and suggests it is one reason why processes of constitutional construction will ultimately end up being pragmatic in nature, even if they pass by the way-station of functionalism. My argument, however, is that this way-station matters a great deal to the legitimacy of judicial review by the Court: it represents an attempt by judges to ensure that their own subjective judgements about values (eg, their concrete content or relative priority)

[109] cp with the judgments of Gageler J in *Murphy* (2016) 90 ALJR 1027 and *McCloy* (2015) 257 CLR 178; see also S Gageler, 'The Underpinnings of Judicial Review of Administrative Action: Common Law or Constitution' (2000) 28 *Federal Law Review* 303, emphasising the importance of process-based approaches to judicial review as usefully guiding the application of constitutional norms, including implicitly the scope and weight to be given by the Court to various constitutional values.

[110] See, eg, Mason, 'Rights, Values and Legal Institutions', above n 42, 9. Mason suggests that 'identification of values is not a major problem; assessment of their interaction or of their relationship with competing policy considerations is': at 14.

[111] P Daly, *A Theory of Deference in Administrative Law: Basis, Application and Scope* (New York, Cambridge University Press, 2012).

[112] Allsop, above n 44, 130

[113] See the chapter by Gabrielle Appleby and Brendan Lim in this collection, pp 241–42.

play a role only where relevant objective 'guideposts' for making such judgements run out.[114]

The collection also only touches indirectly on what might legitimately be considered the most important values-based question of all—ie, the meta-value of judicial versus legislative supremacy in the resolution of various constitutional controversies. I have clear views on these questions, which I have explored elsewhere,[115] and these are questions that I have suggested are put front and centre by a functionalist approach.[116] They are also questions that are indirectly addressed, at various points, by various chapters, such as those on democratic deliberation and political equality.[117] But they are also meta-theoretical, process-based questions that can only adequately be addressed in their own terms, distinct from an exploration of questions of constitutional substance. They are thus questions I leave explicit for another day.

Further, there are important potential questions, not addressed by this collection, as to the degree to which various constitutional values may legitimately be enforced, or recognised, via various quasi-constitutional constitutional principles, such as the principle of legality. The High Court, in recent years, has placed strong and consistent reliance on the principle of legality as a basis for a form of weak-form constitutional review, or sub-constitutional enforcement of common law rights and liberties.[118] Yet an important, open question relates to the degree to which the principle of legality might apply or extend to the protection of other constitutional values of the kind addressed in the collection.

The turn to constitutional values, therefore, is in no way a turn to some new clear or determinate set of decisional criteria. Rather, it is a turn to an additional set of substantive arguments, which can enrich rather than resolve the need for political deliberation about questions of constitutional justice. The aim of the collection is to contribute to this process of constitutional deliberation—by highlighting the diverse and complex ways in which values-based constitutional arguments might play out, if the High Court were to endorse a more explicitly functionalist approach to constitutional interpretation. The project would not have been possible without the support of the UNSW Faculty of Law, the HSF Law & Economics Initiative and the outstanding research assistance of Amelia Loughland, Anna Rienstra and Melissa Vogt, and I offer them my warmest thanks.

[114] For the language of guideposts, see US case law on their constitutional due process clause: *BMW of North America, Inc v Gore*, 517 US 559 (1996); *State Farm Mutual Automobile Insurance Co v Campbell*, 538 US 408 (2003).

[115] See, eg, Dixon, 'Amending Constitutional Identity', above n 6.

[116] Dixon, 'The Functional Constitution', above n 37, 480–81; see further Waldron, above n 37.

[117] See especially ch 3 by Jeffrey Goldsworthy; ch 8 by Scott Stephenson; ch 10 by James Stellios; and ch 9 by Joo-Cheong Tham in this collection.

[118] See, eg, *Lee v New South Wales Crime Commission* (2013) 251 CLR 196; *X7 v Australian Crime Commission* (2013) 248 CLR 92; *Momcilovic v The Queen* (2011) 245 CLR 1 (see especially French CJ, Crennan and Kiefel JJ). For discussion, see also D Meagher, 'The Principle of Legality as Clear Statement Rule: Significance and Problems' (2014) 36 *Sydney Law Review* 413; J Gans, 'Legality, Lenity and Responsibility' (paper presented at The Principle of Legality in Australia and New Zealand Conference, Deakin Law School, 20 February 2015); B Lim, 'The Normativity of the Principle of Legality' (2013) 37 *Melbourne University Law Review* 372; R Dixon (Comment), 'A New (Inter)National Human Right Experiment for Australia' (2012) 23 *Public Law Review* 69, 75.

I am particularly grateful to the many distinguished Australian public lawyers who agreed to join me in the task of exploring what a functionalist project could mean in practice. Not all of them agree with the basic tenets of the project, and yet all engage generously and thoughtfully with the questions it poses for the Court and debates over constitutional construction. They also embrace the broader academic vision that has guided me in producing this collection: the idea that, while the labels that structure the collection may be ones I have chosen as a means of guiding the conversation, the conversation only makes sense as a collaborative one, which draws on the insights and expertise of a vast array of scholars. I thus hope that this collection will be the beginning of a long-running and much broader conversation about what it would mean to take seriously the idea of distinctly *Australian* constitutional values.

2

The Justification of Judicial Review: Text, Structure, History and Principle[*]

NICHOLAS ARONEY[*]

I. INTRODUCTION

THE INSTITUTION OF judicial review is a vital part of the substructure on which the entire body of Australian constitutional law rests. Constitutional law would not exist as we know it today if it wasn't for the exercise by the courts, especially the High Court, of the power to review statutes for their constitutionality and to declare them to be invalid and void if they are considered to be inconsistent with the Constitution.

Judicial review is a monumental power. It is a capacity of the courts to determine what can and cannot be law. Its existence flatly contradicts the principle of parliamentary sovereignty, the doctrine that the power of the Parliament is 'so transcendent and absolute' that it 'cannot be confined either for causes or any bounds'.[1] Judicial review proposes that our legislatures are not sovereign in the sense that AV Dicey maintained was the case with the British Parliament, which he said could 'make or unmake any law whatever', and which 'no person or body' could 'override or set aside'.[2]

The remarkable thing about judicial review in Australia is that although it is a formidable power of immense significance and is exercised routinely by the High Court, its exact constitutional basis is exceedingly difficult to pin down. In many constitutions of the world, the power of judicial review is expressly conferred on the courts.[3] However, like the American and Canadian Constitutions on which it was

[*] This chapter was first presented as a paper at the Constitutional Theory Scholars' Workshop, Centre for Comparative Constitutional Studies, Melbourne Law School, 20 July 2017. Thanks are due to the organisers of the workshop and especially to Patrick Emerton, James Stellios, Scott Stephenson, Adrienne Stone and Fiona Wheeler for comments on the paper. The support of ARC grant FT100100469 is also gratefully acknowledged.

[1] Edward Coke, *The Fourth Part of the Institutes of the Laws of England: Concerning the Jurisdiction of Courts*, 1st edn (London, Flesher, Lee and Pakeman, 1644) 36.

[2] AV Dicey, *Introduction to the Study of the Law of the Constitution*, 10th edn (London, Macmillan, 1959) 40. See J Goldsworthy, *The Sovereignty of Parliament: History and Philosophy* (Oxford, Clarendon Press, 1999) ch 1.

[3] eg, *Österreichische Bundesverfassung* [Austrian Federal Constitution] art 140; *Grundgesetz für die Bundesrepublik* [Basic Law of the Federal Republic of Germany] arts 93 and 100; *Bunreacht na hÉireann* [Constitution of Ireland] arts 15 and 26; *Constitución Española de 1978* [Spanish Constitution] arts 161–64.

partly modelled, there is no provision in the Australian Constitution which expressly confers the power. This fact alone has led two distinguished scholars to conclude that judicial review is constitutionally unjustified. Thus, after a careful review of the relevant provisions, Pat Lane found that he could find no constitutional basis for the practice.[4] Rather, he concluded, the institution was historically adopted and became part of Australian law by prescription: the High Court had copied the practice of the US Supreme Court, the Privy Council, and the pre-federation colonial courts, and the Parliament and people had acquiesced in it.[5] James Thomson, following an even closer examination of the relevant constitutional provisions, came to a similar conclusion. Judicial review is a 'prodigious power', he observed, which rests on a 'slender reed'.[6]

It does seem to be the case, however, that the framers of the Australian Constitution anticipated the High Court would exercise judicial review. It was expected that the Court would, in the words of Josiah Symon, 'safeguard the liberties of the subject and the rights of the individual States against the encroachment of the Legislature'.[7] As the 'supreme interpreter' of the Constitution, said Edmund Barton, the federal judiciary would function as the 'bulwark of the Constitution', settling any dispute over whether the Parliament had attempted to 'transgress the law of the land'.[8] Such a role was understood by the framers to be essential to the operation of a genuinely federal constitution modelled on the United States example. Citing the famous decision of Marshall CJ of the US Supreme Court in *Marbury v Madison*,[9] Barton observed:

> It is only such Acts of Congress as are within the scope of their powers as conferred by the Constitution that became the supreme law of the land. Where such Acts are in violation of the Constitution, it is the province of the courts of the United States to declare the law void and refuse to execute it. The final appellate power upon all such questions is in the Supreme Court of the United States.[10]

Relying on statements such as these, Brian Galligan argued that the framers 'fully intended' and 'clearly specified' judicial review as 'an integral part of the system's design and structural logic'.[11] Sir Owen Dixon put it this way:

> To the framers of the Commonwealth Constitution the thesis of *Marbury v Madison* was obvious. It did not need the reasoned eloquence of Marshall's utterance to convince them that simply because there were to be legislatures of limited powers, there must be a question of ultra vires for the courts.[12]

[4] P Lane, 'Judicial Review or Government by the High Court' (1965) 5 *Sydney Law Review* 203, 203.
[5] ibid 207–08.
[6] JA Thomson, 'Constitutional Authority for Judicial Review: A Contribution from the Framers of the Australian Constitution' in G Craven (ed), *The Convention Debates 1891–1898: Commentaries, Indices and Guide* (Sydney, Legal Books, 1986) 201.
[7] *Official Report of the National Australasian Convention Debates*, Adelaide, 20 April 1897, 950.
[8] ibid 952.
[9] *Marbury v Madison*, 5 US (1 Cranch) 137 (1803).
[10] *Official Report of the National Australasian Convention Debates*, Melbourne, 4 March 1898, 1875.
[11] B Galligan, 'Judicial Review in the Australian Federal System: Its Origin and Function' (1979) 10 *Federal Law Review* 367, 372.
[12] O Dixon, 'Marshall and the Australian Constitution' in *Jesting Pilate and Other Papers and Addresses* (Melbourne, Law Book Company, 1965) 166, 174.

Accordingly, the High Court has from the beginning been very willing to play the role that Symon and Barton expected of it. In its very first exercise of constitutional judicial review the Court—which consisted of three of the most prominent framers, Griffith CJ, Barton and O'Connor JJ—asserted the power without much explanation at all, stating baldly that it was the duty of the Court, not the executive government, to determine questions of constitutional validity.[13] Almost half a century later, in the *Communist Party Case*, Fullagar J famously said that in Australia the principle established in *Marbury v Madison* has been regarded as 'axiomatic'.[14] In *Cormack v Cope*, Barwick CJ went so far as to adopt the words of Lord Pearce in *Bribery Commissioner v Ranasinghe* when he said that the High Court has a 'duty to see that the Constitution is not infringed and to preserve it inviolate'.[15] In subsequent cases justices of the High Court have occasionally referred to particular provisions of the Constitution as affirming the Court's jurisdiction to exercise judicial review in particular respects,[16] but none of these provisions justifies the exercise of the power as a whole. Rather, the power seems to arise by way of implication.

Certainly, that was the view of Geoffrey Lindell, who argued that the High Court is not only authorised, but is under a duty to exercise its jurisdiction, even when that involves the exercise of judicial review.[17] According to Lindell, the exercise of judicial review is an outworking of the principle that it is the recognised function of courts to determine and interpret every law that is relevant to the disposition of a matter, and that the Constitution is such a law.[18] This power was exercised prior to federation by Australian colonial courts with respect to Imperial statutes operating by paramount force, and it necessarily continued after federation, for the Constitution was, after all, enacted as an Imperial statute.[19]

In this chapter, I propose that the various rationales for constitutional judicial review in Australia are deeply intertwined. There are specific provisions in the text of the Constitution from which its exercise may be inferred, but such inferences depend on an understanding of the operation of those provisions within the wider structural features of the Constitution and the context of the institutions that the Constitution was intended to establish. To use the language popularised by Philip Bobbitt (but *not* his meaning), the modalities of text, structure and history all seem necessary to the argument, as well as the wider modalities of ethics and doctrine.[20] No single modality of argument is sufficient to establish the constitutional legitimacy of judicial review. It is only when the modalities are brought into a mutually illuminating and disciplining relationship that judicial review can be constitutionally justified.

[13] *D'Emden v Pedder* (1904) 1 CLR 91, 117–18.

[14] *Australian Communist Party v Commonwealth* (1951) 83 CLR 1, 262 (*Communist Party Case*). See also *Victoria v Commonwealth* (1975) 134 CLR 338, 379–80 (Gibbs J).

[15] *Cormack v Cope* (1974) 131 CLR 432, 452, quoting *Bribery Commissioner v Ranasinghe* [1965] AC 172, 194.

[16] See, eg, *Plaintiff S157/2002 v Commonwealth* (2003) 211 CLR 476, 513–14 (*Plaintiff S157/2002*).

[17] G Lindell, 'Duty to Exercise Judicial Review' in L Zines (ed), *Commentaries on the Australian Constitution: A Tribute to Geoffrey Sawer* (North Ryde, Butterworths, 1986) 158.

[18] ibid 160–69.

[19] ibid 169–83.

[20] P Bobbitt, *Constitutional Fate: Theory of the Constitution* (New York, Oxford University Press, 1982); P Bobbitt, *Constitutional Interpretation* (Oxford, Blackwell Publishers, 1991).

In particular, while the text of the Constitution comes close to suggesting that the High Court will exercise constitutional judicial review, this is only when the text is read in the light of what Brian Galligan called its 'structural logic and original design'.[21] The logic and design of the Constitution only becomes apparent, I argue, when the relevant evidence and argument adduced by each modality is considered in an integrated, mutually illuminating and mutually disciplining manner.[22] Moreover, this justification of judicial review has implications for how the Constitution ought to be interpreted. Each of the modalities—text, structure, history, and ethics—must be brought into mutually illuminating and disciplining relationship if our interpretations of the Constitution are to possess explanatory power. Principles and values have a legitimate role to play in constitutional interpretation, but only as they are grounded in and disciplined and illuminated by the Constitution's text, structure and history.

II. TEXTUAL PROVISIONS

The textual provisions of the Constitution relevant to the justification of judicial review are of three kinds. First, there are the provisions that confer or authorise the conferral of particular heads of jurisdiction on the High Court, other federal courts, and State courts invested with federal jurisdiction. The second are the provisions that confer or presuppose the conferral of judicial power on the courts. The third are those that establish a hierarchy between particular categories of law, with the Constitution at the apex of that hierarchy.

Section 76 is the only provision that refers explicitly to the interpretation of the Constitution. It authorises the conferral of jurisdiction in the following terms:

> The Parliament may make laws conferring original jurisdiction on the High Court in any matter:
>
> (i) arising under this Constitution, or involving its interpretation;
> (ii) arising under any laws made by the Parliament;
> (iii) of Admiralty and maritime jurisdiction;
> (iv) relating to the same subject-matter claimed under the laws of different States.

Does this provision authorise the High Court to exercise the power of constitutional judicial review? There are several barriers to such a conclusion. First, there is the problem that this is a head of jurisdiction, not a conferral of judicial power as such. Section 76(i) enables the conferral of jurisdiction in respect of matters arising under the Constitution or involving its interpretation, but it does not of itself

[21] Galligan, above n 11, 370.

[22] For more detail, see N Aroney, 'Originalism and Explantory Power' (paper presented at the Workshop in Honour of Professor Jeffrey Goldsworthy, Monash University Chambers, Melbourne, 17–18 July 2017); N Aroney, 'Explanatory Power, Theory Formation and Constitutional Interpretation: Some Preliminaries' (2013) 38 *Australian Journal of Legal Philosophy* 1; N Aroney, 'Towards the "Best Explanation" of the Constitution: Text, Structure, History and Principle in *Roach v Electoral Commissioner*' (2011) 30 *University of Queensland Law Journal* 145.

confer judicial power; and the exercise of constitutional judicial review is a kind of judicial power, not a kind of jurisdiction. As Griffith CJ explained in *Ah Yick v Lehmert*, '"federal jurisdiction" means the authority to exercise the judicial power of the Commonwealth',[23] and it is section 71 of the Constitution, not sections 75 and 76, that confers judicial power. Jurisdiction, as such, refers to the categories of matters in respect of which a court has authority to adjudicate, and such categories of matters may be defined by reference to geography, classes of persons or particular subject matters.[24] Accordingly, as James Stellios has explained, while judicial power is a particular kind of governmental power, jurisdiction is the authority to exercise that power in a particular respect.[25]

Secondly, the heads of original jurisdiction referred to in section 76 are not conferred directly by the Constitution but depend on a decision of the Parliament to grant the jurisdiction. The fact that the Parliament conferred this particular head of jurisdiction when it enacted the Judiciary Act in 1903,[26] suggests that such matters were always intended to be included within the jurisdiction of the High Court. But it would be curious if the Court's authority to exercise such a profoundly important power as constitutional judicial review, at least in its original jurisdiction, should depend on parliamentary enactment.[27]

Thirdly, it is notable that section 76(i) refers to matters 'arising under' and 'involving [the] interpretation' of the Constitution. The High Court has held that for a matter to 'arise under the Constitution' it is sufficient that the right or duty in question 'owes its existence' to a provision of the Constitution; it is not necessary, therefore, that the resolution of the controversy involves the interpretation of the Constitution or a determination of the constitutional validity of the law.[28] Likewise, a matter 'involving the interpretation of the Constitution' need not involve a determination that a Commonwealth or State law is constitutionally invalid. Such a matter may simply involve the direct operation of the Constitution in some particular respect. Thus, the exercise of jurisdiction in respect of the matters referred to in section 76(i) need not involve constitutional judicial review. If, as a matter of construction, they need not involve it, then section 76(i) can have a conceivable operation that does not include judicial review. If it can have this operation, then it does not of itself authorise, or mandate, the exercise of constitutional judicial review by the High Court, although it is not inconsistent with the exercise of judicial review either.

[23] *Ah Yick v Lehmert* (1905) 2 CLR 593, 603.

[24] See *Lipohar v The Queen* (1999) 200 CLR 485, 516–517; *Minister for Immigration and Multicultural and Indigenous Affairs v B* (2004) 219 CLR 365, 377, 394–95.

[25] J Stellios, *The Federal Judicature: Chapter III of the Constitution* (Sydney, LexisNexis Butterworths, 2010) 109.

[26] Judiciary Act 1903 (Cth) s 30. See H Irving, 'The Framers' Vision of the High Court' in P Cane (ed), *Centenary Essays for the High Court of Australia* (Sydney, LexisNexis Butterworths, 2004) 28–30.

[27] This point is underscored by the fact that general jurisdiction over the other matters referred to in s 76 has not been conferred on the High Court: N Aroney, P Gerangelos, J Stellios and S Murray, *The Constitution of the Commonwealth of Australia: History, Principle and Interpretation* (Melbourne, Cambridge University Press, 2015) 525–26.

[28] *R v Commonwealth Court of Conciliation and Arbitration; Ex parte Barrett* (1945) 70 CLR 141, 154; *LNC Industries v BMW* (1983) 151 CLR 575, 581; *British American Tobacco Australia Ltd v Western Australia* (2003) 217 CLR 30, discussed in ibid 536–37.

The appellate jurisdiction of the High Court, which is conferred directly by section 73 of the Constitution, is similar. Section 73 provides:

> The High Court shall have jurisdiction, with such exceptions and subject to such regulations as the Parliament prescribes, to hear and determine appeals from all judgments, decrees, orders, and sentences:
>
> (i) of any Justice or Justices exercising the original jurisdiction of the High Court;
> (ii) of any other federal court, or court exercising federal jurisdiction; or of the Supreme Court of any State, or of any other court of any State from which at the establishment of the Commonwealth an appeal lies to the Queen in Council;
> (iii) of the Inter-State Commission, but as to questions of law only;
>
> and the judgment of the High Court in all such cases shall be final and conclusive.

Apart from the difference between jurisdiction and judicial power already noted, there are two reasons why this provision is insufficient to provide a decisive basis for judicial review. The first is that the appellate jurisdiction of the High Court is subject to such exceptions as the Parliament prescribes. Again, it would be odd that such an important power should be capable of being qualified in this way. The second problem is that the nature of the judicial power exercised by the High Court in any particular appeal depends on the nature of the judicial power exercised by the court from which the appeal has been brought. Whether such cases can involve questions of constitutional judicial review depends on the kind of judicial power being exercised by those lower courts. The question thus turns on a larger one, concerning the power exercised by Australian courts generally, and not the particular jurisdiction conferred on the High Court by section 73 of the Constitution.

Similar observations can be made about paragraphs 75 (iii) and (v). These provide that the High Court shall have original jurisdiction in all matters in which the Commonwealth is a party, in which a person suing or being sued on behalf of the Commonwealth is a party, and in which a writ of Mandamus, prohibition or injunction is sought against an officer of the Commonwealth. Such matters can often involve the interpretation of the Constitution or of a law made by the Commonwealth. They can also often involve matters of administrative judicial review such as a determination of whether the Commonwealth, a person on behalf of the Commonwealth or an officer of the Commonwealth has undertaken action that contravenes or is not authorised by a law of the Commonwealth.[29] However, this is not constitutional judicial review per se, and even when cases arising under paragraphs 75(iii) and (v) involve judicial review of legislation, there is nothing in the language of those provisions, semantically understood, that expressly confers the power to do so. More is needed.

Section 74 of the Constitution is another possibility. It relevantly provides:

> No appeal shall be permitted to the Queen in Council from a decision of the High Court upon any question, howsoever arising, as to the limits inter se of the Constitutional powers

[29] See P Cane and L McDonald, *Principles of Administrative Law: Legal Regulation of Governance*, 2nd edn (Melbourne, Oxford University Press, 2012) ch 5.

> of the Commonwealth and those of any State or States ... unless the High Court shall certify that the question is one which ought to be determined by Her Majesty in Council.

This section contemplates that the High Court may make decisions concerning the limits inter se of the constitutional powers of the Commonwealth and the States. Assuming such decisions to be final and binding, section 74 seems to assume, without saying so explicitly, that the Court may in the course of making such decisions declare that Commonwealth and State laws have exceeded their limits and are for that reason unconstitutional and therefore invalid. Of all the provisions considered so far, section 74 accordingly provides the strongest support for Geoffrey Sawer's claim that these provisions are 'unintelligible' unless the power of constitutional judicial review was intended to be exercised.[30] However, as Thomson has observed, section 74 does not itself grant the power to make such decisions. Moreover, inter se questions are not the only kind of question that may involve constitutional judicial review.[31] Again, more is required.

The jurisdiction provisions of the Constitution do not, of themselves, confer the power to exercise judicial review. The power itself must be an aspect of the judicial power of the Commonwealth. Section 71 of the Constitution provides:

> The judicial power of the Commonwealth shall be vested in a Federal Supreme Court, to be called the High Court of Australia, and in such other federal courts as the Parliament creates, and in such other courts as it invests with federal jurisdiction.

Read solely in terms of its semantic meaning, the 'judicial power' conferred by section 71 might or might not include constitutional judicial review. The canonical definition of judicial power proposed by Griffith CJ in *Huddart, Parker v Moorehead* makes no mention, however, of judicial review. It merely refers to 'the power which every sovereign authority must of necessity have to decide controversies between its subjects, or between itself and its subjects, whether the rights relate to life, liberty or property'.[32] Later cases clarified that these must be understood as pre-existing rights, and that an essential element of judicial power is that it involves the application of pre-existing law to some controversy about the meaning or application of that law.[33] This is not constitutional judicial review, however; it is merely a description of the ordinary adjudicative functions of a court. The judicial power conferred on the High Court might include judicial review, but section 71 does not require this to be so. To get to constitutional judicial review, more therefore is needed than the bare words of section 71, even when read with the jurisdiction referred to and conferred by sections 73, 74, 75 and 76 of the Constitution. Something more is still required.

Judicial review involves a determination of whether a law enacted by a legislature is constitutionally valid. The assessment of the constitutional validity of a law in turn depends on a legal hierarchy of laws in which the Constitution is higher than the ordinary statute and therefore prevails over it in the event of an inconsistency between them. Two provisions of the Constitution refer to relationships of

[30] G Sawer, *Australian Federalism in the Courts* (Melbourne, Melbourne University Press, 1967) 76.
[31] Thomson, above n 6, 200–01.
[32] *Huddart, Parker & Co Pty Ltd v Moorehead* (1909) 8 CLR 330, 357.
[33] Aroney et al, above n 27, 564, 567–68.

supremacy and inferiority between particular categories of law and law-interpreting institutions. The first is covering clause 5. It relevantly provides:

> This Act, and all laws made by the Parliament of the Commonwealth under the Constitution, shall be binding on the courts, judges, and people of every State and of every part of the Commonwealth, notwithstanding anything in the laws of any State.

The second is section 109. It provides:

> When a law of a State is inconsistent with a law of the Commonwealth, the latter shall prevail, and the former shall, to the extent of the inconsistency, be invalid.

These provisions suggest a hierarchy consisting of (a) the Commonwealth of Australia Constitution Act 1900 (UK) and the Constitution contained therein; (b) laws made by the Parliament of the Commonwealth; and (c) laws made by the Parliaments of the States.[34] Here the text of the Constitution comes close to stating expressly that an ordinary statute that is inconsistent with the Constitution must be regarded as invalid. But not quite. The term 'invalid' is used only in respect of State laws that are inconsistent with Commonwealth laws; it is not used to refer to laws that are inconsistent with or repugnant to the Constitution. And, in any case, the kind of invalidity contemplated by s 109 is not of the kind contemplated by constitutional judicial review. If the relevant federal law is subsequently repealed, the state law springs back into operation. It is not void ab initio.

Likewise, while covering clause 5 requires that the courts and judges named therein are bound to apply the Constitution and Commonwealth laws notwithstanding anything contained in a State law, it does not quite say that they are bound to find a State law invalid if it is inconsistent with the Constitution. While such a conclusion would not be inconsistent with the language of covering clause 5, it is not required by the clause as a matter of its semantic and syntactical meaning. Moreover, the judges and courts referred to in covering clause 5 are those 'of every State' and 'of every part of the Commonwealth'. There is reason to think that this latter phrase encompasses Territory courts, but not the High Court and other federal courts.[35] It is true that covering clause 5 refers to Commonwealth laws made 'under the Constitution' and this might be taken to imply, as Quick and Garran argued, that any law made 'in excess of the authority conferred by the Constitution is no law' and that it is the duty of the courts to regard any such law as ultra vires and invalid.[36] However, in the reasoning of Quick and Garran such a conclusion depended not on the language of covering clause 5 itself, but upon the practices of American courts under the US Constitution and the opinions of scholarly authorities such as AV Dicey. Neither covering clause 5 nor section 109 of themselves provide a textual basis for constitutional judicial review of Commonwealth and State laws generally. Something more is still needed.

[34] See *Joosse v Australian Securities and Investment Commission* (1998) 159 ALR 260, 264 (Hayne J).

[35] Thomson, above n 6, 191.

[36] J Quick and R Garran, *The Annotated Constitution of the Australian Commonwealth* (Sydney, Angus & Robertson, 1901) 346–47. Remarkably, while Quick and Garran discussed at this point the doctrine that colonial laws repugnant to imperial laws will be void, they did not offer this as a reason why constitutional judicial review might be exercised, on the basis that the Constitution is contained in an imperial statute: ibid 347–52. Edmund Barton likewise did not ground the exercise of judicial review on the imperial doctrine of repugnancy: Thomson, above n 6, 182.

III. STRUCTURAL PRINCIPLES

Here we come to an important juncture. The bare text of the Constitution does not tell us that the High Court is authorised to exercise constitutional judicial review; that is, to declare, conclusively, that a statute inconsistent with the Constitution is invalid, void ab initio, and therefore of no legal effect. But what, then, of the structure of the Constitution? Do the provisions of the Constitution canvassed so far, when read together, add up to the institution of judicial review? If the judicial power conferred by section 71, as Griffith CJ maintained, authorises the courts to determine the meaning, content and application of the law, and if covering clause 5 and section 109 indicate a hierarchy of laws in which the Constitution is regarded as superior to ordinary statutes enacted by the Commonwealth and State Parliaments, then two of the vital premises in Marshall CJ's argument in *Marbury v Madison* appear to be supplied by the Constitution. It is the province of the courts to determine what the law is, and the relevant law to be determined includes a written constitution that is hierarchically superior to ordinary statute law. Marshall CJ's conclusion might therefore be thought to follow: in the case of an inconsistency between the Constitution and an ordinary statute, it is the Constitution that must be applied and the ordinary statute disregarded. Perhaps, this does indeed follow, but only if the premises in the argument are sound. However, as noted, while covering clause 5 and section 109 might be thought to suggest a kind of hierarchy among the laws, they do not quite spell this out. Supplementary principles and understandings are required.

Geoffrey Lindell has suggested that the separation of powers implies that the courts are authorised to exercise judicial review. He has stated that judicial review is 'an essential feature of any system of government which recognises the distinction between the exercise of judicial, executive and legislative powers'.[37] However, this is not a compelling argument. First, it begs the question. Just because there is a distinction between judicial, legislative and executive power tells us nothing of the content of those powers. It is quite conceivable that a rigorous separation of powers could exist and yet the functions of the courts be restricted to the determination of disputes concerning the meaning and application of the law without including a power to declare that laws inconsistent with the Constitution are invalid and void. Indeed, on one view, the principle of the separation of powers requires that courts should not exercise constitutional judicial review, for this involves them in trespassing on the domain of the legislature. It is for this very reason that the exercise of constitutional judicial review in France has historically been reserved to the *Conseil constitutionnel* and is denied to the ordinary judiciary.[38]

In *Plaintiff S157/2002*, Gaudron, McHugh, Gummow, Kirby and Hayne JJ suggested two other principles that might underwrite constitutional judicial review: the rule of law and federalism.[39] The rule of law, we may suppose, entails the proposition that all persons and institutions are, as Dicey maintained, subject to and

[37] Lindell, 'Duty to Exercise Judicial Review', above n 17, 158.

[38] M Cappelletti, 'Judicial Review in Comparative Perspective' (1970) 58(5) *California Law Review* 1017, 1024–26.

[39] *Plaintiff S157/2002* (2003) 211 CLR 476, 513–14.

bound by the law.[40] This might be thought to imply that the power of the Parliament to make laws is not only conferred by the Constitution, but is also subject to and limited by it. For, after all, the legislative power of the Commonwealth is expressed in section 51 to be 'subject to' the Constitution. If it is the province of the courts to apply the law, it seems to follow that it is within the province of the courts to determine whether a statute enacted by the Parliament contravenes those limits.

The principle of federalism also supports this sort of conclusion. As the justices said in *Plaintiff S157/2002*, some authority is required to 'maintain the federal compact by ensuring that propounded laws are constitutionally valid and ministerial or other official action lawful and within jurisdiction'. In 'any written constitution where there are disputes over such matters', they observed, 'there must be an authoritative decision-maker', and under the Australian Constitution, that 'ultimate decision-maker' is the High Court.[41] Such reasoning has often been expressed by members of the High Court. In the *Boilermakers* case, it was said:

> In a federal form of government a part is necessarily assigned to the judicature which places it in a position unknown in a unitary system or under a flexible constitution where Parliament is supreme. A federal constitution must be rigid. The government it establishes must be one of defined powers; within those powers it must be paramount, but it must be incompetent to go beyond them. The conception of independent governments existing in the one area and exercising powers in different fields of action carefully defined by law could not be carried into practical effect unless the ultimate responsibility of deciding upon the limits of the respective powers of the government were placed in the federal judicature.[42]

As John Quick and Robert Garran put it in their *Annotated Constitution*:

> The Federal Parliament and the State Parliaments are not sovereign bodies; they are legislatures with limited powers, and any law which they attempt to pass in excess of those powers is no law at all it is simply a nullity, entitled to no obedience. The question whether those powers have in any instance been exceeded is, when it arises in a case between parties, a purely judicial question, on which the courts must pronounce.[43]

Arguments like this, drawing on fundamental principles of the rule of law and federalism, would seem to be needed in order to conclude that constitutional judicial review is a legitimate function of the High Court.

IV. ENACTMENT HISTORY

But here is an important question: are text, structure and principle sufficient? The problem is this: while the inferences we draw about the rule of law, federalism and judicial review seem obvious, this is only due to our tendency to interpret the Constitution in the light of the historically situated culture in which it was enacted and of which we are still a part. If an alien, literally, was to interpret the Constitution solely

[40] Dicey, above n 2, 183–205.

[41] *Plaintiff S157/2002* (2003) 211 CLR 476, 513–14.

[42] *R v Kirby; Ex parte Boilermakers' Society of Australia* (1956) 94 CLR 254, 267–68 (Dixon CJ, McTiernan, Fullagar and Kitto JJ) (*Boilermakers' Case*). See also *Forge v Australian Securities and Investments Commission* (2006) 228 CLR 45, 73.

[43] Quick and Garran, above n 36, 791.

with aid of a dictionary,[44] there is little if anything in its text or structure that would lead the alien to the idea of the 'rule of law', 'federalism' or 'judicial review', as these expressions are nowhere used in the text. Only fragments of those expressions are used in the Constitution: 'law', 'federal' and 'judicial'.[45] The semantic meaning of those terms and the syntactical meaning of the sentences in which they are located do not give rise to the larger concepts. And nor does a careful assessment of the structural relationships established by the Constitution quite get us there. Combining the semantic and syntactical meaning and strictly logical implications of the relevant sections in Chapters I and III the Constitution does not of itself generate the 'rule of law', 'federalism', or 'judicial review'. It is our reading of these provisions in the light of our shared cultural understandings that leads us to discern these larger concepts. The text and structure of the Constitution is consistent with them because, as a matter of history, the framers of the Constitution intended and designed the document to provide a constitutional framework in which the rule of law, a federal system and judicial review would operate.

Indeed, there was a very broad consensus among the framers of the Constitution that the High Court would, and should, exercise constitutional judicial review. According to two of the most influential academic authors of the time, James Bryce and AV Dicey, judicial review was a vital means by which both federal and state governments are kept within their respective constitutional bounds.[46] At the time, constitutional judicial review existed in the United States, Canada and Switzerland, although in the latter case, judicial review applied only to cantonal, and not to federal, legislation. In Switzerland, the integrity of the federation was (and is) guarded through the effective representation of the cantons in not only the federal legislature, but also in the federal executive.[47] While the framers of the Australian Constitution drew significantly on the Swiss model in other respects, Robert Garran expressed the consensus view when he said that 'the superior sanctity of the Constitution' was 'ineffectually guarded' in Switzerland.[48]

[44] *Baxter v Commissioners of Taxation (NSW)* (1907) 4 CLR 1087, 1106 (Griffith CJ, Barton and O'Connor JJ): 'It is true that what has been called an "astral intelligence," unprejudiced by any historical knowledge, and interpreting a Constitution merely by the aid of a dictionary, might arrive at a very different conclusion as to its meaning from that which a person familiar with history would reach'.

[45] The intention of the framers to establish a 'federal commonwealth' is declared in the preamble and in covering clause 3. If there is one general principle of government that is expressed, as distinct from implied, by the Constitution, it is federalism. But federalism can be of many kinds. To discern the exact kind of federalism established by the Australian Constitution, close attention has to be given to the text, structure and history of the Constitution. I sought to demonstrate this in N Aroney, *The Constitution of a Federal Commonwealth: The Making and Meaning of the Australian Constitution* (Cambridge, Cambridge University Press, 2009).

[46] J Bryce, *The American Commonwealth*, 2nd edn (London, Macmillan and Co, 1889) vol I, 225–28, 235–36, 237–43, 247; Dicey, above n 2, 130–55, 410–13.

[47] T Stauffer et al, 'Switzerland' in AL Griffiths and K Nerenberg (eds), *Handbook of Federal Countries* (Montreal, McGill–Queen's University Press, 2005) 347–48; A Lienhard et al, 'The Federal Supreme Court of Switzerland: Judicial Balancing of Federalism without Judicial Review' in J Kincaid and N Aroney (eds), *Courts in Federal Countries: Federalists or Unitarists?* (Toronto, University of Toronto Press, 2017).

[48] R Garran, *The Coming Commonwealth: An Australian Handbook of Federal Government* (Sydney, Angus & Robertson, 1897) 80. Today, virtually all federations rely on judicial review, as well as the representation of the States in the federal legislature, to ensure that the federal and state institutions of government are kept within their constitutional bounds. See N Aroney and J Kincaid (eds), *Courts in Federal Countries: Federalists or Unitarists?* (Toronto, University of Toronto Press, 2017).

The views of Josiah Symon and Edmund Barton on the importance of constitutional judicial review have been noted already. Andrew Inglis Clark plainly expected the High Court to exercise judicial review and exerted considerable influence on the other framers in thinking likewise.[49] Thus William Trenwith spoke of the need for the High Court to function as 'custodian of the Constitution' so as to ensure that the Parliament did not exceed its powers.[50] It was because the Court was to exercise such an important function that figures such as Bernhard Wise, Josiah Symon, Charles Kingston and John Downer considered it essential that the Court be established in a manner that made it wholly independent of the Parliament and executive.[51]

Only three of the delegates to the federal conventions tried to control the powers or limit the functions of the High Court in one way or another. Patrick Glynn proposed that the Court consist of a Chief Justice and, until Parliament otherwise provided, the Chief Justices of the several States, principally so that it would be more representative of the States.[52] Frederick Holder proposed that decisions of the High Court be reviewable by referendum.[53] John Gordon proposed that only the Commonwealth and State Attorneys-General have the right to plead the unconstitutionality of State and Commonwealth laws respectively.[54] However, such was the framers' confidence in the High Court and in the institution of judicial review that Glynn's proposal failed by a vote of 29 to nine,[55] Holder withdrew his proposal in the face of extensive opposition,[56] and Gordon's proposal was negatived without a division and without an additional voice speaking on its behalf.[57] The framers were thus strongly united on the importance of judicial independence as a means to the end of keeping both the Commonwealth and the States within their respective spheres. As John Downer put it, the High Court would exercise 'vast powers of judicial decision' in determining what would be 'the relative functions of the Commonwealth and of the States'. And he seemed to speak for many when he added that the Court would have

> the obligation of finding out principles which are in the minds of this Convention in framing this Bill and applying them to cases which have never occurred before, and which are very little thought of by any of us. With this Supreme Court, particularly in the earlier days of the Commonwealth, rests practically the establishment on a permanent basis of the Constitution, because with them we leave it not to merely judicially assert the

[49] Galligan, above n 11, 373–78. See A Clark, 'The Supremacy of the Judiciary Under the Constitution of the United States, and Under the Constitution of the Commonwealth of Australia' (1903) 17 *Harvard Law Review* 1.

[50] *Official Report of the National Australasian Convention Debates*, Adelaide, 25 March 1897, 940.

[51] ibid 935 (Wise), 942 (Symon), 947 (Kingston), 957 (Downer).

[52] *Official Report of the National Australasian Convention Debates*, Melbourne, 28 January 1898, 265–68. See also *Official Report of the National Australasian Convention Debates*, Adelaide, 25 March 1897, 117 (John Gordon) and *Official Report of the National Australasian Convention Debates*, Melbourne, 28 January 1898, 272 (Charles Cameron Kingston).

[53] *Official Report of the National Australasian Convention Debates*, Melbourne, 28 January 1898, 1717–19.

[54] ibid 1679–83.

[55] ibid 285.

[56] ibid 1730–32.

[57] ibid 1690.

> principles which we have undoubtedly asserted, but with them rests the application of those principles, and the discovery as to where the principles are applicable and where they are not.[58]

As I have noted elsewhere, no one ventured to contradict him.[59]

V. CONCLUSIONS

It is only when the Constitution is read in the light of its enactment history that its specific provisions, and the structural relationships between them, begin to make sense. Judicial review was not expressly referred to in the Constitution because the framers thought it was not necessary to spell it out explicitly.[60] The framers knew that judicial review had been exercised in the Australian colonies prior to federation; they were aware it operated in the United States and Canada; and they expected the legal community to understand that judicial review was meant to operate within the Australian federation as well. The framers designed the judicial system so that it mimicked, in certain vital respects, the corresponding provisions in the American and Canadian Constitutions. When they provided in section 71 that the judicial power of the Commonwealth would be vested in the High Court, they understood that this would include the power of constitutional judicial review. When they provided that the High Court's jurisdiction would include general appellate jurisdiction (section 73), original jurisdiction in matters where the Commonwealth is a party or a particular remedy is sought against an officer of the Commonwealth (section 75), and could include original jurisdiction in matters arising under the Constitution or involving its interpretation (section 76), they anticipated that the High Court would exercise constitutional judicial review in many such matters. Likewise, the exercise of judicial review in matters inter se between the Commonwealth and the States was assumed in the drafting of section 74 because its existence went without saying. Judicial review was so obvious, it was simply unnecessary to spell it out.

In order to secure obedience to the Constitution, the framers considered it necessary to provide explicitly that the Constitution would be binding on State courts (covering clause 5), but it did not occur to them that it was necessary to say the same thing with respect to the High Court and other federal courts because they would owe their very existence to the Constitution (section 71). While a separation of powers does seem to have been intended by the framers (at least to some extent), it was more central and important to them that they were drafting a constitution for a 'federal commonwealth' (preamble and covering clause 3), by which they meant a self-governing commonwealth constructed out of constituent self-governing

[58] ibid 275.

[59] Aroney, *The Constitution of a Federal Commonwealth*, above n 44, 298.

[60] See J Goldsworthy, 'Implications in Language, Law and the Constitution' in G Lindell (ed), *Future Directions in Australian Constitutional Law: Essays in Honour of Professor Leslie Zines* (Sydney, Federation Press, 1994) 158–61, 168–70; J Goldsworthy, 'Constitutional Implications Revisited' (2011) 30 *University of Queensland Law Journal* 9, 19–21.

commonwealths, as James Bryce had said.[61] This meant, among other things, that the constituent States would continue to exercise the powers they possessed prior to federation, subject only to what was required to establish the federation (sections 106 and 107); that the Commonwealth Parliament would only have the legislative powers specifically conferred on it (sections 51 and 52); and that the executive power vested in the Commonwealth would extend only to the execution and maintenance of the Constitution and of laws constitutionally enacted by the Parliament (section 61). The structure and design of the federal judicature supported this scheme: partly as a dual system of courts operating at a State and federal level (federal courts being invested with particular heads of jurisdiction (sections 75, 76 and 77)); partly as an integrated hierarchy of courts in which the High Court would operate as the highest court of appeal (section 73); and partly to ensure that the courts would exercise the vital power of constitutional judicial review, with the High Court having ultimate control over the determination of the powers of the Commonwealth and the States inter se (section 74).

The text and structure of the Constitution illuminated by its history and by the principles and values that demonstrably influenced its framers, makes adequately clear that the exercise of constitutional judicial review is a legitimate function of the High Court. This does not mean, however, that it is legitimate for the Court to inflate ideas about judicial review, federalism, the separation of powers or representative government into domains and with implications that cannot be justified by reference to the text, structure, and history of the Constitution. Ethical and political principles can illuminate our understanding of the Constitution, but they must themselves be grounded in and illuminated and disciplined by its text and structure, and informed by its history. Otherwise such principles will threaten to overwhelm and displace the Constitution itself. Indeed, since constitutional judicial review is only justifiable on the basis of the text, structure, history and principles of the Constitution, its exercise ought to be calibrated in terms of their disciplining constraints. For it is in the mutually illuminating and disciplining considerations of text, structure, history and principle that we are able to arrive at an interpretation that makes the best sense of the Constitution and most fully acknowledges its authority.

Elsewhere I have spelt out how I think this mutually illuminating and disciplining relationship between the modalities of argument produces an interpretation that makes the best sense of the Constitution.[62] The master concept, I have proposed, is explanatory power. A theory has explanatory power in so far as it can explain a relatively large and complex array of facts with a relatively simple set of concepts or ideas. The simpler the concepts used to explain the data, and the larger, more complex and more detailed the array of facts explained, the greater the explanatory power of the theory. As a consequence, the explanatory power of a theory is a function of its simplicity, its descriptiveness, and its consilience with other theories: the greater the simplicity, descriptiveness and consilience of a theory, the greater its explanatory power. Here, *simplicity* concerns the economy of entities or concepts that are postulated by a theory, *descriptiveness* concerns the range and complexity

[61] N Aroney, 'A Commonwealth of Commonwealths: Late Nineteenth-Century Conceptions of Federalism and Their Impact on Australian Federation, 1890–1901' (2002) 23(3) *Journal of Legal History* 253.

[62] See the sources cited in above n 22.

of the things that a theory purports to explain, and *consilience* concerns the coherent integration of the primary theory with other theories.

The explanatory power of an interpretation of the Constitution will be maximised in proportion to the simplicity of the concepts it uses, the specificity and generality of the constitutional data it explains, and the consilience of the interpretation with cognate interpretations that deal with other aspects of the Constitution. Fundamental principles and values—such as the rule of law, representative democracy, federalism and the separation of powers—contribute to the simplicity of our theories about the Constitution, but they do not of themselves render any particular theory more explanatory than another. This is because the explanatory power of an interpretation also depends on its descriptiveness, which turns on the extent to which it is able to explain the text and structure of the Constitution. The more specific the textual details and the more general the structural features that can be explained, the greater the explanatory power of the interpretation. The specificity of the interpretation is measured by its capacity to explain each particular word, each particular phrase and each particular sentence of the Constitution, considered in the context of the whole, while the generality of the interpretation is measured by its capacity to explain the structure of the constitution as a whole, considered in terms of its organisation into interlocking chapters, parts, paragraphs, sentences and so on.

In arriving at an interpretation of the Constitution that has explanatory power, an understanding of its enactment history is essential. History contributes to the explanatory power of an interpretation by illuminating our understanding of the Constitution's most specific characteristics as well as its most general structural features. Many characteristics of the text and structure of the Constitution that might otherwise be overlooked are often highlighted, and illuminated through an understanding of the Constitution's history. History also serves to discipline interpretation, by helping to ensure that meanings are not attributed to the Constitution as a result of the interpreter's personal preferences and predilections. History brings to light the exact purposes, principles and values that demonstrably motivated those who drafted the Constitution and helps us to understand how those purposes, principles and values were specifically implemented in the Constitution's text and structure. Provided they are appropriately disciplined, these purposes, principles and values can be used to propose, with some elegance, an interpretation of the Constitution that accounts for many of its specific and general features in a coherent way. In other words, they can contribute to an interpretation of the Constitution that has explanatory power. But they can only do this when they are disciplined by the other modalities, so that the content that is ascribed to the general principles is not allowed to become more, or to imply more, than is warranted when the text, structure and history of the Constitution are taken fully into account.

Such an approach explains why constitutional judicial review is genuinely an implication of the Australian Constitution. It also offers an account of why judges routinely rely on textual, structural, historical and ethical modalities of interpretation, and why in our assessment of the legitimacy of particular interpretations of the Constitution we evaluate those interpretations by reference to their capacity to explain both the specific textual details and the general structural relationships of the Constitution, and why an understanding of the enactment history of the Constitution is essential in arriving at an interpretation that has explanatory power.

3

Functions, Purposes and Values in Constitutional Interpretation

JEFFREY GOLDSWORTHY

I. INTRODUCTION

PROFESSOR ROSALIND DIXON has called for a functionalist approach to constitutional interpretation, lying somewhere 'between the extremes of pure formalism, and pragmatism or policy-oriented legal reasoning'.[1] Formalism involves 'a strong, if not exclusive, emphasis on formal legal materials', such as legal texts and court decisions.[2] Pragmatism maintains that such materials are frequently indeterminate, necessitating judicial choices based on 'a purely open ended policy-based approach' allowing 'resort to any form of policy or consequentialist-based reasoning'.[3] Functionalism, like pragmatism, acknowledges the existence of indeterminacies,[4] and 'invites courts directly and openly to rely on substantive constitutional values';[5] but it does not agree that the judges' choice of values is unconstrained—they must have their 'source ... in the text, history or structure of the ... constitution'.[6]

In this chapter I will explore Dixon's call for functionalism from the perspective of mainstream modern originalism.[7] This will require distinguishing between three different activities that are often bundled together under the label 'interpretation', but which I will call clarification, supplementation and rectification.[8] Two main issues are raised: one concerns the nature and source of the values that a functionalist should use, and the second concerns when and how they should be used in the course of these three activities. I will argue that Dixon's functionalism either is a modest extension of formalism—in effect, a kind of purposive formalism—or collapses into

[1] R Dixon, 'The Functional Constitution: Re-reading the 2014 High Court Constitutional Term' (2015) 43 *Federal Law Review* 455, 456.

[2] ibid 455.

[3] ibid 458, 460–61.

[4] ibid 461.

[5] ibid 456, 459, 461.

[6] ibid 456.

[7] See LB Solum, 'What is Originalism? The Evolution of Contemporary Originalist Theory' in G Huscroft and BW Miller (eds), *The Challenge of Originalism: Theories of Constitutional Interpretation* (New York, Cambridge University Press, 2011).

[8] See section IV below.

pragmatism. I will also suggest that, when judges engage in supplementation rather than clarification or rectification, there may be a greater role for pragmatism than Dixon acknowledges.

II. THE NATURE AND SOURCE OF CONSTITUTIONAL VALUES

The Australian Constitution notoriously lacks express statements of national values, aspirations or fundamental principles.[9] This may be for the better.[10] But every constitution is enacted in order to further the purposes of its makers. Different kinds of purpose can be distinguished including, first, the purpose of establishing particular legal norms (rules or principles) by enacting the constitution's text, and second, the purpose of achieving particular beneficial consequences for the community by establishing those norms. These purposes are relevant to the interpretation of the constitution, but many other purposes are not, including ulterior motives such as gratifying personal ambition, acquiring or retaining political power, and so on. The purposes that are relevant to interpreting a law are not all the motivations that led individual lawmakers to enact it, but the main reasons by which they publicly justified doing so.[11]

The purpose of a piece of legal text is to establish a legal norm, and the purpose of the norm is to achieve beneficial consequences for the community. Purposes of the second kind necessarily embody value commitments: to regard a particular consequence as beneficial is to value it. These purposes amount to intentions to achieve particular valued consequences. Purposes are therefore inseparable from value commitments, as Dixon recognises when she frequently refers to 'values or purposes'.[12]

There is usually a chain of linked purposes and values: for example, constitution-makers may enact a set of words in order to establish a particular constitutional norm, that judicial salaries be fixed, in order to secure judicial independence, in order to secure the impartiality of judicial decision-making, in order to secure justice and the rule of law, in order to promote human dignity (and the chain may or may not end there). Until the final link of the chain, purposes and values are instrumental; they contribute to some deeper purpose or value. The final link involves some value or values regarded as intrinsically good—good for its or their own sake. I will subsequently use the term 'chain of purposes' to refer to this phenomenon.

In this context, purposes and functions are identical.[13] The function or purpose of a legal norm is to achieve something valued. Of course, strictly speaking legal

[9] E Arcioni and A Stone, 'The Small Brown Bird: Values and Aspirations in the Australian Constitution' (2016) 14 *International Journal of Constitutional Law* 60, 60–63; C Saunders and M Donaldson, 'Values in Australian Constitutionalism' in D Davis, A Richter and C Saunders (eds), *An Inquiry into the Existence of Global Values: Through the Lens of Comparative Constitutional Law* (Oxford, Hart Publishing, 2015) 15–17.

[10] J Goldsworthy, 'Constitutional Cultures, Democracy, and Unwritten Principles' [2012] *University of Illinois Law Review* 683; J Goldsworthy, 'Redemptive Originalism' [2012] *Ethics* 785.

[11] S Soames, 'Toward a Theory of Legal Interpretation' (2011) 6 *New York University Journal of Law & Liberty* 231, 250.

[12] Dixon, 'The Functional *Constitution*', above n 1, 462, 464–66, 491.

[13] They may not be the same in other contexts; eg, bodily organs such as the heart can intelligibly be said to have functions, but not purposes. In that context, a function is a contribution to the operation of

norms—like other inanimate objects—do not have purposes. A purpose is a kind of intention: an intention to achieve something. Only intelligent, reasoning beings can have intentions and purposes. It is true that we casually say things such as: 'the purpose of a hammer is to bang in nails'. But a hammer does not have a purpose of its own, which is independent of the purposes of human beings. Its purpose must be the purpose for which it was either designed, or acquired, in order to be used, or for which it is in fact used, and that must be a purpose of the person or people who either designed, acquired or use it. The purpose of a hammer that has not yet been purchased might differ from that of a hammer that has been purchased for some idiosyncratic purpose, such as to form part of a sculpture. The purpose of a legal norm must, similarly, be the purpose of either the people who made it, or other people who subsequently use it, such as (a majority of) the community as a whole, or perhaps the judiciary, acting on the community's behalf.

Since purposes and functions are identical, Dixon's references to functions could be replaced by references to purposes. 'Functionalism' therefore seems synonymous with 'purposivism'. Dixon almost accepts this, but distinguishes the two on the ground that purposivism concerns the original purposes of the lawmakers, whereas functionalism may also concern functions that develop or are acquired later on.[14] But there are versions of purposivism, such as that defended by Professor Aharon Barak, that give priority to supposedly contemporary, 'objective' purposes of the community over the historical, 'subjective' purposes of the lawmakers.[15] So the choice is not between formalism and purposivism, but between originalist and non-originalist versions of both.

In several places, most explicitly in her 'Response to Commentators', Dixon raises the possibility that a court could legitimately ascribe to constitutional provisions contemporary values or purposes that the founders may not have endorsed.[16] She distinguishes a 'largely historical or backward-looking approach' concerned with 'textual confirmation of pre-existing values', from a 'more forward-looking approach', for example, one that takes into account 'comparative constitutional law, experience and scholarship to ascertain the possible functions or values served by the relevant structures'.[17]

Even judges who rely on original values might sometimes be justified in taking the experience of other jurisdictions into consideration. For example, as I have observed elsewhere,

> any argument that an implied principle is necessary to fulfil one of the constitution's purposes (such as federalism, democracy, or the separation of powers) could possibly be

a larger system that may or may not have been intelligently designed. In this and later paragraphs in this section, I draw on material in J Goldsworthy, 'The Implicit and the Implied in a Written Constitution' in R Dixon and A Stone (eds), *The Invisible Constitution in Comparative Perspective* (Cambridge University Press, 2017, forthcoming).

[14] Dixon, 'The Functional Constitution', above n 1, 465.

[15] A Barak, *Purposive Interpretation in Law* (Princeton, Princeton University Press, 2005): see especially at chs 7–8.

[16] See, eg, Dixon, 'The Functional Constitution', above n 1, 465; R Dixon, 'Response to Commentators' (2015) 43 *Federal Law Review* 517, 517–18.

[17] Dixon, 'Response to Commentators', above n 16, 517–18.

> tested by reference to experience in other countries whose constitutions have the same purpose. If they get by perfectly well without the principle in question, then its necessity is doubtful.[18]

But that is a matter of using factual evidence of what is necessary for given purposes or values to be fulfilled. Identifying those purposes or values in the first place is a different matter. They cannot be whatever purposes or values the interpreter thinks are most desirable; that would not be functionalism, but instead, the 'purely open ended policy-based approach' that Dixon calls pragmatism.[19] Indeed, it would be hyper-pragmatism, because pragmatism as she defines it resorts to extra-constitutional values and policies only when the constitution's meaning is indeterminate, whereas this approach would make that meaning itself dependent on such values and policies. The same surely goes for laudable purposes or values served by other constitutions; in the absence of evidence that our Constitution was also designed to serve them, they have no genuine place within it, and an interpreter's belief that it would be better if they did could be relevant only if one were to embrace hyper-pragmatism. At one point, Dixon refers to looking 'forward' to likely consequences, in order to identify values (as distinct from working out how best to apply given values).[20] But this implies that those values have no pre-existing connection to the Constitution, so this forward-looking approach is also vulnerable to the objection that it collapses into pragmatism. Dixon adverts to this problem.[21]

As previously observed, only intelligent, reasoning beings can have intentions and purposes. The purpose of a legal norm must therefore be the purpose of either the people who made it, or other people who subsequently use it, such as (a majority of) the community as a whole, or perhaps the judiciary, acting on the community's behalf. The most promising attempt to justify resort to contemporary purposes or values is to argue that the relevant purposes of a constitution are not those of the people who made it, but those of the people who maintain and use it—namely, the contemporary community. This is associated with the popular, but mistaken, view that the contemporary validity or legitimacy of a constitution rests on its acceptance by the community—or in other words, on the 'sovereignty of the (contemporary) people'.[22]

Barak defends this approach. He argues that a constitution has 'objective purposes' that are independent of the subjective purposes of the constitution's makers.[23] Objective purposes consist of 'the goals, values, and principles that the constitutional text is designed [sic] to achieve in a modern democracy at the time of interpretation ... [In other words] society's basic normative positions at the time

[18] J Goldsworthy, 'Questioning the Migration of Constitutional Ideas' in S Choudhy (ed), *The Migration of Constitutional Ideas* (New York, Cambridge University Press, 2006) 141.

[19] Dixon, 'The Functional Constitution', above n 1, 460.

[20] Dixon, 'Response to Commentators', above n 16, 517–18.

[21] Dixon, 'The Functional Constitution', above n 1, 463–64.

[22] For why this view is mistaken, see J Goldsworthy, 'The Case for Originalism' in G Huscroft and BW Miller (eds), *The Challenge of Originalism: Theories of Constitutional Interpretation* (New York, Cambridge University Press, 2011) 57–59.

[23] Barak, *Purposive Interpretation in Law*, above n 15, ch 7 (see especially at 152–55, 190).

of interpretation'.[24] His version of purposivism emphasises 'public understanding at the time of interpretation'.[25]

But it is surely difficult to attribute purposes or values to the contemporary community other than at the most abstract level ('democracy', 'equality', 'justice', and so on), which provides little or no assistance in resolving concrete constitutional disputes. Given that very few citizens have any knowledge of the particular constitutional provisions in question, or of their functions, to attribute helpful purposes to them would usually be to indulge in blatant fiction.

In descending from the community's unhelpfully abstract basic commitments to identify more specific 'purposes' that can actually assist in resolving interpretive disputes, the judges would have to rely on their own contestable value judgements ('what does democracy, equality, justice and so on require *in this situation*?').[26] This would amount to the judges, starting from the ultimate and most abstract purposes in the chains of purposes discussed previously, reasoning backwards and substituting their own judgements of how those abstract purposes are best served, for the judgements actually made by the lawmakers. But to allow the judges to attribute to laws whatever intermediate purposes they deem best would once again return us to pragmatism. It would also undermine the essential role of elected lawmakers, which is precisely to represent the community in intelligently designing laws (including constitutions) to serve chosen purposes. The purposes the constitution's makers chose to pursue on behalf of the community by enacting it have better credentials than anyone else's to be deemed the purposes of the community itself.

The distinction between 'objective' and 'subjective' intentions and purposes can be a source of confusion. In common law jurisdictions, objective intentions have been described as *expressed* or *outwardly manifested* intentions.[27] The distinction is between the actual intentions and purposes of the lawmakers, some of which might be obscure or inaccessible, and what they appear to have been according to objective (publicly manifested) evidence. An objective intention or purpose, then, is an objectively manifested subjective intention or purpose: what a reasonable interpreter would conclude was the lawmaker's subjective intention or purpose, given only the publicly manifested (textual and contextual) evidence of it.[28] Given the fallibility of such evidence, this might differ from the actual subjective intentions and purposes of the lawmakers.

It is hard to conceive of any plausible alternative theory of 'objective' purposes, other than Barak's reliance on the supposed purposes of the contemporary community.

[24] ibid 190. See also at 148, 152–53, 155. 'Sic' is inserted because any constitution was designed by those who made it; even if it is later put to different purposes than theirs, it is not redesigned. Perhaps Barak meant 'intended'.

[25] A Barak, 'On Constitutional Implications and Constitutional Structure' in D Dyzenhaus and M Thorburn (eds), *Philosophical Foundations of Constitutional Law* (Oxford, Oxford University Press, 2016).

[26] Barak, Purposive Interpretation in Law, above n 15, 152–53.

[27] *Byrnes v Kendall* (2011) 243 CLR 253, 273, 274, 274–75, 275 (Gummow and Hayne JJ), 282 (Heydon and Crennan JJ).

[28] See further R Ekins and J Goldsworthy, 'The Reality and Indispensability of Legislative Intentions' (2014) 36 *Sydney Law Review* 39.

Any alternative theory would have to somehow explain how legal purposes or values can be both created by acts of law-making, yet also objective in the sense of being independent of the lawmakers' or even the community's intentions or purposes. This seems impossible. We can at least understand how moral values might be objective in this sense even if, after philosophical analysis, we do not accept that they are. But that is because we do not think of moral values as being deliberately created by human beings, although they can be deliberately incorporated into a law by lawmakers. By contrast, laws are deliberately created by human lawmakers. How, then, could those laws possibly have 'objective' purposes or values that are independent of the intentions and purposes of the people who made them (or, as Barak would have it, of the community that maintains them)? Even when a law incorporates an objective moral value, that is only because the law in its context objectively manifests or evidences the lawmakers' subjective intention to do so. If the notion of an 'objective purpose' is supposed to have some other meaning, it should be regarded with deep suspicion: it is too metaphysically queer to be believable.

The next best alternative for a non-originalist is to rely on purposes or values that have been erroneously attributed to a constitution by its highest court in a previous decision or line of decisions that should be accepted as binding for reasons of *stare decisis*. This does not, of course, provide any justification for the court departing from the constitution's original purposes and values in the first place. It also raises difficult questions, including: (a) whether a *clearly* erroneous prior decision or line of decisions should be regarded as binding, which depends on other factors such as the extent to which it or they have since been relied on, and (b) how much of the reasoning in the previous decision or decisions is binding. The orthodox view is that only the ratio decidendi—the immediate reason for the decision—is binding, rather than more abstract purposes. But pursuing such questions is beyond the scope of this chapter.

III. THE USE OF PURPOSES/FUNCTIONS AND VALUES

In relying on purposes, must interpreters go beyond formalism? As Dixon defines formalism, it places a 'strong, if not exclusive, emphasis on formal legal materials'.[29] These include not only the text of the Constitution and prior court decisions, but 'formal sources relating to the aims and understandings of the framers of the Constitution, or other aspects of our constitutional history'.[30] These sources include the 'formal record' of their aims and understandings[31]—in other words, the Convention Debates which, along with other historical evidence of original understandings, have been used since *Cole v Whitfield* to determine the originally intended purposes (or functions) of constitutional provisions.[32] From what other sources could their aims and understandings possibly be inferred? Apart from rightly inadmissible sources such as the founders' private diaries—inadmissible because they are not on

[29] Dixon, 'The Functional Constitution', above n 1, 455, 457.
[30] ibid 455.
[31] ibid 461.
[32] *Cole v Whitfield* (1988) 163 CLR 360.

the public record, and therefore not objectively 'manifested'—it is hard to see what else could be relevant. If admissible, publicly manifested evidence discloses an aim—which is another word for a purpose—then formalist judges can (and should) take that into account. In other words, they should be purposive formalists.

But if so, how would functionalist judges differ? Dixon says that they would 'directly and openly rely on substantive constitutional values, not simply more "formal" legal sources', *provided that* there is a way 'to source the particular values ... in the text, history or structure of the relevant provision'.[33] The verb 'to source' may be deliberately ambiguous, in order to include an array of possibilities; Dixon variously suggests that these values must be 'traced' to, 'anchored' in, 'directly sourced in', 'grounded' in, 'underlie' or 'underpin', or be 'implicit in', the text and structure of the constitution.[34] But surely values can be inferred, in any of these ways, from a law's text, history and structure only insofar as these sources are evidence of the lawmakers' value commitments, which are their 'aims'. If so, the formalist and the functionalist would appear to infer purposes and values from exactly the same sources.

The question then is: how does the formalist's purposive reasoning differ from the functionalist's substantive value reasoning? Dixon refers to 'direct and *open* engagement with substantive criteria that go beyond the scope of the constitution, prior cases, or the formal record of the aims and understandings of those who drafted the constitution'.[35] This suggests two possible differences. One is that the functionalist but not the formalist engages with 'substantive criteria that go beyond' the formal record of the aims and understandings of the drafters, and the other is that although both of them engage with substantive criteria, only the functionalist does so 'directly and openly'.

It is not clear how the functionalist can engage with substantive criteria that go beyond the formal record of the aims and understandings of the drafters. This is because Dixon herself insists that the functionalist should only engage with substantive values that can be inferred from the text, structure or history of the constitution. It might be argued that the interpreter cannot derive practical conclusions from the drafters' purposes or values without, in effect, stepping into their shoes and, from their perspective, making substantive purposive or value judgements. In this sense, the interpreter must go beyond the 'formal record'. But a purposive formalist would have to do the same thing. The formal record may disclose a relevant purpose or value, but cannot determine what that purpose or value entails in a particular, practical context.

Perhaps, then, Dixon intends the second difference: functionalists, but not formalists, are both able and willing to make substantive value judgements 'directly and openly'. This seems to be corroborated when Dixon distinguishes formalism from functionalism on the ground that formalists do not explicitly acknowledge the existence of judicial discretion and the need to make policy choices, and even conceal the policy choices that in fact guide their decision-making.[36] Dixon suggests that

[33] Dixon, 'The Functional Constitution', above n 1, 456.
[34] ibid 457, 460–63, 466.
[35] ibid 461 (emphasis in original).
[36] ibid 462, 464–65.

functionalism comes into play in 'hard cases' where constitutional meaning is relevantly indeterminate, and creative construction is required: '[a] functional approach … [is committed to] a focus on a range of substantive legal goals and values in resolving areas of formal legal indeterminacy'.[37] It then makes evaluative judgements openly, based on the lawmakers' likely purposes that have been inferred from formal legal sources. Dixon says that '[i]n many ways' functionalism 'simply represents an extension of existing, purposive approaches'.[38] On this view, functionalism is simply purposive formalism practised frankly and openly in hard cases involving indeterminate law.[39]

It should be noted that if the constitution-makers' purposes clarify the meaning of a legal text, then no legal indeterminacy needs to be resolved. For example, the meaning of the words 'absolutely free' in section 92 was unclear and controversial, but in *Cole v Whitfield* historical evidence helped to clarify the meaning that was originally intended.[40] The indeterminacy of its literal meaning was resolved by what Dixon describes as 'formal sources relating to the aims and understandings of the framers of the Constitution'.[41] It was therefore resolved by formalist methods, as she herself describes them. There was no remaining legal indeterminacy, and therefore no need for functionalism as we have just defined it.

This case shows how formalism must sometimes be purposive in order to clarify the meaning of a constitutional provision. But when clarification remains elusive, then according to Dixon, functionalism is required, and it extends the methodology of purposive formalism to the resolution of legal indeterminacies. Actually, the judicial role is somewhat more complicated, because judges do not only clarify meanings and then creatively resolve residual indeterminacies; they sometimes change determinate meanings in order to advance the lawmaker's purposes. It is useful to explore in more depth the kinds of interpretive problems that judges are called upon to resolve. The role of purposes and values in constitutional interpretation, and whether purposive formalism or functionalism (as we have now defined it) is called for, depends on the nature of the interpretive difficulty.

IV. INTERPRETATION AND CONSTRUCTION

Consider the variety of activities that are all bundled together under the label 'interpretation', in relation to both statutes and constitutions. Mainstream American originalists distinguish between 'interpretation' *stricto sensu*, and 'construction'.[42] 'Interpretation' refers to revealing and clarifying the pre-existing linguistic or communicative content of a constitutional provision: the meaning or meanings—express

37 ibid 459.

38 ibid 465–66: '[i]n many ways' functionalism 'simply represents an extension of existing, purposive approaches'.

39 Dixon herself uses this term: ibid 455–56, 466–67, citing P Gerangelos, 'Interpretational Methodology in Separation of Powers Jurisprudence: The Formalist/Functionalist Debate' (2005) 8 *Constitutional Law & Policy Review* 1.

40 (1988) 163 CLR 360.

41 Dixon, 'The Functional Constitution', above n 1, 455.

42 See L Solum, 'The Interpretation/Construction Distinction' (2010) 27 *Constitutional Commentary* 95.

and implied—that it communicates to its intended audience. I will refer to this as 'clarification'. 'Construction' is a more creative process, which must be resorted to when clarification is unable to resolve an interpretive difficulty, and the Constitution's communicative content or meaning is relevantly indeterminate. It involves supplementing the Constitution's meaning—adding more meaning to it in order to resolve a stubborn ambiguity, vagueness[43] or 'gap'. I will call this 'supplementation'. But as we will see, courts sometimes go even further and change or rectify, rather than just supplement, the meanings of constitutional provisions. I will refer to that activity as 'rectification'.

The meaning, or communicative content, of a constitution is determined by both its text and context; both provide evidence from which the meaning or meanings that the lawmakers intended to communicate can be inferred. The literal meaning of the text is governed by conventional rules of semantics (word meanings) and syntax (rules of grammar). The relevant semantic conventions are those of the language used (eg, English), including specialised legal terminology. The contribution of context to meaning is governed by what philosophers of language call 'pragmatics'. Context can inform both the express meaning communicated by the text, through what is called 'contextual enrichment', and various kinds of implied meanings.[44]

One example of contextual enrichment is the resolution of ambiguities; when a word has two or more dictionary meanings, the context in which it appears often makes clear which meaning was intended. Another example involves what are sometimes called 'implicitures' (from 'implicit'), as in: 'everyone [in some contextually identified group] is going to Paris' or: 'the Commonwealth Parliament has power to make laws with respect to [its own] taxation'.[45] Here, a crucial term (appearing in the square brackets) goes unmentioned because the context makes it so obvious that it can safely be taken for granted and left unsaid. Section 92 of the Australian Constitution provides that interstate trade and commerce is to be 'absolutely free', but fails to expressly specify from what it is free. The High Court in *Cole v Whitfield* correctly interpreted its communicative content as 'absolutely free [from discriminatory protectionism]'.[46] In addition, contextual as well as textual evidence of the lawmakers' communicative intentions can reveal various kinds of implications and implicit assumptions.[47]

When the Constitution's meaning cannot be clarified in some crucial respect, and remains partly indeterminate, the courts must resort to supplementation because they are obligated to resolve the difficulty even if the law does not provide them

[43] For my purposes 'vagueness' can be treated (inaccurately) as encompassing what has been called 'incommensurate multidimensionality', an example of which is the term 'child neglect' which encompasses multiple possible dimensions that are incommensurable. See H Asgeirsson, 'On the Instrumental Value of Vagueness in the Law' (2015) 125 *Ethics* 425, which explains how incommensurate multidimensionality entails vagueness. See also S Evans, 'The Meaning of Constitutional Terms: Essential Features, Family Resemblance and Theory-Based Approaches' (2006) 29 *UNSW Law Journal* 207, for a discussion of the same phenomenon (as in the case of 'judicial power') without using the same label for it.

[44] See Goldsworthy, 'The Implicit and the Implied', above n 13.

[45] Australian Constitution s 51(ii).

[46] See text accompanying above n 40.

[47] For further details, see Goldsworthy, 'The Implicit and the Implied', above n 13; J Goldsworthy, 'Constitutional Implications Revisited' (2011) 30 *University of Queensland Law Journal* 9, 13–15.

with a resolution. Due to the principle of *stare decisis*, the courts' resolution of the indeterminacy in effect adds new content to the meaning of the provision or provisions in question. For example, when vague expressions, or vague implications, are concerned, courts often construct sub-principles or 'doctrines' that determine how these expressions or implications should be applied.

Dixon attributes the recognition of (something like) supplementation to legal realism.[48] But it is also a prominent feature of standard legal positivism. Positivists hold that in 'easy cases', sufficiently determinate express or implied meanings can be identified, even if only with some difficulty, but in 'hard cases' they cannot, and judges then need to exercise creative, lawmaking discretion guided by extra-legal norms.[49] The difference between standard positivism and realism seems to be that realists regard legal indeterminacy as much more pervasive than do legal positivists; in other words, they regard many more cases as 'hard' rather than 'easy'.[50] I side with the legal positivists, because I do not believe that indeterminacy is as pervasive as realists seem to believe; in other words, there are many more easy cases—especially among those cases that are not taken to appellate courts—than realists acknowledge.[51]

I had previously tended to assume that in hard cases, courts must rely on considerations external to the Constitution, such as extra-legal moral and political considerations; in other words, they must resort to pragmatism. But Dixon suggests that judges should still rely on purposes and values that can be 'sourced', 'anchored', 'grounded' (and so on) in the text and structure of the Constitution.[52] Her position is similar to that of Scott Soames, an eminent philosopher of language:

> Courts are not to legislate, but … [w]hen the content of the laws fails to provide reliable guidance in determining a unique acceptable legal outcome—either because it leads to inconsistent outcomes, or because it fails to lead to any outcome … the task of the judicial authority is (i) to discern the predominant legislative rationales of the lawmaking bodies in adopting the laws or legal provisions, and (ii) to fashion the minimal modification of existing legal content that removes the deficiency and allows a decision to be reached, while maximizing the fulfilment of the discernible legislative rationales of the relevant laws or legal provisions.[53]

These same rationales, or purposes, are taken into account by purposive formalists at the clarification stage of the enquiry. Dixon and Soames argue that they have a continuing role at the supplementation stage.

[48] Dixon, 'The Functional Constitution', above n 1, 458.

[49] Positivists do not use the interpretation/construction terminology, but refer to judges in hard cases using discretion guided by extra-legal values.

[50] According to Dixon, legal realists argue that evaluative judgements are needed in 'almost any concrete legal controversy': Dixon, 'The Functional Constitution', above n 1, 458.

[51] See L Solum, 'On the Indeterminacy Crisis: Critiquing Critical Dogma' (1987) 54 *University of Chicago Law Review* 462.

[52] Dixon, 'The Functional Constitution', above n 1, 457, 460–63, 466.

[53] Soames, 'Toward a Theory of Legal Interpretation', above n 11, 233; see also at 252–53; see further S Soames, 'Deferentialism: A Post-Originalist Theory of Legal Interpretation' (2013) 82 *Fordham Law Review* 597, 613.

Supplementation is necessary when clarification fails to resolve ambiguity, vagueness or other kinds of indeterminacy. In cases of stubborn ambiguity, it is hard to see how, having failed to tip the scales in favour of one of the alternative possible meanings of a provision, the founders' purposes could assist in guiding supplementation of the provision's meaning. If one of the alternative possible meanings is more conducive to fulfilling the founders' purpose in enacting the expression, that would have been a reason to resolve the ambiguity accordingly, through clarification. If purposive formalism has failed to resolve an ambiguity, then resort to the lawmakers' purposes has presumably been exhausted and supplementation must appeal to extraneous values. At that point pragmatism becomes inescapable.

By contrast, in resolving problems caused by vagueness, which requires supplementation, the purposes or values that the Constitution was intended to fulfil may remain relevant. The lawmakers' purpose in using a vague expression cannot dissolve the vagueness; a vague term (consider 'tall' or 'bald') remains vague even when we understand that purpose. But our understanding of it might help us to apply the term in accordance with the purpose.[54]

On the other hand, it might be argued that when lawmakers deliberately enact vague standards, such as abstract principles, rather than precise rules, they do so because they realise that they cannot anticipate all the circumstances that might be relevant to the just determination of individual cases in the distant future, and therefore intend to give future judges—who can be informed of those circumstances—discretion to assess their relative weights and reach appropriate decisions. In other words, the lawmakers' main purpose in using vague terms may sometimes be to enable future judges—within limits—to be guided by their own evaluation of all the relevant circumstances that may come to light when the law must be applied in particular cases, rather than to be controlled by the lawmakers' own less well-informed preferences or expectations. If so, judges in applying vague terms should be guided by their own sense of appropriateness, in the light of contemporary circumstances, knowing that in doing so they are exercising a discretionary power deliberately conferred on them.[55]

There is an argument against using purposivism to resolve indeterminacies in the meaning of old constitutional provisions. Non-originalists argue that in interpreting constitutions, judges should be guided by contemporary values rather than the purposes of the constitution's long dead makers. In the case of clarification, this argument must overcome the powerful objection that it would authorise judges to change the meanings of constitutional provisions, contrary to the constitution's own mandatory procedures for amendment.[56] But when the meaning of a provision remains relevantly

[54] See S Soames, 'What Vagueness and Inconsistency Tell Us about Interpretation' in A Marmor and S Soames (eds), *Philosophical Foundations of Language in the Law* (Oxford University Press, 2011) 36–37, 43, 49–50.

[55] T Endicott, 'The Value of Vagueness' in A Marmor and S Soames (eds), *Philosophical Foundations of Language in the Law* (Oxford, Oxford University Press, 2011) 26. Jack Balkin's theory of 'living constitutionalism' is based heavily on just this argument: see J Balkin, *Living Originalism* (Cambridge, Mass, Harvard University Press, 2014). Dixon touches on these issues when discussing the debate over rules versus standards: Dixon, 'The Functional Constitution', above n 1, 468–69.

[56] Goldsworthy, 'The Case for Originalism', above n 22.

indeterminate, after all admissible evidence of the constitution-makers' communicative intentions has been exhausted, then this objection has no force. Judges who are obligated to supplement the meaning of a partially indeterminate provision are not changing its meaning contrary to the proven intentions of its makers. In that situation, the non-originalist argument that judges are free to be guided by contemporary values has much more force, and originalist objections to that argument much less. Pragmatism is then more plausible.

V. CONSTRUCTION AS RECTIFICATION

Courts sometimes change or rectify, rather than just supplement, the meaning of constitutional provisions. Arguably, there are various situations in common law systems in which rectification is tacitly accepted as legitimate, even if it is rarely explicitly acknowledged. The following four examples may not be comprehensive. It is notable that in all four, the lawmakers' purposes are crucial both in justifying and limiting the changes that judges are (arguably) entitled to make. The judges act as the constitution-makers' 'faithful agents' by adjusting the meanings of provisions in order to give better effect to their purposes.

(a) It is accepted that judges may sometimes correct obvious drafting errors, including inconsistencies, although these are very rare in constitutions. A drafting error is obvious when there is an obvious discrepancy between what a provision expressly provides, and what the lawmaker clearly intended to provide, given the law's subject matter and purpose. The error is corrected by adjusting the law's meaning to give better effect to its purpose.[57] An inconsistency should be resolved by adjusting the meaning of one or both of the inconsistent provisions in order to eliminate the inconsistency, while optimising the fulfilment of the lawmakers' purposes. This may require deciding which of two inconsistent purposes is the dominant one; usually, a specific purpose prevails over and qualifies a more general one.[58]

(b) What used to be called the 'equitable interpretation' of provisions has often been used to add qualifications to laws in order to avoid unintended and undesirable consequences in unusual and unanticipated circumstances.[59] The interpretation of section 117 of the Australian Constitution may provide an example. This prohibits the imposition within any State of a 'disability or discrimination' on anyone who is a resident of any other State, but it would not be held to require that temporary visitors from other States must be able to vote in elections for the State Parliament, even though the section is not expressly qualified.[60] Once again, the lawmaker's

[57] DC Pearce and RS Geddes, *Statutory Interpretation in Australia*, 7th edn (Australia, LexisNexis Butterworths, 2011) 50–52; A Scalia and BA Garner, *Reading Law: The Interpretation of Legal Texts* (St Paul, MN, Thomson/West, 2012) 234–39.

[58] Pearce and Geddes, above n 57, 146–48; P Herzfeld and T Prince, *Statutory Interpretation Principles* (Sydney, Lawbook Co, 2014) 98–99.

[59] See, eg, J Evans, 'A Brief History of Equitable Interpretation in the Common Law System' in J Goldsworthy and T Campbell (eds), *Legal Interpretation in Democratic States* (Farnham, Ashgate, 2002); J Evans, 'Reading Down Statutes' in R Bigwood (ed), *The Statute: Making and Meaning* (Australia, LexisNexis, 2004); R Ekins, *The Nature of Legislative Intent* (Oxford University Press, 2012) 275–84.

[60] See Goldsworthy, 'The Implicit and the Implied', above n 13.

apparent purpose is crucial in determining whether a consequence is unintended and undesirable.

(c) The meanings of provisions may sometimes be adjusted incrementally to enable them to achieve their intended purposes, if unanticipated social or technological developments would otherwise have made that impossible.[61] For example, the United States Constitution vests exclusive power in Congress to raise and maintain 'armies' and 'a navy' and to regulate 'the land and naval forces'.[62] When military aircraft were developed, it would have defeated the provision's obvious purpose if Congress had been denied the power to raise an air force. It is widely accepted that in such cases, the judges may adopt a purposive rather than a literal interpretation, by stretching the provision's literal meaning to give effect to its original purpose in contemporary circumstances. Elsewhere I have argued that this justifies the High Court adopting an interpretation of the word 'marriage' in the Australian Constitution that includes same-sex marriage; even though the word was not used in that sense in 1900, this would better serve the founders' purpose in giving power over marriage to the Commonwealth Parliament.[63]

(d) A so-called 'implied term' can be 'read into' or 'implied into' (in other words, inserted into) a law on the ground that it is practically necessary for the law to achieve one of its intended purposes. Here, too, purpose is crucial, both to justify and to limit the change that is made. Elsewhere, I have distinguished these 'fabricated implications', which are inserted by rectification, from genuine implications that are revealed by clarification.[64] The implied freedom of political communication, which the High Court purported to find in the Constitution in 1992, is an example of a fabricated implication.[65] So too, presumably, are the implications recognised in the *Kable* line of cases.[66]

VI. FABRICATED IMPLICATIONS

The process by which such implications are fabricated warrants further analysis, because it represents potentially the most fertile vehicle for judicial creativity. Consider the chains of purposes and values discussed previously, which can end with extremely abstract purposes such as to advance democracy, justice, liberty or human dignity. May judges legitimately start with such an abstract purpose, and then reason that—despite the lawmakers having taken a different view—some provision not included in the Constitution is in fact necessary to achieve that purpose, and therefore should be 'implied into' the Constitution? If so, what is to stop the judges using such purposive reasoning to rewrite the Constitution?

[61] Goldsworthy, 'The Case for Originalism', above n 22, 62–63; J Goldsworthy, 'Interpreting the Constitution in Its Second Century' (2000) 24 *Melbourne University Law Review* 677, 699–701.

[62] United States Constitution art I § 8.

[63] Goldsworthy, 'Interpreting the Constitution in Its Second Century', above n 61, 699–701.

[64] Goldsworthy, 'Constitutional Implications Revisited', above n 47, 18–22, where I referred to 'spurious' instead of 'fabricated' implications.

[65] ibid.

[66] J Goldsworthy, '*Kable*, *Kirk* and Judicial Statesmanship' (2014) 40 *Monash University Law Review* 75.

One obstacle is the need to accommodate other, competing purposes, whether abstract or more concrete. The Constitution's makers did not pursue a single, overarching purpose, but a variety of purposes, and made many compromises in attempting to accommodate all of them. The result is a qualified, partial pursuit of most purposes in order to accommodate others. A provision that might, in the abstract, seem necessary to achieve one of them, may have been deliberately excluded for that reason.

But the main obstacle is the requirement of humility on the part of judges, through their acceptance of a high standard of proof of 'necessity'. Disagreements about what concrete measures are necessary to pursue abstract purposes are commonplace, as shown by perennial debates about what democracy, liberty, justice and so on require in particular circumstances. Given that conflicting opinions are often all reasonable ones, judges should be reluctant to conclude that the Constitution's makers erred by omitting something truly necessary to achieve one of their own purposes. As the great American jurist Learned Hand observed: '[i]n construing written documents it has always been thought proper to engraft upon the text such provisions as are necessary to prevent the failure of the undertaking'. But because this is 'a dangerous liberty, not lightly to be resorted to', it is essential that the need be 'compelling' and the interpolated provision be confined 'to the need that evoked it'.[67]

Dixon is aware of the difficulty. Discussing the implied freedom of political communication, she observes that 'the prime focus of a functional approach is on how courts interpret *express* constitutional provisions or norms'; it does not, by itself, answer the question of 'when courts should identify additional principles as implicitly protected by the text and structure of the Constitution'. That requires 'an account of the underlying approach to judicial, versus legislative, power under a particular constitutional order'.[68] She then discusses a recent speech by Stephen Gageler, before his appointment as a Justice of the High Court of Australia, which is an example of functionalist reasoning along the lines that Dixon advocates.[69]

Gageler argued, in my view rightly, that the bare text of the Constitution is not sufficiently determinate to explain the major developments in Australian constitutional law since 1920. This is because '[t]he largest and most emphatic words in the Constitution ... have no fixed or intrinsic meaning'; 'language is inherently ambiguous and ... [this] is compounded the bigger is the idea and the more enduringly it is expressed'.[70] Those developments must be explained, instead, 'through the prism of some over-arching understanding of the structure and function of the Australian Constitution'.[71] He purports to reject originalism, although apparently only because he misunderstands it.[72] But then he adopts a plainly originalist version

[67] L Hand, *The Bill of Rights* (Cambridge, Mass, Harvard University Press, 1958) 29; see also at 14 where he uses the term 'interpolate'.

[68] Dixon, 'The Functional Constitution', above n 1, 480 (emphasis in original).

[69] S Gageler, 'Beyond the Text: A Vision of the Structure and Function of the Constitution' (2009) 32 *Australian Bar Review* 138.

[70] ibid 141.

[71] ibid 140.

[72] ibid 141–43. Gageler seems (erroneously) to regard originalism as committed to giving effect to how the constitution-makers intended particular constitutional provisions to be applied in the circumstances of their own era: at 143; see also the quote at 141, fn 11. That must be why he (erroneously) regards originalism in Australia as 'a relatively new phenomenon' that was not endorsed by the constitution-makers: at 141–42.

of functionalism. For example, just after rejecting the idea that the High Court in *Cole v Whitfield* used history in 'an attempt to tie the course of modern constitutional developments to the original intention of the framers', he acknowledges that the Court 're-align[ed] the legal operation of s 92 to the function originally conceived for it'—'the mischief to which s 92 was directed'.[73] His subsequent explanation of broader constitutional developments is also based on a historical account of 'the purpose of federation', which he argues was 'conceived not as a means of dividing and constraining government but as a means of empowering self-government by the people of Australia'.[74] He provides evidence that this was 'the underlying purpose of the Constitution'.[75] There is in our pre-Federation history 'no hint ... of any intention' of giving effect to the American conception of federalism as a means of avoiding majoritarian excesses.[76]

Gageler goes on to deploy this 'vision' of the structure and function of the Constitution to justify the High Court's 'discovery' of the implied freedom of political communication.[77] Given that political accountability is 'the primary mechanism by which the Constitution achieves [its] purpose' of enlarging the self-government of the people of Australia, judicial vigilance is required 'where ... political accountability is inherently weak or endangered'.[78] It follows that 'where a process of communication by which that political accountability is maintained is burdened by law, judicial deference must give way to judicial vigilance'.[79]

This reasoning is plausible, but insufficient to vindicate the implied freedom. Even Dawson J, who rejected the implied freedom, agreed that the Court should strike down any burden on political communication that would in fact prevent Members of Parliament from being 'directly chosen by the people', since 'chosen' must refer to the making of a genuine, informed choice.[80] Dawson J would have relied on express words, not a much broader implication. The problem is that the implied freedom is applied independently of the Constitution's express words, and has led to the invalidation of laws in situations that could not plausibly be regarded as preventing a genuine, informed electoral choice. To be soundly based, a structural implication such as the implied freedom must be 'necessary' to ensure the fulfilment of some constitutional purpose—as Judge Learned Hand put it, the need must be 'compelling'—and the implied freedom was never convincingly shown to be either necessary or compelling.[81] It cannot be the case that any norm that would *enhance* the capacity of some institution to perform its constitutional functions should be 'implied into' the Constitution. That would give the Court far too broad a power to rewrite the Constitution in order to improve it. That is why the test of necessity should still

[73] ibid 143.
[74] ibid 145.
[75] ibid 151.
[76] ibid.
[77] ibid 154–55.
[78] ibid 152.
[79] ibid 154–55.
[80] *Australian Capital Television Pty Ltd v Commonwealth* (1992) 177 CLR 106, 187.
[81] Goldsworthy, 'Constitutional Implications Revisited', above n 47; Goldsworthy, '*Kable*, *Kirk* and Judicial Statesmanship', above n 66.

be required: any proposal that a new norm should be 'implied into' the Constitution must show that the norm is necessary to enable that institution to perform its constitutional functions. That requirement is—and should be—very difficult to satisfy when taken seriously.

Another example of a structural implication is the so-called '*Kable* doctrine', which Dixon says has 'frequently invoked quite explicitly functionalist concerns as a guide to application of the doctrine'.[82] This doctrine prohibits State courts being given powers or procedures that would undermine their 'institutional integrity', a term that has yet to be given a clear meaning. This doctrine is itself based on functionalist reasoning: the need to protect the institutional integrity of State courts supposedly follows from the fact that they either are or could be invested with federal jurisdiction. But it has not yet been satisfactorily explained why a perceived or even actual diminution of their institutional integrity, which is confined to cases involving State jurisdiction and has no discernible effect on their exercise of federal jurisdiction, must be prohibited.[83] According to Dixon, the High Court has often justified the doctrine on the ground that it is designed to prevent the risk of arbitrary interferences with individual liberty.[84] But that takes the doctrine far beyond its underlying rationale, and therefore far beyond what is genuinely necessary or compelling. A structural implication can only be justified by a functionalist or purposive argument: the implication must be truly necessary for a constitutional 'structure' to function (that is, to achieve its intended purposes) effectively. That argument establishes the relevant purpose or value whose fulfilment the implication is supposed to guarantee. No other purpose or value would appear to be relevant.

VII. THE LIMITS OF PURPOSE

Recourse to the lawmakers' purposes may not be able to resolve every interpretive difficulty without the need for substantial moral or political choice on the part of the interpreter. The lawmaker's purposes may be too abstract and vague, or they may be in conflict with one another.

Western Australia v Commonwealth (*First Territory Senators Case*)[85] is an example of conflicting purposes. It is notorious for there being both textual and contextual, including purposive, arguments on both sides, for those arguments being evenly balanced, and for the judges ultimately having to choose (even if they did not acknowledge this) on the basis of their own value judgements.[86] The textual arguments pitted section 7 of the Constitution—which states that: 'The Senate shall be composed of Senators from each State'—and other provisions in Chapter I pt II which seem to presuppose that the Senate must be comprised only of Senators

[82] Dixon, 'The Functional Constitution', above n 1, 472.
[83] Goldsworthy, '*Kable*, *Kirk* and Judicial Statesmanship', above n 66.
[84] Dixon, 'The Functional Constitution', above n 1, 472–73.
[85] *Western Australia v Commonwealth* (1974) 134 CLR 201.
[86] The case is used to illustrate precisely this point in both J Stellios, *Zines's the High Court and the Constitution*, 6th edn (Sydney, Federation Press, 2015) 677–82; and S Joseph and M Castan, *Federal Constitutional Law: A Contemporary View*, 4th edn (Sydney, Lawbook Co, 2014) 40–42.

from the States—against the express provision in section 122 that Parliament 'may allow the representation of such territory in either House of the Parliament to the extent and on the terms which it thinks fit'. The word 'representation' was ambiguous, given that the Territories of both Australia and the United States had enjoyed non-voting representation in their respective Senates. The practical consequences of the alternative interpretations were also explored without clear resolution. The question ultimately became whether the principle of federalism (in the form of the Senate as a 'States' House') prevailed over that of representative democracy, or vice versa. But it was unclear which of the two principles the founders themselves would have prioritised, so the judges arguably had to decide which principle was morally more compelling. But that amounted to a pragmatic decision in Dixon's sense; it was not determined by functionalist/purposive considerations, because they were evenly divided—two functions or purposes, both fairly attributable to the Constitution and its makers, were in conflict.

VIII. CONCLUSION

Dixon has advocated a functionalist approach to constitutional interpretation in 'hard cases' where the meaning of the Constitution is relevantly indeterminate. She depicts functionalism as lying somewhere between formalism and pragmatism.[87] I have argued that:

1. In this context, functionalism is a kind of purposivism, because the function of a constitutional provision is to achieve a purpose, which is an intention to achieve something believed to be of value.
2. The purposes of a constitution are primarily the purposes of those responsible for creating or amending it, although erroneous judicial decisions that are binding due to *stare decisis* may introduce extraneous purposes. For judges to implement other purposes—such as the supposed purposes of the contemporary community—would be tantamount to adopting pragmatism. True purposivism is inherently originalist.
3. The purposes of constitutional provisions are often crucial to clarifying their meanings, because the literal meanings of their words must often be contextually enriched by taking into account contextual evidence of the constitution-makers' intentions and purposes. Express as well as implied meanings often depend on contextual enrichment. Sensible formalists who strive to clarify the meanings of constitutional provisions must therefore be purposive formalists.
4. In a 'hard case', where the meaning of a crucial provision is insufficiently determinate to resolve an interpretive controversy, judges must resolve it through supplementation. Dixon argues that even here, they should be guided by purposes and values that can be 'sourced in' the constitution. That would make functionalism an extension of purposive formalism. But I have suggested that in these situations, pragmatism may be defensible, because it is much less vulnerable

[87] See the definitions in section I above.

to the originalist objection that it amounts to amending the Constitution contrary to the prescribed amendment procedure. Purposive formalism during clarification, combined with pragmatism during supplementation, may be the ideal compromise between originalism and non-originalism.

5. As well as clarifying the meanings of constitutional provisions, and supplementing them when necessary, judges sometimes change them in order to advance the purposes of the constitution's makers. Here, too, those purposes are crucial, both in justifying and limiting the changes that may be made. One prominent example of such changes involves terms being 'read into' or 'implied into' a constitution when truly necessary to ensure that its purposes can be achieved.
6. In rare cases, resort to the constitution-makers' intentions and purposes is unable to resolve an interpretive controversy, even through supplementation, because those intentions and purposes are conflicting or otherwise insufficiently determinate. In these cases, resort to pragmatism seems inescapable.

4

Functions, Context and Constitutional Values

JONATHAN CROWE*

I. INTRODUCTION

WHAT ARE CONSTITUTIONAL values and where do they come from? One plausible answer is that constitutional values reflect the functions or purposes of the Australian Constitution and its provisions.[1] Representative government, it might be said, is a constitutional value because sections 7 and 24 of the Constitution (among other provisions) have the function or purpose of creating a representative system of government; similarly, federalism is a constitutional value because the Constitution as a whole has the function or purpose of creating a federal Commonwealth. This functional explanation of constitutional values strikes me as broadly correct. However, it is susceptible to at least two competing interpretations.

The idea that constitutional values reflect functions or purposes raises the question of where those functions or purposes themselves come from. One possible answer to this question is that the functions or purposes of the Constitution reflect the intentions of its framers. The functions of the Constitution, in other words, are those functions that the framers intended it to have. This account of functions is defended by Jeffrey Goldsworthy in his contribution to the present volume.[2] It yields an intentionalist or originalist account of constitutional functions and, therefore, of constitutional values. Constitutional values, on this view, are created with the Constitution and remain in place thereafter.

The intentionalist account of constitutional functions is plausible, as far as it goes. The intentions of the framers are certainly one possible source of constitutional functions and values. However, they are not the only source. A second possible answer to the question posed above is that the functions or purposes of the Constitution

* I would like to thank Peta Stephenson for her helpful comments on an earlier version of this chapter.

[1] See, eg, R Dixon, 'The Functional Constitution: Re-reading the 2014 High Court Constitutional Term' (2015) 43 *Federal Law Review* 455.

[2] See ch 3 by Jeffrey Goldsworthy in this collection. See also R Ekins and J Goldsworthy, 'The Reality and Indispensability of Legislative Intention' (2014) 36 *Sydney Law Review* 39.

reflect contemporary beliefs about the Constitution by members of the community. The functions of the Constitution, on this view, are those functions conferred on it by social agreement; their content can be discerned by examining social practices and narratives. This explanation yields what I will call a contextualist account of constitutional values.[3]

The intentionalist and contextualist accounts of constitutional functions and values are not necessarily mutually exclusive. Indeed, it seems to me that a combination of the two explanations is appropriate. Some constitutional values reflect the intentions of the framers of the Constitution, while others reflect contemporary beliefs and attitudes towards it. Goldsworthy and other originalists typically reject this kind of proposal on the ground that contemporary understandings of constitutional functions and purposes cannot be used to interpret the Constitution without illegitimately changing its meaning.[4] My aim in this chapter is to show that this objection is mistaken.

I begin by examining the concept of a function as it applies to legal texts and other artifacts. I explore the relationship between functions and intentions, showing how functions can arise from contemporary beliefs and attitudes, not just authorial intentions. I discuss the implications of this argument for the notion of ordinary meaning, explaining how the role of contemporary context in shaping the meaning of constitutional texts creates a problem for originalism. I then introduce the idea of constitutional narratives, showing how this helps to make sense of the role of contemporary practices in grounding constitutional values. I argue that constitutional narratives can provide a sound basis for constitutional implications (even when not grounded in authorial intentions). I conclude with a brief comment on functionalist theories of constitutional interpretation.

II. THE CONCEPT OF A FUNCTION

It is all very well to say that constitutional values can be explained in terms of functions, but what are functions in the first place? It is useful to begin by distinguishing broad and narrow senses of the term as applied to artifacts generally. A function, in the broadest sense, is any causal role an artifact plays in the plans of its creators or intentional acts of its users. An artifact such as a screwdriver, for example, may have numerous functions in this broad sense, including stirring tins of paint, prying open stuck doors and so forth. This broad concept of a function, however, is distinguishable from what is sometimes described as an artifact's *proper function*.[5]

[3] *cf* J Crowe, 'The Role of Contextual Meaning in Judicial Interpretation' (2013) 41 *Federal Law Review* 417.

[4] See, eg, J Goldsworthy, 'Constitutional Interpretation: Originalism' (2009) 4 *Philosophy Compass* 682; J Goldsworthy, 'The Case for Originalism' in G Huscroft and BW Miller (eds), *The Challenge of Originalism: Theories of Constitutional Interpretation* (Cambridge, Cambridge University Press, 2011).

[5] See, eg, R Millikan, *Language, Thought and Other Biological Categories* (Cambridge, MIT Press, 1984) 17; P Griffiths, 'Functional Analysis and Proper Functions' (1993) 44 *British Journal for the Philosophy of Science* 409, 410–12.

The proper function of a screwdriver is to drive screws, notwithstanding that it may also routinely be used in various other ways.

How, then, can we distinguish the proper function of an artifact from its other causal roles? It is tempting to say that the proper function of an artifact reflects the causal role its creator *intends* it to play, as opposed to other incidental roles invented by its users. However, a more subtle account is needed to distinguish the proper function of an artifact from foreseen or intended side effects. The designer of a pistol foresees that it will expel spent bullet casings, but the expulsion of spent shells is not the proper function of the pistol. The proper function of a pistol is, rather, to shoot bullets towards a target. The expulsion of spent shells is merely incidental to that function (notwithstanding that pistol designers may seek to ensure that shells are ejected in an optimal manner).

The proper function of an artifact, then, does not simply reflect the item's actual or intended causal role. It seems more illuminating to say that an artifact's proper function itself plays a particular causal role in both our *explanations* of what kind of artifact it is and our *evaluations* of its success or failure.[6] The proper function of a screwdriver, on this view, plays a central role in explaining why something counts as a screwdriver in the first place. An artifact normally counts as a screwdriver only if its creator both has in mind an appropriate concept of a screwdriver (including its proper function) and intends the created item to substantially fulfil that concept.[7] The type of intention that is necessary to produce a screwdriver is therefore partly defined by its proper function.[8]

Proper functions also play an evaluative role in relation to artifacts. They are not, of course, the only standards by which artifacts are evaluated. The proper function of a screwdriver is to drive screws, but a screwdriver is nonetheless deficient if it snaps easily when being used to pry open doors or for other purposes. Proper functions, however, play a particularly *fundamental* evaluative role, insofar as they enable artifacts to be placed on a continuum ranging all the way from complete failures to paradigmatic examples. Furthermore, evaluations of artifacts based on their functions play a particularly *salient* role in conditional evaluative descriptions such as 'an excellent screwdriver', 'a poor pistol' and so forth. A screwdriver that cannot drive screws without great effort is a poor screwdriver. However, a screwdriver that snaps when used as a prying tool, but drives screws well and with little effort, seems to be a good screwdriver with a flaw.

The proper function of an artifact of kind K, then, is a characteristic causal attribute of Ks which is both: (a) an essential component of any adequate explanation of why a K counts as a member of the kind; and (b) a fundamental evaluative standard for judging a K as a more or less successful example of the kind.[9] The proper

[6] For further discussion, see J Crowe, 'Law as an Artifact Kind' (2014) 40 *Monash University Law Review* 737, 749–50.

[7] ibid 740–43.

[8] This type of intention may not be sufficient to create a screwdriver, because the creator must also succeed in producing something that is constitutively capable of performing the screwdriver's proper function. For further discussion, see ibid 748–50.

[9] ibid 750.

function of a screwdriver, for example, is to drive screws. This is a characteristic causal feature of screwdrivers that plays a fundamental role in both explaining why something counts as a screwdriver in the first place and evaluating something as a good or bad example of a screwdriver. Similar accounts can be advanced for a wide range of other kinds of artifact.

I have so far been discussing the concept of a function as it applies to artifacts generally. We are now in a position to apply this analysis to law. It is generally accepted that law is a kind of artifact.[10] Individual laws, then, are artifact tokens that fall within the wider category of law. Specific laws will share the proper function of law in general (which I have argued elsewhere is to serve as a deontic marker by creating a sense of social obligation).[11] However, they will also have their own specialised proper functions in addition to sharing the function of law as a whole. A magnetic screwdriver, for example, shares the proper function of screwdrivers in general (driving screws), but it also has a more specialised proper function (driving screws while holding them magnetically in place).

It is in this sense, then, that we can speak about the function of the Constitution or a constitutional provision. References to functions or purposes in constitutional or statutory interpretation can be understood as appeals to the specialised proper functions of the laws or provisions in question. They cannot be understood as appeals to functions in the broad sense discussed at the start of this chapter, because that would mean the function of a law is however it is used or interpreted. There must be a more refined concept of a function in play. The notion of a proper function seems well suited to this role.

III. FUNCTIONS AND INTENTIONS

The account of proper functions advanced above places heavy emphasis on the intentions of artifact creators. It might therefore seem to yield an intentionalist account of where functions come from. Importantly, however, it is also possible for artifacts to obtain proper functions without being intentionally created with this in mind. The way an object is used and regarded by members of a social group can, in some cases, transform it into a particular kind of artifact with a proper function. Consider this case:

> *Tree Bench:* A tree falls down in the middle of a village. Workers in the village begin to regularly use the tree as a place to sit while they eat their lunch. They think and speak about the tree as they would a bench placed there for their use. They say things to each other like, 'I'll meet you on the bench at lunchtime'.[12]

[10] See, eg, JL Coleman and O Simchen, '"Law"' (2003) 9 *Legal Theory* 1; B Leiter, 'The Demarcation Problem in Jurisprudence: A New Case for Scepticism' (2011) 31 *Oxford Journal of Legal Studies* 663, 666; J Gardner, 'The Legality of Law' (2004) 17 *Ratio Juris* 168.

[11] Crowe, 'Law as an Artifact Kind', above n 6, 750–53.

[12] ibid 740. The example is based on a case discussed in J Searle, *The Construction of Social Reality* (New York, Free Press, 1995) 39.

It seems plausible that the fallen tree in this example has become a bench. However, its membership of the artifact kind *bench* cannot be traced to an authorial intention. Rather, its status as a bench is a matter of social fact involving the collective assignment of a status (bench) associated with a function (serving as a seat for multiple people). This status arises not from authorial intentions, but from social acceptance.[13]

Notice that what makes the tree a bench is not merely its physical form or even the fact that people may sit on it from time to time. It is not the case that anything people choose to sit on becomes a bench, even if it possesses many of the salient features normally attributed to benches. Rather, its membership of the artifact kind *bench* arises when it is collectively accepted as a member of that kind. The collective acceptance of the tree as a bench gives it a new *status function*:[14] it means that the item's status and function are now linked. It is no longer just a tree that people happen to sit on at lunchtime. Rather, it is collectively recognised as the *kind of thing* that characteristically performs that role.

We are now in a position to distinguish two general categories of artifact. *Intentional artifacts* are those artifacts whose status functions are best explained by reference to the intentions of their creators. *Institutional artifacts*, by contrast, are those artifacts whose status functions are best explained by reference to social beliefs and practices. The content of the collective acceptance that is necessary to create an institutional artifact plausibly mirrors the content of the intention required to create an intentional artifact.[15] That is, an item normally counts as an institutional artifact of kind K only if members of a social group have in mind an appropriate concept of K (including its proper function) and the item in question is collectively accepted as largely fulfilling that concept.

I have argued so far in this section that artifact functions can arise from both authorial intentions and social acceptance in appropriate cases. There are some artifacts whose status functions are best understood by reference to the intentions of their creators and others whose status functions are best attributed to social beliefs and practices. Furthermore, some artifacts plausibly possess status functions of both kinds. Consider, for example, a packet of cigarettes that is used as a form of money by prisoners in jail. The cigarettes do not cease to be cigarettes: they still have the proper function of being smoked by virtue of the intention with which they were created. However, they also have an additional function—serving as a medium of exchange—conferred by social acceptance.

I can see no reason, in principle, why a similar analysis should not be applied to law. A particular law, such as the Constitution or its individual provisions, is likely to have functions or purposes conferred on it by its creators. It may also have other functions or purposes conferred on it by social acceptance. There is no obvious reason to maintain—as Goldsworthy does—that the former explanation should generally be preferred to the latter.[16] There are, however, two further

[13] Crowe, 'Law as an Artifact Kind', above n 6, 743–46.

[14] *cf* Searle, above n 12, 40.

[15] *cf* Crowe, 'Law as an Artifact Kind', above n 6, 745–46.

[16] See ch 3 by Jeffrey Goldsworthy in this collection. See also Ekins and Goldsworthy, above n 2, 57–58.

questions arising from this account. The first concerns what happens when a function conferred on a law by its creators conflicts with a function conferred subsequently through social acceptance. The second concerns how we can determine the content of a socially conferred function when the interpretation of the law is in dispute. I will deal with the first question now and the second later.

IV. THE PROBLEM WITH ORIGINALISM

What happens when the function of a law intended by its framers clashes with a function attributed to it by social agreement? Both kinds of function, as explained above, may be correctly described as proper functions of the law. The question of which should prevail in a specific context, it seems to me, turns on which function is more salient for the interpretive task at hand. Consider, for example, the cigarette example described above. Suppose that a prisoner is discovered with several packets of cigarettes and accused of black market trading. The prison disciplinary hearing may have to determine the meaning or significance of the packets. It seems clear that, in this setting, the salient meaning of the packets corresponds to their function as a medium of exchange. They have not ceased to have the function of being smoked, but that function is less salient in this context.

I wish to argue that, in the context of legal interpretation, the socially accepted function of a law or provision is generally more salient than its intended function where these are in conflict. This is because the socially accepted function of a law is more likely than its intended function to reflect the ordinary meaning of the law for members of the community. Legal interpretation, as I have argued in detail elsewhere,[17] should presumptively follow ordinary meaning. This is both fair, because it helps ensure that the meaning of the law is transparent to its subjects, and conducive to law's function as a means of social coordination. It follows that, where legal interpreters must choose between the function intended for a law by its framers and the function attributed to it by contemporary social beliefs and practices, they should presumptively choose the latter option.

This argument, if correct, poses a deep challenge to originalist theories of legal interpretation. Goldsworthy has outlined in a book chapter published several years ago what he regards as 'the best argument for originalism'.[18] A central component of his argument is the claim that the original meaning of a legal text is its 'utterance meaning' at the time of enactment.[19] Goldsworthy distinguishes utterance meaning from both 'sentence meaning' (literal or dictionary meaning) and 'speaker's meaning' (the meaning intended by the speaker).[20] Utterance meaning, Goldsworthy says,

[17] Crowe, 'The Role of Contextual Meaning', above n 3, 426–31.

[18] Goldsworthy, 'The Case for Originalism', above n 4, 42.

[19] ibid 48.

[20] ibid 46–48. See also J Goldsworthy, 'Implications in Language, Law and the Constitution' in G Lindell (ed), *Future Directions in Australian Constitutional Law: Essays in Honour of Professor Leslie Zines* (Sydney, Federation Press, 1994) 151; J Goldsworthy, 'Constitutional Implications and Freedom of Political Speech' (1997) 23 *Monash University Law Review* 362, 362.

is 'the full meaning of an utterance, implied as well as expressed, and it depends on what the speaker's meaning appears to be, given evidence that is readily available to his or her intended audience'.[21] I agree with Goldsworthy that the original meaning of a legal text is best identified with its utterance meaning at enactment. However, the utterance meaning of a text at enactment may diverge significantly from the ordinary (or utterance) meaning of that text today.

Goldsworthy correctly observes that when we are unsure about the meaning of a text, we try to work out what the author was trying to communicate. However, this does not mean that the ordinary meaning of a text corresponds to its originally intended meaning. Nor does it mean that the ordinary meaning of a text reflects the beliefs people would have held about its intended meaning at the time of enactment. Rather, the ordinary meaning of a text reflects the best attempt of current interpreters to *reconstruct* its intended meaning from a contemporary standpoint.[22] Contemporary interpreters will often be in a position where the actual intentions of the authors are opaque or underdetermined. The ordinary meaning of a text, in such cases, will not reflect the actual intentions of the authors, but rather the most plausible reconstruction of their intentions from the interpreter's perspective.

Let us imagine a case where the intended function of a legal text diverges from its socially accepted function. The text will then have two competing proper functions. A contemporary interpreter, when encountering the text, will try to work out what the authors intended. However, the interpreter will do this from her contemporary point of view. The original intentions of the authors may be opaque from a contemporary standpoint, in which case the interpreter will have no choice but to follow current social understandings. In other cases, however, the interpreter may have some awareness that the author's intentions are likely to diverge from contemporary meanings. It is nonetheless likely in such cases that the author's intentions will be underdetermined by the evidence available to the interpreter in a way that favours applying contemporary viewpoints.

Take, for example, the term 'marriage' in section 51(xxi) of the Constitution. This term would have been understood by the drafters of the Constitution to mean 'the union of a man and a woman to the exclusion of all others, voluntarily entered into for life'.[23] However, the High Court has recently interpreted it to include same-sex marriages.[24] What, then, is the term's ordinary meaning? I think it is obvious that the ordinary meaning of 'marriage' in contemporary Australia includes same-sex unions.[25] A contemporary reader of the Constitution who knows that it was drafted more than a century ago is likely to be aware that the drafters would have understood 'marriage' in a more restrictive sense. However, this does not mean that the ordinary meaning of 'marriage' in the Constitution corresponds to its intended or original meaning at the time of drafting. How, then, can we explain this?

[21] Goldsworthy, 'The Case for Originalism', above n 4, 48.

[22] Crowe, 'The Role of Contextual Meaning', above n 3, 431–34.

[23] Marriage Act 1961 (Cth) s 5.

[24] *Commonwealth v Australian Capital Territory* (2013) 250 CLR 441.

[25] Some people, of course, think same-sex marriage is normatively objectionable. However, even those people typically find it *intelligible* (albeit, in their view, undesirable) for the term 'marriage' to be used to refer to certain kinds of same-sex unions.

Some people may be tempted to conclude from such examples that the ordinary meaning of a text bears no relation to its intended meaning, but I think this would be too hasty. Rather, contemporary interpreters seek to reconstruct the intended meaning of the text, but they do not necessarily do this solely at the level of lexical definitions.[26] Rather, they take into account the social milieu of the drafters and seek to understand why they understood 'marriage' in that way. Effectively, contemporary interpreters ask themselves: would the drafters understand the term 'marriage' in the same way today? If the answer is 'no', then the current meaning of the term prevails, because it is the most plausible reconstruction of the framer's intentions from a contemporary standpoint.

The socially accepted function of a law, then, is generally more likely than its intended function to determine the law's ordinary meaning. This is because current interpreters will understand the law by attempting to reconstruct the author's intentions from a contemporary point of view. The author's intentions may be opaque (if we simply cannot know what they intended) or underdetermined (if we know more or less what they intended at the time, but we cannot know what they would intend if they were here today). In either case, contemporary interpreters are likely to be guided by current social understandings. This explains why the ordinary meanings of terms like 'marriage' and 'adult' in the Constitution are not the same today as they were when the text was drafted.[27]

V. CONSTITUTIONAL NARRATIVES

Those who favour an intentionalist view of legal interpretation often do so because they worry that otherwise the meaning of legal texts will be indeterminate.[28] How, then, can we determine the content of a law's socially conferred function when the meaning or application of the law is disputed? I want to argue that determining the content of a law's socially accepted function involves interpreting what I will call *social narratives*. The idea of a narrative, in this context, refers to the ways members of a community think about, talk about and interact with a law or other artifact. Consider the example of the *Tree Bench* discussed above. It is because members of the local community think about, talk about and use the fallen tree as a bench that it becomes a member of the relevant artifact kind.

Narratives about artifacts are not purely abstract. Rather, they revolve around the artifact itself. The ways members of the local community talk about the tree bench are anchored in their causal interactions with the bench. Similarly, constitutional narratives—the ways members of a community think about, talk about and interact

26 Crowe, 'The Role of Contextual Meaning', above n 3, 434–36.

27 I have argued elsewhere that the originalist interpretation of the term 'adult' in s 41 of the Constitution adopted by the High Court in *King v Jones* (1972) 128 CLR 221 was mistaken. See Crowe, 'The Role of Contextual Meaning', above n 3, 436; Jonathan Crowe and Peta Stephenson, 'An Express Constitutional Right to Vote? The Case for Reviving Section 41' (2014) 36 *Sydney Law Review* 205, 228–29.

28 *cf* Goldsworthy, 'Constitutional Interpretation', above n 4, 688–89.

with the Constitution—are anchored in the constitutional document. The Constitution tells a story about an 'indissoluble Federal Commonwealth' created by the Australian people.[29] It conveys information about a variety of people and entities and stipulates norms governing their conduct. The people and entities mentioned in the Constitution are presumed to exist outside the text. Otherwise, there would be no point in mentioning them.

Constitutions work: they do things in the world. In order for this to happen, constitutions need to refer to people and entities in the real world: a constitution that existed purely in a fictional universe would be causally inert. The lighthouses, corporations and railways featured in the Constitution are actual lighthouses, corporations and railways.[30] Legal officials take the normative framework set out in the Constitution and apply it to govern our interactions with these entities. The Constitution, then, bears some resemblance to a factual narrative. It refers to things and events that take place in the actual world. The Constitution itself is a sparse document containing many gaps, but we can fill in the gaps in its narrative by referring to the way things actually are.

The way things are, of course, changes over time. The reference to lighthouses in section 51(vii) of the Constitution refers to around 350 lighthouses presently existing in Australia, most of which would have been unknown to the framers.[31] The reference to 'trading or financial corporations formed within the limits of the Commonwealth' in section 51(xx) refers to those corporations established under Australian law from time to time.[32] The reference to 'postal, telegraphic, telephonic, and other like services' in section 51(v) covers television[33] and plausibly the internet, although the framers could never have imagined them. The Constitution, in this sense, tells a story about a world that exists outside its boundaries. The meaning of the Constitution shifts as this factual backdrop changes.

The Constitution takes for granted a large collection of background facts and norms that cannot be found in the document itself. It does not, however, take these facts and norms exactly as it finds them. The Constitution also creates new entities and norms. The Senate (section 7), House of Representatives (section 24), Governor-General (section 61) and High Court of Australia (section 71) did not exist until the Constitution created them. The Constitution also creates numerous new powers and duties relating to various persons and entities. The Constitution, then, changes the factual and normative universe: this is how it works in the world. It follows that the Constitution is not fully analogous to a factual narrative. It is also like a fictional narrative in the way that it creates its own factual and normative universe.

The factual backdrop for the Constitution is partly a function of social institutions and practices. Chapter II of the Constitution, for example, concerns the executive.

[29] Commonwealth of Australia Constitution Act 1901 (Imp).

[30] Australian Constitution ss 51 (vii), (xx), (xxxii).

[31] National Geospatial Intelligence Agency, *List of Lights, Radio Aids and Fog Signals* (Report, United States Government, 2017) 117–215.

[32] *New South Wales v Commonwealth* (1990) 169 CLR 482.

[33] *Jones v Commonwealth [No 2]* (1965) 112 CLR 206.

Section 61 of the Constitution vests the executive power of the Commonwealth in the Queen and makes it exercisable by the Governor-General as the Queen's representative. Sections 62 and 63 refer to a Federal Executive Council with the function of advising the Governor-General, while section 64 refers to Ministers of State who are members of the Federal Executive Council. There is no reference to the office of Prime Minister and no express limitations on the Governor-General's power to act without advice. The established practice in the Westminster system of government, however, was for the ministers to select a leader and the Queen (or her representative) to act on that person's advice except in exceptional cases.[34]

The office of Prime Minister, then, is an institutional artifact: it arises from a status function conferred upon a person who fulfils certain criteria. This status function is a product of social acceptance. The resulting institutional artifact forms an integral part of the Australian constitutional narrative. The Constitution and its provisions, as we saw earlier, are themselves artifacts with proper functions arising from both authorial intentions and social convention. Their functions depend, in part, on their interaction with other institutional artifacts, such as the office of Prime Minister. The Constitution, in this sense, takes its meaning at least partly from a wider constitutional narrative to be found in the thought, speech and actions of those who interact causally with its provisions.

VI. CONSTITUTIONAL IMPLICATIONS

The role of social narratives in giving meaning to the constitutional text has not gone unnoticed by the High Court. Indeed, it figures prominently in a number of important constitutional decisions. The cases that established the implied constitutional freedom of political communication—*Nationwide News v Wills*[35] and *Australian Capital Television v Commonwealth*[36]—provide striking examples. The High Court in those cases sought to make sense of the system of representative government embodied in the Constitution. The majority judges, in so doing, clearly recognised the role of social narratives in shaping the meaning and function of the constitutional provisions.

Sections 7 and 24 of the Constitution, along with the other sections relating to the legislature, clearly evince an intention to set up a representative form of government.[37] 'The purpose of the Constitution', as McHugh J observes, 'was to further the institutions of representative and responsible government'.[38] However, the content and significance of this function, as the majority judges understood, cannot be fully determined by looking at the provisions themselves. It depends on

[34] See generally A Blick and G Jones, *Premiership: The Development, Nature and Power of the Office of the British Prime Minister* (Exeter, Imprint Academic, 2010).

[35] *Nationwide News Pty Ltd v Wills* (1992) 177 CLR 1.

[36] *Australian Capital Television Pty Ltd v Commonwealth* (1992) 177 CLR 106.

[37] See, eg, ibid 137 (Mason CJ), 227–28 (McHugh J).

[38] ibid 228.

how those provisions interact with other social practices and institutions. It is these institutions, rather than the constitutional text alone, that provide the basis for the implied freedom and render it a legitimate part of Australian constitutional jurisprudence. As Deane and Toohey JJ put it:

> Inherent in the Constitution's doctrine of representative government is an implication of the freedom of the people of the Commonwealth to communicate information, opinions and ideas about all aspects of the government of the Commonwealth, including the qualifications, conduct and performance of those entrusted ... with the exercise of any part of legislative, executive or judicial powers of government.[39]

This freedom is not, strictly speaking, inherent in the constitutional text. Rather, it is inherent in the doctrine of representative government, which is an institutional artifact forming part of the wider narrative surrounding the Constitution.

Institutional artifacts such as the office of Prime Minister and the doctrine of representative government form an indispensable part of the context for interpreting the Constitution. The Constitution would make little sense without them. The High Court, for its part, has recognised the role played by these institutions and social narratives in a range of different fields of constitutional jurisprudence. For example, the High Court has held that the separation of judicial power is reflected in the structure of the Constitution, giving rise to more robust protections for judicial independence than can be found in the text alone.[40] The doctrine of the rule of law has been found to underpin the Constitution as a whole and to play a role in the interpretation of Commonwealth powers.[41] The federal distribution of powers likewise forms the basis of the doctrine of intergovernmental immunities, despite the lack of any express provisions enshrining this protection.[42]

These diverse constitutional implications—some of them hotly disputed, others largely uncontroversial—all have their basis in a common form of reasoning. They involve looking at the constitutional provisions, discerning the functions given to them by authorial intention and social convention, then interpreting these against the wider backdrop of social institutions. The end result is that entrenched social norms and expectations concerning topics such as the separation of judicial power, the rule of law and the autonomy of the executive governments of the States play an integral role in how the Constitution and its provisions are understood and interpreted. The Constitution, in each of these areas, has been from time to time 'read in a new light ... [as] a consequence of developments that had occurred outside the law courts as well as a cause of further developments there'.[43]

The role of contemporary social narratives in shaping (and effectively changing) the meaning of the Constitution can be clearly discerned in Gleeson CJ's finding in

[39] *Nationwide News Pty Ltd v Wills* (1992) 177 CLR 1, 74.

[40] *R v Kirby; Ex parte Boilermakers' Society of Australia* (1956) 94 CLR 254, 270 (Dixon CJ, McTiernan, Fullagar and Kitto JJ).

[41] *Australian Communist Party v Commonwealth* (1951) 83 CLR 1, 95 (Dixon J).

[42] See, eg, *Melbourne Corporation v Commonwealth* (1947) 74 CLR 31; *Clarke v Commissioner of Taxation* (2009) 240 CLR 272.

[43] *Victoria v Commonwealth* (1971) 122 CLR 353, 396 (Windeyer J).

the case of *Roach v Electoral Commissioner* that 'the words of ss 7 and 24, because of changed historical circumstances including legislative history, have come to be a constitutional protection of the right to vote'.[44] Gleeson CJ is quite explicit that this implied (albeit conditional) constitutional right to vote did not exist when the Constitution was first adopted. It is not a product of the constitutional text alone—although it is anchored in sections 7 and 24—nor of the intentions of the framers. It is, rather, a result of new functions and values imposed upon those sections by surrounding constitutional narratives.

VII. FUNCTIONS AND CONTEXT

I have argued in this chapter that constitutional values—such as representative government, federalism, and the rule of law—reflect the proper functions of the Constitution and its provisions. These functions may arise from authorial intentions, social acceptance, or a combination of both sources. The functions given to constitutional provisions by contemporary understandings are generally more salient in constitutional interpretation than those stemming from authorial intentions, because they are more likely to reflect the ordinary meaning of the provisions. The process of identifying and interpreting functions conferred on the Constitution by social acceptance involves engaging with constitutional narratives. These narratives, in turn, give content to constitutional values.

I want to conclude with a brief comment on functionalism as an approach to constitutional interpretation. Functionalism as a theory of law was popularised in the early twentieth century by Felix Cohen. Cohen argued that law is best understood as a pattern of judicial decisions exhibiting a certain regularity, not because it follows underlying norms, but because it reflects the influence exerted on law by social and political ideologies. Functionalism, for Cohen, means that 'a thing *is* its manifestations, its effects, and its relation with other things'.[45] Law, then, is nothing more or less than a network of relations with other material and social phenomena. The central question of the functionalist method, as Cohen conceives it, is 'what is the human meaning of the law?' This is very different, he thinks, from traditional jurisprudential questions about law's nature or purpose.[46]

Rosalind Dixon has recently defended a somewhat different form of functionalism in the Australian constitutional context.[47] Dixon's functionalism 'invites courts directly and openly to rely on substantive constitutional values, not simply more "formal" legal sources'.[48] This approach, she argues, strikes an attractive middle

[44] *Roach v Electoral Commissioner* (2007) 233 CLR 162 [7]. A similar line of reasoning was applied by McTiernan and Jacobs JJ in *Attorney-General (Cth) ex rel McKinlay v Commonwealth* (1975) 135 CLR 1, 36. For further discussion, see Crowe and Stephenson, above n 27, 223–26.

[45] FS Cohen, 'The Problems of a Functional Jurisprudence' (1937) 1 *Modern Law Review* 5, 7.

[46] ibid 6–7.

[47] Dixon, 'The Functional Constitution', above n 1. See also S Gageler, 'Beyond the Text: A Vision of the Structure and Function of the Constitution' (2009) 32 *Australian Bar Review* 138.

[48] Dixon, 'The Functional Constitution', above n 1, 456.

ground between formalism and pragmatism (including the version of pragmatism embraced by Cohen).[49] Dixon's vision of functionalism is, I think, to be welcomed, particularly if it encourages High Court judges to be more open about their reliance on constitutional values. However, the central place the theory gives to constitutional values invites precisely the question posed at the start of this chapter: what are these values and where do they come from?

Dixon makes it clear that constitutional values should not simply be policy based, but must be sourced 'in some way' from 'the text, structure and history of the relevant constitution'.[50] However, this comment—as foreshadowed above—is susceptible of at least two different interpretations. It could be interpreted in an intentionalist sense as meaning that constitutional values should have some basis in the intentions of the framers of the constitutional document. Alternatively, it could be interpreted in a contextualist light as meaning that constitutional values at least sometimes reflect contemporary beliefs and attitudes. Dixon seems inclined towards the latter interpretation,[51] although she also appears cautious about the extent to which functionalism may appeal to principles that go beyond the express words of constitutional provisions.[52]

I have argued throughout this chapter that the role of functions and values in constitutional interpretation is best understood by adopting a contextualist perspective. A contextualist theory best explains both what constitutional values are and where they come from. Authorial intentions undoubtedly play some role in generating constitutional functions, purposes and values, but whether they should be followed by contemporary interpreters ultimately depends on their salience for current constitutional narratives. Contextualism also offers a response to two important further issues confronting functionalist theories: first, how we should resolve conflicts between a law's intended and socially accepted functions; and, second, how the function of a law should be determined when its meaning is in dispute. Functionalism, then, offers a promising account of constitutional interpretation: provided that it is understood in a contextualist light.[53]

[49] ibid 455–56.
[50] ibid 456.
[51] R Dixon, 'Response to Commentators' (2015) 43 *Federal Law Review* 517, 517–18.
[52] Dixon, 'The Functional Constitution', above n 1, 480.
[53] *cf* Crowe, 'The Role of Contextual Meaning', above n 3.

Part II

Legality and Constitutionalism

5

The Rule of Law

LISA BURTON CRAWFORD*

THE RULE OF law is assumed to be a goal of any good legal system. In *Australian Communist Party v Commonwealth* (*Communist Party Case*), Dixon J stated that 'the rule of law forms an assumption' of the Australian Constitution.[1] That statement has been frequently repeated, but its meaning remains uncertain—not least because Dixon J did not explain what he meant by the 'rule of law'.

At a certain level of abstraction, the phrase is easy to define. As Joseph Raz said, the rule of law 'means literally what is says: the rule of law'.[2] This captures a potent belief, rooted in antiquity: that those who hold public power should not be able to do whatever they want, however they want, but rather that their will should be constrained by law. If this is achieved, then it can be said that citizens are ruled, not by the people who happen to hold public power but by law itself: that there is 'a government of laws and not of men'. Most people would agree with these broad and general statements. But if we scratch beneath the surface, differences of opinion soon emerge. Reasonable people disagree upon exactly what the rule of law entails, and how it can be achieved—if indeed, it could ever be achieved at all.

This chapter will examine whether and the sense in which the rule of law is an Australian constitutional value, and its role in constitutional interpretation. Section I discusses the meaning of 'the rule of law'. Section II discusses the relationship between the rule of law and the text and structure of the Constitution. Section III examines whether and how, in light of the preceding discussion, the rule of law should inform constitutional interpretation.

This chapter seeks to show that the rule of law is indeed an important value of Australian constitutionalism. At some level of abstraction, it may be a value that we share with many other legal orders. However, there is no definitive recipe for achieving law's rule: the rule of law 'might be—and ha[s] been—pursued in a variety

* This chapter draws upon research published as Lisa Burton Crawford, *The Rule of Law and the Australian Constitution* (Sydney, Federation Press, 2017). Thank you to Professor Jeffrey Goldsworthy, Professor Rosalind Dixon, Associate Professor Patrick Emerton, Dr Janina Boughey and the other attendees of the Constitutional Values Workshop, especially Professor Martin Krygier and Associate Professor Gabrielle Appleby, for their help in formulating these ideas. I also thank the anonymous reviewer of this volume for their very useful comments.

[1] *Australian Communist Party v Commonwealth* (1951) 83 CLR 1, 193.

[2] J Raz, *The Authority of Law: Essays on Law and Morality* (Oxford, Oxford University Press, 2009) 212.

of ways'.[3] Hence, it is more apt to speak of an Australian rule of law tradition, which may guide constitutional interpretation, but only in a certain way.

I. WHAT IS THE RULE OF LAW?

At its most basic level, the rule of law denotes the existence of a system of laws. If there are no laws, then the law cannot rule. If there are laws, but no one obeys them, then the rule clearly does not rule, either. Thus the rule of law represents the antithesis of lawlessness.

As the foregoing suggests, the rule of law seems to require that everyone be subject to the law, 'ordinary' citizen and government official alike. But when legal philosophers discuss the rule of law, they tend to focus upon the legal constraints of governmental power.[4] They also tend to focus upon 'the law's contribution to maintaining the rule of law':[5] the shape that law must be in in order for it to rule. Given the subject of this volume, it is appropriate to adopt the same focus—but it is important to note at the outset, that the rule of law can never be achieved by legal means alone. [6]

When we say that the rule of law requires that the government be subject to the law, we convey the basic idea that government actors should not be able to do whatever they want, however they want to do it: rather, they should only do what they are legally authorised to do, in the manner that the law authorises them to do it. No one is above the law, no matter his or her position. If that goal can be achieved, then it can be said that citizens are ruled, not by those who hold public power, but by the law itself—metaphorically, at least. So understood, the rule of law represents the antithesis of law by men (or people).

This seems a worthy ideal. It is one that has a clear presence in Australian legal discourse. Yet, it lacks precision. To describe the rule of law as the ideal of a government of laws rather than of men raises a series of further questions. What kinds of things can government actors be empowered to do? What should be the limits of their powers? How should those limitations be enforced? And finally, what is the point of all this: the purpose or value of the rule of law itself? Does it produce an efficacious system of laws? Or does it create a system of laws that is morally just? These are matters upon which reasonable people disagree.

Thus the rule of law is the subject of a seemingly intractable academic debate, which is said to have two competing sides: those who advocate a 'thin' or 'formal'

[3] M Krygier, 'Ethical Positivism and the Liberalism of Fear' in T Campbell and J Goldsworthy (eds), *Judicial Power, Democracy and Legal Positivism* (Farnham, Ashgate, 2000) 71–72.

[4] This makes no specific claim about who or what 'the government' is. Indeed, the changing face of government creates a real difficulty for the rule of law.

[5] J Gardner, 'The Supposed Formality of the Rule of Law' in J Gardner, *Law as a Leap of Faith: Essays on Law in General* (Oxford, Oxford University Press, 2012) 195. Note, this comment was made with respect to the works of Lon Fuller.

[6] See further M Krygier, 'The Rule of Law: Legality, Teleology, Sociology' in G Palombella and N Walker (eds), *Relocating the Rule of Law* (Portland, OR, Hart Publishing, 2009); M Krygier, 'Why the Rule of Law is too Important to Be Left to Lawyers' (2012) 2(2) *Prawo i Więź* 30. See also LB Crawford, *The Rule of Law and the Australian Constitution* (Sydney, Federation Press, 2017) ch 10.

account of the rule of law, and those who advocate a 'thick' or 'substantive' version.[7] A thin account of the rule of law may focus upon the requirements that ensure that law is calculable,[8] or capable of guiding human conduct.[9] For example, it may require that laws should be prospective, clear and stable.[10] By contrast, a thick conception of the rule of law may focus upon the requirements that are needed to ensure that the legal system is morally legitimate.[11] For example, it may require that government action be a proportionate means of achieving some legitimate end,[12] or authorised by law that is compatible with fundamental human rights norms.[13]

These labels of thick and thin can serve as a useful device for marshalling the enormous amount that has been written about the rule of law. They will be used for that purpose here. However, they must be used with a significant degree of caution, for several reasons.[14] Only some are mentioned here, as they inform the manner and extent to which the rule of law can guide constitutional interpretation.

First, the labels simplify the nature of the rule of law debate. There is no one 'thick' or 'thin' conception of the rule of law. Rather, there are differences—from the subtle to the significant—between most individual accounts of the rule of law. The labels also tend to suggest that the two conceptions of the rule of law are like concentric circles, with the thick requiring all that the thin conception does, and more. There is some truth to this, as a thick conception will typically require that law satisfy substantive criteria that a thin conception does not. But the differences between the two accounts run deeper than this. Conflicting conceptions of the rule of law are often premised upon different methodologies of constitutional interpretation and adjudication, and often linked to fundamental disagreements about the concept of law, and the role of the judiciary.[15]

Further, the rule of law is internally complex no matter which way it is defined. Take for example the thin conception of the rule of law. Labelling it as such suggests that it is easier to wield: that is, that it would be easier to assess whether a particular law is or is not incompatible with the rule of law thinly conceived. But that is not necessarily the case. The individuated requirements of this conception of the rule of law are complex. For example, the formal conception of the rule of law is often said to require that the

[7] See P Craig, 'Formal and Substantive Conceptions of the Rule of Law: An Analytical Framework' [1997] *Public Law* 466.

[8] W Scheuerman, *Between the Norm and the Exception: The Frankfurt School and the Rule of Law* (Cambridge, MIT Press, 1994) 68–69.

[9] See, eg, Raz, above n 2.

[10] ibid 214–18; L Fuller, *The Morality of Law* (New Haven, Yale University Press, 1969) 39. Note, the complexity of these requirements is explored further below.

[11] See, eg, TRS Allan, *The Sovereignty of Law: Freedom, Constitution and Common Law* (Oxford, Oxford University Press, 2013) (see especially at 119).

[12] See, eg, ibid 91.

[13] See, eg, ibid 89, 91; T Bingham, *The Rule of Law* (London, Penguin Books, 2011) 67–69.

[14] See, eg, Gardner, above n 5; Krygier, 'Why the Rule of Law is too Important to Be Left to Lawyers', above n 6.

[15] Craig, above n 7, 477. See further N Simmonds, 'Law as a Moral Idea' (2005) 55 *University of Toronto Law Journal* 61 (see especially at 63); L McDonald, 'Positivism and the Formal Rule of Law: Questioning the Connection' (2001) 26 *Australian Journal of Legal Philosophy* 93; M Bennett, '"The Rule of Law Means Literally What It Says: The Rule of the Law": Fuller and Raz on Formal Legality and the Concept of Law' (2007) 32 *Australian Journal of Legal Philosophy* 90.

law be relatively stable—not constantly changing, and especially not in unpredictable ways. But law must necessarily change, as society does. It would become absurd if it did not. The real and more difficult question for the rule of law is, is the law *stable enough*? This is a question of legislative craft, which may be inappropriate for or incapable of judicial determination.[16] Its answer will depend on myriad legal, political and social factors: on the very nature of the legal system in question.

However it is defined, the rule of law is also exceptionally broad. It is said to inform every aspect of a legal system, from the character of legislation, to the manner in which executive power is exercised, and the nature of judicial reasoning. The rule of law is linked to relatively distinct principles and practices (like, for example, the requirement that statute law have only prospective effect) as well as broad structural features of the legal system (such as the separation of powers, or representative democracy).

Further difficulties arise, by virtue of the fact that the phrase 'the rule of law' is often used at two levels of abstraction: as a device for commenting upon the health of a legal system as a whole, as well as the quality of individual laws or government decisions. As the rule of law operates at these two levels of meaning, it is difficult to determine whether an individual law or government decision diminishes the rule of law. That difficulty is not alleviated by the fact that the ideal of a government of laws has been dissected into a set of more specific criteria, for the relationship between those specific criteria and the broader concept is itself complex.[17]

For example, it is often said that judicial review of governmental action is one necessary ingredient of the rule of law. But at what point does a lack of judicial review diminish law's ability to rule? Is it enough if the majority of government action is subject to judicial review, or must it be all of it? In Australia, the High Court can invalidate legislation, but in the UK, the Supreme Court cannot—the orthodox position being that the powers of the Parliament in Westminster are legally unlimited. But it would be highly contestable to assert that Australia 'has' the rule of law whereas the UK does not. It would be difficult even to assert that one country has made better progress towards attaining that ideal.[18]

This suggests that there are many different ways of pursuing the rule of law, the suitability of which will depend in part upon the social, political and legal cultures that exist within a given legal system.[19] Furthermore, the suitability of those measures cannot be answered without first determining the ultimate purpose of the rule of law. The individuated demands of the rule of law 'do not stand on their own. They must constantly be interpreted in light of the basic idea'.[20] For example, if one thinks that

[16] See further T Endicott, 'The Value of Vagueness' in A Marmor and S Soames (eds), *Philosophical Foundations of Language in the Law* (Oxford University Press, 2011).

[17] T Endicott, 'The Impossibility of the Rule of Law' (1999) 19 *Oxford Journal of Legal Studies* 1.

[18] This distinction between the minimum and aspirational content of the rule of law is discussed at length in Fuller, above n 10 (see especially at 38–44).

[19] Krygier, 'Ethical Positivism and the Liberalism of Fear', above n 3. Note also Krygier's broader critique, of this tendency to treat the rule of law as a recipe for institutional design.

[20] Raz, above n 2, 218.

the purpose of the rule of law is to produce law that can guide human behaviour, then one might tolerate a different degree of instability in the law from one who thinks that the purpose of the rule of law is to create a morally legitimate system of government. On the other hand, we cannot assume that the rule of law is overly robust. It may well be destroyed by a thousand smaller cuts.

Finally, the distinction between thick and thin is not the only axis of the rule of law debate. Scholars disagree, not only about what the concept of the rule of law entails, but what *kind* of concept it is. Some portray the rule of law as a political ideal—a 'value', if you like—to which a legal system should aspire.[21] Others see the rule of law differently. For example, TRS Allan argues that '[t]he rule of law is not merely an ideal or aspiration *external* to the law—a yardstick by which the law can be measured for its compliance with an important political value, and against which it may fall short'.[22] On his view, a law that fails to comply with his conception of the rule of law is not merely a bad law but no law at all: it lacks moral *and* legal validity. Thus the rule of law can be directly enforced by the courts, even if there is no apparent support for this in the text or structure of the relevant constitutional documents. Though important, this issue is outside the scope of this enquiry.[23]

So the rule of law is complex and contested. Indeed, it has been suggested that the rule of law is an 'essentially contested concept', as defined by WB Gallie.[24] This does not just mean that it is contested with particular intensity, or that it is contested at the borderlines. Rather, reasonable people disagree about the very essence of the concept. The same or similar could potentially be said about many other values, like 'democracy' or 'justice'.

Contested concepts are not useless. Their use encourages discussion and debate, including about the very thing that the concept is invoked to capture.[25] Furthermore, we cannot deny that the rule of law is important, despite all the disagreement it has engendered. One doubts we would have spent so much time debating the rule of law if we did not care about it. It seems that we would much rather live in a legal system that values 'the rule of law' than one that does not, even though we cannot agree upon what it means.[26]

However, real difficulties do emerge, if the rule of law is looked to as a source of legal rules—as some commentators and judges argue that it ought to. This chapter does not engage directly with those claims. Rather, it asks whether the rule of law is a constitutional value that can and should guide the interpretation of the Australian Constitution. The complexities discussed in this section will inform the answer to that question.

[21] See, eg, ibid 196.
[22] See, eg, Allan, *The Sovereignty of Law*, above n 11, 88–89 (emphasis in original).
[23] It is the central enquiry of Crawford, *The Rule of Law and the Australian Constitution*, above n 6.
[24] J Waldron, 'Is the Rule of Law an Essentially Contested Concept (in Florida)?' (2002) 21(2) *Law and Philosophy* 137.
[25] ibid 152.
[26] See also Bingham, above n 13, 9.

II. TEXTUAL AND STRUCTURAL SUPPORT FOR THE RULE OF LAW

The Australian Constitution does not expressly refer to the 'rule of law'.[27] The framers did not expressly mention this concept in debating what it should (or should not) contain. Yet, there is a clear relationship between the Australian Constitution and the rule of law.

The first reason for that is that the rule of law denotes the existence of a legal system, and the Constitution brought such a system into being. The Constitution is a legal instrument that established the federal government and its respective branches, and conferred and delimited their powers.[28] It was always assumed that the government so constituted would be subject to this law. Covering clause 5 provides: 'This Act, and all laws made by the Parliament of the Commonwealth under the *Constitution*, shall be binding on the courts, judges, and people of every State and of every part of the Commonwealth'. Many other provisions impose limitations on governmental power. The High Court has express or implied authority to enforce most of those limitations,[29] against most government actors.[30] Thus the federal government is constituted and limited by law, which is enforced by the courts. In this simple but fundamental sense, the rule of law is enshrined in Australian constitutional law.

Many of these principles were confirmed in the *Communist Party Case*.[31] This considered the constitutional validity of the Communist Party Dissolution Act 1950 (Cth)—a sweeping piece of legislation that attempted to eradicate the Communist ideology from Australian public life, by outlawing the Communist Party, confiscating its property, and making it an offence to in any way support its teachings. The Act was prefaced by a set of recitals, which asserted that the Communist Party posed a threat to the Australian community, and that the federal Parliament had power to enact the Act.

By majority, the Court found the Act invalid. This finding was premised upon two fundamental principles. First, the federal Parliament could not enact laws that fell outside the enumerated powers conferred on it by the Constitution. Second, it was for the High Court to decide whether a law was within power.[32] The Act in question did not bear any obvious connection to the heads of power enumerated in the Constitution, and hence it failed.

[27] *cf*, eg, *Grundgesetz für die Bundesrepublik Deutschland* [Basic Law of the Federal Republic of Germany] arts 16, 22.

[28] Of course, some of this work was done by legislation—but such laws must be a valid exercise of the 'legislative power of the Commonwealth' conferred by the Constitution.

[29] Some are said to be non-justiciable, see, eg, s 53: *Osborne v Commonwealth* (1911) 12 CLR 321; *Western Australia v Commonwealth* (1995) 183 CLR 373, 482 (*Native Title Case*); *Permanent Trustee Australia Ltd v Commissioner of State Revenue* (2004) 220 CLR 388, 409.

[30] Not all judicial review remedies are available against all government actors. See further the discussion of the limits of judicial power, below.

[31] *Communist Party Case* (1951) 83 CLR 1. The significance of this case, especially for the rule of law, is explored at length in Crawford, *The Rule of Law and the Australian Constitution*, above n 6, ch 5.

[32] *Communist Party Case* (1951) 83 CLR 1, 262 (Fullagar J). See further R Sackville, 'The Changing Character of Judicial Review in Australia: The Legacy of *Marbury v Madison*?' (2014) 25 *Public Law Review* 245; LB Crawford and J Goldsworthy, 'Constitutionalism' in C Saunders and A Stone (eds), *The Oxford Handbook of the Australian Constitution* (Oxford, Oxford University Press, 2018, forthcoming).

This decision is often described as a victory for the rule of law. That phrase was only mentioned by one member of the Court: Dixon J. At the point of the judgment in question, Dixon J was discussing the scope of the federal Parliament's incidental legislative power, and whether it supported the Act. His Honour explained that this power

> is ancillary or incidental to sustaining and carrying on government. Moreover, it is government under the *Constitution* and that is an instrument framed in accordance with many traditional conceptions, to some of which it gives effect, as for example, in separating the judicial power from other functions of government, others of which are simply assumed. *Among these I think that it may fairly be said that the rule of law forms an assumption.*[33]

His Honour continued:

> In such a system I think that it would be impossible to say of a law of the character described, which depends for its supposed connection with the power upon the conclusion of the legislature concerning the doings and the designs of the bodies or person to be affected [is within power. If it were] the Act would have the effect of making the conclusion of the legislature final and so the measure of the operation of its own power.[34]

Thus the Act was invalid because it did not conform to the law of the Constitution. Parliament could not wield any power greater than that conferred by the Constitution, even in an actual or perceived emergency: 'a stream cannot rise higher than its source'.[35]

In the course of argument, the Court made its principled aversion to the legislation clear.[36] Yet, as Fullagar J explained:

> [N]othing depends on the justice or injustice of the law in question. If the language of an Act of Parliament is clear, its merits and demerits are alike beside the point. It is the law, and that is all ... It is only because the legislative power of the Commonwealth Parliament is limited by an instrument emanating from a superior authority that it arises in the case of the Commonwealth Parliament.[37]

The High Court has explained its role in similar terms in many other cases.[38]

Accordingly, Fullagar J noted that the legislation could have been enacted in the Australian States, or the UK, where legislative power is not subject to the same constraints found in sections 51 and 52 of the Australian Constitution,

33 *Communist Party Case* (1951) 83 CLR 1, 193 (emphasis added).

34 ibid 193.

35 ibid 258 (Fullagar J).

36 G Winterton, 'The Significance of the *Communist Party Case*' (1991) 18 *Melbourne University Law Review* 630, 656–57; G Williams, 'Reading the Judicial Mind: Appellate Argument in the *Communist Party Case*' (1993) 15 *Sydney Law Review* 3.

37 *Communist Party Case* (1951) 83 CLR 1, 262.

38 See, eg, *South Australia v Commonwealth* (1942) 65 CLR 373, 429 (Latham CJ) (*First Uniform Tax Case*); *Amalgamated Society of Engineers v Adelaide Steamship Co Ltd* (1920) 28 CLR 129, 142, 151–52 (Knox CJ, Isaacs, Rich and Starke JJ) (*Engineers Case*); *Burton v Hogan* (1952) 86 CLR 169, 179 (Dixon J); *Leask v Commonwealth* (1996) 187 CLR 579, 602 (Dawson J), 616 (McHugh J); *The Grain Pool of Western Australia v Commonwealth* (2000) 202 CLR 479, 492 [16] (Gleeson CJ, Gaudron, McHugh, Gummow, Hayne and Callinan JJ), 522–25 [111]–[118] (Kirby J); *New South Wales v Commonwealth* (2006) 229 CLR 1, 203–04 [477] (Kirby J), 103–04 [142] (Gleeson CJ, Gummow, Hayne, Heydon and Crennan JJ) (*Work Choices Case*).

notwithstanding its patent effect on civil liberties.[39] Dixon J was clearly of a similar view. His Honour stated, 'I am deciding the case on the ground of want of affirmative legislative power'.[40]

A. The Rule of Law and Executive Power

The Communist Party Case was primarily concerned with the limits of legislative power. However, the Court also commented upon the powers of the executive branch. Just as the validity of a federal Act could not depend on the assertion of the legislature, 'the validity of ... an administrative act done under a law cannot be made to depend on the opinion of ... the person who is to do the act'.[41] Later cases have confirmed the fundamental proposition that in every case the executive must be able to point to legal authority for its actions. Relatedly, the executive has no authority to excuse itself from the limitations or requirements of the law.[42] Once again, the stream cannot rise above its source.[43]

Like the validity of legislative action, the validity of executive action is adjudicated by the courts. Section 75(v) of the Constitution gives the High Court original jurisdiction to hear matters in which certain remedies are sought against 'officers of the Commonwealth'. It is assumed that section 75(iii) also confers some judicial review-type jurisdiction,[44] though it remains relatively unexplored. These sub-sections delineate spaces in which the High Court is, when approached by an applicant with standing, entitled to exercise the 'judicial power of the Commonwealth', which is vested in the High Court and other courts by section 71 of the Constitution.

While the concept of 'judicial power' defies precise definition,[45] it is tolerably clear that it includes the power to interpret legislation, and to decide whether an executive act or decision is within the scope of the power conferred.[46] Together, these provisions authorise the High Court to review the legality of executive action and to remedy unlawful executive action, at least within certain circumstances. As these functions are constitutionally conferred, they are constitutionally

[39] *Communist Party Case* (1951) 83 CLR 1, 262–63. See also Winterton, above n 36, 657.

[40] ibid 200. For an alternative interpretation of the case, see D Dyzenhaus, 'Constituting the Enemy: A Response to Carl Schmitt' in A Sajó (ed), *Militant Democracy* (The Netherlands, Eleven International Publishing, 2004).

[41] *Communist Party Case* (1951) 83 CLR 1, 258 (Fullagar J).

[42] *A v Hayden [No 2]* (1984) 156 CLR 532, 540 (Gibbs CJ), 550 (Mason J), 562 (Murphy J), 580 (Brennan J); *Plaintiff M79/2012 v Minister for Immigration and Citizenship* (2013) 252 CLR 336, 366–67 [87] (Hayne J); *Plaintiff M68/2015 v Minister for Immigration and Border Protection* (2016) 257 CLR 42, 98–99 [135]–[136] (Gageler J). This principle is not unique to Australia, as recent cases concerning the executive branch of the UK government's power to trigger 'Brexit' demonstrate. See *Miller for Secretary of State for Exiting the European Union* [2017] UKSC 5.

[43] See further Crawford, *The Rule of Law and the Australian Constitution*, above n 6, ch 7.

[44] See, eg, *Plaintiff M61/2010E v Commonwealth* (2010) 243 CLR 319.

[45] *TCL Air Conditioner (Zhongshan) Co Ltd v Judges of the Federal Court of Australia* (2013) 251 CLR 533, 553 [27] (French CJ and Gageler J).

[46] *Attorney-General (NSW) v Quin* (1990) 170 CLR 1, 35–38 (Brennan J); *Corporation of the City of Enfield v Development Assessment Commission* (2000) 199 CLR 135, 153 [43] (Gleeson CJ, Gummow, Kirby and Hayne JJ); S Gageler, 'The Legitimate Scope of Judicial Review' (2001) 21 *Australian Bar Review* 279 (see especially at 280). See further LB Crawford, 'Who Decides the Validity of Executive Action? No-Invalidity Clauses and the Separation of Powers' (2017) 24 *Australian Journal of Administrative Law* 81; Crawford, *The Rule of Law and the Australian Constitution*, above n 6, ch 7.

entrenched.[47] This is frequently described as an important implementation of the rule of law ideal.[48]

The relationship between section 75 of the Constitution and the rule of law was given fresh emphasis in *Plaintiff S157/2002 v Commonwealth* (*Plaintiff S157*).[49] This case confirmed that the federal Parliament could not prevent the High Court from exercising the jurisdiction that that section conferred, by way of a privative clause. More specifically, this meant that the federal Parliament could not prevent the Court from hearing an application for mandamus, prohibition or injunction against an officer of the Commonwealth, at least not on the grounds of a jurisdictional error of law. Towards the end of their judgment, the plurality judges stated that

> the issues decided in these proceedings are not merely issues of a technical kind ... [Section 75], and specifically s 75(v), introduces into the *Constitution* of the Commonwealth an entrenched minimum provision of judicial review. There was no precise equivalent to s 75(v) in either of the Constitutions of the United States of America or Canada. The provision of the constitutional writs and the conferral upon this Court of an irremovable jurisdiction to issue them to an officer of the Commonwealth *constitutes a textual reinforcement for what Dixon J said about the significance of the rule of law for the Constitution in Australian Communist Party v The Commonwealth*.[50]

This seems to make a statement about the purpose or value served by section 75: that being, the rule of law. However, the plurality did not articulate what it understood the rule of law to mean; nor did Gleeson CJ, who listed the rule of law as one principle of statutory interpretation.[51]

A similar point about s 75(v) was made by Chief Justice Wayne Martin, in recounting the following anecdote:

> When the New South Wales Bar Association commissioned a portrait of the Honourable Mary Gaudron AC upon her retirement from the High Court she insisted that the text of section 75(v) of the *Constitution* be stencilled across the top of the portrait ... 'As Mary Gaudron acknowledged in her speech at the unveiling of the portrait, the text is hardly Jeffersonian: it is the "technical language of lawyers". Her fondness for it is because it provides a signal guarantee of protection under the rule of law. It is a protection that is not found in the constitutions of other liberal democracies. The jurisdiction of the High Court to restrain an officer of the Commonwealth from exceeding his or her legal duty or, conversely, to compel an officer of the Commonwealth to perform his or her legal duty, cannot be ousted'.[52]

[47] See also the decision with respect to State Supreme Courts in *Kirk v Industrial Court (NSW)* (2010) 239 CLR 531.

[48] There are too many to sensibly note here, but see, eg, L Zines, *Cowen and Zines's Federal Jurisdiction in Australia* (Sydney, Federation Press, 2002) 35; A Mason, 'The Foundations and Limitations of Judicial Review' (2001) 31 *Australian Institute of Administrative Law Forum* 1, 6–7; *Church of Scientology Inc v Woodward* (1982) 154 CLR 25, 70 (Brennan J). See also the passages of *Plaintiff S157/2002 v Commonwealth* (2003) 211 CLR 476, discussed below (*Plaintiff S157/2002*).

[49] *Plaintiff S157/2002* (2003) 211 CLR 476.

[50] ibid 513 [103] (Gaudron, McHugh, Gummow, Kirby and Hayne JJ) (emphasis added) (citations omitted).

[51] ibid 492 [31]. The principles of statutory interpretation are explored in section II.D.

[52] Chief Justice Wayne Martin, 'Peripheral Vision? Judicial Review in Australia: 2014 Australian Institute of Administrative Law National Lecture on Administrative Law' (paper presented at the Australian Institute of Administrative Law National Conference, 24 July 2014, University of Western Australia) 19; quoting Justice Virginia Bell, 'The Legal Content of the "Fair Go"' (speech delivered at Redfern Town Hall, 20 April 2011) 9.

Neither of these passages should be taken to suggest that Australia is the only legal system in which it is thought that executive actors should be subject to legal rules, judicially enforced. Nor is Australia the only place in which this is described as an important element of the rule of law. But section 75(v) is one of the particular means by which this aspect of the rule of law ideal is pursued in Australian law, and as a result the authority of the High Court to review executive action cannot be denied. The institution has not suffered the same crises of legitimacy seen in some other jurisdictions.[53] However, its ambit is clearly limited by the express and implied terms of the Constitution from which it derives its authority. These limitations are explored in the following sections.

B. The Rule of Law and Judicial Power

The federal judicature is also subject to the law. Like the other branches of the federal government, the judicature owes its existence to the Constitution, and its powers are limited thereby. While Chapter III empowers the judicature to perform certain important functions, it forbids it from performing others.[54]

The only power which the High Court is constitutionally authorised to exercise is the 'judicial power of the Commonwealth' vested by section 71.[55] This constrains the ambit of judicial review. For example, the High Court would exceed the boundaries of judicial power if it rewrote the legislation that conferred executive power,[56] or reviewed the substantive merits of executive action.[57] The latter is well captured by the now canonical statement of Brennan J:

> The duty and jurisdiction of the court to review administrative action do not go beyond the declaration and enforcing of the law which determines the limits and governs the exercise of the repository's power. If, in so doing, the court avoids administrative injustice or error, so be it; but the court has no jurisdiction simply to cure administrative injustice or error. The merits of administrative action, to the extent that they can be distinguished from legality, are for the repository of the relevant power and, subject to political control, for the repository alone.[58]

Finally, the scope of statutory executive power is determined by the statute by which it is conferred—albeit interpreted in accordance with a set of strong interpretative presumptions. This point is explained in further detail below. Its immediate

[53] I allude to the 'ultra vires debate' that plagued the UK. For an overview, see C Forsyth (ed), *Judicial Review and the Constitution* (Oxford, Hart Publishing, 2000).

[54] See further Crawford, *The Rule of Law and the Australian Constitution*, above n 6, ch 9.

[55] *R v Kirby; Ex parte Boilermakers' Society of Australia* (1956) 94 CLR 254 (*Boilermakers' Case*). This extends to functions incidental to the exercise of judicial power.

[56] *Momcilovic v The Queen* (2011) 245 CLR 1 [45] (French CJ); 158 [398] (Heydon J).

[57] Of course, these are general statements, and their application is sometimes complex. For example, the principle that courts can review findings of jurisdictional fact would appear to strain the boundary between legality and merits review; it might be justified on the basis of the countervailing concern, to ensure that within the Australian legal system, no stream rises above its source.

[58] *Attorney-General (NSW) v Quin* (1990) 170 CLR 1, 35–36.

significance is that Australia must retain a distinction between jurisdictional and non-jurisdictional errors of law.[59]

In light of these and other constraints, Australian administrative law is sometimes described as formalist and rule-bound.[60] It is also sometimes said to fall short of all that the rule of law requires.[61] But that latter criticism is contestable, given there is no one definition of the rule of law. It is also incongruent with the fact, explained above, that judicial review in Australian law is often proclaimed as an important means of protecting the rule of law. It seems that Australian administrative law serves a particular conception of the rule of law, which coheres with the limits of judicial review of legislative action revealed by the *Communist Party Case*.

Both practices reflect the fact that government is subject to the law. But 'the law' here means that found in the Constitution, or else validly enacted by the Parliament. These laws guarantee that the High Court shall have authority to ensure the other branches of government act within the boundaries of their legal powers, but no more. The judicature would itself act beyond the law if it attempted to go further. The limits of the judicial role are said to ensure its independence and impartiality—a feature which is also frequently described as vital to the rule of law in case law and commentary.[62]

For example, Kirby J explained that the courts have an 'obligation' to maintain the rule of law, and '[i]nherent in that obligation'

> is the notion that courts, disposing of matters within the Judicature, will give effect to the commands of the several legislatures of the States and the Commonwealth, as expressed in the statutes which they enact, or in the subordinate laws which they thereby authorise.[63]

On the other hand, '[a]n aspect of the rule of law under the *Constitution* is that the role or function of Ch III courts does not extend to the performance of the legislative function of translating policy into statutory form or the executive function of administration'.[64]

[59] J Boughey and LB Crawford, 'Jurisdictional Error: Do We Really Need It?' in M Elliott, J Varuhas and S Wilson Stark (eds), *The Unity of Public Law? Doctrinal, Theoretical and Comparative Perspectives* (Oxford, Hart Publishing, 2018, forthcoming).

[60] See, eg, T Poole, 'Between the Devil and the Deep Blue Sea: Administrative Law in an Age of Rights' in L Pearson, C Harlow and M Taggart (eds), *Administrative Law in a Changing State: Essays in Honour of Mark Aronson* (Oxford, Hart Publishing, 2008).

[61] See, eg, Allan's arguments concerning the interpretation of statutory conferrals of executive power: Allan, *The Sovereignty of Law*, above n 11, 213–14. This issue is revisited below.

[62] *White v Director of Military Prosecutions* (2007) 231 CLR 570, 634 [178] (Kirby J); *Abebe v Commonwealth* (1999) 197 CLR 510, 586 [220] (Kirby J); *Thomas v Mowbray* (2007) 233 CLR 307, 342 [61] (Gummow and Crennan JJ); *South Australia v Totani* (2010) 242 CLR 1, 40 [61] (French CJ), 52 [131] (Gummow J), 111 [423] (Crennan and Bell JJ); *Momcilovic* (2011) 245 CLR 1, 224 [593] (Crennan and Kiefel JJ).

[63] *Central Bayside General Practice Association Ltd v Commissioner of State Revenue* (2006) 228 CLR 168, 196 [77] (Kirby J).

[64] *Re Minister for Immigration and Multicultural and Indigenous Affairs; Ex parte Lam* (2003) 214 CLR 1, 24–25 (McHugh and Gummow JJ). See also *City of Enfield v Development Assessment Commission* (2000) 199 CLR 135, 152–54 (Gleeson CJ, Gummow, Kirby and Hayne JJ); A Mason, 'The Tension between Legislative Supremacy and Judicial Review' (2003) 77 *Australian Law Journal* 803, 807–08.

A similar view was expressed by Gleeson CJ in *Plaintiff S157*, in explaining the nature and purpose of section 75(v). In keeping with the authorities described above, Gleeson CJ described that provision as 'secur[ing] a basic element of the rule of law':[65]

> Judicial review is neither more nor less than the enforcement of the rule of law over executive action; it is the means by which executive action is prevented from exceeding the powers and functions assigned to the executive by law and the interests of the individual are protected accordingly.[66]

Yet, Gleeson CJ acknowledged that, '[w]ithin the limits of its legislative capacity, which are themselves set by the *Constitution*, Parliament may enact the law to which officers of the Commonwealth must conform'.[67] Thus:

> The Parliament cannot abrogate or curtail the Court's constitutional function of protecting the subject against any violation of the *Constitution*, or of any law made under the *Constitution*. However, in relation to the second aspect of that function, the powers given to Parliament by the *Constitution* to make laws with respect to certain topics, and subject to certain limitations, enable Parliament to determine the content of the law to be enforced by the Court.[68]

So understood, the core of the 'judicial power of the Commonwealth' is to interpret and enforce the law found in the Constitution, or validly enacted thereunder—and not to ensure that the law is just, effective, or satisfies any other such extraneous standards. However, this should not be taken to suggest that the judiciary is somehow subordinate to the legislature. Rather, the foregoing reflects a particular conception of the rule of law, according to which the powers of the various governmental institutions—including the judicature—are derived from, distributed and limited by a higher law. These ideas will be revisited below.

C. The Individuated Requirements of the Rule of Law

The preceding sections explained that all branches of the federal government are subject to the law of the Constitution, and (where applicable) laws validly enacted thereunder. This represents a clear commitment to the rule of law ideal, in a simple but fundamental sense. But the rule of law has come to be understood in a far more particularised sense: as a device for denoting a more specific set of principles and practices thought necessary to adequately constrain governmental power.

Section I explained that it is problematic to treat the rule of law as a list of check-a-box requirements. In any event, the Australian Constitution does not enshrine any of these more particularised conceptions of the rule of law, whether they be categorised as thick or thin.

For example, thick conceptions of the rule of law typically require the legal recognition and protection of human rights. But one of the most notable features

[65] *Plaintiff S157/2002* (2003) 211 CLR 476, 482 [5].
[66] ibid 492 [31], quoting *Church of Scientology Inc v Woodward* (1982) 154 CLR 25, 70 (Brennan J).
[67] *Plaintiff S157/2002* (2003) 211 CLR 476, 482 [5].
[68] ibid 483 [6].

of the Australian Constitution is that it has no bill of rights. Indeed, the Australian Constitution says very little about the relationship between the citizen and the state at all. However it is interpreted, it is doubtful that the text of the Australian Constitution could ever be legitimately be found to 'guarantee' the full catalogue of individual rights and freedoms associated with the thick conception of the rule of law.[69]

On the other side of the debate, thin conceptions of the rule of law typically require that all government action be authorised by law enacted in advance.[70] But there is no express prohibition of retrospective laws in the Constitution,[71] and the High Court has found that no such prohibition is implied. Thus it is accepted that the federal Parliament may enact retrospective legislation, including so as to provide government actors with legal authority which may have been lacking in the past.[72] Similarly, it is often argued that the rule of law requires that the law be clear, accessible and stable,[73] but the Constitution does not require this,[74] or at least not directly.[75] There has been some suggestion that an entirely uncertain statute might simply not be a 'law' at all,[76] but that seems doubtful, for reasons I explore at length elsewhere.[77]

Other elements of the rule of law are implemented by the Constitution, but only in a particular and limited way. One important example was described above. That is, that while the Constitution gives the High Court authority to review the validity of executive action, it is for Parliament to confer statutory executive power and define its scope. Therefore, the executive may be validly empowered to act in a manner that (some may argue) is repugnant to the rule of law. For example, procedural fairness is often described as a requirement of the rule of law. But it is quite clear that Parliament can confer statutory executive powers that are not subject to any requirement of procedural fairness, provided that it does so by express and unambiguous words.[78]

Thus the Constitution does not 'guarantee' all the individuated requirements of any particular conception of the rule of law. But this does not mean that those individuated principles (or the rule of law more broadly) are not valued within the

[69] See further Crawford, *The Rule of Law and the Australian Constitution*, above n 6, ch 8.

[70] See, eg, Raz, above n 2, 214–18; Fuller, above n 10 (see especially at 39). See further C Sampford, *Retrospectivity and the Rule of Law* (Oxford, Oxford University Press, 2006).

[71] cf, eg, United States Constitution art 1 § 9 cl 3.

[72] See, eg, *Polyukhovich v Commonwealth* (1991) 172 CLR 501; *Plaintiff M68/2015 v Minister for Immigration and Border Protection* (2016) 257 CLR 42.

[73] See, eg, Raz, above n 2, 214–18; Fuller, above n 10, 39.

[74] *Giris Pty Ltd v Federal Commissioner of Taxation* (1968) 119 CLR 365, 372–73 (Barwick CJ), 375–76 (McTiernan J), 378–80 (Kitto J); and somewhat similarly *Work Choices Case* (2006) 229 CLR 1, 175 [399] (Gleeson CJ, Gummow, Hayne, Heydon and Crennan JJ).

[75] As to whether a degree of clarity is required by ss 51 and 52 of the Constitution, see LB Crawford, 'Can Parliament Confer Plenary Executive Power? The Limitations Imposed by ss 51 and 52 of the *Australian Constitution*' (2016) 44 *Federal Law Review* 287.

[76] See, eg, *Plaintiff S157/2002* (2003) 211 CLR 476, 512–13 [102] (Gaudron, McHugh, Gummow, Kirby and Hayne JJ).

[77] LB Crawford, 'The Entrenched Minimum Provision of Judicial Review and the Limits of "Law"' (2017) 45 *Federal Law Review* 1. See further Crawford, *The Rule of Law and the Australian Constitution*, above n 6, ch 6.

[78] M Groves, 'Exclusion of the Rules of Natural Justice' (2013) 39 *Monash University Law Review* 285. Note, procedural fairness may be an essential characteristic of 'judicial power'.

Australian legal system. Indeed, principles that are not fully enshrined in constitutional rules would seem to fit more squarely within the realm of values than those that are. Further, though many of the individuated requirements of the rule of law are not constitutionally entrenched, they are recognised and protected by the principles of statutory interpretation.

D. The Rule of Law and Statutory Interpretation

Though the principles of statutory interpretation are sometimes described as creatures of the common law, they have a clear constitutional foundation. For the power to interpret statutes is part of the judicial power vested in the judicature by section 71 of the Constitution, and the principles of statutory interpretation must reflect the constitutional distribution of powers between the legislative, executive and judicial branches.[79] They reflect and serve the rule of law in various ways.

First, Australian courts emphasise the importance of interpreting statutes in such a way that their legal meaning reflects the ordinary grammatical meaning of the words used 'on the page'.[80] French J explained:

> In a representative democracy those who are subject to the law, those who invoke it and those who apply it are entitled to expect that it means what it says ... 'that rule is dictated by elementary considerations of fairness, for, after all, those who are subject to the law's commands are entitled to conduct themselves on the basis that those commands have meaning and effect according to ordinary grammar and usage'.[81]

This reflects the view that law ought to be capable of guiding human conduct, and cannot do so if courts routinely add an artificial gloss to the words on the page of the statute book. They also suggest that there is some injustice in subjecting an individual to legal obligations they are incapable of knowing in advance. The importance attributed to ordinary grammatical meaning also serves the value of transparency, and judicial independence. For when the legal meaning of a statute bears no resemblance to its ordinary grammatical meaning, one may wonder whether courts have made statute law rather than interpreted it.

But of course, there are many reasons why a court may conclude that the legal meaning of a statute is not the same as its ordinary grammatical meaning. One is that the courts employ a catalogue of interpretative presumptions—many of which reflect other, individuated requirements of the rule of law.

For example, it is presumed that statutory conferrals of executive power are subject to certain implied limitations.[82] Thus even an ostensibly unlimited conferral

[79] *Zheng v Cai* (2009) 239 CLR 446, 455 [28] (French CJ, Gummow, Crennan, Kiefel and Bell JJ); *Plaintiff S10/2011 v Minister for Immigration and Citizenship* (2012) 246 CLR 636, 666 [97] (Gummow, Hayne, Crennan and Bell JJ).

[80] See, eg, *Engineers Case* (1920) 28 CLR 129, 161–62 (Higgins J); *Cooper Brookes (Wollongong) Pty Ltd v Federal Commissioner of Taxation* (1981) 147 CLR 297, 320–21 (Mason and Wilson JJ), and the quotations that follow.

[81] *NAAV v Minister for Immigration and Multicultural and Indigenous Affairs* (2002) 123 FCR 298, 410 [430], quoting *Corporate Affairs Commission (NSW) v Yuill* (1991) 172 CLR 319, 340 (Gaudron J).

[82] M Aronson, M Groves and G Weeks, *Judicial Review of Administrative Action and Government Liability* (Sydney, Thomson Reuters, 2017) 116–22.

will be read subject to the subject matter, purpose and scope of the statute in which it appears, and broader norms concerning the proper exercise of executive power. Often, this will include a requirement to exercise the power in a manner that is procedurally fair. Second, it is presumed that statutes—and especially, penal statutes—do not have retrospective effect.[83] Finally, it is presumed that statutes do not abrogate fundamental rights, such as the right to liberty, or property rights, or freedom from speech. This presumption is known as the principle of legality.[84]

This demonstrates that many of the more discrete principles associated with the rule of law are recognised and valued in Australian law. For example, the courts' approach to construing statutory conferrals of executive power reflects the view that executive power should not be arbitrary, and discretionary power should be constrained: ideas that are central to many conceptions of the rule of law.

But except and insofar as they are enshrined in the text or structure of the Australian Constitution, these principles are vulnerable to legislative abrogation. Presumptions of statutory interpretation must yield to clear statutory provision to the contrary. As Stephen Gageler explained, with respect to the presumed limitations of statutory executive power: 'The traditional grounds are in truth no more than the default position to be applied in the absence of a contrary legislative intention to define the boundaries of a decision-maker's jurisdiction differently'.[85] French CJ made a similar point, with regard to the limits of the principle of legality. A statute may be drafted in such a way that it is only open to one legitimate interpretation: 'an interpretation … which infringe[s] one or more rights or freedoms. The principle of legality … is of no avail against such language'.[86] This does not mean that individual rights and freedoms have no value in the Australian legal system—rather, that their protection is ultimately entrusted to the legislative branch.

E. Conclusion: An Australian Rule of Law Tradition?

The powers of all branches of the federal government are conferred and limited by law, as found in the Constitution or legislation validly enacted thereunder. But the content of that law does not necessarily conform to the 'rule of law', as that phrase has come to be defined in the realms of legal theory, or as it may be understood in other jurisdictions.

We may *expect* that government should act in a way that is consistent with those broader conceptions of the rule of law. That expectation is reflected in and supported by the principles of statutory interpretation—as well as the public criticism that often ensues, when government acts in such a way as to disappoint it. But the judiciary cannot, within the lawful scope of its powers, invalidate legislative or executive

[83] *Director of Public Prosecutions (Cth) v Keating* (2013) 248 CLR 459, 479 [48] (French CJ, Hayne, Crennan, Kiefel, Bell and Keane JJ).
[84] See generally, D Meagher and M Groves (eds), *The Principle of Legality in Australia and New Zealand* (Sydney, Federation Press, 2017).
[85] Gageler, above n 46, 287.
[86] *Momcilovic v The Queen* (2011) 245 CLR 1, 47 [45].

action that conforms to the requirements of the Constitution: the stream cannot rise above its source.[87] The constitutional function of the court is to interpret and enforce the Constitution, and laws validly made thereunder, and not to otherwise ensure that the law is effective or just.

Some theorists argue that these conclusions are unacceptable—indeed, illogical. For example, Allan argues that it was simply 'not open to the framers [of the *Australian Constitution*] to choose only partial implementation of the rule of law', in the expansive sense that he defines it, 'or to leave its enforcement to other organs of government [than the courts]'.[88] Those well-known cases in which the High Court has found that the Constitution does not provide the kinds of protections Allan's theory requires 'should be treated as unacceptable legal errors, reflecting failures to understand the full implications of the rule of law'.[89] These are remarkable claims, that seem incongruent with the nature of the Constitution, and the process by which it acquired legal force. They are inherently contestable, for they are premised upon but one conception of the rule of law.

It seems altogether more implausible that, in all the many and different constitutional orders that exist across the world, the limits of governmental power are in fact the same. The rule of law encapsulates the basic idea that government should be subject to the law. But it remains up to each legal system to make a choice—indeed, a series of choices—as to how that broad and nebulous goal should be pursued. That will include a choice as to the nature of the limitations on governmental power, and how those limitations are enforced. One may well argue that the choices made in a particular legal order are not the best means of pursuing the rule of law, but any such argument is inherently contestable. If those choices are enshrined in a rigid constitution (like the Australian Constitution), then they can only be undone in accordance with the process stipulated therein. Those choices will in turn engender differing legal cultures, and even different understandings of what the rule of law entails.

To be quite clear, this is not to say that *any* understanding of the rule of law must be legitimate; that any legal system in which there are laws can profess to abide by the rule of law. There are perverse legal systems with the trappings of legality, but in which certain government actors effectively wield unfettered power. But Australia is not such a system. Government power is constrained by law—albeit perhaps not to the full extent, or in the precise manner, that some may desire.

III. THE RULE OF LAW AND CONSTITUTIONAL INTERPRETATION

The rule of law is undoubtedly an Australian constitutional law, served and reflected by the basic nature and structure of the Constitution as well as many of its more

[87] This makes no comment on whether the judiciary may sometimes have a moral obligation to do so: see J Goldsworthy, 'The Limits of Judicial Fidelity to Law' (2011) 24 *Canadian Journal of Law & Jurisprudence* 305.

[88] TRS Allan, *Constitutional Justice: A Liberal Theory of the Rule of Law* (Oxford, Oxford University Press, 2001) 264.

[89] ibid.

specific parts. Let us assume that the High Court should take into account such values in interpreting the Constitution. How might the rule of law assist it in that task?

In answering that question, the nature of the rule of law must be kept in mind. If the rule of law can sensibly guide constitutional interpretation, then it is only insofar as that broad and nebulous value is understood and practised in Australian law. The interpretative use of the rule of law must reflect the reasons for which, it is concluded, the rule of law is an Australian constitutional value, and the manner and extent to which it is reflected in the constitutional text.

This chapter has sought to show that, in Australian constitutional discourse, the rule of law is most closely associated with the rigorous and impartial enforcement of the Constitution, and laws validly enacted thereunder. This emphasises the fact that the powers of the various branches of the federal government are derived from, distributed and limited by a higher law: that is, the Constitution. Indeed, Australia's rule of law tradition emphasises the fact that the legal order of Australia was created by the Constitution. This provides the historical and logical foundation for that constitutional maxim: the stream cannot rise above its source.

The interpretative powers of the High Court must be understood within this paradigm. It is clear that in interpreting the Constitution, the High Court cannot exceed the boundaries of the 'judicial power of the Commonwealth', or otherwise act contrary to the Constitution. It would undoubtedly do so if it purported to change the Constitution, or invalidate a law that was within the scope of constitutionally conferred legislative power. This would diminish the rule of law at it is understood in Australian law. It may eventually prove self-defeating. For the efficacy of judicial decision-making depends in large part upon the attitude taken towards it by the other branches of government, which may in practical reality choose to respect and abide by a court's decision, or not. In Australia, judicial decisions are routinely obeyed by the legislature and executive—even though, undoubtedly, the legislature or executive sometimes think that the decision is wrong in principle. This further demonstrates a deep commitment to a particular rule of law ideal. For the courts to give effect to some alien conception of the rule of law, and hence subject governmental power to limitations not firmly rooted in the Constitution on the basis that the rule of law requires it, would seem to undermine this rule of law tradition.[90]

This is a rule of law tradition that requires us to take the text and structure of the Constitution seriously. However, it should not be mistaken as a call for literalism, nor necessarily formalism, or an overly truncated judicial role. Indeed, close analysis of constitutional text and structure might well reveal far greater rule of law protections than would at first appear.

It is necessary to demonstrate this with some examples. Given the breadth of the rule of law, that concept could inform the answer to a great many constitutional questions. Some comment is made in Section IV about the relationship between the rule of law and judicial deference, especially during times of emergency. The following section examines another issue, that has attracted significant attention

[90] This should not be taken to suggest that the High Court seeks to do so.

in recent years: Parliament's power to evade the entrenched minimum provision of judicial review of executive action.[91]

A. Interpreting the Entrenched Minimum Provision of Judicial Review

As explained above, it is well settled that the jurisdiction conferred upon the High Court cannot be ousted by ordinary legislation. Less clear is whether and to what extent Parliament may design statutory conferrals of executive power in such a way that the exercise of the power is largely or entirely immune from judicial review. There are many ways in which that could be attempted, of varying degrees of plausibility. For example, Parliament could include a 'no-invalidity clause' in a statute that confers executive power. These clauses assert that the exercise of executive power shall be valid, notwithstanding certain legal errors made along the way. The High Court has limited capacity to review non-jurisdictional errors of law. Moreover, the federal Parliament may be able to preclude judicial review on non-jurisdictional grounds.[92] Thus no-invalidity clauses have the potential to diminish judicial review, and perhaps, the rule of law. Yet, they are not obviously contrary to the Australian Constitution.

It is well established that the courts have constitutional authority to independently review the legality of executive action, but only within the parameters of Chapter III. There is nothing necessarily illogical about a legal limitation on executive power, breach of which does not lead to invalidity—that is, is a non-jurisdictional error.[93] The High Court clearly accepts the possibility of non-jurisdictional errors of law. Indeed, the distinction between jurisdictional and non-jurisdictional errors is central to Australian administrative law. It reflects the constitutional distribution of powers between the legislative, executive and judicial branches.[94] For it is the role of Parliament to confer executive power, and define its scope. The only legal limitations on its capacity to do so are those imposed by the Constitution, and few if any of the established 'grounds of review' are constitutionally entrenched.[95] The courts could not, therefore, simply ignore the content of the statute by which executive power is conferred, or enforce legal limitations thereon that Parliament had validly excluded.

However, this does not mean that Parliament can completely hollow out the entrenched minimum provision of judicial review. To the contrary, the constitutional allocation of powers significantly constrains Parliament's ability to do so. Parliament cannot dictate that an exercise of statutory executive power is valid, any more than it can dictate the validity of federal legislation. It is the courts' role to ascertain the scope of the executive power that has been conferred, in accordance with the

[91] See, eg, W Bateman, 'The Constitution and the Substantive Principles of Judicial Review: The Full Scope of the Entrenched Minimum Provision of Judicial Review' (2011) 39 *Federal Law Review* 463; L McDonald, 'The Entrenched Minimum Provision of Judicial Review and the Rule of Law' (2010) 21 *Public Law Review* 14.

[92] Recall the discussion in section II.A and B.

[93] See, eg, *Kirk v Industrial Court NSW* (2010) 239 CLR 531, 571 [65], 581 [100].

[94] See further, Boughey and Crawford, above n 59.

[95] See further Aronson, Groves and Weeks, above n 82.

established principles of statutory construction, and whether the executive has acted within or without power in a given case. This deprives no-invalidity clauses of some of their most destructive potential, as I have explained at length elsewhere.[96]

Understood in this sense, the rule of law also reveals the proper treatment of other legislative devices thought to jeopardise the entrenched minimum provision of judicial review. For example, Parliament's ability to confer plenary executive power is also constrained (though to a lesser extent) by sections 51 and 52 of the Constitution, and the requirement that each and every law demonstrates the requisite connection to a head of power listed therein, to the satisfaction of the High Court.[97] Finally, in exercising the judicial power of the Commonwealth, the courts may legitimately presume that broadly worded statutory conferrals of executive power are subject to implied limitations—like, perhaps, a requirement to afford procedural fairness. If Parliament wishes to confer a power free from those limitations, it must do so expressly. In terms typically used to describe the principle of legality, it must 'accept the political cost'.[98] This does not constrain Parliament's ability to confer such powers as such, but it does make it more difficult to do so; ideally, it may deter Parliament from trying.[99]

The recent decision of the High Court in *Graham v Minister for Immigration* and Border Protection (*Graham*) demonstrates the potential application of these principles to other legislative devices that might indirectly restrict judicial review.[100] This case considered powers conferred on the Minister by the Migration Act 1958 (Cth), to cancel a person's visa on character grounds. Section 503A(2) of the Act provided (inter alia) that the Minister must not be required to disclose information relevant to the exercise of this power to a court, if that information was communicated to the Minister by certain law enforcement or intelligence agencies on the condition that it be kept confidential.

Two of the Minister's decisions were challenged on the ground that he had acted unreasonably. It was accepted that the power to cancel a visa was subject to an implied condition of reasonableness. However, the Minister admitted that he had based his decision, in part, upon 'undisclosed information' pursuant to section 503A(2). The plaintiffs challenged the constitutional validity of section 503A(2). It was argued that, in practical effect, the legislation impaired judicial review by denying the information upon which this depends. A majority of the High Court agreed.

The majority judgment placed explicit emphasis on section 75(v) of the Constitution. Yet, their Honours' decision must be understood—if it is to be accepted at all—as grounded in the separation of powers. The first reason for this is that section 503A(2) was found to be invalid in its application to both the High Court and Federal Court, the latter of which derives its judicial review jurisdiction from statute. The second reason is that section 75(v) of the Constitution is best understood as a

[96] See further Crawford, 'Who Decides the Validity of Executive Action?', above n 46.

[97] See further Crawford, 'Can Parliament Confer Plenary Executive Power?', above n 75.

[98] *R v Secretary of State for the Home Department; Ex parte Simms* [2000] 2 AC 115, 131 (Lord Hoffman).

[99] See further Crawford, 'Can Parliament Confer Plenary Executive Power?', above n 75.

[100] *Graham v Minister for Immigration* [2017] HCA 33.

conferral of jurisdiction and not of power.[101] As explained above, section 75 marks out a space in which the judicial power of the Commonwealth, conferred by section 71, can be used.[102] In these circumstances, the relevant content of the judicial power is to declare and enforce the law that limits executive power and grant appropriate remedies, by the ascertainment of facts and the application of legal rules to those facts. Section 503A(2) did not, in substance or form, impede access to the section 75(v) *jurisdiction*.[103] But it is arguable that section 503A(2) impeded the exercise of the judicial *power* of the Commonwealth, in circumstances where these courts were authorised to use it. The majority concluded that this was the case: that section 503A(2) would prevent the courts from accessing the facts necessary to determine whether the Minister had acted within the legal limits of his power.[104]

On the majority's view, the combined protection afforded by sections 71 and 75 of the Constitution seems greater than was previously supposed. As Edelman J explained in his powerful dissent, legislation which restricted the courts' access to information, to a far greater extent than section 503A(2), had been upheld in the past.[105] Similar cases can be found in the context of constitutional review. For example, in *Dawson v Commonwealth*, the High Court held that the fact it could not ensure power conferred upon the Treasurer pursuant to section 51(vi) of the Constitution would in fact be exercised for defence-related purposes (as the Treasurer might conceal or mispresent the purposes for which he acted) did not mean that the conferral was invalid. Dixon J explained: 'that is a complaint against the inadequacy of the judicial process to uphold the law. It does not go to the intrinsic validity of the supposed acts of the Treasurer'.[106]

This aspect of the decision will require further analysis. For present purposes, *Graham* stands as authority for a simple but significant proposition: if executive power is subject to legal limits, then the courts must be able to *properly* enforce those limits, in circumstances where they are given jurisdiction to do so. In other words, Parliament cannot substantially impede the exercise of judicial power by a court, in order to resolve a case that the court has jurisdiction to hear. This is an important protection of the rule of law, but that protection is limited. The case proceeded from the premise that the power to cancel a visa was subject to an implied requirement of

[101] *Harris v Caladine* (1991) 172 CLR 84; *Re Refugee Tribunal; Ex parte Aala* (2000) 204 CLR 82, 139 [156] (Hayne J); *Minister for Immigration and Multicultural and Indigenous Affairs v B* (2004) 219 CLR 365, 377 [6] (Gleeson CJ and McHugh J); 395 [69] (Gummow, Hayne and Heydon JJ). See further LB Crawford, 'Why These Three? The Significance of the Selection of Remedies in Section 75(v) of the Australian Constitution' (2014) 42(2) *Federal Law Review* 253; G Lindell, *Cowen and Zines's Federal Jurisdiction in Australia* (Federation Press, 2016) 5–6.

[102] As implied at [2017] HCA 34 [48].

[103] Hence the analogy drawn to *Bodruddaza v Minister for Immigration and Multicultural Affairs* (2007) 228 CLR 651 (at [49]) seems strained. That case concerned a strict statutory limit on the time in which an application for review could be made.

[104] [2017] HCA 34 [52].

[105] [2017] HCA 33 [80]–[84], [123]–[167].

[106] (1946) 73 CLR 157, 182. See similarly *Giris* (1968) 119 CLR 365, 384–85 (Barwick CJ), 376 (McTiernan J), 379 (Kitto J), 381–82 (Menzies J), 368 (Owen J). See further Crawford, 'Can Parliament Confer Plenary Executive Power?', above n 75, 308–09; J Stellios, *Zines's The High Court and the Constitution* (Sydney, Federation Press, 2015) 318, 328.

reasonableness. But it is generally accepted that Parliament can confer power that is not subject to this limitation,[107] and nothing in the majority's decision suggests to the contrary.

Hence, the case does not support the broader proposition, that section 75(v) of the Constitution implicitly forbids the conferral of executive powers that are not readily amenable to the writs listed in that section. As Edelman J explained, such a principle would be contrary to precedent and inconsistent with the general understanding of the limited, albeit important, constitutional function of section 75(v).[108]

The decision in *Graham* also demonstrates the broader limits of judicial review, and confirms that the Australian Constitution does not require the government to comply with all those requirements which, theoretical enquiry may reveal, is necessary to ensure law's rule. I have stated that the rule of law cannot be secured by judicial action alone: it requires, amongst other things, that the other branches of government respect and obey the courts' decisions. I also stated that in Australia, judicial decisions are typically obeyed by the legislature and executive, which may be taken as evidence of a broader rule of law culture. However, there is a difference between complying with the letter of a judicial decision, and its spirit. Soon after the decision in *Graham*, the federal Parliament enacted legislation retrospectively authorising decisions made in (at the time, unlawful) reliance on undisclosed information.[109] On the basis of authority outlined in preceding sections, this legislation appears to be constitutionally valid—even though retrospective validation of unlawful executive action would be repugnant to most conceptions of the rule of law.

IV. CONCLUSION

The rule of law is a fundamental value of Australian constitutionalism, with a clear presence in the text and structure of the Constitution. This value is implemented and practised in certain, specific ways: this is unsurprising, given there is no authoritative conception of the rule of law, and very clear institutional and doctrinal differences between the many legal systems which could share this same broad value. If the rule of law is to guide constitutional interpretation, this must be borne in mind. It is the Australian rule of law tradition that should be looked to as the guide, and not the abstract conceptions of the rule of law that proliferate in the realms of legal theory, nor necessarily the mechanisms for pursuing that value that exist in other jurisdictions.

[107] eg *Minister for Immigration and Citizenship v Li* (2013) 249 CLR 332, 362 [63], 369 [86] (Hayne, Kiefel and Bell JJ), 371 [92] (Gageler J); *Minister for Immigration and Border Protection v Singh* (2014) 231 FCR 437, 445 [43]. Arguably, if the legal standard of reasonableness truly depends upon the statutory context, then s 503A(2) should have been read as affecting the standard of reasonableness required. It is not necessary to pursue that line of enquiry here.

[108] eg the decision in *Plaintiff M61/2010 v Commonwealth* (2010) 243 CLR 319 (see, eg, [174]–[175], citing Crawford, *The Rule of Law and the Australian Constitution*, above n 6).

[109] Migration Amendment (Validation of Decisions) Act 2017 (Cth). This Act did not apply to matters previously adjudicated or reserved by a court: s 503E(2).

Thus the limitations on governmental power imposed by the Constitution must be carefully ascertained, and rigorously and impartially enforced. That will not only help to uphold the rule of law, but support the realisation of other constitutional values discussed in this volume, such as government accountability, impartial justice, and representative democracy; it may potentially temper the untrammelled pursuit of others, such as national security. That said, courts can only play one part in this process. The extent to which law rules in Australia will depend greatly upon the way in which other branches of government respond to judicial decisions.

The *Communist Party Case* demonstrates this exercise in practice. There, the High Court insisted on careful legal analysis of the legislation in question, despite the hysteria of the times; it did not defer to the government's claims that the legislation was necessary to protect Australia against an existential threat. The legislation was found to be invalid because it did not conform to the Constitution. In doing so, the High Court confirmed that the legislative power of the Commonwealth was subject to the legal limitations found in the Constitution: no more, but no less. In doing so, the Court played its part in upholding the rule of law—in the sense that it is understood in Australian law.

6

Government Accountability as a 'Constitutional Value'

JANINA BOUGHEY AND GREG WEEKS*

I. INTRODUCTION

ACCOUNTABILITY IS FREQUENTLY described as one of the key 'values' or 'ideals' that administrative law is designed to uphold.[1] Accountability's greatest claim to hold the status of a value might be its ubiquity: it has been described as the 'buzzword of modern governance',[2] the '*über*-concept of the 21st century',[3] and a 'theme ... central to all discussion of government'.[4] Yet the modern meaning of accountability has developed very recently. The word 'accountability' can be found in Australian cases over the last century but most refer to the accountability of fiduciaries (such as liquidators and executors) in equity,[5] of taxpayers, of tortfeasors, in electoral matters and of public companies, rather than of

* The authors would like to thank Ellen Rock and those who commented on this paper at the Australian Constitutional Values workshop held at UNSW on 10 June 2016, particularly Gabrielle Appleby, Lisa Burton Crawford, Rosalind Dixon, Patrick Emerton and Jeff Goldsworthy. The usual caveat applies.

[1] See, eg, M Aronson, M Groves and G Weeks, *Judicial Review of Administrative Action and Government Liability* (Sydney, Thomson Reuters, 2017) [1.10], [3.370]; M Taggart, 'The Province of Administrative Law Determined?' in M Taggart (ed), *The Province of Administrative Law* (Oxford, Hart Publishing, 1997) 1, 3; P Craig, *UK, EU and Global Administrative Law: Foundations and Challenges* (Cambridge, Cambridge University Press, 2015) 15; P Cane, 'Theory and Values in Public Law' in P Craig and R Rawlings (eds), *Law and Administration in Europe: Essays in Honour of Carol Harlow* (Oxford, Oxford University Press, 2003), 15. *cf*, however, Allsop CJ's almost total omission of accountability from his oration on values in public law: J Allsop, 'Values in Public Law' (2017) 91 *Australian Law Journal* 118.

[2] M Bovens, T Schillemans and RE Goodin, 'Public Accountability' in M Bovens, RE Goodin and T Schillemans (eds), *The Oxford Handbook of Public Accountability* (Oxford, Oxford University Press, 2014) 1.

[3] M Flinders, 'The Future and Relevance of Accountability Studies' in M Bovens, RE Goodin and T Schillemans (eds), *The Oxford Handbook of Public Accountability* (Oxford, Oxford University Press, 2014) 661.

[4] R Creyke, J McMillan and M Smyth, *Control of Government Action: Text, Cases & Commentary*, 4th edn (Sydney, LexisNexis, 2015) 14. The authors of this text use accountability as the organising concept around which the entire book is arranged.

[5] Finn has repeatedly, and more expansively, characterised the relationship between government and the people of Australia as fiduciary: see, eg, PD Finn, 'A Sovereign People, A Public Trust' in PD Finn (ed), *Essays on Law and Government* (Sydney, LawBook Co, 1995) vol 1, 9–10. The only reference to accountability in Allsop CJ's oration on public law values was in relation to trustees in bankruptcy: Allsop, above n 1, 124–25.

government bodies.[6] The concept of the 'accountability' of government to those governed has become prominent only fairly recently.[7]

There is a school of thought which suggests that there are few values which can be explicitly discerned from the text of the Australian Constitution, and not many more by implication.[8] In the absence of a clear link to the Constitution, to describe any purported value as 'small-c' *constitutional* might be seen merely as a proxy for saying that it is important.[9] Government accountability, as we will see, has claims of various strength to being described as a 'constitutional value' in this sense. The fact that it regularly features on lists of 'public law values' can be taken predominantly to indicate that accountability is generally regarded as being of immense importance.[10]

However, there is a lively debate as to the existence of a set of values which are distinctive to public law.[11] Central to this problem is the fact that 'public' and 'private' are labels of convenience[12] rather than categories with particular normative force; there is no 'bright line' by which one can be discerned from the other.[13] More importantly, as Cane pointed out, such a distinction is unhelpful:

> The meaning and goals of accountability, and judgments about the success of accountability mechanisms, are likely to remain contested and ultimately dependent on normative legal and political theories. Putting the point quite crudely, people who believe that a public/private distinction is normatively justified and an important accountability tool are unlikely to be shaken in this belief by the observable facts that the line between state and non-state is blurred, and that the social universe is characterised by complex and interacting networks of accountability. Nor will the assertion that it is difficult to impose public law values on

[6] Early uses of accountability in the latter sense include *Re Control Investment Pty Ltd and Australian Broadcasting Tribunal* (1980) 50 FLR 1, 14 and *R v Toohey; Ex parte Northern Land Council* (1981) 151 CLR 170, 230 (Murphy J).

[7] See, eg, P Finn, 'The Abuse of Public Power in Australia: Making Our Governors Our Servants' (1994) 5 *Public Law Review* 43, 53; C Harlow, *Accountability in the European Union* (Oxford, Oxford University Press, 2002) 6.

[8] Indeed, while it is frequently asserted that Australians share certain values which are not necessarily able to be traced to the Constitution at all, 'it is easier to assert that people in Australia share [such] "values" than it is to nominate the individual values that are shared': M Groves and G Weeks, 'Substantive (Procedural) Review in Australia' in H Wilberg and M Elliott (eds), *The Scope and Intensity of Substantive Review: Traversing Taggart's Rainbow* (Oxford, Hart Publishing, 2015) 151.

[9] Spigelman CJ suggested a wider conception of the Constitution, which hinted that functionally entrenched constitutional statutes, frameworks and traditions have laid the ground for newer statutory forms of accountability: JJ Spigelman, 'Foundations of Administrative Law: Toward General Principles of Institutional Law' (1999) 58 *Australian Journal of Public Administration* 3, 8.

[10] This might extend to accountability being described as a 'core' public law value: E Rock, 'Fault and Accountability in Public Law' in M Elliott, J Varuhas and S Wilson Stark (eds), *The Unity of Public Law? Doctrinal, Theoretical and Comparative Perspectives* (Oxford, Hart Publishing, 2018).

[11] As opposed to judicial review: M Aronson, 'Public Law Values in the Common Law' in M Elliott and D Feldman (eds), *The Cambridge Companion to Public Law* (Cambridge, Cambridge University Press, 2015).

[12] Aronson suggested that the convenience is for the benefit of those who design law school curriculums, rather than practising lawyers who are generally suspicious of such a compartmentalised approach to law: Aronson, 'Public Law Values', above n 11, 134; *cf* C Scott, 'Accountability in the Regulatory State' (2000) 27 *Journal of Law and Society* 38, 59.

[13] See, eg, C Harlow, '"Public" and "Private" Law: Definition without Distinction' (1980) 43 *Modern Law Review* 241; P Cane, 'Accountability and the Public/Private Distinction' in N Bamforth and P Leyland (eds), *Public Law in a Multi-Layered Constitution* (Oxford, Hart Publishing, 2003); M Taggart, '"The Peculiarities of the English": Resisting the Public/Private Law Distinction' in P Craig and R Rawlings (eds), *Law and Administration in Europe: Essays in Honour of Carol Harlow* (Oxford, Oxford University Press, 2003).

complex accountability networks convince them to abandon the attempt to do so and instead to be satisfied with judging the 'success' of such networks according to other criteria.[14]

On this view, to analyse accountability as a 'public law value' causes one to miss the complexities of how accountability is able to be imposed because it is rooted in an outmoded distinction. Further, such an approach ignores the dual applications of accountability: the various mechanisms through which accountability might be imposed, on one hand, and the functions and activities which we might want to make accountable, on the other. Seddon provides an example of the latter point in relation to government contracting, which has become the preferred mechanism for delivery of some public services,[15] by noting that commonly cited public law values are almost[16] entirely contradictory to contractual principles.[17] Contracting has long been viewed as quintessentially incompatible with judicial review,[18] yet to categorise government contracting as private would be to complicate unnecessarily the fact that we have every right to demand that government 'behave impeccably' in its contractual dealings.[19]

This chapter, therefore, undertakes no easy task in attempting to place accountability within the scope of 'capital-C' 'Constitutional values'. We will address this task by setting aside, for now, the difficult questions raised above and take it as established that accountability is something that is both desired and desirable in public governance. We will seek to discover how accountability works and the nature of its claim to be a 'constitutional value'.

We do so by first defining what we take the phrase 'government accountability' to mean, in section II of the chapter. We then consider, in section III, the extent to which government accountability is constitutionally entrenched—as distinct from the question of whether it is a value. In the context of government accountability, the scope of constitutional entrenchment is crucial to the question of whether it may also have broader application as a 'constitutional value'. There are two reasons for this. First, we will argue that any 'constitutional value' of government accountability has sprung from the particular constitutional provisions and principles that give effect to that value. Particular provisions of the Constitution, and principles arising therefrom, have been found to have been included for the purpose of ensuring government accountability. Any suggestion of government accountability being a constitutional value, its scope, application and limits, must therefore be understood in the context of what the Constitution has been found to entrench. Secondly, section IV of the chapter moves on to the question of whether government accountability can

14 Cane, 'Accountability and the Public/Private Distinction', above n 13, 272.

15 Subject to the presence of executive power (*Pape v Commissioner of Taxation* (2009) 238 CLR 1) or the existence of a valid legislative scheme (*Williams v Commonwealth [No 1]* (2012) 248 CLR 156 (*Williams [No 1]*); *Williams v Commonwealth [No 2]* (2014) 252 CLR 416 (*Williams [No 2]*)).

16 Honesty is required in both contractual relationships and public service.

17 N Seddon, *Government Contracts: Federal, State and Local*, 5th edn (Sydney, Federation Press, 2013) 18.

18 See, eg, *General Newspapers Pty Ltd v Telstra Corporation* (1993) 45 FCR 164; *Griffith University v Tang* (2005) 221 CLR 99. These cases dealt with the Administrative Decisions (Judicial Review) Act 1977 (Cth) and, while it is usually assumed that the same principles would apply under the general law, declaratory or injunctive relief might nonetheless be granted in appropriate circumstances: Aronson, Groves and Weeks, above n 1, [2.560], [3.180].

19 Seddon, above n 17, 18.

be said to be a value that has force beyond the specific provisions of the Constitution that have the practical effect of achieving government accountability in limited circumstances. We argue that there is both explicit and implicit evidence from the High Court which suggests that government accountability may go beyond these express guarantees and be a constitutional value. In section V, we examine the possible effects of the Court giving more explicit and consistent recognition to the value of accountability in hard cases, and explore the limits of this approach in the context of government accountability.

II. DEFINING GOVERNMENT ACCOUNTABILITY

Like accountability itself,[20] the word 'government' is ambiguous. It is often used to refer compendiously to all state institutions, including Parliament, courts and the administration. In other contexts, 'government' refers to the political party that controls the Lower House and encompasses all the party's members in the legislature, as well as the administration. 'Government' is also frequently used more narrowly, to mean the executive branch. We take the last of these definitions for the purposes of this chapter, because other chapters in this collection cover parliamentary accountability.

As the changing use of the word in case law indicates, 'accountability' itself says nothing about *who* is accountable to *whom*, for *what*, *how*, and according to what *criteria*.[21] It is not the task of this chapter to resolve the many contested questions surrounding the definition of accountability. For our purposes, it is sufficient to make the point that, at its core, in both public law and equitable senses, accountability refers to an obligation to provide answers and justifications.[22] In the context of government, Mashaw states that this has tended to take three forms:[23]

— *Legal accountability* whereby government officials are responsible to aggrieved individuals (and corporations), via the process of judicial review, to act within the law.[24]
— *Administrative accountability* whereby government officials are responsible to their superiors and external administrative institutions, such as ombudsmen and anti-corruption agencies, for acting in accordance with 'good government' principles and standards,[25] and not just strict legality.
— *Political accountability* whereby, in a Westminster system, government officials and Ministers are answerable to the Parliament, and ultimately the electorate, for their policies, expenditure and actions.

[20] Whose precise meaning remains 'nebulous, contested, and vague': Flinders, above n 3, 661.

[21] JL Mashaw, 'Accountability and Institutional Design: Some Thoughts on the Grammar of Governance' in MW Dowdle (ed), *Public Accountability: Designs, Dilemmas and Experiences* (Cambridge, Cambridge University Press, 2006) 117–18.

[22] Bovens, Schillemans and Goodin, above n 2, 3; Mashaw, above n 21, 117.

[23] Mashaw, above n 21, 120.

[24] 'In this context, "accountability" can be taken to refer to the need for the executive government and administrative bodies to comply with the law and, in particular, to observe relevant limitations on the exercise of their powers': *Corporation of the City of Enfield v Development Assessment Commission* (2000) 199 CLR 135, 157 (Gaudron J) (Enfield Corporation).

[25] See the APS Values and APS Code of Conduct: Public Service Act 1999 (Cth) ss 10, 13.

Even this taxonomy, however, is contested. For instance, Creyke, McMillan and Smyth bundle judicial review and most administrative accountability mechanisms under a single 'administrative law accountability' label, but have separate categories for 'financial accountability' mechanisms such as Auditors-General[26] and ethics and integrity bodies.[27] It is also not clear where merits review would fit within Mashaw's taxonomy in the Australian context. In some ways it is more like a form of legal accountability, because it relies on individuals bringing claims, but in others it is more similar to administrative accountability, as tribunals are usually empowered to examine issues and issue remedies beyond 'strict legality' and more similar to those Mashaw describes as characteristics of an administrative accountability regime.

Acknowledging the lack of consensus about the content and taxonomy of government accountability, we propose to take a broad view of the definition for the purposes of this chapter. We do so largely because it allows consideration of some of the interesting issues that are developing in Australian law. We take the view that 'government accountability' encapsulates the basic idea that the executive branch and its delegates must be answerable, and as a general principle justify their actions, to the public, the Parliament, the courts or any administrative agency (ombudsmen, tribunals, anti-corruption agencies etc). We propose to examine both process and substance questions: is answerability/justification as a process a 'constitutional value'; and is there any content attached to that 'value'?

III. CONSTITUTIONAL GUARANTEES OF ACCOUNTABILITY

There is certainly some textual and structural support for accountability processes within the Constitution, both legal accountability to the courts and political accountability to the Parliament. This comes explicitly from the subsections of section 75 and from the doctrines of the separation of powers and responsible government which are implicit in the structure of the Constitution. The most practical and useful methods through which the executive is held to account by the Australian public—tribunals, ombudsmen and other independent executive oversight bodies—are, however, not constitutionally entrenched, and rely almost entirely on political will. This section examines express constitutional support for accountability via legal, political and administrative mechanisms, and the limits of each.

A. Legal Accountability: Judicial Review of Administrative Action

i. Judicial Review under the Constitution

The jurisdiction of the High Court to review certain government action is entrenched in sections 75(iii) and 75(v) of the Constitution. The text of these provisions itself does nothing more than confer original jurisdiction on the Court to hear certain matters: those in which the Commonwealth, or a person suing, or being sued on

[26] Creyke, McMillan and Smyth, above n 4, 22–24.
[27] ibid 28.

its behalf, is a party; and those in which particular remedies are sought against an 'officer of the Commonwealth', respectively. This conferral of jurisdiction gives no right of action and says nothing about the protection of any substantive content of judicial review. For instance, section 75(iii) does not, on its face, prohibit Parliament from legislating to exclude the Commonwealth from liability for any of its actions. It simply states that wherever suit is brought, the High Court has original jurisdiction to hear the case. And section 75(v) says nothing about whether the Court has jurisdiction only in matters in which the listed remedies are in fact available—and whether the Parliament can make them unavailable, either expressly or by conferring unlimited jurisdiction on the executive.

The Court has interpreted section 75(v) as entrenching more than just its jurisdiction to hear cases. Its reasons for doing so are, at least in part, based on an understanding that the provision performs an accountability function. Section 75(v) has been found to entrench a 'minimum provision of judicial review' which prevents the Parliament from ousting judicial review of the jurisdictional limits of administrative powers.[28] Andrew Inglis Clark's intent in including the provision in the original draft of the Constitution[29] was to prevent the High Court from needing to face the jurisdictional difficulties that had become apparent to the Supreme Court of the US in *Marbury v Madison*.[30] However, others at the constitutional conventions who were not as well versed in US constitutional law, understood section 75(v) as serving a broader accountability function.[31] For instance, Edmund Barton believed that section 75(v) had been included 'so that the High Court may exercise its function of protecting the subject against any violation of the *Constitution*, or of any law made under the *Constitution*'.[32] Upon receiving a telegram from Inglis Clark which revealed the true purpose behind his inclusion of the draft clause which would become section 75(v), and why its removal should be opposed, Barton was frank about his ignorance of the relevant US constitutional arrangements.[33] However, as Stellios has explained, it is Barton's original accountability explanation which has come to dominate the story of section 75(v) in recent years.[34]

[28] *Plaintiff S157/2002 v Commonwealth* (2003) 211 CLR 476, 513 (Gaudron, McHugh, Gummow, Kirby and Hayne JJ) (*Plaintiff S157/2002*); *Graham v Minister for Immigration and Border Protection* [2017] HCA 33, [48] (Graham).

[29] See *Ah Yick v Lehmert* (1905) 2 CLR 593, 609 (Barton J); *R v Commonwealth Court of Conciliation and Arbitration; Ex parte Brisbane Tramways Co Ltd* (1914) 18 CLR 54, 82 (Gavan Duffy and Rich JJ); *Ruddock v Vadarlis [No 2]* (2001) 115 FCR 229, 242–43 [31] (Black CJ and French J); Aronson, Groves and Weeks, above n 1, [2.120]. A brief history of the discussions relating to the clause that would become s 75(v) in the Convention Debates appears in L Zines, *Cowen and Zines's Federal Jurisdiction in Australia*, 3rd edn (Sydney, Federation Press, 2002) 21–22.

[30] *Marbury v Madison*, 5 US (1 Cranch) 137 (1803). See M Leeming, *Authority to Decide: The Law of Jurisdiction in Australia* (Sydney, Federation Press, 2012) 244.

[31] See J Stellios, 'Exploring the Purposes of Section 75(v) of the *Constitution*' (2011) 34 *UNSW Law Journal* 70.

[32] Official Record of the Debates of the Australasian Federal Convention, Melbourne, 4 March 1898, 1885 (Edmund Barton).

[33] JM Williams, *The Australian Constitution: A Documentary History* (Melbourne, Melbourne University Press, 2005) 846, cited in JT Gleeson and RA Yezerski, 'The Separation of Powers and the Unity of the Common Law' in JT Gleeson et al (eds), *Historical Foundations of Australian Law* (Sydney, Federation Press, 2013) vol 1, 317.

[34] Stellios, above n 31, 71.

The High Court has frequently said that section 75(v) must be read in conjunction with section 75(iii)[35] and indicated that even if section 75(v) had not been included in the Constitution, the Court would nevertheless have had original jurisdiction under section 75(iii) to review the actions of Commonwealth officers and issue the remedies listed in section 75(v).[36] While it is not usual to refer to a request for an order nisi for a writ of mandamus, certiorari or prohibition as a suit, nor to the applicant and decision-maker as 'parties',[37] it is clear that at least some of the framers thought that section 75(v) was unnecessary as the Court would have had such jurisdiction in any case.[38] The Court does not seem to have ever doubted its jurisdiction to issue mandamus under section 75(iii).[39] It has thus been said that the combined effect of the provisions is

> to ensure that there is available, to a relevantly affected citizen, a Ch III court with jurisdiction to grant relief against an invalid purported exercise of Commonwealth legislative power or an unlawful exercise of, or refusal to exercise, Commonwealth executive authority.[40]

Leeming JA has concluded in light of such statements of the law that section 75(v) may be inessential but we are nonetheless fortunate to have it:

> The provision [which became s 75(v)] was probably unnecessary in order to avoid the outcome in *Marbury v Madison*, given that, in contrast with the position in the United States, all litigation to which the Commonwealth was a party was to be in the High Court's original jurisdiction. However, it serves a more useful purpose, namely, of ensuring that jurisdictional error by a federal court may be reviewed by the High Court (this would otherwise be outside the scope of s 75(iii)).[41]

The High Court has also interpreted 'the Commonwealth' more broadly than the equivalent provisions of the United States Constitution have been interpreted as result of the additional references in section 75(iii) to 'a person suing or being sued on behalf of the Commonwealth'. The purpose behind including this additional jurisdiction was held by Dixon J to be 'to cover the enforcement of actionable rights and liabilities of officers and agencies in their official and governmental capacity, when in substance they formed part of or represented the Commonwealth'.[42] This suggests that section 75(iii) also performs an accountability function, alongside

[35] See, eg, *Bank of New South Wales v Commonwealth* (1948) 76 CLR 1, 363 (Dixon J) (*Bank Nationalisation Case*).

[36] *Deputy Commissioner of Taxation v Richard Walter Pty Ltd* (1995) 183 CLR 168, 204 (Deane and Gaudron JJ), 221 (Dawson J), 231–32 (Toohey J); *Re Refugee Review Tribunal; Ex parte Aala* (2000) 204 CLR 82, 92 (Gaudron and Gummow JJ). This point is still something which 'requires fuller attention': W Gummow, 'The Scope of Section 75(v) of the *Constitution*: Why Injunction but No Certiorari?' (2014) 42 *Federal Law Review* 241, 241.

[37] PH Lane, 'The High Court's Jurisdiction to Issue Writs' (1967) 41 *Australian Law Journal* 130, 131.

[38] See J Quick and R Garran, *The Annotated Constitution of the Australian Commonwealth* (Angus & Robertson, 1901) 779.

[39] *R v Registrar of Titles for Victoria; Ex parte Commonwealth* (1915) 20 CLR 379.

[40] *Deputy Commissioner of Taxation v Richard Walter Pty Ltd* (1995) 183 CLR 168, 204–05 (Deane and Gaudron JJ), cited with approval in *Re Refugee Tribunal; Ex parte Aala* (2000) 204 CLR 82, 92 [20] (Gaudron and Gummow JJ).

[41] Leeming, above n 30, 247 (emphasis added, citations omitted).

[42] *Bank Nationalisation Case* (1948) 76 CLR 1, 366–67 (Dixon J).

section 75(v). However, any support that section 75(iii) gives to the suggestion that government accountability is a constitutional 'value' is heavily qualified by the limits on that section's own ability to perform an accountability function. The Court does not seem to have been willing to find that section 75(iii) protects any substantive right of action against the Commonwealth. There are judgments going both ways,[43] but it seems that the prevailing view is now that section 75(iii) confers jurisdiction only, leaving the Commonwealth free to alter its liability via legislation.[44] In other words, it is up to the Parliament to decide those actions for which the Commonwealth will be liable.

ii. The Separation of Powers

The separation of powers, and conferral of judicial power exclusively on the judicial branch,[45] have been given as an additional constitutional basis for the entrenchment of judicial review of administrative action.[46] It is to some extent unclear precisely what would be constitutionally entrenched under a separation of powers rationale for judicial review of administrative action. On the other hand, it has been clear for some time that the separation of powers is central to any understanding of judicial review in Australia. Brennan J's canonical judgment in *Attorney-General (NSW) v Quin*[47] (*Quin*) places the separation of powers above even the terms of the Constitution itself[48] in explaining the limits of judicial review:

> The duty and the jurisdiction of the courts are expressed in the memorable words of Marshall CJ in *Marbury v Madison*: 'It is, emphatically, the province and duty of the judicial department to say what the law is'.[49]
>
> The duty and jurisdiction of the court to review administrative action do not go beyond the declaration and enforcing of the law which determines the limits and governs the exercise of the repository's power. If, in so doing, the court avoids administrative injustice or error, so be it; but the court has no jurisdiction simply to cure administrative injustice or error. The merits of administrative action, to the extent that they can be distinguished from legality, are for the repository of the relevant power and, subject to political control, for the repository alone.

[43] See, eg, *Commonwealth v New South Wales* (1923) 32 CLR 200; *Bank Nationalisation Case* (1948) 76 CLR 1, 363 (Dixon J).

[44] *Commonwealth v Mewett* (1997) 191 CLR 471. The majority comprised Brennan CJ, Gaudron, Gummow and Kirby JJ while Dawson, Toohey and McHugh JJ dissented. The majority held that s 75(iii) removed the procedural bar (misleadingly described as 'sovereign immunity') to the Commonwealth's common law liability in tort. See G Weeks, *Soft Law and Public Authorities: Remedies and Reform* (Oxford, Hart Publishing, 2016) 185.

[45] *R v Kirby; Ex parte Boilermakers' Society of Australia* (1956) 94 CLR 254.

[46] *Plaintiff S157/2002* (2003) 211 CLR 476, 484 (Gleeson CJ), 511–12 (Gaudron, McHugh, Gummow, Kirby and Hayne JJ). Daly saw this doctrine more generally as creating checks and balances between different branches of government on the basis that 'foxes should not guard henhouses': P Daly, 'Administrative Law: A Values-based Approach' in J Bell et al (eds), *Public Law Adjudication in Common Law Systems: Process and Substance* (Oxford, Hart Publishing, 2016) 30 (citations omitted).

[47] *Attorney-General (NSW) v Quin* (1990) 170 CLR 1.

[48] See M Groves, 'Federal Constitutional Influences on State Judicial Review' (2011) 39 *Federal Law Review* 399, 402.

[49] 5 US (1 Cranch) 137 (1803), 177.

> The consequence is that the scope of judicial review must be defined not in terms of the protection of individual interests but in terms of the extent of power and the legality of its exercise. In Australia, the modem development and expansion of the law of judicial review of administrative action have been achieved by an increasingly sophisticated exposition of implied limitations on the extent or the exercise of statutory power, but those limitations are not calculated to secure judicial scrutiny of the merits of a particular case.[50]

The separation of powers, on this reading, forms the basis upon which judicial review is prevented from exceeding its limitations and imposing itself on the domain of legislative and administrative decision-making.[51] The separation of powers therefore *informs* the standards of accountability to which judicial review is subject; the doctrine is not itself a method of imposing accountability. This point extends further if it is accepted that accountability itself is a term which lacks detail but is rich in rhetorical appeal, less an organising principle than a 'catch-cry to denote values of transparency, democracy and justice'.[52] Accountability represents values, on this view, but is not a value in its own right.

iii. Limits of Judicial Review as an Accountability Mechanism

Although the text and structure of the Constitution entrench a 'minimum provision of judicial review',[53] which in practice ensures that Commonwealth decision-makers are held to account for some of their actions by the courts, this is far from a complete form of government accountability. Ultimately the jurisdiction of government decision-makers is a matter for the Parliament. And Parliament can, if it chooses, confer extremely broad powers on the executive (though probably not unlimited powers, due to the fact that Parliament's own powers are limited by the Constitution).[54] Ultimately, the Court's role is simply to enforce the jurisdictional limits that Parliament has chosen, in addition to any constitutional limits.

Further, there are other limits on the ability of courts to hold the executive to account via judicial review. These include the concept of justiciability, standing rules, and the limited remedies available, which generally mean that an official whose decision has been quashed is free to re-make the decision and reach the same substantive outcome, provided he or she does so according to law.

[50] *Quin* (1990) 170 CLR 1, 35–36.

[51] Brennan J cited review for *Wednesbury* unreasonableness as coming closest to crossing over into merits review, which belongs to the executive branch, but insisted that it is an 'extremely confined' ground of review and that 'properly applied' it does not interfere with the merits of a matter at 36. There remains some doubt as to whether this interpretation has survived the High Court's decision in *Minister for Immigration and Citizenship v Li* (2013) 249 CLR 332, in which Hayne, Kiefel and Bell JJ denied that unreasonableness was 'limited to what is in effect an irrational, if not bizarre, decision': at 364. By contrast, Gageler J held that the 'stringency' of the *Wednesbury* test remains and that the ground will continue to be made out rarely: at 377–78.

[52] Rock, above n 10.

[53] *Plaintiff S157/2002* (2003) 211 CLR 476, 513 (Gaudron, McHugh, Gummow, Kirby and Hayne JJ).

[54] See, eg, the broad power conferred on the Minister for Immigration by the Migration Act 1958 (Cth) s 198AB and the discussion of the breadth of that discretion in *Plaintiff S156/2013 v Minister for Immigration and Border Protection* (2014) 254 CLR 28. On the scope of Parliament's power to confer 'plenary' power on the executive, see L Burton Crawford, 'Can Parliament Confer Plenary Executive Power? The Limitations Imposed by ss 51 and 52 of the *Australian Constitution*' (2016) 44 *Federal Law Review* 287.

The High Court highlighted these limits on its role:

> [J]udicial review of administrative action stands on a different footing from constitutional adjudication, both historically and functionally. In part no doubt because alternative methods of control, both political and administrative in nature, are available to confine agencies within bounds, there has never been a pervasive notion that limited government mandated an all-encompassing judicial duty to supply all of the relevant meaning of statutes. Rather, the judicial duty is to ensure that the administrative agency stays within the zone of discretion committed to it by its organic act.[55]

B. Political Accountability: Responsible Government

i. Responsible Government in the Australian Constitutional Context

Sections 49 and 64 of the Constitution together entrench the principle of responsible government in Australia, forming a framework through which the executive is accountable to the Parliament. The third paragraph of section 64 provides that 'no Minister of State shall hold office for a longer period than three months unless he is or becomes a senator or member of the House of Representatives'. The provision was intended by the framers, and has consistently been interpreted by the High Court, to import the Westminster system of responsible government.[56] Section 49 gives each House of Parliament the same powers, privileges and immunities as were possessed by the UK House of Commons in 1901. These include inquisitorial powers, which involve the ability to: summon persons, including Commonwealth Ministers[57] and government officials; order the production of government documents; and punish contempt.[58] Together sections 49 and 64 underpin the main mechanisms through which the Commonwealth Parliament holds ministers responsible for their own actions and those of officials within their portfolio, including question time, appearances before a Senate Estimates Committee, and other committee inquiries.

The principle of responsible government, derived from sections 49 and 64, has also been applied more generally to determine the content and scope of other constitutional provisions, including the scope of executive power under section 61. Section 61 simply vests 'the executive power of the Commonwealth' in the Queen, exercisable by the Governor-General, and provides that this power 'extends to the execution and maintenance of this Constitution, and of the laws of the Commonwealth'. The High Court held in *Williams [No 1]*[59] and *Williams [No 2]*[60]

[55] *Enfield Corporation* (2000) 199 CLR 135, 153 (Gleeson CJ, Gummow, Kirby and Hayne JJ), quoting HP Monaghan, '*Marbury* and the Administrative State' (1983) 83 *Columbia Law Review* 1, 32–33.

[56] Quick and Garran, above n 38, 708–11; *New South Wales v Commonwealth* (1915) 20 CLR 54, 89 (Isaacs J) (*Wheat Case*); *Amalgamated Society of Engineers v Adelaide Steamship Co Ltd* (1920) 28 CLR 129, 146–48 (Knox CJ, Isaacs, Rich and Starke JJ); *New South Wales v Commonwealth* (1975) 135 CLR 337, 364–65 (Barwick CJ) (*Seas and Submerged Lands Case*).

[57] But excluding Ministers from the other House: H Evans and R Laing, *Odgers' Australian Senate Practice*, 13th edn (Canberra, Department of the Senate, 2012) 76.

[58] ibid 75–79.

[59] *Williams [No 1]* (2012) 248 CLR 156.

[60] *Williams [No 2]* (2014) 252 CLR 416.

that expenditure by the Commonwealth executive must be authorised by legislation and must fall within the Commonwealth's legislative power. The effect is that the Commonwealth Parliament retains ultimate control over most Commonwealth government expenditure. One of the central rationales for the Court finding that section 61 was restricted in this way was the principle of responsible government.[61] For instance, Crennan J explained:

> The Commonwealth defendants' wider submission, based on the common law freedom to contract enjoyed by the Commonwealth, must be assessed in the light of: the text and structure of the Constitution as it bears on the Executive's powers to protect or benefit the body politic or nation of Australia; the distribution of executive powers between the Commonwealth and the States as polities; financial relations between the Commonwealth and States; and relations between the Commonwealth Parliament and the Commonwealth Executive affecting spending, which include the Executive's obligations of accountability to Parliament.[62]

It seems to be becoming fairly common for members of the Court to refer to section 64 in particular, and responsible government generally, as performing an accountability function. For instance, in *Williams [No 1]*, in addition to the above passage, Crennan J spoke at length about the notion of the executive being accountable to the legislature via section 64, and other, unwritten, constitutional sources.[63]

ii. Limits of Responsible Government as an Accountability Mechanism

Although the Australian Constitution clearly establishes a system of ministerial responsibility to Parliament, there are practical and possibly legal limits on the ability of Parliament to hold governments to account.

One likely constitutional limit is that the Parliament's enquiry power is limited to matters within its legislative competence.[64] The enquiry powers of the US Congress have been held to be limited in the same way.[65] While the Commonwealth executive's spending power is similarly limited to matters within the legislative competence of the Commonwealth Parliament,[66] there may nevertheless be other ways in which the executive might act outside these matters, which might result in gaps in its accountability to the Parliament.

A more significant limit on responsible government concerns the ability of ministers to withhold information and documents from Parliament on the basis of public

[61] See *Williams [No 1]* (2012) 248 CLR 156, 232–33 [136] (Gummow and Bell JJ), 350–51 [512]–[516] (Crennan J), 370 [581] (Kiefel J). See also *Pape v Commissioner of Taxation* (2009) 238 CLR 1, 36–45 (French CJ), which preceded the *Williams* cases. Note that other constitutional principles, including federalism, were also relied on in the Court's reasoning in these cases.

[62] *Williams [No 1]* (2012) 248 CLR 156, 346 [495].

[63] ibid (2012) 248 CLR 156, 350–51 [512]–[516]. See also *Egan v Willis* (1998) 195 CLR 424, 451 [42] (Gaudron, Gummow and Hayne JJ).

[64] See obiter dicta in *Attorney-General (Cth) v Colonial Sugar Refinery Co Ltd* (1913) 17 CLR 644, 656; *Lockwood v Commonwealth* (1954) 90 CLR 177, 182–83.

[65] *Quinn v United States*, 349 US 155 (1955).

[66] *Williams [No 1]* (2012) 248 CLR 156.

interest immunity. Ministers frequently refuse to comply with Senate orders to produce documents on the ground that doing so would not be in the public interest. While most claims of public interest immunity are accepted by the Senate, in some instances the Senate disputes a claim,[67] which leads to an as yet unanswered question: who decides whether it is in the public interest for the executive to refuse to release a document to the Senate? The Senate asserts that it does, though successive governments have rejected that claim and refused to present information to the Senate despite its demands.[68] Allowing ministers to be the sole judges of whether or not release of a document is in the public interest has obvious implications for the ability of Parliament to hold them to account. On the other hand, 'the point of maintaining privilege may be destroyed if the documents are revealed to the Senate for it to decide upon the claim of privilege'.[69]

The Senate has not yet tested the issue. In practice, what occurs in situations where the Senate and government disagree on whether a document attracts immunity or privilege is that the Senate may resolve to impose political penalties which frustrate the government in the Senate, such as refusing or delaying the passage of legislation, and extending question time. The Senate has never attempted to impose a more severe penalty that might force the question of its constitutional powers to compel the production of documents over which privilege is claimed into the courts, such as imprisoning or fining a minister, or ejecting them from the Senate.[70] This solution is broadly similar to that reached by courts where legislation places a certain decision in the hands of a minister, to be made 'in the national interest'. Some matters are outside the competence of bodies exercising legal standards and are better left in the political realm.[71]

The issue of how to deal with a minister who refuses to release documents to the Parliament has been tested and resolved in NSW. In 1996, the NSW Legislative Council passed an order suspending the Treasurer and Leader of the Government in the Legislative Council, the Honourable Michael Egan, as a result of his refusal to produce documents. Mr Egan was forcibly removed from the chamber, and sued the President of the Legislative Council and the Usher of the Black Rod for trespass. One of his arguments was that the NSW Legislative Council did not have the power to compel the production of documents. The NSW Court of Appeal dismissed his case, as did the High Court on appeal, holding that the NSW Legislative Council has the powers 'reasonably necessary' to fulfil its functions, one of which is to scrutinise the executive.[72] This includes powers to order the government to produce documents

[67] See, eg, a recent report resulting from such a refusal by the Assistant Minister for Immigration and Border Protection: Senate Legal and Constitutional Affairs References Committee, Parliament of Australia, *A Claim of Public Interest Immunity Raised Over Documents* (2014).

[68] See H Evans, 'The Senate's Power to Obtain Evidence' (Papers on Parliament No 50, 2010) 5.

[69] A Twomey, 'Executive Accountability to the Senate and the NSW Legislative Council' (2008) 23 *Australian Parliamentary Review* 257, 259.

[70] Evans and Laing, above n 57, 624–25.

[71] Note, however, that terms like the 'national interest' can sometimes be given more substantive content by a court determining the extent of its jurisdiction: see, eg, *NEAT Domestic Trading Pty Ltd v AWB Ltd* (2003) 216 CLR 277, 290 (Gleeson CJ).

[72] *Egan v Willis* (1998) 195 CLR 424, 453 (Gummow, Gaudron and Hayne JJ).

and to suspend a member for non-compliance with such an order.[73] The following year the NSW Court of Appeal held that a claim by the executive that a document is privileged or immune from release on public interest grounds does not affect the Legislative Council's powers. The only exception is Cabinet documents.[74]

However, it is not clear that the same argument could be made in respect of the Commonwealth Senate's powers, as the powers of the two legislatures rest on different foundations.[75] While the matter has been the subject of debate, the better view at law is that the Senate has powers to order documents and punish a failure to comply with such an order. Regardless of practice at various points in time, the Senate has never accepted that it does not have the *power* to compel the production of privileged documents.[76] Yet, even if it is within the constitutional competence of the Senate to compel the executive to produce documents and other evidence, this does nothing to resolve the practical problems inherent in such attempts, particularly if the Senate refuses to issue anything more than political penalties for contempt.

Similar issues have arisen in relation to the power of the Senate to compel ministerial advisers to appear and give evidence before them.[77] In recent decades, there have been suggestions from governments on both sides that there is a 'convention' that ministerial advisers not appear before Senate committees. Most notably, this claim was made in response to the Senate Select Committee for the *Inquiry into A Certain Maritime Incident*, formed to investigate the 2001 'Children Overboard' incident. Ministerial advisers had played a central role in the incident, and the Committee asked them to appear to give evidence in its inquiry. However, the government refused to allow advisers to appear, claiming they were immune. The Committee sought legal advice which concluded that no such immunity exists.[78] Former Clerk of the Senate, Harry Evans, has also argued that there is no basis in law for such an immunity, and there has never been any such question in the UK.[79] The Senate Committee, however, ultimately decided not to compel the advisers' attendance on the basis that it would 'it would be unjust for the Senate to impose a penalty on a person who declines to provide evidence on the direction of a minister'.[80] This highlights

[73] ibid 453–56 (Gummow, Gaudron and Hayne JJ).

[74] *Egan v Chadwick* (1999) 46 NSWLR 563, 574 (Spigelman CJ), 593–95 (Priestley JA), 596–97 (Meagher JA). This is consistent with exceptions to freedom of information legislation: see, eg, *Freedom of Information Act 1982* (Cth) s 34; *Government Information (Public Access) Act 2009* (NSW) s 106, sch 1 cl 2.

[75] H Evans, 'The Parliamentary Power of Inquiry: Any Limitations?' (2001) 17 *Australasian Parliamentary Review* 131, 133. The powers of the NSW Legislative Council have never been codified, so that the Courts' reasoning in the *Egan* cases was based on common law principles of what is 'reasonably necessary' for the proper functioning of the Houses of the NSW Parliament, as those principles have evolved over time. By contrast, the powers of the Senate under s 49 of the Constitution are set in time—as those held by the House of Commons at Federation—until otherwise defined by the Parliament.

[76] G Lindell, 'Parliamentary Inquiries and Government Witnesses' (1995) 20 *Melbourne University Law Review* 383, 398; E Campbell, 'Parliamentary Inquiries and Executive Privilege' (1986) 1 *Legislative Studies* 10. In the US, the power to compel testimony has been held to be an inherent power of the legislature: *McGrain v Daugherty*, 273 US 135 (1927).

[77] On the accountability problems posed by ministerial advisers generally, see Y Ng, *Ministerial Advisors in Australia: The Modern Legal Context* (Sydney, Federation Press, 2016).

[78] Commonwealth Senate Select Committee, Parliament of Australia, *A Certain Maritime Incident* (2002) xxxiv.

[79] Evans, 'The Senate's Power to Obtain Evidence', above n 68, 6.

[80] Commonwealth Senate Select Committee, above n 78, xxxiv–xxxv.

that even if there are no legal limits on the Parliament's powers to hold the government to account, there are significant practical limits which, for several reasons, the Senate does not appear to be prepared to push.

C. Administrative Accountability

There is, quite simply, no constitutional support for, or guarantee of, many of the most important practical methods through which the Australian public holds government to account.[81] These administrative accountability mechanisms include: merits review tribunals, such as the Administrative Appeals Tribunal (AAT); oversight and investigatory bodies such as the Commonwealth Ombudsman, Office of the Australian Information Commissioner (OAIC), and anti-corruption agencies; freedom of information laws; and law reform advisory bodies, including the Australian Law Reform Commission (ALRC) and former Administrative Review Council (ARC). From a practical perspective, these are the methods that provide the cheapest, fastest forms of accountability over the executive and carry most of the accountability burden in Australia. For instance in the 2014–15 financial year major merits review tribunals (the AAT, Migration Review Tribunal, Refugee Review Tribunal and Social Security Appeals Tribunal—all of which now form part of the AAT) finalised over 40,000 applications for review. The Commonwealth Ombudsman finalised almost 20,000 complaints against Commonwealth agencies the same year. Just over 5,000 judicial review applications were resolved in federal courts in that year, the vast majority (around 90 per cent) of them in the migration jurisdictions.[82]

However, each of these methods designed to ensure good administration via accountability tools was created by, and so can be abolished by, statute. Recent experience has shown that, even where these bodies cannot, for political reasons, be abolished by statute, they are also vulnerable to the whims of the government of the day—the very government they were designed to hold to account. Over the past few years, the Commonwealth Government has abolished (either de jure or de facto) a number of accountability agencies. The first step is usually to reduce or eliminate their funding. Bodies dealt with in this way include the ARC and OAIC. The ALRC funding has also been reduced substantially.

The OAIC is a particularly salutary example. The government first attempted to abolish this body, which had only been created as a statutory authority in 2010, via legislation. However, the Senate refused to pass the legislation, and the government simply withdrew the bulk of the office's funding.[83] Some has since been restored,

[81] Spigelman CJ seemed to infer that constitutional gaps were responsible for the fact that the rise of accountability (which he termed 'administrative responsibility') owed more to administrative statutes than to the Constitution: above n 9, 7.

[82] Administrative Appeals Tribunal, *Annual Report 2014–15* (2015); Commonwealth Ombudsman, *Annual Report 2014–15* (2015); Federal Circuit Court of Australia, *Annual Report 2014–15* (2015); Federal Court of Australia, *Annual Report 2014–15* (2015); High Court of Australia, *Annual Report 2014–15* (2015).

[83] G Weeks, 'Comment from Australia: A Disappointing Backward Step in Information Policy' (*UK Constitutional Law Blog*, 6 September 2014): ukconstitutionallaw.org/2014/09/06/greg-weeks-comment-on-australia-a-disappointing-backward-step-in-information-policy/.

but not before the office lost almost all its staff, including its head, Professor John McMillan.[84] The following year, the ARC's budget was abolished, yet it too remains on the statute books.[85]

Bodies like the OAIC and ARC, along with tribunals and other accountability agencies, do much of the heavy lifting in holding government to account. The oversight provided by the courts and Parliament is limited due to resourcing constraints and due to the constitutional balance struck between the powers of those branches and the executive. Yet the government is able to control the extent to which executive accountability agencies are able to hold it to account through its control of the purse strings. To a large extent, government accountability in Australia is therefore dependent on government's own willingness to be held to account. As the OAIC incident demonstrated, even political accountability counts for little when legislation is required to repeal the existence of a statutory body, but not to neutralise it.

IV. HIGH COURT RECOGNITION OF ACCOUNTABILITY AS A 'VALUE'

As discussed above, members of the High Court have referred to section 64, and the principle of responsible government more generally, as performing an accountability function on several occasions. It is less common for the Court to refer expressly to 'accountability' in the context of section 75(v) alone, though Kirby J did so on several occasions.[86] So too, did Edelman J in his dissenting judgment in *Graham*, however, only to highlight the limited nature of the accountability role played by section 75(v).[87] However, the view the majority of the High Court has taken of the purpose of the provision clearly reflects such a function, even in the absence of the word 'accountability' being used frequently as it is with section 64.[88]

Furthermore, there are several examples of judgments suggesting that the two provisions act together to secure accountability of the Commonwealth executive. For instance, in *Re Patterson; Ex parte Taylor*, Gaudron J said:

> The concluding sentence of s 64 of the Constitution provides the machinery by which a Minister is accountable to Parliament, a core aspect of the notion of responsible government. Of equal significance to the concept of responsible government is the conferral, by s 75(v) of the Constitution, of original jurisdiction on this Court in all matters 'in which a writ of Mandamus or prohibition or an injunction is sought against an officer of

[84] However, not before the funding for a Canberra office was lost, which led to a substantial period of time during which Professor McMillan was conducting his statutory functions from his own house and using his own phone and internet connections. It is impossible to say whether the government officials responsible for this state of affairs were embarrassed. They should have been.

[85] J Boughey and G Weeks, 'Comment from Australia: Australian Government Scraps Peak Administrative Law Advisory Body' (*UK Constitutional Law Blog*, 25 May 2015): ukconstitutionallaw.org/2015/05/20/janina-boughey-and-greg-weeks-comment-from-australia-australian-government-scraps-peak-administrative-law-advisory-body/.

[86] See, eg, *NEAT Domestic Trading v AWB Ltd* (2003) 216 CLR 277, 300 [67], 311 [105]; *Minister for Immigration and Multicultural Affairs v Jia* (2001) 205 CLR 507, 545 [124] (Jia).

[87] [2017] HCA 33, [104]–[105].

[88] See, especially, the majority's judgment in *Graham* [2017] HCA 33.

> the Commonwealth'. That provision provides the mechanism by which the Executive is subjected to the rule of law. To the extent that there is ambiguity in the terms of s 64 of the Constitution, the notion of responsible government, as embodied in the concluding sentence of s 64 and in s 75(v) of the Constitution, may shed light on its proper construction.[89]

Similar comments were made by Gleeson CJ and Gummow J in *Minister for Immigration and Multicultural Affairs v Jia* (*Jia*).[90] That case raised the question of whether public comments by the Minister, criticising a tribunal's leniency in criminal deportation cases, amounted to bias in a subsequent criminal deportation decision. In holding that the comments did not constitute actual or apprehended bias, Gleeson CJ and Gummow J said:

> [P]owers conferred upon the minister by ss 501 and 502 [of the Migration Act 1968 (Cth)] form part of a statutory scheme which involves a complex pattern of administrative and judicial power, and differing forms of accountability. The minister is a member of parliament, with political accountability to the electorate, and a member of the executive government, with responsibility to parliament. As French J recognised in his decision at first instance in the case of Mr Jia, the minister functions in the arena of public debate, political controversy, and democratic accountability. At the same time, the minister's exercise of statutory powers is subject to the rule of law, and the form of accountability which that entails. In relation to an applicant for, or holder of, a visa the minister, either personally or through a delegate, may be an initial decision-maker, a party to proceedings for administrative or judicial review, and the holder of a power of cancellation and exclusion under ss 501 and 502.[91]

Note that the result of reading responsible government and judicial review as together providing for executive accountability in *Jia* was to reduce the strictness of the applicable judicial review principles. The Court was of the view that alternative, and better-suited accountability mechanisms were available to hold the Minister to account for his political statements, making a lesser standard of bias appropriate in judicial review of his actions.

Along similar lines, Gleeson CJ emphasised in *Re Minister for Immigration and Multicultural Affairs; Ex parte Fejzullahu* that responsible government and judicial review perform distinct accountability functions, and operate together, so that each is not required to go beyond its limits:

> Under s 75(v) of the Constitution, the court is empowered, in the exercise of its responsibility to maintain the rule of law, to make orders of specified kinds aimed at ensuring observance of the law by officers of the Commonwealth. It is not invested with an appellate jurisdiction, enabling the court to set aside decisions, lawfully and regularly made, upon the ground that the court disagrees with such decisions. The rule of law is not maintained by subverting the democratic process. The Constitution, which is the instrument of government of a democratic, and therefore political, society, has not substituted general judicial review for political accountability. The question raised by the principal proceedings is whether the minister has acted according to law; not whether his decisions are wise, or humane, or in the public interest.[92]

[89] *Re Patterson; Ex parte Taylor* (2001) 207 CLR 391, 415 (Gaudron J).
[90] *Jia* (2001) 205 CLR 507, 528 [61].
[91] ibid.
[92] *Re Minister for Immigration and Multicultural Affairs; Ex parte Fejzullahu* (2000) 171 ALR 341 [6].

These statements lend support to the argument that government accountability is a constitutional value.[93] It should be noted that the High Court has also occasionally referred to executive accountability as being guaranteed by other constitutional provisions and principles, including representative government.[94]

In addition to these express references to accountability as a principle or value protected by sections 64 and 75, we suggest there are several examples of the High Court having been implicitly guided by the value of government accountability. For instance, it appears to us that accountability also played a role in the decision in *Commissioner of Taxation v Futuris* (*Futuris*).[95] In that case the Court upheld the validity and effectiveness of provisions in the Income Tax Assessment Act 1936 (Cth) which stated that:

> The validity of any assessment shall not be affected by reason that any of the provisions of this Act have not been complied with.[96]

And:

> The production of a notice of assessment, or of a document under the hand of the Commissioner, a Second Commissioner, or a Deputy Commissioner, purporting to be a copy of a notice of assessment, shall be conclusive evidence of the due making of the assessment and, except in proceedings under Part IVC of the Taxation Administration Act 1953 on a review or appeal relating to the assessment, that the amount and all the particulars of the assessment are correct.[97]

The majority of the Court found that the first of these provisions simply expressed the Parliament's intent as to the effect of a breach of a provision, resulting in the breach being a non-jurisdictional error.[98] The second simply gave 'evidentiary effect' to the first, and made proceedings under pt IVC of the Taxation Administration Act 1953 (Cth) the only method of challenging the validity of an assessment based on an alleged breach of the provisions of the Income Tax Assessment Act 1936 (Cth).[99] The Court did make an exception for deliberate breaches.[100]

The practical effect of the majority's judgment was that the Federal Court could not exercise its jurisdiction under section 39B of the Judiciary Act 1903 (Cth), nor the High Court its jurisdiction under section 75(v) of the Constitution to review a tax assessment on the ground that the decision-maker who made the assessment had failed to comply with a provision of the Act under which the decision was made. This result might appear to contradict any assertion that accountability is a constitutional value.

However, we suggest that the fact that the relevant tax legislation provided for a comprehensive appeals mechanism, which included both merits and judicial review,

93 Ng, above n 77, 13.
94 See, eg, *McCloy v New South Wales* (2015) 257 CLR 178, 229–30 [122] (Gageler J).
95 *Commissioner of Taxation v Futuris* (2008) 237 CLR 146.
96 Income Tax Assessment Act 1936 (Cth) s 175.
97 ibid s 177(1).
98 *Futuris* (2008) 237 CLR 146, 157 [24] (Gummow, Hayne, Heydon and Crennan JJ).
99 ibid 167 [67] (Gummow, Hayne, Heydon and Crennan JJ).
100 ibid 165 [55]–[56] (Gummow, Hayne, Heydon and Crennan JJ).

was critical to the High Court's conclusion in the case. We suggest that the majority was likely only prepared to give the impugned provisions their full effect because there was an alternative, and comprehensive, method through which the decision-maker was accountable to the courts for acting outside the scope of his or her statutory authority.[101]

Therefore, the notion that government accountability is a constitutional value—which is underpinned by, but also goes beyond, its specific application in sections 49, 64 and 75 of the Constitution—has some force. The Court has expressly endorsed the idea that the particular legal and political accountability mechanisms which are entrenched in the Constitution operate together to ensure that the executive branch is held to account. This suggests that the value of accountability has some force that is independent of the particular provisions which have been said to entrench it. In other words, sections 49, 64 and 75 give practical effect to the broader norm of government accountability, and that norm, or value, shapes the way the provisions are interpreted, and interact with one another.

The way the Court responded to the 'no-invalidity' clause in *Futuris*, and its approach to the scope of the Commonwealth's power to spend in the *Williams* cases, add further force to the possibility that government accountability is a constitutional value. *Futuris*, we argue, indicates that, although administrative accountability mechanisms are not entrenched in the Constitution, they are seen as supporting the value of accountability and thus operate alongside, and may even be a substitute for, legal accountability. The *Williams* cases demonstrate how the value of accountability, tied specifically to responsible government in that case, has shaped the interpretation of other constitutional provisions and powers. These examples suggest that there is a sound basis for arguing that government accountability is a constitutional value.

V. ACCOUNTABILITY UNDER A FUNCTIONALIST APPROACH

If accountability were explicitly, and more consistently, recognised as a 'constitutional value' by the High Court, what effect might this have on the resolution of 'hard' cases, in which the text and structure of the Constitution itself yields no clear answer? There are several areas of law in which the value of accountability might assist the Court in resolving lingering uncertainties. One is the power of Parliament to compel the executive to provide documents over which immunity is claimed. As discussed above, the text of the Constitution and historical material yield no definitive answer. If asked to answer this question and, if emphasis were placed on accountability as a constitutional value, the Court would likely answer the question in favour of parliamentary power. We have identified two further examples, both of which deal with aspects of judicial review of administrative action, in which a constitutional value of accountability may resolve existing uncertainties.

[101] See ibid 153 [10], 156 [21]–[22], 167 [64]–[67] (Gummow, Hayne, Heydon and Crennan JJ).

A. Review of Outsourced Decision-Making

The first is in defining the phrase 'officer of the Commonwealth' in section 75(v): and specifically whether a private company exercising public functions (most commonly under contract or as a result of privatisation) is capable of falling within the definition. We have discussed the significant problems that privatisation and outsourcing present for judicial review generally, and for review under section 75(v) specifically, elsewhere.[102] For the purposes of this chapter it is sufficient to note that the extent to which the High Court has jurisdiction to review outsourced decisions under section 75(v) depends on the unresolved question of whether the people making those decisions are 'officers of the Commonwealth'. To date the Court has avoided answering this question.[103]

There is a similar lack of High Court authority, and legal certainty, surrounding the question of whether the actions of statutory corporations can be reviewed under section 75(v). The weight of Federal Court authority suggests that they cannot.[104] There is more certainty with respect to statutory corporations under section 75(iii). The High Court has set out several factors which it will consider in determining whether a statutory corporation is an agency or instrumentality of 'the Commonwealth' for the purposes of section 75(iii). These include:

— The degree of control able to be exerted over the body by the Commonwealth executive.
— Whether the Commonwealth executive has the power the appoint directors to the board.
— The presence or absence of shareholders or corporators.
— Whether the income of the corporation is paid into the consolidated revenue and the consolidated revenue is appropriated to meet expenses and liabilities of the body.
— Whether the body is subject to scrutiny by the Auditor-General.
— Whether the body's functions and objectives have a public character, such as, for example, administration of a statute or a role as a regulator.[105]

These factors make it unlikely that the actions of a private company exercising administrative discretion under a contract with the Commonwealth could be challenged using judicial review under section 75(iii).

If the same approach were taken to defining 'officer of the Commonwealth' under section 75(v), as it is to defining 'the Commonwealth' under section 75(iii), the result would be that government could avoid also the scrutiny of judicial review by outsourcing decision-making in contentious areas, such as the processing of offshore

[102] J Boughey and G Weeks, 'Officers of the Commonwealth in the Private Sector: Can the High Court Review Outsourced Exercises of Power?' (2013) 36 *UNSW Law Journal* 316.

[103] See, eg, *Plaintiff M61/2010E v Commonwealth* (2010) 243 CLR 319, 345 (*Offshore Processing Case*).

[104] See Aronson, Groves and Weeks, above n 1, [2.160].

[105] For a discussion of the cases on this issue, see D Barnett, 'The Commonwealth: A Multitude of Manifestations—Federal Jurisdiction under s 75(iii) of the Constitution' (2007) 81 *Australian Law Journal* 195, 201–02.

asylum claims,[106] and determining whether a social security recipient has met their activity requirements.[107]

Aronson, Groves and Weeks have criticised this position, arguing that:

> The main point of s 75(v) should be to ensure judicial supervision of the execution of Commonwealth statutes and the exercise by the Commonwealth Executive of its common law and executive powers. Whether the Commonwealth chooses to perform its tasks via central departments, statutory authorities, its own companies or private sector firms is surely irrelevant to that point. This is particularly important in view of the drive to reduce the size of the traditional forms of government to the core functions, whilst outsourcing service delivery functions.[108]

If the High Court were to give greater weight to the 'value' of government accountability, it may take a broader approach to interpreting the phrases 'the Commonwealth', 'on behalf of the Commonwealth' and 'officer of the Commonwealth' in sections 75(iii) and 75(v), as Aronson, Groves and Weeks suggest they should. For instance, the level of departmental or ministerial control over contracted-out decision-making (via guidelines and directives) may be weighed as a more central factor in analysing whether a person is acting on behalf of, or is an officer of, the Commonwealth. Less weight would thereby be given to the identity of the decision-maker's direct employer.

B. Jurisdictional Error

A second area in which reliance on the value of accountability might resolve current uncertainties in the scope of the entrenched minimum of judicial review under the Constitution is in relation to the concept of jurisdictional error. A jurisdictional error is broadly understood to be an error that Parliament intended would take a decision-maker outside the scope of their authority and invalidate an order or decision of the decision-maker. Whether an error is jurisdictional is determined by the statutory context and by the nature of the decision and error within that context.[109] This means that Parliament can expressly state its intention as to whether an error results in a decision being invalid, as it did in the legislation at issue in *Futuris*.

Presently, it remains unclear whether Parliament is capable of effectively ousting judicial review in respect of a statutory power, by stating its intention that *all* errors of law made in the exercise of that power are within jurisdiction. The Court has suggested that it might not be possible; that, for instance, it may be outside Parliament's authority to protect a decision made in bad faith.[110] The Court has also

[106] See M Groves, 'Outsourcing and s 75(v) of the Constitution' (2011) 2 *Public Law Review* 3, 5–6.

[107] See discussion in R Harris, 'Avoiding the Worst of All Worlds: Government Accountability for Outsourced Employment Services' (2007) 54 *AIAL Forum* 3.

[108] Aronson, Groves and Weeks, above n 1, [2.160].

[109] *Kirk v Industrial Court (NSW)* (2010) 239 CLR 531, 567–68, 577 (French CJ, Gummow, Hayne, Crennan, Kiefel and Bell JJ); M Aronson, 'Jurisdictional Error and Beyond' in M Groves (ed), *Modern Administrative Law in Australia: Concepts and Context* (Melbourne, Cambridge University Press, 2014) 267.

[110] *Futuris* (2008) 237 CLR 146, 165 [55]–[58] (Gummow, Hayne, Heydon and Crennan JJ); *Plaintiff S157/2002* (2003) 211 CLR 476, 508 [82] (Gaudron, McHugh, Gummow, Kirby and Hayne JJ); *Bodruddaza v Minister for Immigration and Multicultural and Indigenous Affairs* (2007) 228 CLR 651, 663 [28] (Gleeson CJ, Gummow, Kirby, Hayne, Heydon and Crennan JJ).

recently found that it is not possible for Parliament effectively to prevent the Court from determining whether a jurisdictional error has been made, by providing that certain information must be withheld from the Court.[111] However, the Court has not given any serious consideration to why it may be beyond Parliament's authority to protect certain errors from judicial review, nor to whether there may be other limits on Parliament's capacity to confer jurisdiction on an administrative decision-maker to make legal errors.

If the Court were to give greater weight to a constitutional value of accountability, it is possible that the Court might place more limits on the effectiveness of 'no-invalidity' clauses. For instance, it might not be possible for Parliament to simultaneously place 'core' limits on a decision-maker's jurisdiction and to declare that a breach of those limits is a non-jurisdictional error by the use of a 'no-invalidity' clause. Similar issues arise with respect to the question of whether Parliament is constitutionally capable of conferring extremely broad statutory discretion on a minister or other decision-maker.[112]

C. Constitutional Limits on Accountability

It is important to note that the extent to which any constitutional value of accountability can be applied is limited to circumstances of genuine ambiguity in the Constitution. There are several areas in which the High Court's reasoning suggests that if government accountability is a constitutional value, it is limited by the text and structure of the Constitution. A good example is the High Court's rejection of arguments that the law protects the substance of a person's legitimate expectations. In several other jurisdictions including the UK, South Africa and the EU,[113] courts will hold governments to the promises they have made to individuals and, sometimes, to policy positions, provided certain conditions are met. In essence, this has a similar effect to estopping governments from changing their policies with retrospective effect, and from reneging on promises made to individuals.

For example, in a famous UK decision, the Court of Appeal held that the respondent health authority was prevented from closing a nursing care facility and relocating its residents because of a promise made to the residents, inducing them to move in, that the facility would be their 'home for life'.[114] The High Court of Australia rejected the adoption of a similar principle on the basis that a court ordering an administrative decision-maker to exercise their discretion in a particular way, based on a promise or earlier policy, amounts to the court exercising an executive or legislative function.[115]

[111] *Graham* [2017] HCA 33 (Kiefel CJ, Bell, Gageler, Keane, Nettle and Gordon JJ).

[112] On this issue, see Crawford, above n 53.

[113] See M Groves and G Weeks (eds), *Legitimate Expectations in the Common Law World* (Oxford, Hart Publishing, 2016).

[114] *R v North and East Devon Health Authority; Ex parte Coughlan* [2001] QB 213.

[115] *Re Minister for Immigration and Multicultural and Indigenous Affairs; Ex parte Lam* (2003) 214 CLR 1, 24–25 [76] (McHugh and Gummow JJ).

VI. CONCLUSION

Accountability is generally accepted as belonging in the highest echelon of constitutional or public law values. Its importance is unquestioned. It is perhaps surprising therefore that it is a value with a frequently tenuous hold on the mechanisms of Australian public law. It is implicit in the High Court's constitutional jurisdiction to exercise judicial review and in the implied constitutional separation of powers doctrine. However, these are limited accountability mechanisms, not least because the effectiveness of judicial review in this regard is often overstated.[116] Political accountability has roots in the Constitution but is generally more potent electorally than in any other way. The power of Parliament to hold the executive to account may be stronger in law than in practice as, in practice, both major parties appear unwilling to push the boundaries of the Senate's powers against one another, lest it backfire when they themselves are next in government. Administrative accountability can be immensely effective, but statutory accountability bodies are generally subject to whatever constrains the government of the day from choosing to defund them.

For all these limitations, it is notable that the High Court has commented in several cases on accountability as a value. In other judgments, the value is implicit in the Court's reasoning, or the outcome that was reached. This in turn leads to the possibility that areas currently beyond the scope of judicial review will be subject to accountability reasoning and that accountability will bring uncertainties in other areas closer to resolution. Regardless of its precise place in the public law taxonomy—whether as a value or something else—accountability has grown as an analytical tool and will continue to do so.

[116] J McMillan, 'Re-thinking the Separation of Powers' (2010) 38 *Federal Law Review* 423, 425–26.

7

Impartial Justice

SARAH MURRAY

In the government of men, a great deal may be done by severity, more by love, but most of all by clear discernment and impartial justice which pays no respect to persons.[1]

I. INTRODUCTION

Prompted by Dixon's invitation for greater functionalist engagement in Australian constitutional debate,[2] this chapter engages with impartial justice as a constitutional value. While not an express constitutional guarantee,[3] a constitutional creed of impartial justice has considerable force through the meanderings of Chapter III in the Commonwealth Constitution. More recent judicial exegesis has only strengthened the claim for a constitutional value of impartial justice from within the Chapter III patchwork. This chapter will explore the features of impartial justice in the Australian constitutional landscape, whether it might have wider application than 'judicial impartiality', the sources of the concept and the potential impact of a more fervently functionalist Court wielding such a value. It will also ponder any vulnerabilities inherent within this value's ascendance.

II. IMPARTIAL JUSTICE: ISOLATING ITS CONSTITUTIONAL CONTENT AND SOURCE

Inevitably, values intersect and interweave with others. To speak of 'impartial justice' raises the twin, but conceptually distinct, concept of 'independent justice'.[4]

[1] Johann Wolfgang von Goethe and John Stuart Blackie, *The Wisdom of Goethe* (Folcroft, Folcroft Library Edition, first published 1883, 1974 edn) 97.

[2] R Dixon, 'The Functional Constitution: Re-reading the 2014 High Court Constitutional Term' (2015) 43 *Federal Law Review* 455.

[3] *cf* United States Constitution amendments VI, XIV: ET Kasper, *Impartial Justice: The Real Supreme Court Cases that Define the Constitutional Right to a Neutral and Detached Decisionmaker* (Canham, Lexington Books, 2013).

[4] See *Ebner v Official Trustee in Bankruptcy* (2000) 205 CLR 337 [60] (Gleeson CJ, McHugh, Gummow and Hayne JJ) (*Ebner*); M Groves, 'The Rule Against Bias' (2009) 39 *Hong Kong Law Journal* 485, 488–89; M Groves, 'Waiver of the Rule Against Bias' (2009) 35(2) *Monash University Law Review* 315, 324.

Put simply, impartial justice refers to whether a decision-maker remains open-minded. Judicial independence, on the other hand, is concerned with whether a decision is made without interference or influence. Below, I will explore the degree to which impartial justice might be distinguishable from judicial impartiality and may have a wider berth.

Impartial justice, at a minimum, connotes a judge who is free from bias, whether real or apprehended. A judge who is tainted by their own interests, or is not in a position to listen fairly to both sides, not only compromises the integrity of the case at hand but also public confidence in the courts as an institution. The legitimacy of the courts is therefore closely tied to the degree to which they are seen as impartial and independent bodies. Indeed, it could be said that judicial independence is a precondition for impartial justice. If a judicial officer lacks independence in the first place they cannot be free from real or perceived bias.[5] As Cappelletti explains, 'independence, far from being an end in itself, is but an *instrumental* value, the goal of which is to safeguard another value—connected for sure, but different and much more "ultimate": the impartiality of the judge'.[6]

In *Ebner v Official Trustee in Bankruptcy* (*Ebner*),[7] the Court validated the importance of impartiality within Australia's legal landscape. As well as having a well-documented legal heritage, as far back even as the Magna Carta, the Court referred to its common law roots.[8] In separate judgments, Gaudron J and Kirby J identified Chapter III of the Constitution as a crucial source for the requirement of judicial impartiality. For Kirby J this was achieved by a process of implication.[9] For Gaudron J impartiality was wrapped up in the concept of judicial power conferred by Chapter III[10] with the common law rule against bias mirroring the Chapter III position.[11]

Impartial justice must be understood in the context of the separation of powers. The separation of the judiciary derives from the Constitution's structural and textual separation of the courts from the parliamentary and executive governmental arms. As Stellios has explained, the need for an impartial and independent judiciary was a leading motivation for the framers and for the separation of powers.[12] He explains:

> At the core of all the separation and checks and balances arguments for limiting powers is the idea of an independent and impartial judiciary ... in establishing the broad separation principles, the need to protect the independence and impartiality of the judiciary was the driving force during the Convention Debates, and has proved to be the most stable foundation within High Court jurisprudence.[13]

[5] See C Saunders, 'The Separation of Powers' in B Opeskin and F Wheeler (eds), *The Australian Federal Judicial System* (Carlton South, Melbourne University Press, 2000) 10.

[6] M Cappelletti, *The Judicial Process in Comparative Perspective* (New York, Clarendon Press, 1989) 70 (emphasis in original).

[7] *Ebner* (2000) 205 CLR 337.

[8] ibid [3] (Gleeson CJ, McHugh, Gummow and Hayne JJ).

[9] ibid [115].

[10] ibid [79]–[80], [91].

[11] ibid [84]. See also *Grollo v Palmer* (1995) 184 CLR 348, 394 (Gummow J). *cf Forge v Australian Securities and Investments Commission* (2006) 228 CLR 45 [68] (Gummow, Hayne and Crennan JJ). See further F Wheeler, 'Due Process, Judicial Power and Chapter III in the New High Court' (2004) 32 *Federal Law Review* 205, 216.

[12] J Stellios, *The Federal Judicature: Chapter III of the Constitution Commentary and Cases* (Chatswood, LexisNexis, 2010) 72, 96–102.

[13] ibid 103.

For instance, Stellios recounts that there was concern expressed in the Convention Debates that impartiality, or its perception, might be compromised if State judges were to fill the High Court bench.[14] As Higgins noted: '[s]upposing you drag in the Chief Justice of each state, there will be a strong tendency for him to feel himself the representative of his colony, and nothing could be more damaging to the cause of the Federal Court than that'.[15] In *R v Kirby; Ex parte Boilermakers' Society of Australia* (*Boilermakers'*),[16] the joint judgment quoted Isaacs J, in identifying the High Court's position as an 'impartial tribunal' as its 'essential feature'.[17] However, justifications for this judicial characteristic, and for the separation of powers, are less easy to pin down. Possible candidates are the protection of individual rights, the rule of law or the preservation of the federation.[18] Or, impartiality could ultimately be in the service of ensuring adequate checks on the executive and legislative branches. In *Ebner*, Gaudron J observed that the constitutional requirement of impartiality serves the greater purpose of public confidence in the courts, and that this in turn, is not just in the service of the rule of law but also the 'federal compact' which the 'judiciary has a central role in maintaining'.[19] What Gaudron J suggests, and which will be explored further below, is that impartial justice is to be understood as an intermediate constitutional value rather than an end in itself.

What is the constitutional foundation of impartial justice? Section 71 of the Commonwealth Constitution, and the way it has been interpreted by the High Court, is crucial here. For a federal court to exercise judicial power in the absence of impartiality would contravene the *Boilermakers'* doctrine. The almost proverbial twin-limbed *Boilermakers'* doctrine provides that Commonwealth judicial power can only be housed in a section 71 'court' and that the Commonwealth Parliament cannot confer non-judicial power, subject to some limited exceptions. Gaudron J in *Ebner* contended that impartiality, as well as its perception, form a vital core of judicial power.[20] Her Honour stated:

> Impartiality and the appearance of impartiality are so fundamental to the judicial process that they are defining features of judicial power. And because the only power that can be conferred pursuant to Ch III of the Constitution is the judicial power of the Commonwealth, that Chapter operates to guarantee that matters in federal jurisdiction are determined by a court constituted by a judge who is impartial and who appears to be impartial. And that is

[14] ibid 70.

[15] *Official Record of the Debates of the Australasian Federation Convention*, Melbourne, 28 January 1898, 281 (Henry Higgins).

[16] *R v Kirby; Ex parte Boilermakers' Society of Australia* (1956) 94 CLR 254. See also *Attorney-General (Cth) v The Queen; Ex parte Australian Boilermakers' Society* (1957) 95 CLR 529.

[17] *Boilermakers'* (1956) 94 CLR 254, 271 (Dixon CJ, McTiernan, Fullagar and Kitto JJ), quoting *New South Wales v Commonwealth* (1915) 20 CLR 54, 93 (Isaacs J).

[18] J Stellios, 'Conceptions of Judicial Review: Commentary on Dixon' (2015) 43 *Federal Law Review* 511, 513. See also H Patapan, *Judging Democracy: The New Politics of the High Court of Australia* (Cambridge, Cambridge University Press, 2000) 150. See further comments as to the vagaries of the framers' intentions in the separation of powers context: F Wheeler, 'Original Intent and the Doctrine of the Separation of Powers in Australia' (1996) 7 *Public Law Review* 96; P Gerangelos, 'Interpretational Methodology in Separation of Powers Jurisprudence: The Formalist/Functionalist Debate' (2005) 8 *Constitutional Law & Policy Review* 1, 9.

[19] *Ebner* (2000) 205 CLR 337 [103].

[20] ibid [80]. See also *Wilson v Minister for Aboriginal and Torres Strait Islander Affairs* (1996) 189 CLR 1, 22 (Gaudron J).

so whether the matter is before a federal court or a State or Territory court invested with federal jurisdiction.[21]

In *TCL Air Conditioner (Zhongshan) Co Ltd v Judges of the Federal Court of Australia* French CJ and Gageler J saw 'judicial power' as connoting a number of attributes including:

> the overriding necessity for the function always to be compatible with the essential character of a court as an institution that is, and is seen to be, both impartial between the parties and independent of the parties and of other branches of government in the exercise of the decision-making functions conferred on it.[22]

In *Forge v Australian Securities and Investments Commission*, Gleeson CJ maintained that '[f]or a body to answer the description of a court it must satisfy minimum requirements of independence and impartiality. That is a stable principle, founded on the text of the Constitution'.[23] While at times the distinction becomes judicially opaque,[24] Gleeson CJ recognises that one possibility is to source impartial justice, within the Chapter III notion of a 'court' rather than within the 'judicial power' phraseology. Such a 'court' is accordingly an appropriate repository of federal jurisdiction.[25]

Section 72 of the Commonwealth Constitution, in regulating the appointment, guaranteed tenure and set remuneration of federal justices, protects their independence but also the perception of their impartiality. Even beyond Chapter III and the judicial context, the contours of impartiality are evident in constitutional provisions such as section 99 (Commonwealth not to give preference to a State or any part of a State) and section 102 (Parliament may forbid preferences by State).

Relatedly, while the Commonwealth Constitution lacks an express entrenched right of due process, there is extensive judicial support closely traced in the work of Wheeler for the constitutionalisation of procedural fairness, of which impartiality forms a crucial limb, namely, the rule against bias.[26] In *International Finance Trust Co Ltd v New South Wales Crime Commission* French CJ explained that:

> Procedural fairness or natural justice lies at the heart of the judicial function. In the federal constitutional context, it is an incident of the judicial power exercised pursuant to Ch III of the Constitution. It requires that a court be and appear to be impartial, and provide

[21] *Ebner* (2000) 205 CLR 337 [80] (citations omitted).

[22] *TCL Air Conditioner (Zhongshan) Co Ltd v Judges of the Federal Court of Australia* (2013) 251 CLR 533, [28] (*TCL Air Conditioner*).

[23] *Forge v Australian Securities and Investments Commission* (2006) 228 CLR 45 [41].

[24] *Chu Kheng Lim v Minister for Immigration, Local Government and Ethnic Affairs* (1992) 176 CLR 1, 27 (Brennan, Deane and Dawson JJ); *TCL Air Conditioner* (2013) 251 CLR 533 [27] (French CJ and Gageler J).

[25] *Leeth v Commonwealth* (1992) 174 CLR 455, 487 (Deane and Toohey JJ); *Polyukhovich v Commonwealth* (1991) 172 CLR 501, 607 (Deane J). See also Wheeler, 'Due Process, Judicial Power and Chapter III in the New High Court', above n 11, 209–10.

[26] F Wheeler, 'The Doctrine of Separation of Powers and Constitutionally Entrenched Due Process in Australia' (1997) 23 *Monash University Law Review* 248, 261.

each party to proceedings with an opportunity to be heard, to advance its own case and to answer, by evidence and argument, the case put against it.[27]

It is clear that the constitutional value of impartial justice filters down from the federal level to the courts of a State[28] and even to the courts of the Territories.[29] This permeation occurs by virtue of the intrepid *Kable*[30] principle. This principle posits that State and Territory courts must continue to be appropriate repositories for federal judicial power and, as a result, their institutional integrity must not be compromised. The curial language has increasingly sought to peg the *Kable* principle to the constitutional text by focusing on whether a judicial body is required to depart from features which form part of its characteristic as a 'court'.[31] For Gaudron J in *Ebner*:

> Because State courts are part of the Australian judicial system created by Ch III of the Constitution and may be invested with the judicial power of the Commonwealth, the Constitution also requires, in accordance with *Kable* ... that, for the maintenance of public confidence, they be constituted by persons who are impartial and who appear to be impartial even when exercising non-federal jurisdiction.[32]

In *South Australia v Totani*,[33] French CJ referred to the 'histor[ical]', 'text[ual]' and 'structur[al]' requirement[34] that '[t]he courts of the States continue to bear the defining characteristics of courts and, in particular, the characteristics of independence, impartiality, fairness and adherence to the open-court principle'.[35] While the *Kable* principle does not spring from the separation of powers itself, there is an increasing recognition that, in practice, albeit with some tweaks[36] and jurisdictional differences,[37] Chapter III applies broadly similar standards to both federal and State courts.[38] Within these standards, the value of impartial justice seems unassailable.

[27] *International Finance Trust Co Ltd v New South Wales Crime Commission* (2009) 240 CLR 319 [54]; *Assistant Commissioner Condon v Pompano Pty Ltd* (2013) 252 CLR 38 [67] (French CJ); See also *TCL Air Conditioner* (2013) 251 CLR 533 [27] (French CJ and Gageler J). For a recent consideration of fairness and the judicial role see: J Allsop, 'Values in Public Law' (2017) 91 *Australian Law Journal* 118, 123.

[28] *Ebner* (2000) 205 CLR 337 [82] (Gaudron J), [116] (Kirby J). See also *Smits v Roach* (2006) 227 CLR 423 [121]–[122] (Kirby J).

[29] *North Australian Aboriginal Legal Service Inc v Bradley* (2004) 218 CLR 146.

[30] *Kable v Director of Public Prosecutions* (NSW) (1996) 189 CLR 51.

[31] *South Australia v Totani* (2010) 242 CLR 1 [70] (French CJ), [438] (Kiefel J).

[32] *Ebner* (2000) 205 CLR 337 [81].

[33] ibid.

[34] ibid [61].

[35] ibid [62]. See also *Wainohu v New South Wales* (2011) 243 CLR 181 [44] (French CJ).

[36] *International Finance Trust Co Ltd v New South Wales Crime Commission* (2009) 240 CLR 319 [53] (French CJ); *K-Generation Pty Ltd v Liquor Licensing Court* (2009) 237 CLR 501 [84], [88] (French CJ), [229] (Kirby J); *Assistant Commissioner Condon v Pompano Pty Ltd* (2013) 252 CLR 38 [125]–[126] (Hayne, Crennan, Kiefel and Bell JJ).

[37] *Re Wakim; Ex parte McNally* (1999) 198 CLR 511.

[38] S McLeish, 'The Nationalisation of the State Court System' (2013) 24 *Public Law Review* 252; J Stellios, 'The Centralisation of Judicial Power within the Australian Federal System' (2014) 42 *Federal Law Review* 357, 371; S Murray, 'Dual Federal and State Judicial Appointments: An Australian Impossibility?' (2014) 25 *Public Law Review* 284, 293. See also *South Australia v Totani* (2010) 242 CLR 1 [69] (French CJ).

III. FUNCTIONALISM IN ACTION: A CONSTITUTIONAL VALUE OF IMPARTIAL JUSTICE

What if, through a functionalist lens, even greater weight was placed on impartial justice as a constitutional value? What if it became a more overt interpretive tool in constitutional cases? Take the case of *Hogan v Hinch*.[39] While the case ultimately determined that the relevant suppression order made pursuant to the Serious Sex Offenders Monitoring Act 2005 (Vic), and which qualified the open justice principle, was constitutionally valid, the judicial phraseology is particularly noteworthy. French CJ determined that '[u]nder the Constitution courts capable of exercising the judicial power of the Commonwealth must at all times be and appear to be independent and impartial tribunals. The open-court principle serves to maintain that standard'.[40]

Even more expressly, Gummow, Hayne, Heydon, Crennan, Kiefel and Bell JJ held that '[t]he criterion for the exercise of power under s 42 is not such as to impair impermissibly the character of the State courts as independent and impartial tribunals and thus to render them inappropriate repositories of federal jurisdiction'.[41] The impact on impartial and independent justice becomes the central enquiry here. The open-court principle, while serving these values, must be weighed up against the need for in-camera proceedings in some instances.[42]

A similarly seismic role for impartial justice could occur via a functionalist shift away from the second limb of *Boilermakers*' that proscribes the conferral of non-judicial power of the Commonwealth on Chapter III courts. Criticism of the non-judicial power prohibition of *Boilermakers*' as an overreach is very much old news[43] when the due administration of justice is not dependent upon it. As Stellios contends, '[t]he same values that we might rely on to support an argument for a strict separation of judicial power also supports arguments for what is and what is not exclusively judicial in character'.[44]

I have argued elsewhere that several recent trends evident in Chapter III decisions make a functionalist shift towards an incompatibility test,[45] or 'contextual incompatibility' enquiry feasible.[46] This approach moves away from the initial focus

[39] *Hogan v Hinch* (2011) 243 CLR 506.
[40] ibid [20].
[41] ibid [80].
[42] ibid [46] (French CJ).
[43] See, eg, G Winterton, 'The Separation of Judicial Power as an Implied Bill of Rights' in G Lindell (ed), *Future Directions in Australian Constitutional Law: Essays in Honours of Professor Leslie Zines* (Sydney, Federation Press, 1994) 188; F Wheeler, 'The Boilermakers Case' in HP Lee and G Winterton (eds), *Australian Constitutional Landmarks* (Cambridge, Cambridge University Press, 2003) 172; Sir Anthony Mason, 'Judicial Review: Constitutional and Other Perspectives' (2000) 28 *Federal Law Review* 331, 339; J Stellios, *Zines's The High Court and the Constitution*, 6th edn (Sydney, Federation Press, 2015) 331.
[44] Stellios, *The Federal Judicature*, above n 12, 103.
[45] Something long championed ever since Williams J's dissent in *Boilermakers* (1956) 94 CLR 254, 314–15. See also Sir Anthony Mason, 'A New Perspective on Separation of Powers' (1996) 82 (December) *Canberra Bulletin of Public Administration* 1, 6; G Winterton, *Parliament, the Executive and the Governor-General: A Constitutional Analysis* (Melbourne, Melbourne University Press, 1983) 62; J Stellios, 'Reconceiving the Separation of Judicial Power' (2011) 22 *Public Law Review* 113, 130.
[46] S Murray, 'Giving Chapter III Back Its Constitutional Mojo: Lessons from State Courts and Beyond' (2014) 40 *Monash University Law Review* 198, 207–09, discussing *TCL Air Conditioner* (2013) 251 CLR 533 and *Magaming v The Queen* (2013) 252 CLR 381.

upon whether a federal role is judicial or not and has the potential to apply flexibly across the court hierarchy and across the *Boilermakers'/Kable* divide. In interpreting Chapter III for the purposes of State or federal courts, incompatibility would put the spotlight on whether a role, or its manner of exercise, is incompatible with the relevant standards applying to the 'court', as required by Chapter III. It would therefore bring to the fore the question of whether a curial task may compromise the independence or impartiality of a particular court or its ability to duly administer justice. Even a non-judicial role might be acceptable within this reformed approach.

For instance, this might mean that one could look at a federal judge mediating (as in facilitating a non-binding settlement between the parties) from a different constitutional perspective. Traditionally, judicial mediation is foreclosed by Chapter III as amounting to a non-judicial, and possibly non-incidental, conferral.[47] Certainly, within the current confines of Chapter III, it might be argued that a federal judge is mediating in a personal capacity.[48] However, a great deal of artificiality would be avoided by a functionalist loosening of the *Boilermakers'* strictures. This would mean that a non-judicial role, such as mediation, could be exercised by a Chapter III court, provided a federal judge is able to fulfil the constitutional requirements imposed. On such a reading, if a federal judge were to conduct a mediation, the constitutional enquiry would narrow in on the substance of the role instead of the form. Section 71 might be interpreted to allow a federal judge to mediate in some limited circumstances provided that judicial impartiality can still be maintained. It might mean, however, that Chapter III would be read such that the perceived threat to impartiality would require a judge involved in an unsuccessful mediation to withdraw from a later trial.

Incompatibility as an interpretive shift would not necessarily change the outcome in all Chapter III cases but could potentially ease obfuscation. It would set down the factors transparently and in a form that could be revised and analysed by later courts.[49] The enquiry would not be divorced from all subjectivity. There would still be questions as to what could compromise a court's independence or impartiality. However, in the functionalist tradition, the focus would be less on the form of the judicial function and more about its substance.

Functionalism, as Dixon highlights, tends to ensure that the consequences of interpretative choices are given appropriate precedence.[50] The implications of this are that a greater focus on the value of impartial justice may supersede other potential interests and result in an alteration of the status quo.[51] For instance, for Gaudron J in *Ebner*,[52] the fact that impartiality has a constitutional nature means that necessity, as an exception to the rule against bias, may be significantly qualified. Necessity can mean that a judge is required to continue to sit, concerns as to impartiality notwithstanding. Through the constitutional lens, however, the necessity exception could

[47] See S Murray, *The Remaking of the Courts: Less-Adversarial Practice and the Constitutional Role of the Judiciary in Australia* (Sydney, Federation Press, 2014) 142–49.

[48] *Grollo v Palmer* (1995) 184 CLR 348; *Wilson v Minister for Aboriginal and Torres Strait Islander Affairs* (1996) 189 CLR 1.

[49] Dixon, 'The Functional Constitution', above n 2, 456, 461–62, 492.

[50] ibid 459.

[51] ibid 464.

[52] *Ebner* (2000) 205 CLR 337 [102].

only apply if the court could *only* be properly constituted with the inclusion of that particular judge.[53] Were it otherwise, 'constitutional requirements' would be insupportably 'yield[ing] to expediency or convenience'.[54] Indeed, similar constitutional interpretative considerations might also mean that a party would not be able to use waiver to allow a judge, tainted by a perception of bias, to continue to sit in a case.[55]

IV. TRAPS WITHIN THE VALUE OF IMPARTIALITY

While greater engagement with a functional dialectic would mean that values such as impartial justice would play a more explicit role in judicial decision-making, this is not an exercise free of complication.

First, 'impartiality' is not a concept that can be exhaustively defined.[56] In commenting on Dixon's paper, Lim[57] noted that even if a value is identified, pitching it at 'an appropriate level of abstraction' becomes the next real challenge. This is very true with impartial justice and there is the potential for jurists to be using the same value but to mean slightly different things or to be focusing on it differently. Lucy, for example, comments on the intersecting ways which impartiality can apply to a decision-maker's 'attitude' as well as the 'outcome' or 'procedure' applied to resolve a dispute.[58]

Practically, is there is a terminological difference between a value of 'impartial justice' as opposed to a value of 'judicial impartiality'? 'Impartial justice' may be richer and have broader application than 'judicial impartiality' which is arguably more judge-centric. If this is the case, whether the value is crafted as judicial impartiality or impartial justice may make a real difference.

For instance, a value of impartial justice (but not judicial impartiality) could extend to expectations surrounding impartial decisions being made by jurors as well as other decision-makers.[59] Section 80 of the Commonwealth Constitution requires a jury trial for Commonwealth offences tried on indictment. To the extent that there is a risk of juror bias, something that has for instance been raised in the context of the trying of highly publicised terrorism offences,[60] a constitutional value of impartiality may shape the interpretation of 'jury' in section 80. Such a reading would be consistent with the High Court's acceptance of the trial judge's comments in *Brownlee v The Queen* that 'the framers of the constitutional guarantee intended that a jury exercise its function without fear or favour and without undue influ-

[53] ibid.

[54] ibid. See also *Bass v Permanent Trustee Company Ltd* (1999) 198 CLR 334, 369 (Kirby J).

[55] E Campbell, 'Waiver of Judicial Disqualification for Bias or Apprehended Bias: A Constitutional Issue' (1999) 2 *Constitutional Law & Policy Review* 41; Groves, 'Waiver of the Rule Against Bias', above n 4, 327.

[56] See Murray, *The Remaking of the Courts*, above n 47, 247.

[57] B Lim, 'The Convergence of Form and Function: Commentary on Dixon' (2015) 43 *Federal Law Review* 505, 509. See the response of Dixon: R Dixon, 'Response to Commentators' (2015) 43 *Federal Law Review* 518, 520.

[58] W Lucy, 'The Possibility of Impartiality' (2005) 25(1) *Oxford Journal of Legal Studies* 3, 14ff.

[59] *Ebner* (2000) 205 CLR 337, 344 (Gleeson CJ, McHugh, Gummow and Hayne JJ).

[60] F Davis, 'Trial by Jury: Time for a Re-evaluation' (2007) 32 *Alternative Law Journal* 86.

ence in the context of community standards and expectations as current from time to time'.[61]

However, 'impartial justice' might have an even wider connotation, suggesting a breadth that could potentially compromise its utility as a precise constitutional value. Indeed it could even be used in a sense that begins to see it overlap with values such as the rule of law.[62] While contested, the rule of law, in requiring freedom from the exercise of arbitrary and preferential exercises of power,[63] has definite correlations with the value of impartial justice or the 'impartial administration of justice'.[64]

While the open-endedness of impartiality as a value may be beneficial, it may complicate the interpretive exercise in opening up functionalist interpretations to criticisms of latent subjectivity, discretion and even partisanship. Are judges able to conveniently and selectively use impartial justice to strike down legislation which may undermine their own legitimacy? In this regard, drawing on historical and structural references to justify functionalist interpretations can ease, but not prevent, such criticisms.[65]

Second, sourcing a constitutional value of impartial justice is less problematic than addressing the ultimate role it may serve. Does it matter if judges are eluding the 'ultimate constitutional value' at stake?[66] Akin to Sunstein's 'incompletely theorized agreement',[67] does the value of impartial justice typically bring about the same constitutional outcome regardless of the motivation for its prioritisation?[68] Can judges use impartial justice as a 'safe ground' on which they agree before their views as to its function begin to diverge? Is it necessary to unpack whether impartiality is in the service of fundamental and/or individual rights, the rule of law, the federation, or more broadly, just providing suitable governmental checks? Might these different purposes bring about a change in a functionalist constitutional interpretation? If so, stopping at impartial justice may only be masking disagreement in need of greater transparency.

It would seem that the ultimate constitutional value served by impartial justice may in fact bring about a change in constitutional outcome. Take, for example, the possibility of whether waiver can apply to allow a biased judge to remain assigned to a case. A constitutional value of impartiality could suggest that waiver cannot apply in such instances. At least, that is, if the ultimate value being served is the maintenance of public confidence in the administration of justice. It might, however,

[61] *Brownlee v The Queen* (2001) 207 CLR 278 [67] (Gaudron, Gummow and Hayne JJ). See also at [27] (Gleeson CJ and McHugh J). See further *Ebner* (2000) 205 CLR 337 [5]–[8] (Gleeson CJ, McHugh, Gummow and Hayne JJ).

[62] *Australian Communist Party v Commonwealth* (1951) 83 CLR 1, 193 (Dixon J). See also ch 5 by Lisa Burton Crawford in this collection.

[63] Sir Gerard Brennan, 'Judicial Independence' (speech delivered at the Australian Judicial Conference, Canberra, 2 November 1996): <www.hcourt.gov.au/assets/publications/speeches/former-justices/brennanj/brennanj_ajc.htm>.

[64] Wheeler, 'The Doctrine of Separation of Powers', above n 26, 253.

[65] See generally S Murray, 'Australian State Courts and Chapter III of the Commonwealth Constitution: Interpretation and Re-interpretation and the Creation of Australian Constitutional "Orthodoxy"' (2012) 24 *Giornale di Storia Costituzionale* 145. See also *South Australia v Totani* (2010) 242 CLR 1 [1], [50] (French CJ).

[66] Dixon, 'The Functional Constitution', above n 2, 464.

[67] CR Sunstein, 'Incompletely Theorized Agreements in Constitutional Law' (2007) 74 *Social Research* 1.

[68] As Dixon notes, it may therefore have 'the benefit of avoiding the need for a judge to choose between these potentially competing rationales': above n 2, 464.

be permissible if the protection of the rights of the individual is seen as the ultimate value.[69] This presents a real dilemma for a functionalist using impartial justice as a guiding intermediate value.

This suggests that if impartial justice is to be understood as only an intermediate constitutional value,[70] it could be required to give way to other values explored in this collection, such as individual liberty and the rule of law. Ultimately, while there may be some definitional resolutions, finding consensus as to the definitive values in such a setting becomes a vexed exercise and one likely to fuel dissension. One difficulty with equivocating as to the ultimate constitutional values concerned is that, should constitutional values conflict, the muddying of values becomes a much riskier enterprise. How can it be determined which is the fundamental value to take precedence?

Are there values even more ultimate than individual liberty, the rule of law and the maintenance of the federal compact? Cappelletti recognises the complexity inherent within this exercise in acknowledging that 'all human values can be "ultimate" only in a limited and relative sense'.[71] Could impartial justice in fact be in service of more primary values of fairness, accountability, justice, dignity and welfare of the person? While separating or choosing between these is difficult, what seems clear is that the process of sifting for values cannot run out at judicial independence or even impartiality. While indeterminate, the values run deeper. Consensus, of the kind envisaged by Sunstein, may be reachable at the point of impartial justice, but it may not be as tangible an agreement as it may appear. Judges may need to be transparent about the point at which they disagree so that constitutional interpretations are as clear as they are disparate.

V. CONCLUSION

Cohen observed that '[l]egal description is blind without the guiding light of a theory of values'.[72]

Functionalist engagement with constitutional interpretation, as provoked by this collection, provides an opportunity to explore the values shaping public law decision-making. Impartial justice, while it should not be understood as a freestanding constitutional principle, sits as a constitutional interpretative value with considerable support and influence within Chapter III and beyond.

However, as identified here, a value of impartial justice presents a range of complications and potential criticisms which only thicken on closer examination. While directed at the value of impartial justice, such criticisms may also be directed at functionalism and other value-based approaches more generally. Such criticisms therefore do not foreclose the functionalist path but simply highlight the sorts of challenges that must be faced by any enrichment in constitutional approach.

[69] I am indebted to Dr Gabrielle Appleby (UNSW) for this perceptive observation through her commentary at the June 2016 Constitutional Values workshop at UNSW.

[70] As Lucy contends, 'much of its value flows from the value-company it keeps': above n 58, 30.

[71] Cappelletti, above n 6, 70.

[72] F Cohen, 'Transcendental Nonsense and the Functional Approach' (1935) *Columbia Law Review* 809, 849.

Part III

Political Democracy

8

Deliberation as a Constitutional Value

SCOTT STEPHENSON

I. INTRODUCTION

DELIBERATION HAS COME to occupy a prominent position in contemporary political theory.[1] The attraction of deliberation is that it sets out standards for discourse (and other interactions) that help realise the promise of democratic self-government, reducing the risk that the voices of certain segments of society will not be heard and the risk that policy debates will not consider, or will pay insufficient regard to, the full range of arguments that can be made for different positions. While Australia's political system has been carefully studied through the lens of deliberative theory,[2] the same cannot be said of the Australian Constitution.[3] This chapter takes some tentative steps towards addressing this gap, evaluating the extent to which the Constitution presupposes a deliberative form of government and contemplating several ways in which the High Court could draw on deliberation as a value to inform the interpretation of the Constitution.

The first section observes that the Constitution's structural features establish four principal relationships between two or more actors that require mediation through discourse: federalism (the Commonwealth and States), responsible government (the Commonwealth executive and Commonwealth Parliament), bicameralism (the House of Representatives and the Senate) and representative democracy (government and the people). It then argues that the successful maintenance of these relationships not only requires discourse, but discourse that is of a deliberative standard, at least most of the time. The section concludes by noting that, while the Constitution therefore presupposes a broadly deliberative form of government, the Constitution also presupposes that in most circumstances the parties to these four relationships are

[1] The literature on deliberation is too extensive to cite in full. For a critical overview of the major scholarship in the field, see JS Dryzek, *Deliberative Democracy and Beyond: Liberals, Critics, Contestations* (New York, Oxford University Press, 2002).

[2] See, eg, J Uhr, *Deliberative Democracy in Australia: The Changing Place of Parliament* (Cambridge, Cambridge University Press, 1998).

[3] Some aspects of the relationship between the Constitution and deliberation have, however, been studied: see, eg, S Stephenson, 'Federalism and Rights Deliberation' (2014) 38 *Melbourne University Law Review* 709; R Levy and G Orr, *The Law of Deliberative Democracy* (New York, Routledge, 2016); R Levy, N Silva and B Saunders, 'Deliberation at the Founding: Deliberative Democracy as an Original Constitutional Value' (2017) 28 *Public Law Review* 41.

responsible for maintaining the requisite standard of discourse—that is, it is not the role of the judiciary to ensure that deliberation is maintained.

The next section argues that the foregoing conclusion does not entirely erase the judiciary from the picture. As is well known, the High Court has drawn a number of implications to help protect the Constitution's structural features.[4] This section first considers whether the Court has already recognised deliberation as a constitutional value in the course of adjudicating on the freedom of political communication. It finds that the Court has, by narrow margins, tended to prioritise freedom of discourse over the protection of deliberation. This stance does not, however, preclude the recognition of deliberation in other parts of the Constitution. It must be remembered that in the freedom of political communication context the Court is being asked to determine whether the protection of deliberation permits the *regulation* of discourse. In other areas, the protection of deliberation is less contentious because it generally entails the *promotion* of discourse. Three suggestions are made where the Court could interpret the Constitution in a way that helps protect deliberation. First, in relation to section 109 (inconsistency of Commonwealth and State laws), it could interpret the 'covering the field' test in a way that allows more scope for complementary State legislation, which would help protect deliberation between the Commonwealth and States. Second, in relation to section 61 (executive power), it could require the major features of government contracts to be included in the laws authorising the executive to make these contracts and spend money pursuant to them, which would help protect deliberation between the executive and Parliament, between the Houses of Parliament, and between government and the people. Third, in relation to section 71 (judicial power), it could construe judicial power in a manner that permits courts to issue suspended declarations of invalidity, which would help protect deliberation between the Houses of Parliament, and between government and the people.

II. DELIBERATION AS A CONSTITUTIONAL PRESUPPOSITION

A. The Meaning of Deliberation

Before examining the relationship between deliberation and the Constitution, it is necessary to consider briefly what the term 'deliberation' means. The considerable literature on deliberation highlights that a significant degree of complexity arises when mapping its precise contours.[5] Deliberation is ordinarily understood to refer to interactions that have a number of characteristics. One set of scholars identifies those characteristics as *participation* by all citizens in *respectful* exchanges of *truthful* claims that are *logically justifiable* and expressed in terms of the *common good* in circumstances where participants are *willing to yield* to the force of better arguments.[6] It is broadly

[4] See the discussion below in section II.A.

[5] See, eg, the contributions to J Bohman and W Rehg (eds), *Deliberative Democracy: Essays on Reason and Politics* (Cambridge, MIT Press, 1997); J Elster (ed), *Deliberative Democracy* (Cambridge, Cambridge University Press, 1998).

[6] J Steiner et al, *Deliberative Politics in Action: Analyzing Parliamentary Discourse* (Cambridge, Cambridge University Press, 2004) 19–24.

understood that political discourse often falls short of this deliberative standard; it is commonly employed as a normative rather than a descriptive benchmark.[7] Consequently, it would be unreasonable to argue that the Constitution presupposes this level of deliberation for its effective operation.

A more plausible position is that the Constitution presupposes a pared-back conception of deliberation, one that embodies a similar yet less exacting set of characteristics. For the purposes of this chapter, it will define deliberation in its minimal form as discourse that is *inclusive*, *informed* and *reasonable*. Even with this less exigent understanding of deliberation, it continues to require more than the expression of opinions—more than just talk. It is discourse that meets a certain set of standards, albeit standards that are expressed in a flexible, minimalist manner. Understood in this way, the concept of deliberation resembles a number of other concepts that are familiar to constitutionalism. Representative democracy and responsible government, for example, denote respectively democracy and government of a particular standard—they do not mean *any* form of democracy or *any* form of government. Yet those standards are expressed in terms that are sufficiently general that a range of institutional arrangements and that a number of patterns of institutional practice will satisfy them. For example, both presidential and parliamentary systems are capable of meeting the definition of representative democracy.

B. Deliberation and the Australian Constitution

The Constitution does not contain any provisions that directly provide for or require institutional actors to deliberate. The provision that has the strongest link to the concept of deliberation is section 49, which allows Parliament to declare the 'powers, privileges, and immunities' that the House of Representatives and Senate enjoy and, until they are declared, establishes them to be the same as those enjoyed by the House of Commons of UK Parliament at Federation. One of the privileges that UK Parliament enjoyed at Federation and that Commonwealth Parliament continues to enjoy today[8] derives from Article 9 of the Bill of Rights 1688 (UK), which provides that 'the freedom of speech and debates or proceedings in Parliament ought not to be impeached or questioned in any court or place out of Parliament'. While the protection of freedom of speech in Commonwealth Parliament is connected to deliberation insofar as it relates to discourse, it does not require or necessarily even encourage discourse to be of a standard that would merit characterisation as deliberation. To the contrary, absolute freedom of speech may encourage discourse of precisely the opposite persuasion (ie, discourse that is exclusive, uninformed and unreasonable) because it allows persons to make statements without fear of those laws that are designed to protect the quality of discourse (eg, defamation and hate speech laws). Indeed, it is not difficult to find examples of parliamentarians who have employed parliamentary privilege to make false accusations designed to harm

[7] This explains why scholars have developed a range of innovative mechanisms to foster deliberation: see, eg, B Ackerman and J Fishkin, *Deliberation Day* (New Haven, Yale University Press, 2004).

[8] Parliamentary Privileges Act 1987 (Cth) s 16.

the reputation of individuals.[9] It is, therefore, difficult to source any connection between deliberation and the Constitution directly in the terms of the document.

That does not, however, mark the end of the enquiry. A strong argument can be made that the form of government established by the Constitution presupposes the existence of discourse that is of a deliberative standard, at least in most circumstances. It is a two-step argument that involves, first, identifying the features of Australia's constitutional system of government that require discourse to occur either between different institutions of government or between government and the people and, second, demonstrating why this discourse must generally be of a deliberative standard.

In relation to the first step, four structures or principles of the Constitution require a not insubstantial level of interaction and, as a result, discourse between two or more actors. First, the Constitution provides for a federal system of government that introduces two levels of government into the same geographical area. The potential for cooperation and division, agreement and disagreement between governments is evident from many of the Constitution's provisions. For example, sections 51 and 109 foreshadow that Commonwealth and State parliaments will make laws on the same subjects, section 51(xxxvii) allows State parliaments to refer heads of power to Commonwealth Parliament, section 92 requires 'trade, commerce, and intercourse among the States' to be 'absolutely free', and section 96 allows Commonwealth Parliament to 'grant financial assistance to any State on such terms and conditions as the Parliament thinks fit'.

Second, the Constitution establishes a system of responsible government at the federal level that results in a close, interdependent relationship between the executive and Parliament. Section 64 is the principal provision that establishes this relationship, prohibiting any minister from 'hold[ing] office for a longer period than three months unless he is or becomes a senator or a Member of the House of Representatives'. Most other features of responsible government, such as the office of Prime Minister, the role of Cabinet and the procedure by which a party forms government, are a product of constitutional convention, a point to which I return below.

Third, the Constitution establishes a bicameral federal legislature that results in two Houses of Parliament that must work closely together to enact legislation, conduct enquiries and hold the executive to account. Parts II and III of Chapter I establish, respectively, the Senate and the House of Representatives. Importantly, it establishes them as nearly equal chambers with the Senate enjoying broadly the same electoral credentials as the House of Representatives, with sections 7 and 24 stating that both chambers are to be comprised of persons 'directly chosen by the people', and broadly the same legislative powers, with section 53 stating that, apart from money bills, 'the Senate shall have equal power with the House of Representatives in respect of all proposed laws'.

Fourth, the Constitution establishes a system of representative democracy that results in an ongoing, reciprocal relationship between government and the people.

[9] See, eg, Senator Bill Heffernan's false accusations made against High Court Justice Michael Kirby under parliamentary privilege: H Patapan, 'High Court 2002: The Least Dangerous Branch' (2003) 38 *Australian Journal of Political Science* 299, 299–302.

In addition to sections 7 and 24 mentioned above, a large number of provisions, especially those found in part IV of Chapter I, envisage that the Houses of Parliament will be elected. The government's relationship to the people is maintained not only through periodic elections, but also through the system of parliamentary committees envisaged by section 49 that allows the people to participate in the law-making process.

The level of interaction required to mediate these four relationships has, if anything, risen over time. For example, the Commonwealth and States have become increasingly intertwined as a result of the States' growing dependence on the Commonwealth to provide the funds necessary to perform their functions given that the Commonwealth now controls the principal means of raising revenue.[10] The relationship between government and the people has broadened and deepened as the activities of government have expanded with, for example, the development of the welfare state.[11]

Turning to the second step of the argument, it is clear that mediation of these relationships requires actors to engage in discourse with each other. Some discourse may occur through official channels such as standing forums between the levels of government, estimates hearings between the executive and Parliament, messages between the Houses of Parliament, and government statements to the people. Yet discourse may also occur through informal mechanisms, such as comments made to the media.[12] For these relationships to function well, especially over long periods of time, it is strongly arguable that this discourse must be inclusive, informed and reasonable—that is, it must be of a deliberative standard—at least in most circumstances and most of the time. Discourse that is not inclusive, informed and reasonable is likely to result in mistrust, stalemates, tit-for-tat actions, unpredictability and other pathologies that will erode the proper functioning of the relationships and, therefore, the system of government for which the Constitution provides.

To give just a few examples, the Constitution's system of representative democracy is likely to falter if the relationship between the government and people is marked by discourse that is predominantly exclusive—that is, where the public, or certain segments thereof, are marginalised or outright prohibited from engaging in discourse with and about the government. The Constitution's system of responsible government is likely to falter if the relationship between the executive and Parliament is marked by discourse that is predominantly uninformed—that is, where Parliament cannot engage in constructive exchanges with the executive about proposed laws and the implementation of existing laws because it does not have the requisite information. Bicameralism is likely to falter if the relationship between the two Houses of Parliament is marked by discourse that is predominantly unreasonable—that is, where one House makes excessive demands of, or even outright refuses to engage with, the other.

10 T Burton, B Dollery and J Wallis, 'A Century of Vertical Fiscal Imbalance in Australian Federalism' (2002) 36 *History of Economics Review* 26.

11 Indeed, the Constitution was amended in 1946 to empower Parliament to make laws in this field: s 51(xxiiiA).

12 For some examples of discourse conducted through the media along the federal dimension, see Stephenson, above n 3.

To say that the Constitution requires a deliberative form of government is not to say that it requires discourse to be of a deliberative standard at all times and all stages. Indeed, certain institutional arrangements have developed that are well suited to tolerating discourse that is not necessarily of a deliberative standard. Question Time in the House of Representatives has, for example, come to be understood as a space in Parliament's schedule where parliamentarians will engage in grandstanding. Even beyond such spaces, the constitutional system of government can tolerate occasional and minor departures from the deliberative standard of discourse. Representative democracy can withstand minor restrictions on speech, especially in the pursuit of other values such as national security.[13] Bicameralism can withstand the occasional impasse between the Houses of Parliament, as occurred in 1975.[14] Responsible government can withstand the occasional and minor pursuit of institutional self-interest, such as when the Senate estimates process devolves into political point scoring.[15]

The Constitution can tolerate these kinds of departures in part because it contains mechanisms for addressing them. Section 57 contains a procedure for resolving disagreements between the Houses of Parliament. Indeed, it is one that prioritises deliberation insofar as it requires an interval of three months to elapse between the first and second rejection of a proposed law, a period of time where discussions can take place, before the second stage of the procedure (ie, a double dissolution election) can be invoked. Section 75 contains a procedure for resolving disagreements between the Commonwealth and States by giving the High Court original jurisdiction in all matters in which the Commonwealth is a party and in all matters between the States.

While a degree of departure from the standards of deliberation is therefore tolerable, the four constitutional relationships would be imperiled if these departures became frequent or significant. For example, representative democracy would be seriously endangered if parliamentarians did nothing but grandstand, failing to evaluate and discuss complex and unpopular legislative proposals in a reasonable manner. Bicameralism would be threatened if the Senate sought to create an impasse with the House of Representatives at every possible opportunity. Further, the constitutional mechanisms for addressing dysfunction are not a substitute for deliberation. Double dissolution elections and High Court litigation are costly and cumbersome mechanisms for resolving disagreement. As a result, they can only be employed on an infrequent basis.

[13] There are, however, limits. For a discussion of the concerns related to the increasingly large number of security-based restrictions on speech, see Australian Law Reform Commission, *Traditional Rights and Freedoms—Encroachment by Commonwealth Laws*, Report No 129 (2015) ch 4.

[14] For an overview of the events of 1975 and their constitutional implications, see B Lim, *Australia's Constitution after Whitlam* (Cambridge, Cambridge University Press, 2017).

[15] Concerns are sometimes expressed that occasional and minor departures from deliberative standards in Senate estimates are becoming permanent and major: see, eg, Simon Tatz, 'Senate Estimates: We're All Losers in This Game of "Gotcha"' *ABC The Drum* (online) 19 October 2015: www.abc.net.au/news/2015-10-19/tatz-senate-estimates:-we're-all-losers-in-this-game-of-'gotcha'/6860784.

III. DELIBERATION AS AN INTERPRETIVE VALUE

A. Current State of the Law

That the Constitution presupposes the existence of a deliberative form of government does not automatically mean that deliberation becomes a value that the judiciary should recognise let alone enforce. Many constitutional presuppositions are maintained by a combination of convention, culture and institutional forms with little if any involvement of the judiciary. Given the paucity of constitutional provisions on responsible government, this aspect of the system of government operates primarily in accordance with convention. Given the absence of a constitutional bill of rights to secure the electoral and free speech rights necessary to maintain representative democracy, this aspect of the system of government relies in large part on a parliamentary culture of respect for these rights. The same line of reasoning can be extended to deliberation. The necessary standard of discourse is primarily maintained through certain conventions (eg, the convention that the public service is apolitical helps ensure that the executive and Parliament are supplied with evidence and information of a quality necessary to conduct informed discussion);[16] cultural practices (eg, a general practice of refraining from abuse of the free speech entitlements afforded by parliamentary privilege);[17] and institutional forms (eg, the Council of Australian Governments facilitates focused and orderly discourse between the Commonwealth and States).[18]

The High Court has nevertheless taken a role in enforcing aspects of the system of government that the Constitution presupposes. The doctrine of intergovernmental immunities helps protect federalism by prohibiting a government from taking actions that undermine the ability of another government to exercise its constitutional powers.[19] The separation of judicial powers doctrine helps protect the separation of powers by limiting the ability of legislatures to confer judicial functions on non-judicial bodies and to confer non-judicial functions on judicial bodies.[20] The right to vote helps protect representative democracy by limiting the ability of legislatures to restrict the franchise.[21] The limitations on the executive's power to contract and spend help protect federalism and bicameralism by ensuring that the Senate cannot be circumvented.[22] Finally, the freedom of political communication doctrine helps protect representative democracy by limiting the ability

[16] This convention is also reflected in law: Public Service Act 1999 (Cth) s 10(5).

[17] When, for example, Senator Heffernan made the allegations against Justice Michael Kirby mentioned above at n 9, 'Prime Minister John Howard stated that he had counselled Heffernan not to raise these matters under parliamentary privilege, which should be used "carefully and properly"': Patapan, above n 9, 300.

[18] B Galligan and J Wright, 'Australian Federalism: A Prospective Assessment' (2002) 32 *Publius: The Journal of Federalism* 147, 152–55.

[19] *Melbourne Corporation v Commonwealth* (1947) 74 CLR 31.

[20] *R v Kirby; Ex parte Boilermakers' Society of Australia* (1956) 94 CLR 254.

[21] *Roach v Electoral Commissioner* (2007) 233 CLR 162.

[22] *Williams v Commonwealth* (2012) 248 CLR 156 (*Williams [No 1]*).

of government to take actions that suppress the lines of communication between government and the people.[23]

It might be thought that the High Court has already extended a measure of protection to deliberation through the freedom of political communication doctrine. The doctrine is protective of *discourse* given that it prevents restrictions from being placed on political communication that are not compatible with the constitutionally prescribed system of representative and responsible government.[24] However, the Court has been closely divided over whether the doctrine allows Parliament to impose limitations on political communication that help maintain discourse to a standard that is *deliberative* (or, at least, closer to a standard that is deliberative). In other words, there is disagreement as to whether the protection of deliberation is an end or object that is compatible with the constitutionally prescribed system of representative and responsible government. In *Coleman v Power*,[25] Gleeson CJ, Callinan J, and Heydon J held that Parliament can prohibit the use of insulting or offensive language even in circumstances where the words are unlikely to provoke unlawful physical retaliation. Heydon J, for example, was of the view that the protection of deliberation is consistent with the protection of discourse, stating that it is legitimate for Parliament

> to prevent other persons who hear the insults from feeling intimidated or otherwise upset: they have an interest in public peace and an interest in feeling secure, and one specific consequence of those interests being invaded is that *they may withdraw from public debate or desist from contributing to it.* Insulting words are a form of uncivilised violence and intimidation.[26]

By contrast, McHugh J, Gummow and Hayne JJ, and Kirby J held that ensuring civility of discourse is not a legitimate end and that Parliament can only prohibit political communication that is reasonably likely to provoke unlawful physical retaliation. McHugh J, for example, said that the protection of discourse entails rejecting the protection of deliberation:

> The use of insulting words is a common enough technique in political discussion and debates. No doubt speakers and writers sometimes use them as weapons of intimidation. And whether insulting words are or are not used for the purpose of intimidation, fear of insult may have a chilling effect on political debate. However, as I have indicated, insults are a legitimate part of the political discussion protected by the Constitution. An unqualified prohibition on their use cannot be justified as compatible with the constitutional freedom.[27]

In *Monis v The Queen*,[28] the Court once again spilt. Crennan, Kiefel and Bell JJ held that the legislation in question was directed to the legitimate end of preventing intrusion of seriously offensive material into a person's home or workplace. By contrast,

[23] *Australian Capital Television Pty Ltd v Commonwealth* (1992) 177 CLR 106; *Nationwide News Pty Ltd v Wills* (1992) 177 CLR 1.

[24] *Lange v Australian Broadcasting Corporation* (1997) 189 CLR 520, 561–62, 567.

[25] *Coleman v Power* (2004) 220 CLR 1.

[26] ibid 121 [323] (emphasis added).

[27] ibid 54 [105].

[28] *Monis v The Queen* (2013) 249 CLR 92.

French CJ, Hayne J, and Heydon J held that the legislation was directed to the end of ensuring civility of discourse, which was held not to be a legitimate end in *Coleman v Power*.

While the contested character of these decisions might be construed as a reason against relying on the concept of deliberation to aid the interpretation of the Constitution, it should be remembered that the relationship between discourse and deliberation is particularly difficult in the context of political communication and, more generally, free speech. The extent to which discourse should be regulated to promote discourse *of a particular standard* is an issue that has been fiercely debated for centuries in the field of free speech.[29] Not every engagement with the concept of deliberation raises such intractable problems. In many if not most situations, the protection of deliberation also entails the promotion of discourse—that is, the two concepts align rather than conflict. For example, creating opportunities for participation so that discourse is inclusive, ensuring participants are given sufficient evidence to ensure that discourse is informed, and providing opportunities for interlocutors to respond to each other to increase the likelihood that discourse is reasonable, are all scenarios where deliberation is protected *through* the promotion of discourse. Consequently, it is possible for the Court to expand its engagement with the concept of deliberation without necessarily having to take a stand on issues that are characterised by pervasive, intractable disagreement.[30]

Further, greater judicial recognition of deliberation as a constitutional presupposition need not entail the creation of freestanding limitations on power in the mould of the freedom of political communication doctrine. As discussed below, there are alternative means of recognising and utilising the concept of deliberation that result in more modest developments to the state of the law. Indeed, as the Constitution can tolerate contained, occasional and minor deviations from deliberative standards of discourse, it would arguably be inappropriate to draw on the concept of deliberation in a way that imposes a rigid or universal set of restrictions on institutions. The search is, therefore, for ways of acknowledging that the Constitution presupposes a deliberative form of government that are responsive to the fact that the Constitution does not require deliberation at all times and in all places.

B. Future Directions

If a future High Court were minded to draw on the concept of deliberation to aid the interpretation of the Constitution, there are at least two ways in which the Court could accord some weight to the protection of deliberation that would not go so far as to create a freestanding limitation on power.

First, the High Court could interpret existing doctrines and principles in a manner that is consistent with the concept of deliberation where there is uncertainty or

[29] See generally AW Saxonhouse, *Free Speech and Democracy in Ancient Athens* (Cambridge, Cambridge University Press, 2005).

[30] That is not to say that any engagement with the concept of deliberation is free from controversy. Some invocations of the concept are, however, more difficult and contested than others.

contestation about their scope and application. When deciding whether to prefer a narrower or broader interpretation of a power granted to or a limitation placed upon an institution, the effect that the competing constructions would have on deliberation could be considered. The protection of deliberation would not necessarily be the only factor relevant to resolving the issue. Indeed, the other chapters in this book attest to the significant number of other values that might be relevant. However, it would be a not insignificant factor given that it underpins most of the salient features of the system of government that the Constitution establishes: representative democracy, responsible government, bicameralism and federalism.

Second, the High Court could interpret the Constitution in a manner that accords institutions a degree of deference if their actions are taken after engaging in deliberation. The rationale for this form of recognition is that, first, the Constitution presupposes a deliberative form of government; second, an institutional act that upholds and helps further this form of government has demonstrated fidelity to the Constitution; and third, this demonstration of fidelity is one factor that can help determine the constitutional validity of the institutional act. The degree of deference accorded to institutions would be modest. It would not give, for instance, a legislature the ability to exempt itself from the requirements of the Constitution by engaging in careful deliberation before the enactment of a statute. However, if the legislature enacted a statute following careful deliberation, it would allow the Court to err on the side of validity in situations where the arguments for and against validity are finely balanced. Thus, this form of recognition would not disturb the Court's existing interpretations of, for example, the scope of a head of power, but would give the Court an additional tool to help determine whether a law comes within the scope of the head of power in a *particular* case.

In its most direct form, this second form of recognition would involve consideration of the parliamentary record—debates, committee reports and so forth—to determine whether deliberation had occurred. It would not require the Court to abandon its emphasis on the primacy of the text in statutory interpretation because these materials would be used to identify the presence and extent of deliberation rather than to determine the meaning of the statute. However, if this approach would prove to be a step too far, a more indirect method would be to employ a proxy test. The Court could evaluate the terms of the statute against criteria that are more likely to exist if the statute is the product of deliberation. An example is the proportionality framework that the Court has adopted to evaluate the constitutional validity of limitations on political communication.[31] One element of proportionality analysis evaluates whether an 'obvious and compelling alternative, reasonably practicable means of achieving the same purpose which has a less restrictive effect on the freedom' exists.[32] While this element does not require the legislature to deliberate

[31] *McCloy v New South Wales* (2015) 257 CLR 178, 193–95 [2] (French CJ, Kiefel, Bell and Keane JJ). The use of a proportionality framework of analysis in Australia remains the subject of contestation. See, eg, the judgments of Gageler J (at 235–39 [141]–[152]) and Gordon J (at 288–89 [338]–[339]) in *McCloy*.

[32] ibid 193–95 [2] (French CJ, Kiefel, Bell and Keane JJ).

on an issue, the legislature is more likely to satisfy this element if it has engaged in deliberation because an inclusive, informed and reasonable enquiry into a legislative proposal is more likely to have considered the range of less restrictive alternatives, and concluded that no obvious and compelling one exists. Thus, it serves as a proxy, albeit an imperfect one, for determining whether deliberation has occurred.

Three examples of how this approach might work in practice are discussed below.

i. Section 109

The application of section 109, which renders State laws invalid to the extent that they are inconsistent with Commonwealth laws, is straightforward when a Commonwealth law and a State law are incapable of simultaneous obedience. There is little room for interpretive disagreement. Putting these rare situations to one side, however, a significant degree of uncertainty and vagueness attends section 109. The test to which the Court most frequently turns, the 'covering the field' test, holds that a State law is inconsistent with a Commonwealth law where the Commonwealth law 'on its true construction intended to cover the whole ground and, therefore, to supersede' the State law.[33] The test asks two questions: do the Commonwealth and State laws occupy the same field and, if so, does the Commonwealth law intend to cover that field? Where there is room for disagreement about the answers to these questions, which is often the case, there is scope to accord some weight to the answer that will best protect deliberation. This is because inconsistency of Commonwealth and State legislation affects the extent to which and the way in which Commonwealth and State governments engage with each other and with the people.

If section 109 is interpreted in a manner that gives it a broader operation—meaning that it is more likely that a Commonwealth law is found to have entered the same field as a State law and that it is more likely that the Commonwealth law is found to have expressed an intention to cover that field—there is less need for the Commonwealth to consult with the States prior to taking legislative action. The Commonwealth needs to spend less energy and time working with the States to consider the implications of having laws that intersect and to develop a coherent body of law in the field. A broader operation for section 109 also leaves the States with fewer incentives to engage with the Commonwealth in a sustained manner given the higher likelihood that their legislative contributions will be declared invalid. Further, it reduces the number of areas in which the States can legislate and thus contribute to debates between the government and people by serving as policy laboratories. Conversely, a narrower operation generates greater scope for Commonwealth and State laws to coexist, thus creating greater space for engagement to occur in the form of intergovernmental consultation and cooperation as well as for State experimentation. A close connection thus exists between the interpretation of section 109 and deliberation.

Recognising this connection yields two conclusions that map onto the discussion above about the ways in which the Court might recognise this constitutional value.

[33] *Clyde Engineering Co Ltd v Cowburn* (1926) 37 CLR 466, 489 (Isaacs J).

First, in the event of uncertainty, the Court could prefer a narrower rather than a broader application of section 109 to help protect deliberation. In particular, the Court might not readily find an implied intention to cover the field because the Commonwealth can always express its intention to cover the field using express words.[34] An interpretation of section 109 that demonstrates a modest preference for an express rather than implied intention to cover the field has the additional advantage of facilitating deliberation in Commonwealth Parliament by requiring parliamentarians to turn their minds to the issue and make a deliberate, public decision to exclude any State law in the same field.

Second, the Court could accord a degree of deference to State laws that are the product of a deliberative process. If a State has consulted, or perhaps even attempted to consult, with the Commonwealth and enacted a law that demonstrates an inclusive, informed and reasonable attempt to cohere with the Commonwealth law, the Court could err in favour of validity if the arguments for and against validity are finely balanced. In its more ambitious form, this approach would entail looking to parliamentary records and other supplementary materials to determine if State parliamentarians have deliberated on these issues. In its more modest form, this approach would entail looking to the terms of the State law to ascertain whether it has been drafted in a way that minimises the degree of conflict with Commonwealth law—in other words, to ascertain whether or not there is a reasonable, less intrusive or less conflictual means of achieving the purpose of the State law. Here the complementarity of the terms of the State law is employed as a proxy for deliberation because it is more likely that the State has engaged in some form of deliberation if it has taken care to enact complementary legislation. Indeed, the Court has already demonstrated some willingness to adopt reasoning along these lines. In *Jemena Asset Management (3) Pty Ltd v Coinvest Ltd*,[35] the Court found the State law to be valid under section 109 because 'it is possible to infer from the beneficial nature of the federal instruments that the Commonwealth legislature did not intend to exclude *a compatible State law*'.[36] It is possible to strengthen this factor by describing it as one that emanates not from the intention of Commonwealth Parliament, but instead directly from the Constitution as a consequence of the deliberative form of government that it presupposes. A compatible State law demonstrates respect for this constitutional presupposition, which weighs in favour of its validity.

ii. Section 61

The executive's power under section 61 to contract and spend money deeply implicates the system of government that the Constitution establishes. As French CJ observed in *Williams [No 1]*, the 'governmental contract "is now a powerful tool of public administration"'.[37] That tool can be, and has been, used to centralise power in the executive, which affects federalism and bicameralism to the extent that

[34] *Botany Municipal Council v Federal Airports Corporation* (1992) 175 CLR 453.
[35] *Jemena Asset Management (3) Pty Ltd v Coinvest Ltd* (2011) 244 CLR 508.
[36] ibid 528 [57] (French CJ, Gummow, Heydon, Crennan, Kiefel and Bell JJ) (emphasis added).
[37] *Williams [No 1]* (2012) 248 CLR 156, 193 [38].

it diminishes the role of the Senate and affects responsible government to the extent that it erodes the ability of Parliament to hold the executive to account. In *Williams [No 1]*, the Court recognised the potential for the executive's power to contract and spend to undermine the constitutional system of government and sought to ameliorate this issue. In particular, it identified the risk to federalism that arises if the executive can spend money pursuant to a contract without approval of the Senate, the chamber established to represent the States in Commonwealth Parliament. The Court responded to this issue by adopting a narrowing construction of the executive's power to contract and spend money, the result of which is to require the executive to obtain legislative authorisation in many circumstances. The Senate is thus brought back into the picture because legislative authorisation requires approval from both Houses of Parliament.

Two aspects of the Court's decision merit attention for the purposes of the present analysis. First, it held that protection of the federal system of government requires the Court to do more than simply enforce the terms of the Constitution. Section 83 provides a role for the Senate in the approval of the executive's activities by prohibiting the executive from spending money except under appropriation made by law. However, the Court went beyond enforcement of this provision, holding that the federal system of government requires the Senate to exercise a larger degree of control over the executive's power to spend money than that provided by section 83 because section 53 restricts the Senate's powers in relation to proposed laws appropriating money.[38] It was thus concerned not merely with ensuring that the Senate has an *opportunity* to participate, but also with the *quality* of that participation. This distinction broadly mirrors the one between discourse and deliberation—discourse is the opportunity to speak while deliberation refers to speech of a particular quality. *Williams [No 1]* thus demonstrates that the Court has the capacity and willingness to draw on the system of government that the Constitution establishes to impose more requirements on an institution than the terms of the Constitution strictly require.

Second, the Court's form of response was not to create a freestanding limitation on power, but instead to adopt a narrow interpretation of the power. French CJ said:

> There are consequences for the Federation which flow from attributing to the Commonwealth a wide executive power to expend moneys, whether or not referable to a head of Commonwealth legislative power, and subject only to the requirement of a parliamentary appropriation … That is *not a criterion of invalidity*. It is, however, *a reason not to accept the broad contention* that such activities can be undertaken at the discretion of the Executive, subject only to the requirement of appropriation.[39]

Thus, the Court is familiar with the task of drawing on the system of government that the Constitution establishes in subtle ways.

Williams [No 1] generated a number of questions about the executive's power to contract and spend that are yet to be resolved. One of them is the degree or extent of legislative authorisation that the executive requires. The types of authorisation that could be given to the executive can be mapped on a spectrum that varies

[38] ibid 205 [60] (French CJ).
[39] ibid 193 [37] (emphasis added).

according to its scope and level of detail, stretching from a one-line provision empowering the executive to contract and spend on *any subject* within the scope of Commonwealth legislative power through to a provision that grants the executive the power to make *the precise contract* that is appended to the statute and only that contract. If the High Court were minded to draw on the concept of deliberation, it would offer some assistance in resolving this matter. Deliberation is *informed* discourse. A complete absence of detail about the contract in the authorising law thus undermines deliberation between the executive and Parliament. The lack of detail is, however, ultimately one that Parliament accepts. The bigger concern is that a complete absence of detail undermines deliberation between government and the people because members of the public will often not have ready access to the contracts that the executive makes, but will have ready access to the legislation that Parliament enacts. Thus, if the Court were minded to draw on the concept of deliberation in this area, it would counsel against accepting as sufficient legislative authorisation a plenary conferral of power that has no information about the nature and scope of contract that the executive can make. While reliance on the concept of deliberation would not definitively resolve this issue, it would narrow the range of options, excluding those at one end of the spectrum, and suggest that, in developing the law in this area, it should prefer results that require more rather than less detail in the authorising law.

iii. Section 71

The High Court's power to enforce the Constitution is a considerable one. A decision declaring an executive or legislative act to be incompatible with the Constitution can cause considerable inconvenience for a government.[40] To identify just a few examples, the States collectively lost $5 billion in revenue as a result of the Court's decision in *Ha v New South Wales*,[41] the validity of over 400 Commonwealth programmes was called into question following the Court's decision in *Williams [No 1]*,[42] a major plank of the Commonwealth's social security legislation was invalidated in *Attorney-General (Vic); ex rel Dale v Commonwealth* (*Pharmaceutical Benefits Case*),[43] and the cross-vesting scheme created by the Commonwealth and States was undone by the decision in *Re Wakim; Ex parte McNally*.[44] The potential for considerable

[40] For an alternative view that the inconvenience caused by the High Court's decisions is not as significant as most people think, see H Irving, 'Advisory Opinions, the Rule of Law, and the Separation of Powers' (2004) 4 *Macquarie Law Journal* 105, 130–32.

[41] *Ha v New South Wales* (1997) 189 CLR 465. For details of the Commonwealth and States' hurried and, consequently, disorderly response to the decision, see A Twomey, 'Federal Limitations on the Legislative Power of the States and the Commonwealth to Bind One Another' (2003) 31 *Federal Law Review* 507, 523–25.

[42] *Williams [No 1]* (2012) 248 CLR 156. For a discussion of the ramifications of the Court's decision, see the special issue dedicated to the case that begins with J Allan and R Mortensen, 'Special Issue: After Williams' (2014) 33 *University of Queensland Law Journal* vii.

[43] *Attorney-General (Vic); ex rel Dale v Commonwealth* (1945) 71 CLR 237. For a discussion of the significance of this decision for the Commonwealth's social security programmes, see R Sackville, 'Social Welfare in Australia: The Constitutional Framework' (1973) 5 *Federal Law Review* 248.

[44] *Re Wakim; Ex parte McNally* (1999) 198 CLR 511. For a discussion of the implications of this decision, see G Hill, 'The Demise of Cross-Vesting' (1999) 27 *Federal Law Review* 547.

inconvenience to follow from a judicial decision is exacerbated in Australia by the fact that the Court generally refuses to consider inconvenience to government to be a factor counselling against the adoption of a particular position in law.[45]

The inconvenience that judicial decisions can cause is partly a result of the fact that the Court's declarations of invalidity take effect immediately. It is not merely that the government must respond to a decision, but that they must respond in a very short period of time to settle the legal disruption caused or to fill the legal void created by the judiciary. It is not, however, clear that the Constitution requires declarations of invalidity to take effect immediately. The Constitution contains few indications about the scope of 'the judicial power of the Commonwealth' that Chapter III courts exercise under section 71. As Dixon CJ and McTiernan J observed in *R v Davison*, although '[m]any attempts have been made to define judicial power … it has never been found possible to frame a definition that is at once exclusive and exhaustive'.[46] However, the Court has tended to take a view of judicial power that is not particularly supportive of the position that it could issue declarations of invalidity that do not take effect immediately. It has narrowly defined the scope of its activities, holding that, as judicial power entails the making of binding and authoritative decisions, it cannot issue advisory opinions[47] or non-binding declarations of incompatibility.[48] In *Ha v New South Wales*, the joint majority judgment ruled out the possibility of prospectively overruling an existing Court decision on the following basis:

> A hallmark of the judicial process has long been the making of binding declarations of rights and obligations arising from the operation of the law upon past events or conduct. The adjudication of existing rights and obligations as distinct from the creation of rights and obligations distinguishes the judicial power from non-judicial power. Prospective overruling is thus inconsistent with judicial power on the simple ground that the new regime that would be ushered in when the overruling took effect would alter existing rights and obligations. If an earlier case is erroneous and it is necessary to overrule it, it would be a perversion of judicial power to maintain in force that which is acknowledged not to be the law. This would be especially so where, as here, non-compliance with a properly impugned statute exposes a person to criminal prosecution.[49]

While these comments relate to prior judicial decisions, this line of reasoning is arguably applicable to declarations of invalidity, thus suggesting that they must take effect immediately.

If the Court were minded to consider the concept of deliberation in the interpretation of the Constitution, it might adopt a more liberal construction of the term 'judicial power' found in section 71 that would permit the Court to issue suspended declarations of invalidity in some circumstances. A suspended declaration

[45] See, eg, *Re Wakim; Ex parte McNally* (1999) 198 CLR 511, 540 [2] (Gleeson CJ), 548 [34], 554 [49] (McHugh J), 569 [94] (Gummow and Hayne JJ); *Williams v Commonwealth* (2014) 252 CLR 416, 464–65 [65] (French CJ, Hayne, Kiefel, Bell and Keane JJ) (*Williams [No 2]*).

[46] *R v Davison* (1954) 90 CLR 353, 366.

[47] *In Re Judiciary and Navigation Acts* (1921) 29 CLR 257.

[48] *Momcilovic v The Queen* (2011) 245 CLR 1.

[49] (1997) 189 CLR 465, 503–04 (Brennan CJ, McHugh, Gummow and Kirby JJ), 515 (Dawson, Toohey and Gaudron JJ).

of invalidity holds that a law is invalid by reason of incompatibility with the Constitution, but suspends the day on which the invalidation takes effect for a specified period of time (eg, 12 months). It is a remedial mechanism that helps protect deliberation in Parliament and between government and the people by giving the executive time to consider the full range of possible responses to the Court's decision and to consult the public on different options. Declarations of invalidity that take effect immediately can deprive Parliament of the time necessary to conduct enquiries and to debate the merits of various proposals, and can deprive the public of the time necessary to make submissions to government and, more generally, to form an opinion on the issue and for that opinion to filter back to government through the media and other channels. Creating a period of time between the announcement of the Court's decision and the date on which the Court's order takes effect responds to these issues, securing the temporal space that is necessary for deliberation to occur.

Suspended declarations of invalidity are used by courts in other countries such as the Supreme Court of Canada and the Constitutional Court of South Africa.[50] The use of this remedial option in these countries has been praised in terms of its effect on deliberation. In Canada, Mary Liston writes that a suspended declaration of invalidity 'aims to encourage dialogue horizontally among co-equal constitutional actors (eg, the executive, legislature and judiciary) as well as vertically between citizens and the state'.[51] In South Africa, Sandra Liebenberg states that the mechanism 'illustrate[s] a flexible, dialogic approach' to interactions between the judiciary, other branches of government and civil society.[52] By contrast, Robert Leckey identifies a number of harms that suspended declarations of invalidity can cause, including that they may leave the individual claimant without a remedy and that they may leave a law that has been found to violate rights on the statute book such that it can continue to be enforced against other people.[53] These concerns echo the abovementioned observation of the High Court in *Ha v New South Wales* that 'it would be a perversion of judicial power to maintain in force that which is acknowledged not to be the law ... especially ... where ... non-compliance with a properly impugned statute exposes a person to criminal prosecution'.[54]

While suspended declarations of invalidity are not free from criticism, there are two points that attenuate the strength of these concerns. First, the proposed interpretation of section 71 would empower, *not require*, the Court to issue suspended declarations of invalidity. In many, and perhaps even most, cases where a declaration of invalidity is issued, suspension would not be appropriate. The Court would be entrusted to suspend a declaration of invalidity only where such harms would not

[50] For an overview of the types of cases where Canadian and South African courts have issued suspended declarations of incompatibility, see R Leckey, 'The Harms of Remedial Discretion' (2016) 14 *International Journal of Constitutional Law* 584, 587–88.

[51] M Liston, 'Honest Counsel: Institutional Dialogue and the Canadian Rule of Law' (PhD Thesis, University of Toronto, 2007) quoted in ibid 585.

[52] S Liebenberg, *Socio-Economic Rights: Adjudication under a Transformative Constitution* (Claremont, Juta, 2010) 397.

[53] Leckey, above n 50, 591–93.

[54] (1997) 189 CLR 465, 503–04 (Brennan CJ, McHugh, Gummow and Kirby JJ).

follow. While there might be concerns about granting the Court such a discretionary power,[55] it does no more than mirror the discretionary powers that all courts already exercise in relation to many other remedies (eg, the discretion to award an injunction or damages).

Second, the risks presented by suspended declarations of invalidity may be lower in the Australian context due to the absence of a constitutional bill of rights. Declarations of invalidity in Australia tend to, but by no means always,[56] relate to non-compliance with structural provisions or principles such as the separation of powers or the federal division of powers. In many, but again by no means all,[57] of these cases, the cause of invalidity is not that a government took a particular action (eg, that the government enacted a policy that violated a person's rights), but instead that the *wrong* level of government took the action (eg, the States took an action that is reserved to the Commonwealth or the Commonwealth took an action that can only be taken by the States) or that the government did not comply with the necessary *procedures* before taking the action (eg, the executive failed to obtain sufficient legislative authorisation before proceeding). While compliance with these provisions and principles is essential, the need for *immediate* compliance is arguably not essential. This is especially the case given that, first, some of these actions will have taken place for many years prior to the finding of invalidity[58] and, second, the government's response to some of these decisions will simply be to take the exact same action according to the procedure set out in or implied by the Court's ruling.[59] Further, the deliberative benefits of permitting government to delay compliance for a short period of time (eg, six to 12 months) may be significant, for instance, giving government time to consider a broader range of responses to the decision and to consult the public about different options.

IV. CONCLUSION

Delving into the realm of constitutional values is a difficult exercise. Complexity and disagreement surround the identification of the values that the Constitution embodies and the implications of their identification, especially for the judiciary. This chapter attempts to investigate deliberation as an Australian constitutional value in a way that is responsive to these concerns. It argues that the Constitution presupposes a deliberative form of government because four constitutional structures or principles—federalism, bicameralism, responsible government and representative democracy—would be seriously imperilled if discourse between the relevant

[55] See generally Leckey, above n 50.

[56] See, eg, the declarations of invalidity that stem from the implied freedom of political communication.

[57] See, eg, the declarations of invalidity that stem from violations of s 92, which apply to both the Commonwealth and States.

[58] See, eg, *Ha v New South Wales* (1997) 189 CLR 465.

[59] See, eg, the legislation enacted after *Williams [No 1]* (2012) 248 CLR 156 that was the subject of challenge in *Williams [No 2]* (2014) 252 CLR 416. As the invalidation of the response legislation in the latter case demonstrates, attempting to do the bare minimum to comply with a judicial decision does not always succeed.

institutions or actors—the Commonwealth and States, the Houses of Parliament, the executive and Parliament, and government and the people respectively—became exclusive, uninformed and irrational. However, the chapter also argues that the Constitution presupposes only a modest degree of deliberation in terms of its elements—the Constitution does not require all the elements that a scholar of deliberative democracy would require—and its adherence—the Constitution does not require discourse to be of a deliberative standard at all times and all places. The second section of the chapter proposes three areas where the High Court could draw on the concept of deliberation if it were minded to recognise it as a constitutional value. The suggestions are modest in scope. No new freestanding limitations on power are proposed. Instead, the focus is on ways in which provisions of the Constitution could be interpreted more broadly or narrowly to help protect deliberation.

9

Political Equality as a Constitutional Principle: Cautionary Lessons from McCloy v New South Wales

JOO-CHEONG THAM*

I. INTRODUCTION

It is not difficult to see why those sympathetic to the functionalism project would welcome the High Court's decision in *McCloy v New South Wales* (*McCloy*).[1] If 'functionalism, at its core, invites courts directly and openly to rely on substantive constitutional values, not simply more "formal" legal sources',[2] the decision in *McCloy* clearly meets this requirement with the High Court emphatically endorsing political equality as a constitutional principle.[3] The joint judgment of French CJ, Kiefel, Bell and Keane JJ, for one, stated that '[e]quality of opportunity to participate in the exercise of political sovereignty is an aspect of the representative democracy guaranteed by our Constitution'.[4]

Yet direct and open reliance on values in constitutional adjudication is not the only defining feature of functionalism. There is, first, a crucial condition of *legitimacy:* the values relied upon should be 'directly sourced in the text, history and structure of the *Constitution*'.[5] Functionalism in this way is 'backward-looking'[6] (and not dissimilar from formalism).[7] Secondly, there is the goal of *effectiveness* in the sense that functionalism seeks to advance the values relied upon in constitutional adjudication. This goal explains its focus on 'the potential consequences of various legal choices for the

* Special thanks to Jason Goliszek for excellent research assistance and also to Rosalind Dixon and Jeff Goldsworthy for their comments on an earlier draft.

[1] *McCloy v New South Wales* (2015) 257 CLR 178.

[2] R Dixon, 'The Functional Constitution: Re-reading the 2015 High Court Constitutional Term' (2015) 43 *Federal Law Review* 455, 456.

[3] This chapter uses 'constitutional principle' rather than 'constitutional value' principally because this is how the High Court refers to political equality in *McCloy*. Whether there is any difference in meaning between these two terms depends on the level of abstraction at which the principle or value is couched.

[4] *McCloy* (2015) 257 CLR 178, 207 [45].

[5] Dixon, 'The Functional Constitution', above n 2, 462. See also at 456.

[6] R Dixon, 'Response to Commentators' (2015) 43 *Federal Law Review* 517, 517.

[7] See ch 3 by Jeffrey Goldsworthy in this collection.

realisation of these [values]'.[8] It would also seem to inform the 'forward-looking' aspect of functionalism that looks to 'comparative constitutional law, experience and scholarship to ascertain the range of plausible functions or values served by the relevant structures';[9] and also the suggestion that functionalism may provide an antidote to the charge of 'legalistic obfuscation'[10] laid against judicial review.[11] And third, functionalism would seem to place a premium on *clarity* in seeking to provide 'transparency and predictability, and a strong commitment to the rule of law'.[12]

The High Court's decision in *McCloy* highlights how open reliance on a constitutional value—political equality in this case—does not necessarily align with other features of functionalism. It illustrates how such reliance can result in less clarity and indeterminacy; how it can fail to be properly anchored in the text and structure of the Constitution, giving rise to problems of legitimacy; and how it may undermine the realisation of the value itself.

This chapter begins with a brief summary of the judgments in *McCloy* with a focus on how the judges characterised political equality as a constitutional principle. This is followed by a three-part analysis examining the question of the meaning(s) of this principle; the question of its legitimacy in terms of this principle being adequately supported by the text and structure of the Constitution; and its effectiveness in advancing the broader project of political equality.

This chapter's key arguments are that the High Court in *McCloy* failed to provide sufficient clarity in terms of the meaning of this principle; that the High Court's characterisation of political equality as a constitutional principle is not properly sourced in the text and structure of the Constitution; and that this characterisation risks injuring the project of political equality because of a presumption against discriminatory laws and the unresolved balance between legislative competence and judicial oversight.

II. *McCLOY v NEW SOUTH WALES*

Three aspects of the Election Funding, Expenditure and Disclosures Act 1981 (NSW) (EFED Act) were challenged in *McCloy* on the basis that they breached the implied freedom of political communication:

1. The ban on 'property developers' under division 4A part 6 of the EFED Act.
2. The caps on political donations under division 2A part 6 of the EFED Act.
3. The ban on indirect campaign contributions exceeding $1000 under section 96E of the EFED Act.[13]

[8] Dixon, 'The Functional Constitution', above n 2, 459. See also at 464, 466.

[9] Dixon, 'Response to Commentators', above n 6, 518. Jeffrey Goldsworthy has argued that the 'forward-looking' approach 'collapses into pragmatism': see ch 3 by Jeffrey Goldsworthy in this collection.

[10] J Waldron, 'The Core of the Case Against Judicial Review' (2006) 115 *Yale Law Journal* 1346, 1406.

[11] See the introduction by Rosalind Dixon in this collection.

[12] Dixon, 'The Functional Constitution', above n 2, 455, 456. See also at 492.

[13] *McCloy* (2015) 257 CLR 178, 200 [21] (French CJ, Kiefel, Bell and Keane JJ).

These challenges were brought by Jeffrey McCloy and two of his companies, McCloy Admin and North Lakes.[14] North Lakes was a 'property developer' within the meaning of the EFED Act in the sense of being

> a corporation engaged in a business that regularly involves the making of relevant planning applications by or on behalf of the corporation in connection with the residential or commercial development of land, with the ultimate purpose of the sale or lease of the land for profit.[15]

By virtue of being a director of North Lakes, McCloy, a self-described 'walking ATM',[16] was a 'close associate' of North Lakes, and therefore also a 'property developer' within the meaning of the Act.[17] From about October 2010, McCloy had made political donations and thereby breached the ban in relation to 'property developers'. The amounts of these contributions also exceeded the caps on political donations imposed under the EFED Act. McCloy Admin had further made an indirect campaign contribution within the meaning of the EFED Act.[18]

The Court handed down four judgments: a joint judgment by French CJ, Kiefel, Bell and Keane JJ; and separate judgments by Gageler J, Nettle J and Gordon J. All the judges except for Nettle J concluded that the ban on 'property developers' under division 4A part 6 of the EFED Act did not infringe the implied freedom of political communication. The entire Court found that the caps on political donations under division 2A part 6 of the EFED Act and the ban on indirect campaign contributions exceeding $1000.00 under section 96E of the EFED Act did not infringe the freedom.

A. The Joint Judgment of French CJ, Kiefel, Bell and Keane JJ

The joint judgment recast the test for determining whether a law breaches the implied freedom of political communication in the following terms:

> The question whether an impugned law infringes the freedom requires application of the following propositions derived from previous decisions of this Court and particularly *Lange v Australian Broadcasting Corporation* and *Coleman v Power*:
>
> A. The freedom under the Australian Constitution is a qualified limitation on legislative power implied in order to ensure that the people of the Commonwealth may 'exercise a free and informed choice as electors'. It is not an absolute freedom. It may be subject to legislative restrictions serving a legitimate purpose compatible with the system of representative government for which the Constitution provides, where the extent of

[14] ibid 275 [277] (Gordon J).
[15] EFED Act s 96GB(1)(a).
[16] Michaela Whitbourn and Kate McClymont, 'I Feel Like a Walking ATM: Newcastle Lord Mayor Jeff McCloy Admits Giving Tens of Thousands of Dollars to Liberal Candidates' *The Sydney Morning Herald* (online) (15 August 2014): <www.smh.com.au/nsw/i-feel-like-a-walking-atm-newcastle-lord-mayor-jeff-mccloy-admits-giving-tens-of-thousands-of-dollars-to-liberal-candidates-20140813-103plf.html>.
[17] EFED Act ss 96GB(1)(b), (3)(a).
[18] *McCloy* (2015) 257 CLR 178, 275 [277]–[279] (Gordon J).

the burden can be justified as suitable, necessary and adequate, having regard to the purpose of those restrictions.

B. The question whether a law exceeds the implied limitation depends upon the answers to the following questions, reflecting those propounded in *Lange* as modified in *Coleman v Power*:

1. Does the law effectively burden the freedom in its terms, operation or effect?

   If 'no', then the law does not exceed the implied limitation and the enquiry as to validity ends.

2. If 'yes' to question 1, are the purpose of the law and the means adopted to achieve that purpose legitimate, in the sense that they are compatible with the maintenance of the constitutionally prescribed system of representative government? This question reflects what is referred to in these reasons as 'compatibility testing'.

   The answer to that question will be in the affirmative if the purpose of the law and the means adopted are identified and are compatible with the constitutionally prescribed system in the sense that they do not adversely impinge upon the functioning of the system of representative government.

   If the answer to question 2 is 'no', then the law exceeds the implied limitation and the enquiry as to validity ends.

3. If 'yes' to question 2, is the law reasonably appropriate and adapted to advance that legitimate object? This question involves what is referred to in these reasons as 'proportionality testing' to determine whether the restriction which the provision imposes on the freedom is justified.

   The proportionality test involves consideration of the extent of the burden effected by the impugned provision on the freedom. There are three stages to the test—these are the enquiries as to whether the law is justified as suitable, necessary and adequate in its balance in the following senses:

   — *suitable*—as having a rational connection to the purpose of the provision;
   — *necessary*—in the sense that there is no obvious and compelling alternative, reasonably practicable means of achieving the same purpose which has a less restrictive effect on the freedom;
   — *adequate in its balance*—a criterion requiring a value judgment, consistently with the limits of the judicial function, describing the balance between the importance of the purpose served by the restrictive measure and the extent of the restriction it imposes on the freedom.

   If the measure does not meet these criteria of proportionality testing, then the answer to question 3 will be 'no' and the measure will exceed the implied limitation on legislative power.[19]

i. Burden

Following *Unions NSW v New South Wales* (*Unions NSW*), the joint judgment in *McCloy* concluded that the challenged provisions burdened the implied freedom

[19] ibid 193–95 [2] (citations omitted) (emphasis in original).

because they restricted the funds available to New South Wales political parties and candidates to engage in political communication.[20] The joint judgment considered that a burden did not arise because of the communicative content of political donations in themselves—'the act of donation is not itself a political communication'.[21]

They further rejected the plaintiffs' submission that the provisions burdened the freedom because it impinged upon the ability of donors to 'build and assert political power' by making 'substantial political donations in order to access and make representations to politicians and political parties'.[22] This was on the ground that the submission 'appears to mistakenly equate the freedom under our Constitution with an individual right such as is conferred by the First Amendment to the United States Constitution'.[23]

Another reason for the rejection of this submission stemmed from the adoption by the joint judgment of the following statement by Harrison Moore: 'The great underlying principle [of the Constitution] is, that the rights of individuals were sufficiently secured by ensuring, as far as possible, to each a share, and an equal share, in political power'.[24] According to the joint judgment, 'guaranteeing the ability of a few to make large political donations in order to secure access to the those in power would seem to be antithetical to the great underlying principle to which Moore referred'.[25] It is clear here that political equality as a constitutional principle shaped the assessment of the joint judgment as to whether there is a burden on the implied freedom.

ii. Compatibility Testing

The joint judgment concluded that the purposes of the caps on political donations under division 2A part 6 and section 96E of the EFED Act—preventing the reality and perception of corruption and undue influence—are compatible with the system of representative government provided for by the Constitution.[26] The joint judgment also came to the same conclusion in relation to the purpose of the ban on 'property developers' under division 4A, which is 'to reduce the risk of undue or corrupt influence in an area of planning decisions, where such risk may be greater than in other areas of official decision-making'.[27]

Here the joint judgment adopted a broad approach to the meaning of corruption by identifying three types of corruption: 'quid pro quo' corruption; 'clientelism' corruption; and 'war-chest' corruption. The first type occurs when political contributions secure specific favours from the recipient public official. The second,

[20] ibid 201 [24]; *Unions NSW v New South Wales* (2013) 252 CLR 530.
[21] ibid 201 [25].
[22] ibid.
[23] ibid 202 [29].
[24] WH Moore, *The Constitution of the Commonwealth of Australia* (London, John Murray, 1902) 329. Favourably quoted in *McCloy* (2015) 257 CLR 178, 202 [27] (French CJ, Kiefel, Bell and Keane JJ), 226 [110] (Gageler J), 258 [219] (Nettle J), 283–84 [318] (Gordon J).
[25] *McCloy* (2015) 257 CLR 178, 202 [28].
[26] ibid 208 [47].
[27] ibid 209 [53].

'clientelism' corruption, 'arises from an office-holder's dependence on the financial support of a wealthy patron to a degree that is apt to compromise the expectation, fundamental to representative democracy, that public power be exercised in the public interest'.[28]

While the first two types of corruption 'threaten the quality and integrity of governmental decision-making', 'war-chest' corruption arises when 'the power of money … pose[s] a threat to the electoral process itself'.[29] Here the joint judgment made reference again to the principle of political equality. It did so by favourably citing the judgment of Lord Bingham in *R (Animal Defenders International) v Secretary of State for Culture, Media and Sport (Animal Defenders)* for his Lordship's view that 'in a democracy it is highly desirable that the playing field of public debate be so far as practicable level'.[30]

The principle of political equality was also at the forefront of the joint judgment's rejection of United States First Amendment jurisprudence. Referring to '[t]he view that now prevails (in relation to the First Amendment) that an attempt by the legislature to level the playing field to ensure that all voices may be heard is, prima facie, illegitimate',[31] their Honours stated '[t]hat is not the case with respect to the Australian Constitution'.[32] According to the joint judgment, '[l]egislative regulation of the electoral process directed to the protection of the integrity of the process is … prima facie legitimate'.[33]

Their Honours went on to refer to the decision in *Australian Capital Television Pty Ltd v Commonwealth* (*ACTV*) which accepted '[t]he legitimacy of the concerns that the electoral process be protected from the corrupting influence of money and to place "all in the community on an equal footing so far as the use of the public airwaves is concerned"'.[34] They also favourably referred to the Canadian Supreme Court judgment in *Attorney-General of Canada v Harper* (*Harper*) where the majority endorsed 'the egalitarian model of elections adopted by Parliament as an essential component of our democratic society'.[35]

In what is probably the key paragraph of the joint judgment dealing with political equality, their Honours stated that:

> Equality of opportunity to participate in the exercise of political sovereignty is an aspect of the representative democracy guaranteed by our Constitution. In *ACTV*, the law which was struck down was inimical to equal participation by all the people in the political process and this was fatal to its validity. The risk to equal participation posed by the uncontrolled use of wealth may warrant legislative action to ensure, or even enhance, the practical enjoyment of popular sovereignty.[36]

[28] ibid 204–05 [36].
[29] ibid 205 [38].
[30] *R (Animal Defenders International) v Secretary of State for Culture, Media and Sport* [2008] AC 1312, [28], quoted in ibid 205 [39].
[31] *McCloy* (2015) 257 CLR 178, 205–06 [41].
[32] ibid 206 [42].
[33] ibid.
[34] ibid 206–07 [43]; *Australian Capital Television Pty Ltd v Commonwealth* (1992) 177 CLR 106.
[35] ibid 207 [44], quoting *Harper* [2004] 1 SCR 827, 868.
[36] ibid 207 [45] (citations omitted).

Of significance is footnote 67 of the joint judgment, which is the reference accompanying its statement that '[e]quality of opportunity to participate in the exercise of political sovereignty is an aspect of the representative democracy guaranteed by our Constitution'. That footnote—which this analysis will return to—cites paragraphs from four judgments: Deane and Toohey JJ in *Nationwide News Pty Ltd v Wills* (*Nationwide News*); Mason CJ in *ACTV*; Keane J in *Unions NSW* and Keane J in *Tajjour v New South Wales* (*Tajjour*).[37]

iii. Proportionality Test

The joint judgment concluded that the challenged measures were suitable in terms of having a rational connection to their purposes;[38] necessary in the sense that there were no obvious and compelling reasonably practicable alternative means of achieving the same purpose while having a less restrictive effect on the freedom;[39] and also adequate in their balance.[40]

Political equality figured in the third stage of the proportionality test—adequacy in their balance—which, according to the joint judgment, 'present[ed] no difficulty for the validity of the impugned provisions'.[41] Their analysis of this stage is found in the following paragraph:

> The provisions do not affect the ability of any person to communicate with another about matters of politics and government nor to seek access to or to influence politicians in ways other than those involving the payment of substantial sums of money. The effect on the freedom is indirect. By reducing the funds available to election campaigns there may be some restriction on communication by political parties and candidates to the public. On the other hand, the public interest in removing the risk and perception of corruption is evident. *These are provisions which support and enhance equality of access to government, and the system of representative government which the freedom protects.* The restriction on the freedom is more than balanced by the benefits sought to be achieved.[42]

B. Gageler J

In explaining why there is an implied freedom of political communication under the Commonwealth Constitution, Gageler J, like the joint judgment, referred to the 'great underlying principle' of Moore to underscore the constitutional significance of electoral choice:

> Electoral choice is the means of constituting the Parliament of the Commonwealth, and of indirectly constituting the Executive Government of the Commonwealth. Electoral choice thereby constitutes the principal constraint on the constitutional exercise by the Parliament

[37] See text accompanying below nn 102–08.
[38] *McCloy* (2015) 257 CLR 178, 210 [56].
[39] ibid 210–12 [57]–[63].
[40] ibid 220–01 [93].
[41] ibid.
[42] ibid (emphasis added).

> of the legislative power of the Commonwealth, and on the lawful exercise by Ministers and officers within their departments of the executive power of the Commonwealth.[43]

Gageler J proceeded to trace '[t]he necessity for the implication of the constitutional freedom as a limitation on legislative and executive power' to 'a paradox inherent in the nature of the majoritarian principle which governs electoral choice'.[44] According to his Honour:

> The paradox is that communication of information relevant to the making of an informed electoral choice is peculiarly susceptible to being restricted or distorted through the exercise of legislative or executive power precisely because the exercise of legislative or executive power is subject to the ultimately controlling influence of electoral choice.[45]

Gageler J further elaborated by stating that:

> The ever-present risk within the system of representative and responsible government established by Chs I and II of the Constitution ... that communication of information which is either unfavourable or uninteresting to those currently in a position to exercise legislative or executive power will, through design or oversight, be impeded by legislative or executive action to an extent which impairs the making of an informed electoral choice and therefore undermines the constitutive and constraining effect of electoral choice.[46]

For Gageler J:

> The judicial power, insulated from the electoral process by the structural requirements of Ch III of the Constitution, is uniquely placed to protect against that systemic risk. Here, as elsewhere within our constitutional tradition, 'the absolute independence of the judiciary is the bulwark of the constitution against encroachment whether by the legislature or by the executive'.[47]

The principle of political equality also came into the judgment of Gageler J in a different way, and this time around not as a constitutional principle. Like Nettle and Gordon JJ, Gageler J applied the two-limb *Lange v Australian Broadcasting Corporation* (*Lange*)[48] test, rather than the approach adopted by the joint judgment.[49] This was partly because his Honour was not persuaded that 'one size fits all'[50]—'[n]o unitary standard of justification can or should be applied across all categories of cases'.[51]

For Gageler J, the standard of justification in the context of the conduct of elections for political office should be exacting: for restrictions on political communication in this context to be compatible with the implied freedom, they should be

> imposed in pursuit of an end which is appropriately characterised within our system of representative and responsible government as compelling; and that the imposition of

43 ibid 226 [111].
44 ibid 227 [114].
45 ibid.
46 ibid 227 [115].
47 ibid 227–28 [116], quoting *Attorney-General (Cth) v The Queen* (1957) 95 CLR 529, 540.
48 *Lange v Australian Broadcasting Corporation* (1997) 189 CLR 520.
49 See the 'two principal reservations' of Gageler J: *McCloy* (2015) 257 CLR 178, 235–39 [141]–[152].
50 ibid 235 [142].
51 ibid 238–39 [152].

> the restriction in pursuit of that compelling end can be seen on close scrutiny to be a reasonable necessity.[52]

Here, Gageler J resorted to the principle of political equality in order to emphasise the significance of the objectives of the challenged provisions. For Gageler J, 'the elimination of preferential access to government which results from the making of political donations' is not only a legitimate legislative objective but 'a compelling legislative objective'.[53]

C. Nettle J

The principle of political equality was central to Nettle J's judgment. In the concluding paragraph his Honour stated that 'equality of political power ... is at the heart of the Australian constitutional conception of political sovereignty'.[54] Nettle J also referred to Moore's 'great underlying principle' in order to distinguish the implied freedom under the Australian Constitution from the United States First Amendment which 'puts emphasis on individual rights'.[55]

The constitutional principle of political equality also shaped his Honour's application of the *Lange* test. Significantly, Nettle J connected this principle with a presumption against laws that impose a discriminatory burden on the implied freedom. For Nettle J

> an impugned law which restricts the ability of some sections of the electorate to engage in a significant aspect of the political process while leaving others free to do as they choose mandates an inequality of political power which strikes at the heart of the system.[56]

Such discriminatory laws, according to Nettle J, required a 'strong justification',[57] a view that Nettle J supported by reference to Mason CJ and Deane and Toohey JJ's judgments in *ACTV* and also Keane J's judgment in *Unions NSW*.[58]

Hence for Nettle J, a strong justification was required in relation to the ban on 'property developer' donations under division 4A part 6 of the EFED Act because it 'discriminate[s] against a particular segment of the community, and thus against the expression of their particular political views'.[59] According to Nettle J, such a justification was lacking, leading his Honour to find this ban invalid:

> [B]y focussing on property developers, the prohibited donor provisions arbitrarily discriminate against property developers in a manner which deprives them as a section of the electorate of an ability enjoyed by other sections of the electorate of making political donations and so participating in the political system.[60]

[52] ibid 239 [155].
[53] ibid 248 [184].
[54] ibid 273–74 [271].
[55] ibid 258 [219].
[56] ibid 273–74 [271].
[57] ibid 259 [222], 267 [251].
[58] ibid 267 [251].
[59] ibid 270 [257].
[60] ibid 272 [266].

D. Gordon J

Like Gageler and Nettle JJ, Gordon J applied the *Lange* test and did not adopt the joint judgment's method of analysing whether there was a breach of the implied freedom. This was partly because of her Honour's view that '[t]he questions stated for the opinion of the Court in this case are able to be answered by reference to the known questions and tools'.[61] Further, according to Gordon J, '[t]he method or structure of reasoning to which the plurality refers does not yield in this case an answer any different from that reached by the accepted modes of reasoning'.[62]

As if to underscore the last statement, Gordon J, like the joint judgment,[63] referred to Moore's 'great underlying principle' to reject the plaintiffs' submission that the implied freedom protected a right to 'build and assert' political power, as such a right is 'contrary to the "great underlying principle" of the Constitution that the rights of individuals are secured by ensuring *each* individual has an *equal* share in political power'.[64]

This 'great underlying principle' was also relevant to Gordon J's analysis of the second limb of the *Lange* test: whether the challenged provisions pursued a legitimate objective; and if so, whether they were reasonably appropriate and adapted to serve that legitimate end. For Gordon J, the caps on political donations under division 2A part 6 of the EFED Act and the restriction on indirect campaign contributions under section 96E of the Act pursued a legitimate objective, among others, because they sought to 'ensure that the rights of individuals are secured so that *each* individual has an *equal* share, or at least a more equal share than they would otherwise have, in political power'.[65] This (intended) effect was also a reason why these measures and the ban on 'property developer' donations under division 4A were reasonably appropriate and adapted to serve their legitimate ends.[66]

III. OPENLY UNCLEAR

Broadly speaking, the idea of political equality concerns the institutional requirements that flow from an egalitarian ideal.[67] It is, however, neither simple nor straightforward to draw out the institutional implications of an abstract egalitarian ideal—whether it be based on equal political status of citizens,[68] an obligation on the state to act with equal concern for the life of each citizen[69] or an assumption

[61] ibid 282 [311].
[62] ibid.
[63] See text accompanying above nn 24–25.
[64] *McCloy* (2015) 257 CLR 178, 283–84 [318] (emphasis in original).
[65] ibid 285 [324] (emphasis in original); see also at 296 [376].
[66] ibid 290 [344], 294 [365], 297 [381].
[67] See G Sartori, *The Theory of Democracy Revisited* (Chatham, Chatham House Publishers, 1987) vol 1, ch 12; CR Beitz, *Political Equality: An Essay in Democratic Theory* (Princeton, Princeton University Press, 1989); R Dworkin, *Sovereign Virtue: The Theory and Practice of Equality* (Cambridge, Harvard University Press, 2000) ch 4; RA Dahl, *On Political Equality* (New Haven, Yale University Press, 2006).
[68] Beitz, above n 67, 17.
[69] Dworkin, above n 67, 184.

that all human beings are of equal intrinsic worth.[70] Such a task is often attended by a degree of confusion, despite—perhaps because of—widespread acceptance of the principle of political equality.

As Robert Alan Dahl pointedly observed of political equality: 'its meaning and its relation to democracy, and to the distribution of resources that a citizen can use to influence public decisions, are not, I think, well understood'.[71]

Unfortunately, the High Court's decision in *McCloy* fails to provide clarity in this complex area. The lack of clarity is evident when we consider the metric of political equality—equality of what? Is it equality of opportunity to participate, as appears from the joint judgment?[72] Or is it equal participation as also alluded to in the joint judgment?[73] Or is it equality of access to government as appears in the penultimate paragraph of the joint judgment?[74]

Or is power the metric of equality, as Moore would have it? And if it is power, surely not all aspects of power can be equalised in the inherently dynamic political process; what aspect of political power then is to be equalised?[75] Or is it freedom that is to be equalised in the context of the implied freedom? And if so, is it negative freedom (freedom from) and/or positive freedom (freedom to)?

There is also a distinct lack of clarity in terms of the constituency of equality—equality of whom? Does political equality mean equality of electors as seems to be the case with parts of Nettle J's judgment?[76] Or is it political equality of individuals as appears from the quote from Moore? Or is it political equality of citizens, as is suggested from the High Court decisions in *Roach v Electoral Commissioner* (*Roach*),[77] *Rowe v Electoral Commissioner* (*Rowe*)[78] and also *Murphy v Electoral Commissioner* (*Murphy*)[79] (the latter was decided after *McCloy*)?

Or, even broader, is it equality of those subject to the laws of the Commonwealth, including legal entities like corporations? This is an understanding that could be inferred from the High Court's decision in *Unions NSW*; it is also one that seems to find expression in the judgment of Nettle J in *McCloy* where he disturbingly considered 'property developers' under the EFED Act—which are commercial corporations—to be part of the electorate[80] and 'the community'.[81]

Or, finally, is political equality as advanced by the Court in *McCloy* that of 'the people' as referred to in sections 7 and 24 of the Constitution?

Despite the comment by French CJ in *Rowe* that the adoption of universal adult-citizen franchise had caused the concepts of 'electors' and 'the people' to

[70] RA Dahl, *Democracy and its Critics* (New Haven, Yale University Press, 1989) 83–96; Dahl, *On Political Equality*, above n 67, 4.
[71] Dahl, *On Political Equality*, above n 67, ix.
[72] *McCloy* (2015) 257 CLR 178, 207 [45] (French CJ, Kiefel, Bell and Keane JJ).
[73] ibid.
[74] ibid 220–01 [93].
[75] Beitz, above n 67, 7–16. On the absence of an 'unequivocal conception of power', see at 7.
[76] *McCloy* (2015) 257 CLR 178, 257 [216].
[77] *Roach v Electoral Commissioner* (2007) 233 CLR 162.
[78] *Rowe v Electoral Commissioner* (2010) 243 CLR 1.
[79] *Murphy v Electoral Commissioner* (2016) 90 ALJR 1027.
[80] *McCloy* (2015) 257 CLR 178, 272 [266].
[81] ibid 270 [257].

converge, 'the people' in this context is not necessarily coextensive with either electors or citizens.[82] This is for two opposing reasons. The High Court's decision in *Attorney-General (NSW) ex rel McKellar v Commonwealth*[83] and its holding that the 'people of the Commonwealth' under section 24 did not include the people of the Territories—whether citizens or not—would point to an understanding of the 'people' that is narrower than either electors or citizens.

On the other hand, the way in which the 'people of the Commonwealth' has been operationalised under the second paragraph of section 24 would suggest a broader understanding of the 'people'. As this is a neglected paragraph with important implications for understanding the meaning of the 'people' and the constituency of political equality under the Australian Constitution, a slight detour is in order.

The second paragraph of section 24 provides:

> The number of members chosen in the several States shall be in proportion to the respective numbers of their people, and shall, until the Parliament otherwise provides, be determined, whenever necessary, in the following manner:
>
> (i) a quota shall be ascertained by dividing the number of the people of the Commonwealth, as shown by the latest statistics of the Commonwealth, by twice the number of the senators;
>
> (ii) the number of members to be chosen in each State shall be determined by dividing the number of the people of the State, as shown by the latest statistics of the Commonwealth, by the quota; and if on such division there is a remainder greater than one-half of the quota, one more member shall be chosen in the State.

The Commonwealth Parliament has, in fact, 'otherwise provide[d]', by legislating a method of calculating the number of 'the people of the Commonwealth' in a manner that closely conforms to the default method spelled out in section 24 by using the 'latest statistics of the Commonwealth' as the basis of calculations.[84] The Australian Bureau of Statistics (ABS), in turn, determines the population of Australia by reference to the concept of 'usual residence' based on the 12-month rule (a person is considered to have Australia as their 'usual residence' if he or she has stayed in Australia for at least 12 months or intends to do so).[85]

The key point to be made here is that those considered 'people of the Commonwealth' under this approach extends beyond Australian citizens or electors. As the ABS puts it, the estimated population based on this method 'refers to all people, *regardless of nationality or citizenship*, who usually live in Australia' and captures 'permanent residents and long-term visitors from overseas (including students)'.[86]

This approach also highlights how a citizenship-based understanding of the Australian constitutional community as reflected in *Roach*, *Rowe* and *Murphy* can

[82] *Rowe* (2010) 243 CLR 1, 19.

[83] *Attorney-General (NSW) ex rel McKellar v Commonwealth* (1977) 139 CLR 527.

[84] Commonwealth Electoral Act 1918 (Cth) ss 46–47.

[85] See B Pink, 'Population Concepts' (Information Paper No 3107.0.55.006, Australian Bureau of Statistics, 2008); P Harper, 'Population Estimates: Concepts, Sources and Methods' (No 3228.0.55.001, Australian Bureau of Statistics, 2009).

[86] Pink, above n 85, 1–2 (emphasis added). See also A Reilly and T Torresi, 'Voting Rights of Permanent Residents' (2016) 39 *UNSW Law Journal* 401.

disenfranchise many of those who would—from a different perspective—be considered part of the Australian community. The exclusionary effects of a citizenship-based understanding of political community were well illustrated by the case of *Bennett v Commonwealth* (*Bennett*), where long-term residents of Norfolk Island—who were previously able to vote and stand for election to the Legislative Assembly of Norfolk Island—unsuccessfully challenged amendments that made Australian citizenship a necessary qualification for both.[87]

It can be seen here that the question of the constituency of political equality is bound up with understandings of the political community underlying the Constitution or 'the Australian constitutional community'.[88] The failure of the High Court in *McCloy* to engage the latter question, including relevant dicta in *Roach*,[89] explains in part its confusion on the question of the constituency of political equality.

IV. NOT PROPERLY SOURCED IN TEXT AND STRUCTURE OF THE CONSTITUTION

It is surprising to have such a strong endorsement of political equality as a constitutional principle from the High Court. It would seem to fly in the face of the Court's decisions in *Attorney-General (Cth) ex rel McKinlay v Commonwealth* (*McKinlay*)[90] and *McGinty v Western Australia* (*McGinty*),[91] both of which rejected the proposition that the Constitution required an equal number of electors (or persons) in electoral districts.

These decisions, in fact, point to deeper difficulties with wrestling a principle of political equality from the Australian Constitution. As McHugh J stated in *McGinty*, '[e]quality of voting power is not a fundamental feature of the Constitution. On the contrary, inequality of individual voting power is one of its striking features'.[92] This led his Honour to conclude that '[u]nder the Constitution … individual Australians do not have an equal share in the sovereignty of Australia'.[93]

As can be gathered from the quote from McHugh J, the difficulties in concluding that there is a constitutional principle of political equality are two-fold. The text of

[87] *Bennett v Commonwealth* (2007) 231 CLR 91.

[88] E Arcioni, 'The Core of the Australian Constitutional People: "The People" as "The Electors"' (2016) 39 *UNSW Law Journal* 421; E Arcioni, 'Democracy and the Constitution: The People Deciding the Identity of "The People"' in G Patmore and K Rubenstein (eds), *Law and Democracy: Contemporary Questions* (Canberra, ANU Press, 2014); E Arcioni, 'Section 53 of the Constitution: An Overlooked Reference to the Constitutional People' (2013) 87 *Australian Law Journal* 784; E Arcioni, 'Excluding Indigenous Australian from "The People": A Reconsideration of Sections 25 and 127 of the Constitution' (2012) 40 *Federal Law Review* 287; E Arcioni, 'Some Comments on amici curaie and "The People" of the Australian Constitution' (2010) 22 *Bond Law Review* 148. See also discussion in P Emerton, 'Political Freedoms and Entitlements in the Australian Constitution: An Example of Referential Intentions Yielding Unintended Legal Consequences' (2010) 38 *Federal Law Review* 169, 196–200.

[89] See especially the statement by Gummow, Kirby and Crennan JJ in *Roach* that 'the existence and exercise of the franchise reflects notions of citizenship and membership of the Australian federal body politic': *Roach* (2007) 233 CLR 162, 199.

[90] *Attorney-General (Cth) ex rel McKinlay v Commonwealth* (1975) 135 CLR 1.

[91] *McGinty v Western Australia* (1996) 186 CLR 140.

[92] ibid 236.

[93] ibid.

the Constitution, first, makes no direct mention of this principle. In particular, there is no mention of this principle in sections 7 or 24. As Gibbs J said in *McKinlay* of s 24, '[i]t does not mention equality';[94] Mason J similarly said in that case that the submission that section 24 provided for 'one vote, one value … finds no support in the language itself'.[95]

Secondly, there are constitutional provisions that are at odds with a principle of political equality. There is the Senate which provides for equal representation of States but not equal representation of electors, citizens or people.[96] There are also provisions that clearly contemplated disenfranchisement of key groups of Australian society: people of particular races in section 25 and women in sections 41 and 128.

But what about the system of representative government prescribed under the Constitution?[97] Is the joint judgment in *McCloy* not correct in saying that '[e]quality of opportunity to participate in the exercise of political sovereignty is an aspect of the representative democracy guaranteed by our Constitution'?[98]

There are two pathways through which the joint judgment reaches this conclusion: the first is reliance on a statement by Moore and the other is a citation of four decisions in footnote 67. Neither provide a secure foundation for their conclusion.

The statement by Moore favourably quoted by all the judges in *McCloy* is as follows:

> The great underlying principle [of the Constitution] is, that the rights of individuals were sufficiently secured by ensuring, as far as possible, to each a share, and an equal share, in political power.[99]

This statement followed an earlier—broader—claim by Moore that '[t]he predominant feature of the Australian Constitution is the prevalence of the democratic principle, in its modern guise'.[100]

Both statements were made by way of contrasting the American Constitution with the Australian Constitution. As Moore put it:

> The federalism of Australia is the federalism of the United States; her democracy is her own. The American Constitution was born in distrust … The Constitution of the Commonwealth of Australia bears every mark of confidence in the capacity of the people to undertake every function of government.[101]

So according to Moore, the American and Australian constitutions differed significantly in terms of the trust they placed in the government. This, in turn, shaped the constitutional measures adopted to protect rights and freedoms:

> In one notable matter, the Australian Constitution differs markedly from that of the United States. In America, the checks and balances devised by the Fathers of the Constitution

94 *McKinlay* (1975) 135 CLR 1, 45.
95 ibid 61.
96 Australian Constitution s 7.
97 *Lange* (1997) 189 CLR 520, 557–59.
98 *McCloy* (2015) 257 CLR 178, 207 [45] (French CJ, Kiefel, Bell and Keane JJ).
99 Moore, above n 24, 329. Favourably quoted in *McCloy* (2015) 257 CLR 178, 202 [27] (French CJ, Kiefel, Bell and Keane JJ), 226 [110] (Gageler J), 258 [219] (Nettle J), 283–84 [318] (Gordon J).
100 Moore, above n 24, 327.
101 ibid 327–28.

> were deemed an insufficient restraint of power, and were immediately supplemented by a comprehensive Bill of Rights, which placed the liberties of the citizens under the protection of the Constitution, and secured them against any attack by the Federal Government ... From the Australian Constitution such guarantees of individual rights are conspicuously absent ... *The great underlying principle [of the Constitution] is, that the rights of individuals were sufficiently secured by ensuring, as far as possible, to each a share, and an equal share, in political power.*[102]

It can be clearly seen here that for Moore, political equality is a principle that explained the breadth of power conferred upon the Commonwealth Parliament under the Australian Constitution and its trust in parliamentary processes to protect rights and freedoms.

Whatever reservations one might have regarding Moore's arguments, it is incongruous to rely on them—as the judges in *McCloy* did—to invoke a principle of political equality that *constrains* legislative power through the implied freedom of political communication which is informed by more than a hint of *distrust* in Parliament.

Such incongruity was, in fact, recognised in the judgment of Mason CJ in *ACTV* where his Honour treated the statement by Moore not so much as *justification* for the implied freedom but more so as a principle which the implication of the freedom had to be reconciled with. Immediately after quoting Moore on the 'great underlying principle', Mason CJ said:

> In the light of this well recognized background, it is difficult, if not impossible, to establish a foundation for the implication of general guarantees of fundamental rights and freedoms. To make such an implication would run counter to the prevailing sentiment of the framers that there was no need to incorporate a comprehensive Bill of Rights in order to protect the rights and freedoms of citizens. That sentiment was one of the unexpressed assumptions on which the Constitution was drafted.[103]

The incongruity of relying upon Moore's 'great underlying principle' sits alongside the weakness of the decisions cited in footnote 67. As noted earlier, four judgments were cited in this footnote: *Nationwide News* (Deane and Toohey JJ); *ACTV* (Mason CJ); *Unions NSW* (Keane J); and *Tajjour* (Keane J). These judgments are of weak precedential value: none of them are majority decisions; none, except that of Mason CJ in *ACTV*, can be said to be the key judgment of the cases they were part of.

Further, two of these judgments do not lend support to the claim of political equality as a constitutional principle as advanced by the joint judgment (and Gordon J). First, the part of Mason CJ's judgment in *ACTV* that is cited in *McCloy* is the paragraph where his Honour quotes Moore's 'great underlying principle'. As discussed above, this quote was not relied upon to draw out a constitutional principle of political equality informing the operation of the implied freedom. Secondly, the cited paragraphs of the judgment of Keane J in *Unions NSW*, while referring to the 'political sovereignty of the people of the Commonwealth',[104] make no mention of political equality.[105]

[102] ibid 328–29 (emphasis added).
[103] *Australian Capital Television Pty Ltd v Commonwealth* (1992) 177 CLR 106, 137 (Mason CJ).
[104] *Unions NSW v New South Wales* (2013) 252 CLR 530, 578 [135].
[105] ibid 578 [135]–[136].

The absence of a reference to political equality in these paragraphs also affects the cogency of another judgment cited in footnote 67, that of Keane J in *Tajjour*. The cited paragraph of that judgment states that '[t]he constitutional guarantee to the people of the Commonwealth of a free and informed choice as electors ensures free communication between them as equal participants in the exercise of political sovereignty'.[106]

The problem with this statement in *Tajjour* is that it relies upon the abovementioned paragraphs of Keane J's judgment in *Unions NSW* which make no mention of political equality.

This leaves the judgment of Deane and Toohey JJ in *Nationwide News*. In the paragraphs cited in footnote 67, their Honours state that:

> In implementing the doctrine of representative government, the Constitution reserves to the people of the Commonwealth the ultimate power of governmental control … While one can point to qualifications and exceptions, such as those concerned with the protection of the position of the less populous States, *the general effect of the Constitution is, at least since the adoption of full adult suffrage by all the States, that all citizens of the Commonwealth who are not under some special disability are entitled to share equally in the exercise of those ultimate powers of governmental control*.[107]

There are several difficulties with the reference to political equality in Deane and Toohey JJ's judgment. The judgment of McTiernan and Jacobs JJ in *McKinlay* is cited for support when it does nothing of that kind.[108] More significantly, the constitutional provisions their Honours refer to do not support a principle of political equality. These are provisions relating to the constitutionally prescribed system of representative and responsible government (sections 7, 24, 64 and 128). In a broad sense, these sections do provide for 'political sovereignty'[109] by 'reserv[ing] to the people of the Commonwealth the ultimate power of governmental control'. But it is one thing to identify the repository of (ultimate) sovereignty, 'the people', and another to suggest that such a conferral comes with requirements as to *how* such sovereignty is to be exercised, least of all that such sovereignty is to be exercised based on political equality.

This point is consistent with the interpretation placed on 'directly chosen by the people' in sections 7 and 24 by the High Court in *Roach*, *Rowe* and *Murphy*. Whatever the correctness of these decisions,[110] they stand at their broadest[111] for the proposition that a burden on the constitutional mandate of members of the House

[106] *Tajjour v New South Wales* (2014) 254 CLR 508, 593 [197].

[107] *Nationwide News Pty Ltd v Wills* (1992) 177 CLR 1, 72 (emphasis added) (citations omitted).

[108] ibid 72, fn 27. See generally *McKinlay* (1975) 135 CLR 1, 36.

[109] *McCloy* (2015) 257 CLR 178, 207 [45] (French CJ, Kiefel, Bell and Keane JJ), 257 [215]–[217], 273–74 [271] (Nettle J).

[110] See comments in *Murphy* (2016) 90 ALJR 1027, 1065 [222] (Keane J), 1069–70 [243]–[244] (Nettle J). See further R Greenwood, 'A Progressive Court and a Balancing Test: *Rowe v Electoral Commissioner*' (2010) 14 *University of Western Sydney Law Review* 119; G Orr, 'The Voting Rights Ratchet' (2011) 22 *Public Law Review* 83; A Twomey, '*Rowe v Electoral Commissioner:* Evolution or Creationism?' (2012) 31 *University of Queensland Law Journal* 181; J Allan, 'The Three "R"s of Recent Australian Judicial Activism: *Roach*, *Rowe* and (No) 'Riginalism' (2012) 36 *Melbourne University Law Review* 743.

[111] But see the narrow ratio attributed to *Rowe* by Nettle J in *Murphy: Murphy* (2016) 90 ALJR 1027, 1069 [239]–[240].

of Representatives and the Senate being 'directly chosen by the people'—including universal adult citizen suffrage—will be constitutionally invalid unless it is for a substantial reason.[112] The concern here is clearly with *who* is entitled to choose the elected representatives, not how they choose, let alone an implication that the process of choice should accord with a requirement of political equality. Not surprisingly, the High Court in *McCloy* did not cite either *Roach* or *Rowe* in support of its characterisation of political equality as a constitutional principle.

Reasoning from the 'political sovereignty' of 'the people' to a constitutional principle of political equality seems to conflate the vertical and horizontal dimensions of power relationships in a system of representative government.[113] The vertical dimension concerns the relationship between those who govern (elected representatives) and those who are governed ('the people'); it is this dimension that 'political sovereignty' of 'the people' implicates. Political equality, on the other hand, concerns the horizontal dimension—that is how 'the people' exercise political power.

Drawing out a constitutional principle of political equality by such a conflation seems to reason from an understanding of representative democracy not adequately anchored in the text and structure of the Constitution. If so, there is an apparent breach of the following injunction in *Lange*: 'Under the Constitution, the relevant question is not, "What is required by representative and responsible government?" It is, "What do the terms and structure of the Constitution prohibit, authorise or require?"'[114]

V. INJURING THE PROJECT OF POLITICAL EQUALITY?

The functionalism project seeks to be effective in the sense of advancing constitutional values and principles. In the case of *McCloy*, there are grounds for doubting whether the High Court's characterisation of political equality as a constitutional principle will advance the project of political equality (however understood); indeed there are reasons for fearing that *McCloy* might undermine this project. These reasons stem, first, from the presumptive stance against discriminatory laws arising in particular from the judgment of Nettle J; and, secondly, from the unresolved balance between legislative competence and judicial oversight.

A. Proscribing Discrimination without Discernment?

A concern with laws that discriminate in the sense of providing for differential treatment is clear from various judgments involving the implied freedom of political communication.[115] It was prominent in the judgment of Mason CJ in *ACTV* where

[112] See *Murphy* (2016) 90 ALJR 1027, 1036–37 [29]–[31] (French CJ and Bell J), 1047–48 [84]–[86] (Gageler J), 1059 [181], 1063–64 [208]–[210] (Keane J), 1070 [244] (Nettle J), 1078 [291] (Gordon J).

[113] Dworkin, above n 67.

[114] *Lange* (1997) 189 CLR 520, 567.

[115] See ch 11 by Amelia Simpson in this collection on discrimination in other constitutional contexts.

the Chief Justice concluded that 'it is the discriminatory effect of the free time provisions that is the principal reason for the invalidity of the regulatory scheme'[116]—by being 'weighted in favour of the established political parties represented in the legislature immediately before the election and the candidates of those parties',[117] the regime (unconstitutionally) discriminated against new and independent candidates as well as potential participants in the electoral process.[118]

A concern with such discriminatory laws is also evident in the judgment of Keane J in *Unions NSW*. In this case, his Honour found that by restricting the ability to make political donations to those on the electoral rolls, section 96D of the EFED Act breached the implied freedom, among others, because 'it is itself apt to distort the flow of political communication within the federation by disfavouring some sources of political communication and thus necessarily favouring others'.[119] Similarly with sections 96G(6) and 96G(7) of the Act which aggregated the spending of affiliated organisations to the relevant political party:

> Political communication generated by electoral communication expenditure by organisations affiliated with a party is disfavoured relative to political communication by entities which, though actively supportive of, and indeed entirely ad idem with, a given party, are not affiliated with it. To discriminate between sources of political communication in this way, in the sense of the term used by Mason CJ in *ACTV* and discussed above in relation to s 96D, is to distort the flow of political communication.[120]

A concern with such discriminatory laws also arguably informed the plurality's striking down of the challenged provisions in *Unions NSW* with section 96D characterised as 'selective'[121] and sections 96G(6)–(7) said to be 'targeting'[122] particular groups and individuals.

In *McCloy*, the judgment of Gageler J alluded to the centrality of such discrimination to the conclusion of invalidity of Mason CJ in *ACTV*.[123] In her Honour's judgment, Gordon J also asked whether the ban on 'property developer' donations under division 4A was 'discriminatory in its nature in relation to property developers such that it is invalid?' and answered in the negative.[124]

It is the judgment of Nettle J where the concern with discriminatory laws is most acute. Tracing this concern to the constitutional principle of political equality,[125] his Honour insisted on a 'strong justification'[126] for laws imposing a discriminatory burden on the implied freedom. For Nettle J, there is a presumptive stance against such discriminatory laws.

Such a presumptive stance might seem rather compelling. The language of discrimination can, however, be deceptively simple and obscure key complexities. One

[116] *ACTV* (1992) 177 CLR 106, 147.
[117] ibid 146.
[118] ibid 145–46.
[119] *Unions NSW* (2013) 252 CLR 530, 579 [140].
[120] ibid 586 [167] (citations omitted).
[121] ibid 558 (French CJ, Hayne, Crennan, Kiefel and Bell JJ).
[122] ibid 559, 561 (French CJ, Hayne, Crennan, Kiefel and Bell JJ).
[123] *McCloy* (2015) 257 CLR 178, 233–34 [136]–[137].
[124] ibid 294 [366] (Gordon J).
[125] See text accompanying above nn 56–57.
[126] *McCloy* (2015) 257 CLR 178, 259 [222], 267–68 [251].

set of complexities is perhaps surprising: when is a law said to discriminate in the context of the implied freedom? Take for instance the caps on political contributions under the EFED Act challenged in *McCloy*. If discrimination means differential treatment, why were these caps not said to discriminate? True, the caps applied to all donors. At the same time, however, as the lawyers for *McCloy* correctly pointed out, the caps had a disproportionate impact on those who were able to make donations exceeding their maximums, and in that sense discriminated against the wealthy—that was their point. The caps also set different maximums for donations to registered parties, unregistered parties, groups of candidates, candidates and third-party campaigners,[127] and consequently had varied impacts on the political funds these various political actors could use to engage in political communication. Why did such varied impacts not constitute discrimination in the context of the implied freedom?

This brings us to another—more foundational—set of complexities: why should laws that discriminate in the sense of providing for differential treatment be presumptively illegitimate? As caps on political donations illustrate, laws that discriminate against the wealthy are necessary to 'level the playing field' when political 'capital' is unequally shared.

This points to two difficulties with the presumptive stance against discriminatory laws: its formalism and its simplistic normative premise. The presumptive stance is formalistic in the sense that it implies that it is the form of the law that is determinative as to whether the law is compatible with the constitutional principle of political equality. Of course, the form of the law is always a relevant consideration and, in some cases, a decisive consideration (consider the disenfranchisement of Indigenous peoples, women and those from Asian backgrounds). At the same time, the formal provisions of the law must be viewed in their societal context, and this context will often have a profound impact on how we judge the formal provisions. So it is that formal provisions that do not mete out differential treatment are more likely to be seen as fair in the context where there is a high degree of equality among those to whom they apply. On the other hand, the same provisions might warrant the charge of unfairness if they are applied in the context of stark inequalities. The formalism of a presumption against discriminatory laws might then reflect an adherence to equality of formal freedoms blind to societal inequalities. More than a century ago, Anatole France mocked the poverty of such a view, stating '[t]he law, in its majestic equality, forbids the rich as well as the poor to sleep under bridges, to beg in the streets, and to steal bread'.[128]

Such formalism with its neglect of societal inequalities can result in a failure to appreciate how, in some cases, discriminatory laws can be the lesser of two evils. This is well illustrated by the decision in *ACTV*. As noted earlier, a key reason for the invalidity of the laws challenged in *ACTV* was their discrimination in favour of established political parties and against new and independent candidates as well as other potential participants in terms of the allocation of 'free' broadcasting time. The evidence on the effect of the challenged provisions before being struck down,

[127] EFED Act s 95A(1).

[128] A France, *The Red Lily* (London, The Bodley Head, 1894) ch 7.

however, showed that they had a 'levelling' effect in terms of such time.[129] How is this possible? In essence, inequalities due to prohibitively expensive political broadcasts were more severe than those resulting from the statutory regime.[130] To borrow the words of the joint judgment in *McCloy*, whatever the faults of the 'free-time' regime invalidated in *ACTV*, it could be said that it enhanced 'the practical enjoyment of popular sovereignty'.[131]

As to the normative premise of a presumption against discriminatory laws, the assumption would seem to be that differential treatment is prima facie wrong and unconstitutional. This, however, fails to do justice to the moral (and constitutional) complexity attending differential treatment under laws. Gleeson CJ, Gummow, Hayne, Heydon and Crennan JJ alluded to such complexity in *Bennett*:

> Some forms of discrimination in the conferral or withholding of electoral rights may be unjust or unwise, or inconsistent with currently held democratic values. That does not necessarily mean they are unlawful. Other forms of discrimination are generally accepted. Fixing a minimum age for voting is one example.[132]

Such complexity suggests that a presumption against discriminatory laws wrongly reduces equality-as-justice to equality-as-sameness (under the laws).[133] But as Gummow and Hayne JJ correctly observed in *Mulholland v Australian Electoral Commission* (*Mulholland*), 'differential treatment and unequal outcomes may be the product of a legislative distinction which is appropriate and adapted to the attainment of a proper objective'.[134] Rather than the ham-fisted approach of a presumption against discriminatory laws, these statements suggest a need for a more discerning approach that distinguishes between discriminatory laws that are constitutional and those that are not. A useful starting point here is the statement of Gleeson CJ in *Austin v Commonwealth* that '[d]iscrimination is an aspect of a wider principle; and what constitutes relevant and impermissible discrimination is determined by that wider principle'.[135]

While made in the context of the implied intergovernmental immunities, this statement applies to the development of any test in relation to discriminatory laws in the context of the implied freedom of political communication, if there is to be one: such a test should be firmly anchored in the 'wider principle', which is in case is the constitutionally prescribed system of representative government.

B. The Unresolved Balance between Legislative Competence and Judicial Oversight

Contested principles like human rights and democracy yield a range of understandings. All these principles are, as Jeremy Waldron has convincingly argued, subject

[129] GN Rosenberg and JM Williams, 'Do Not Go Gently into That Good Right: The First Amendment in the High Court of Australia' [1997] *Supreme Court Review* 439, 479–86.
[130] ibid 481.
[131] *McCloy* (2015) 257 CLR 178, 207 [45].
[132] *Bennett* (2007) 231 CLR 91, 109.
[133] See discussion in Sartori, above n 67, 338–41.
[134] *Mulholland v Australian Electoral Commission* (2004) 220 CLR 181, 234.
[135] *Austin v Commonwealth* (2003) 215 CLR 185, 217 [24].

to reasonable disagreement.[136] So it is with political equality—as the foregoing discussion has demonstrated—with its concrete meaning dependent upon how the constituency and metric of political equality as well as the political community are understood. Given this, judicial and legislative understandings of political equality will not be necessarily congruent; so much is illustrated by the High Court's decisions in *ACTV* and *Unions NSW*, with the challenged laws in both cases enacted to 'level the playing field' but found to be constitutionally invalid because they disproportionately affected particular groups.

Disagreement on the meaning of political equality between the legislature and judiciary brings the question of the balance between legislative competence and judicial oversight in the area of electoral law to the fore. While the joint judgment in *McCloy* did discuss 'the boundaries between the legislative and judicial functions' in terms of the implied freedom,[137] none of the judges except Gageler J considered what the specific boundaries were to be when it came to the particular context of political equality and electoral law.

As noted earlier,[138] Gageler J traced the justification for the implied freedom of political communication as a constraint on legislative and executive power to 'a paradox inherent in the nature of the majoritarian principle which governs that electoral choice',[139] and that the making of such a choice may be distorted by the exercise of legislative and executive power because such power is 'subject to the ultimately controlling influence of electoral choice'.[140] Further, judicial independence secured through Chapter III of the Constitution meant that the judiciary 'is uniquely placed to protect against that systemic risk'.[141]

These statements of Gageler J[142] have a powerful element of truth—they are nevertheless partial truths. The paradox identified by Gageler J is real but not the only one in this context. In *Judd v McKeon*, Isaacs J stated that:

> The community organized, being seised of the subject matter of parliamentary elections and finding no express restrictions in the Constitution, may properly do all it thinks necessary to make elections as expressive of the will of the community as they possibly can be.[143]

This paragraph suggests that the exercise of legislative power in relation to elections is an expression of 'the will of the community'. As put in another part of his Honour's judgment:

> Each elector may—*if that be the will of the community expressed by its Parliament*—be placed under a public duty to record his opinion as to which of the available candidates shall in relative preference become the representative or representatives of the constituency in Parliament.[144]

136 J Waldron, *Law and Disagreement* (Oxford, Clarendon Press, 1999).
137 *McCloy* (2015) 257 CLR 178, 220 [90].
138 See text accompanying above n 44.
139 *McCloy* (2015) 257 CLR 178, 227 [114].
140 ibid.
141 ibid 227–28 [116].
142 Gageler J made similar statements in *Murphy* (2016) 90 ALJR 1027, 1049 [95]–[96].
143 *Judd v McKeon* (1926) 38 CLR 380, 385.
144 ibid 386 (emphasis added).

Isaacs J's dicta can be summed up in another paradox—the power of the Commonwealth Parliament over federal elections, in particular how it affects democracy, is itself profoundly democratic given that Parliament is supposed to represent the views of the community.[145]

More recently, Gleeson CJ in *Mulholland* expressed similar sentiments:

> Leaving it to Parliament, subject to certain fundamental requirements, to alter the electoral system in response to changing community standards of democracy is a democratic solution to the problem of reconciling the need for basic values with the requirement of flexibility.[146]

By comparison to the scepticism expressed by Gageler J, these statements point to more benign views of legislative power in relation to elections—including communication relating to these elections.[147] Some of these benign views are made on the ground of (democratic) principle like those of Isaacs J and Gleeson CJ above. Others appear to be based more on practice—the legislative record. Take, for example, a House of Lords decision favourably cited by the joint judgment and Gageler J in *McCloy*,[148] *Animal Defenders*. In that decision, which upheld an *ongoing* ban on political advertisements that was far more extensive than that challenged in *ACTV*, Lord Bingham said that 'it is reasonable to expect that our democratically-elected politicians will be *peculiarly sensitive* to the measures necessary to safeguard the integrity of our democracy. It cannot be supposed that others, including judges, will be more so'.[149]

Both principle and practice come together to inform the benign view of legislative power over federal elections expressed by Barwick CJ in *McKinlay* that 'the Australian Constitution is built upon confidence in a system of parliamentary Government with ministerial responsibility'.[150] Barwick CJ stated further:

> Whilst, in my opinion, there is no constitutional guarantee of a universal franchise of equal voting strength or value, nor of practical equality in electoral divisions either in numbers of people or of electors, the Parliament in the Electoral Act has legislated a uniform adult franchise and has, in my opinion, made a real endeavour to secure equality of voting value when providing for the distribution of the States into electoral divisions ... the confidence reposed in the Parliament by s 30 and s 51 (xxxvi) has not, in my opinion, been misplaced.[151]

[145] For Isaacs J, the connection between the scope of power conferred upon the Commonwealth Parliament and the system of representative government under the Commonwealth Constitution went beyond the field of federal elections. In *Federal Commissioner of Taxation v Munro* (1926) 38 CLR 153, 178, his Honour stated that 'the Constitution is for the advancement of representative government' after highlighting the 'necessary constitutional means by which Parliament may in its discretion meet, and is at present accustomed to meet, the requirements of a progressive people'.

[146] *Mulholland* (2004) 220 CLR 181, 189.

[147] For fuller examination of the different judicial perspectives on the power of the Commonwealth Parliament in relation to federal elections, see Joo-Cheong Tham, 'Political Participation' in C Saunders and A Stone (eds), *The Oxford Handbook of the Australian Constitution* (Oxford University Press, 2018, forthcoming).

[148] *McCloy* (2015) 257 CLR 178, 205 [39] (French CJ, Kiefel, Bell and Keane JJ), 248 [182] (Gageler J).

[149] [2008] AC 1312, [33] (emphasis added).

[150] *McKinlay* (1975) 135 CLR 1, 24.

[151] ibid 25.

The legislative record of the Commonwealth Parliament in advancing political equality—again however understood—raises a deeper difficulty for Gageler J's emphasis on judicial oversight as an antidote to the 'systemic risk' he identified: the political process may provide for internal controls that address or alleviate this risk.[152] That Australia's electoral laws—including its regulation of electoral communication—is widely considered to be reasonably fair or more accurately, not grossly unfair,[153] would suggest that these internal controls are not only present but have some degree of efficacy.

A further difficulty with Gageler J's position is his resort to judicial independence as a justification for judicial oversight against 'the systemic risk'. The problem here is that the independence of the judiciary merely removes a negative—the very real risk that those holding legislative and executive power will seek to insulate themselves from the discipline of electoral accountability. Such independence, however, says very little as to the institutional competence of the judiciary to adjudicate over the substance of electoral laws. It was the conscious acknowledgment of the limits of such competence that led the Canadian Supreme Court in *Harper* to 'approach the justification analysis with deference'[154] when it came to electoral law for, in its view, 'the electoral system, which regulates many aspects of an election, including its duration and the control and reimbursement of expenses, reflects a political choice, the details of which are better left to Parliament'.[155] Notably, *Harper* upheld restrictions on political communication in the form of limits on third-party campaign spending.

One does not, however, need to go to Canada to find such judicial self-restraint. Eight years before *Harper* was handed down, Dawson J in *McGinty* affirmed the broad power of the Commonwealth Parliament over federal elections (and rejected a constitutional requirement of equality of voting power). Dawson J's judgment contains important passages on the rationale for the broad power conferred upon the Commonwealth Parliament in relation to federal elections. According to Dawson J, this exercise of this power required the Commonwealth Parliament 'to determine questions of a political nature about which opinions may vary considerably',[156] especially in light of the 'hundreds of electoral systems in existence today by which a form of representative government might be achieved'[157] with '[t]heir merits … judged by a number of different criteria which are likely to be incompatible with one another'.[158] As such, Dawson J considered it 'unwise to freeze into a constitutional requirement a particular aspect of an electoral system the attraction of which might vary at different times, in different conditions and to different eyes'.[159]

[152] See generally RA Dahl, *A Preface to Democratic Theory*, rev edn (Chicago, University of Chicago Press, 2006) 36.
[153] See the collection of essays in M Sawer (ed), *Elections: Full, Free & Fair* (Annandale, Federation Press, 2001).
[154] *Harper* [2004] 1 SCR 827, 879.
[155] ibid 878–79.
[156] *McGinty* (1996) 186 CLR 140, 183.
[157] ibid.
[158] ibid.
[159] ibid 186.

VI. CONCLUDING THOUGHTS

In its 1974 decision, *Buckley v Valeo* (*Buckley*), the United States Supreme Court infamously ruled that 'the concept that government may restrict the speech of some elements of our society in order to enhance the relative voice of others is wholly foreign to the First Amendment'.[160]

Decades later, *Buckley* remains powerfully influential with the Supreme Court in *McCutcheon v Federal Election Commission* stating in 2014 that '[n]o matter how desirable it may seem, it is not an acceptable governmental objective to "level the playing field", or to "level electoral opportunities", or to "equalize the financial resources of candidates"'.[161]

In *McCloy*, the High Court emphatically rejected the approach of the United States Supreme Court as to the illegitimacy of political equality or fairness as a legislative objective. On the contrary, under the Commonwealth Constitution, '[l]egislative regulation of the electoral process directed to the protection of the integrity of the process is … prima facie legitimate'.[162]

This is a very welcome development. If elections are to be 'free and fair', it would seem absurd to deny Parliament the ability to regulate with the view to advancing electoral fairness. As the McLachlin CJ and Major J observed in the Canadian Supreme Court decision in *Harper*, '[c]ommon sense dictates that promoting electoral fairness is a pressing and substantial objective in our liberal democracy'.[163]

Far less welcome, however, is the High Court's characterisation of political equality as a constitutional principle. In doing so, the High Court has opened the possibility of a dystopian (constitutional) vision of political equality insufficiently anchored in the text and structure of the Constitution with constitutional scrutiny exceeding the institutional competence of the judiciary; corporations on the same footing as natural persons; and formal freedoms consecrated to the neglect of societal inequalities.

All this prompts the question: what role is there for political equality in the functionalism project? The difficulties with sourcing such a principle in the text and structure of the Constitution would tend against any role.[164] This, however, is not necessarily an occasion for lament—it may avoid the confusion of meanings[165] and the risks to the broader project of political equality[166] that have arisen from *McCloy*. Standing against the constitutionalisation of political equality may after all prove to be the 'least dangerous' option.[167]

[160] *Buckley v Valeo*, 424 US 1 (1976) 649.
[161] *McCutcheon v Federal Election Commission*, 34 S Ct 1434, 1450 (2014).
[162] *McCloy* (2015) 257 CLR 178, 206 [42] (French CJ, Kiefel, Bell and Keane JJ).
[163] *Harper* [2004] 1 SCR 827, 845.
[164] See text accompanying above nn 90–114.
[165] See text accompanying above nn 57–89.
[166] See text accompanying above nn 115–59.
[167] Borrowing from Alexander Hamilton's Essay No 78 of the *Federalist Papers*; see also AM Bickel, *The Least Dangerous Branch: The Supreme Court at the Bar of Politics* (Indianapolis, Bobbs-Merrill, 1962).

Part IV

Individual Liberty and Equality

10

Liberty as a Constitutional Value: The Difficulty of Differing Conceptions of 'The Relationship of the Individual to the State'

JAMES STELLIOS*

I. INTRODUCTION

HAVING STATED THE principle from *Chu Kheng Lim v Minister for Immigration, Local Government and Ethnic Affairs*[1] that the adjudgement and punishment of criminal guilt requires an exclusive exercise of Commonwealth judicial power, Gageler J in *Magaming v The Queen* said:

> Why that should be so is founded on deeply rooted notions of the relationship of the individual to the state going to the character of the national polity created and sustained by the Constitution ... Chapter III of the Constitution ... reflects and protects a relationship between the individual and the state which treats the deprivation of the individual's life or liberty, consequent on a determination of criminal guilt, as capable of occurring only as a result of adjudication by a court.[2]

As with many of Gageler J's judgments, his Honour's reasons in *Magaming* reveal, what Rosalind Dixon might describe as, a functionalist approach to determining constitutional meaning:[3] one that looks to substantive goals and values to guide the resolution of constitutional controversies.[4] For his Honour, Chapter III of the Constitution identifies a structure through which government power is exercised; that structure marks out, at least in part, the contours of the relationship between

* I would like to thank Professor Rosalind Dixon for arranging this collection and the Workshop on Australian Constitutional Values held at UNSW in June 2016. My thanks also to the participants at that Workshop for their comments on this chapter and to the anonymous referee for helpful suggestions.

[1] *Chu Kheng Lim v Minister for Immigration, Local Government and Ethnic Affairs* (1992) 176 CLR 1, 27 (*Lim*).

[2] *Magaming v The Queen* (2013) 252 CLR 381, 400, 401 (*Magaming*).

[3] R Dixon, 'The Functional Constitution: Re-reading the 2014 High Court Constitutional Term' (2015) 43 *Federal Law Review* 455.

[4] ibid 459.

the individual and the state; and, in determining principles deriving from Chapter III, resort is had to the constitutional value that underpins that structure of government—the protection of an individual's liberty.

However, Gageler J's proposition about the relationship between the individual and the state is not self-evident. Nor is the liberty value that underpins it. One of the difficulties in understanding constitutional freedoms in Australia is that there are differing conceptions of 'the relationship of the individual to the state', and views vary as to the extent to which these different conceptions are embedded within our constitutional framework.

The matter is further complicated by the *federal* character of the Constitution. Constitutions can do more than identify the relationship of the individual to the state. Gageler J referred to the 'character of the *national* polity created and sustained by the Constitution'. However, it is clear that, to a very large extent, the Constitution is a federal compact and that federal character permeates every corner of the constitutional architecture. Thus, while Gageler J spoke of the 'relationship of the individual to the state', there are additional (or perhaps alternative) conceptions of the 'polity' that were 'created and sustained by the Constitution'.

This chapter seeks to explore the idea of liberty as a constitutional value and how a functional approach to determining constitutional meaning might draw on that constitutional value. It will become immediately apparent that liberty is a slippery concept and to speak of it as a constitutional value raises a number of indeterminacies. The chapter will seek to untangle some of the difficulties by exploring the premise of Gageler J's statement: what conception of the state is embedded within the constitutional system? It will be seen that differing conceptions of that relationship *can be* given meaning through the text and structure of the Constitution. Whether they *should be* depends upon a conception of the judicial role within the constitutional system. A functional approach to determining constitutional meaning may assist in exposing the assumptions underpinning various judicial choices and provide a framework for assessing the strength of those chosen positions.

II. LIBERTY AS A CONSTITUTIONAL VALUE: MARKING OUT THE TERRITORY

In grounding the separation of judicial power principles on a liberty-protecting conception of Chapter III, Gageler J did not identify any clear constitutional mandate for doing so. That is not surprising. Nowhere in the constitutional instrument is there a clear statement of its constitutional significance. The protection of liberty is not an express constitutional objective; nor is it captured in the text in the way that it is in the United States Constitution.[5] Yet, it cannot be denied that liberty is at the core of the constitutional system. Whatever it may mean, and conceptions of liberty do vary, the constitutional system identifies the relationship between the individual and the state giving liberty constitutional import. It readily can be accepted, therefore, that

[5] Where it is expressly referred to in the preamble and the Fifth and Fourteenth Amendments.

liberty is a constitutional value of the kind that Rosalind Dixon says might guide the search for constitutional meaning.[6]

However, identification of the nature of this constitutional liberty value is no easy task. The most obvious and common conception of liberty is freedom from detention in the custody of the state. That was the context of Gageler J's reasons in *Magaming*. But, viewing liberty in this way would be too narrow for the purposes of this chapter. The concept of liberty, at least in political theory, has a broader lens than physical security from an assertion of state power. Indeed, it has been an intensely contested concept. Liberal conceptions of 'liberty' have been seen in *negative* ('absence of interference') and *positive* ('gaining control or mastery of' oneself) terms.[7] A quite different conception sees 'liberty as non-domination'.[8] It is not the purpose of this chapter to assess these different conceptions or choose between them. What is important is to observe that each seeks to mark out the contours of the 'relationship between the individual and the state' as Gageler J sought to do. It is that broader relationship that will be applied as a framework in this chapter to explore the idea of liberty as a constitutional value.

However, this broader framework gives rise to further difficulties in marking out the constitutional terrain. Approached in this way, liberty is an ultimate constitutional value which is dependent, for its achievement, on intermediate constitutional values like representative and responsible government, democracy, separation of powers and (perhaps even) federalism. These intermediate constitutional values identify the constitutional structures through which power is organised and exercised, thereby defining the relationship between the individual and the state.

Given the absence of a clear constitutional commitment to liberty, and the range of structural mechanisms organising and controlling government power, it is not surprising that the constitutional system might give rise to differing conceptions of the relationship between the individual and the state and, consequently, differing understandings of liberty and what is necessary for its protection and advancement.

III. DIFFERING CONCEPTIONS OF THE RELATIONSHIP BETWEEN THE INDIVIDUAL AND THE STATE

'What is the extent of the lawful power of the state over its citizens? Or, to put the question the other way round, what is the extent of the freedom and rights of citizens within a state?'[9] As this quote from Quentin Skinner suggests, conceptions of liberty are inextricably tied to conceptions of the state and state power. The political theorists tell us that conceptions of the state are highly contested.[10] It is not necessary

[6] Dixon, 'The Functional Constitution', above n 3, 464.

[7] P Pettit, *Republicanism: A Theory of Freedom and Government* (Oxford University Press, 1997) 17, see generally at 17–50; Q Skinner, 'States and the Freedom of Citizens' in Q Skinner and B Strath (eds), *States & Citizens: History, Theory, Prospects* (Cambridge University Press, 2003) 11–25.

[8] Pettit, above n 7, 51.

[9] Skinner, above n 7, 11.

[10] ibid. See also MJC Vile, *Constitutionalism and the Separation of Powers* (Clarendon Press, 1967) 211.

for the purposes of this chapter to pin down precise conceptions of the state in political theory—that would be an impossible task. Nor is it necessary to determine conclusively the conception upon which the Constitution was founded. It is enough to accept that: (i) there are differing conceptions of the state; (ii) irrespective of the precise conception, the end of the state (at least in the Western constitutional tradition) is the protection or advancement of liberty; (iii) in the Australian constitutional context, the protection and advancement of liberty is primarily, if not entirely, effected through intermediate constitutional structures; and (iv) constitutional provisions and implications might take on different understandings depending on the assumed character of the liberty value and the intermediate structures that give effect to it.

It is useful to begin by recognising two differing, and sometimes incompatible, visions of the relationship between the individual and the state: the first is that the apparatus of the state can be embraced as a positive force for the common good thereby enhancing liberty; the second is that the state can be viewed with suspicion and fear, and the individual is to be protected from an intrusion of government power.[11] Although this dichotomy lacks nuance, it is a useful lens through which to explore the complexion of liberty as a constitutional value.

A. The State as the Protector of Liberty

If, for the moment, we see the Constitution through the lens of the conception of the state as a positive force for the common good, there are obvious features of the constitutional architecture that become prominent, and there is a clear acceptance of such a conception in High Court case law. Legal sovereignty rests with the Parliament and faith is placed in the democratic process for the advancement of the common good.[12] As Dawson J said in *Australian Capital Television Pty Ltd v Commonwealth*:

> Those responsible for the drafting of the Constitution saw constitutional guarantees of freedoms as exhibiting a distrust of the democratic process. They preferred to place their trust in Parliament to preserve the nature of our society and regarded as undemocratic guarantees which fettered its powers. Their model in this respect was, not the United States Constitution, but the British Parliament, the supremacy of which was by then settled constitutional doctrine.[13]

[11] See, eg, the way in which this distinction is used to contrast Australian and American constitutionalism: S Gageler, 'Foundations of Australian Federalism and the Role of Judicial Review' (1987) 17 *Federal Law Review* 162, 164–74.

[12] See D Meagher, 'What is "Political Communication"? The Rationale and Scope of the Implied Freedom of Political Communication' (2004) 28 *Melbourne University Law Review* 438, 454; H Patapan, 'Competing Visions of Liberalism: Theoretical Underpinnings of the Bill of Rights Debate in Australia' (1997) 21 *Melbourne University Law Review* 497, 505–08; Gageler, 'Foundations of Australian Federalism', above n 11, 170–73; WH Moore, 'The Commonwealth of Australia Bill' (1900) 16 *Law Quarterly Review* 35, 40–42; J Goldsworthy, 'The Constitutional Protection of Rights in Australia' in G Craven (ed), *Australian Federation: Towards the Second Century* (Melbourne University Press, 1992) 151–58.

[13] *Australian Capital Television Pty Ltd v Commonwealth* (1992) 177 CLR 106, 186.

Through the system of representative and responsible government the people can exercise their political sovereignty to advance the common weal. This sentiment can also be seen in Isaacs J's judgment in *Federal Commissioner of Taxation v Munro*. When defending the validity of a taxation board of review against a separation of judicial power challenge, his Honour said:

> I would say, speaking with considerable experience in each of the three departments of government, that, if a legislative provision of the present nature be forbidden, then a very vast and at present growing page of necessary constitutional means by which Parliament may in its discretion meet, and is at present accustomed to meet, the requirements of a progressive people, must, in my opinion, be considered as substantially obliterated so far as the Commonwealth is concerned. Administration must be hampered, and either injustice suffered or litigation fostered. The Constitution, it is true, has broadly and, to a certain extent, imperatively separated the three great branches of government, and has assigned to each, by its own authority, the appropriate organ. But the Constitution is for the advancement of representative government, and contains no word to alter the fundamental features of that institution.[14]

For Isaacs J, even the tripartite horizontal allocation of government power was not seen as qualifying the positive force of the state. The High Court's decision in *Amalgamated Society of Engineers v Adelaide Steamship Co Ltd* (*Engineers*),[15] with its emphasis on the permeating 'spirit'[16] of responsible government as a feature that distinguishes Australian from American constitutionalism, can be seen as a doctrinal manifestation of this conception of government.[17]

On this view of the relationship between the individual and the state, the federal allocation of power between the central and regional governments can be seen in the same way. As Gageler J recognised in his influential 1987 article in the *Federal Law Review*, '[f]ederation sprang … from the comparatively mundane recognition within the Australian colonies of the desirability of unified action in matters of common concern, overarched by a sense of common destiny'.[18] Hence the preliminary resolution of the 1897 National Australasian Convention declared that the purpose of federation was 'to enlarge the powers of self-government of the people of Australia'.[19] Far from diminishing the authority of the state, the federal structure can be seen in this way as enhancing the state's capacity to deliver outcomes for the common good. This conception may then provide a platform for viewing federalism as an intermediate constitutional value that enhances participation and engagement to facilitate better outcomes for the public good.[20]

[14] *Federal Commissioner of Taxation v Munro* (1926) 38 CLR 153, 178.

[15] *Amalgamated Society of Engineers v Adelaide Steamship Co Ltd* (1920) 28 CLR 129.

[16] ibid 147.

[17] See Gageler, 'Foundations of Australian Federalism', above n 11.

[18] ibid 167–68.

[19] *Official Record of the Debates of the Debates of the Australasian Federal Convention*, Adelaide, 23 March 1897, 17 (Edmund Barton).

[20] See, eg, S Stephenson, 'Federalism and Rights Deliberation' (2014) 38 *Melbourne University Law Review* 709; B Galligan and C Walsh, 'Australian Federalism—Yes or No?' in G Craven (ed), *Australian Federation: Towards the Second Century* (Melbourne University Press, 1992); B Galligan, R Knopff and J Uhr, 'Australian Federalism and the Debate over a Bill of Rights' (1990) 20(4) *Publius: The Journal of Federalism* 53.

Two key features of the constitutional system—judicial review and constitutional rights—are more difficult to fit with this conception of the state. However, it is not impossible. The institution of judicial review, the counter-majoritarian power to invalidate the acts of the democratically elected arm of government, necessarily embodies a suspicion of government. There was concern at the founding that the Commonwealth might exceed its power or that the States might renege on their promises. Judicial review was seen as a mechanism to provide for impartial adjudication of such questions. It was put in the following way by Edmund Barton during the convention debates:

> [I]t seems to me that if we are to have Federation in all its strength and power we are forced to the conclusion that the power which will best hold the Federation together, and will best preserve the honor of the Constitution, is the peaceful arbitrament of a Federal Court ... One of the strongest guarantees for the continuance and indestructibility of the Federation is that there should be some body of this kind constituted which, instead of allowing the States to fly to secession because they cannot get justice in any other way, will enable them to settle their differences in a calm judicial atmosphere.[21]

The suspicion that animated this basis for judicial review can be attuned to concerns about the preservation of the federal compact. It resonates clearly in the seminal judgments establishing the federal separation of judicial power principles.[22] As Dixon CJ, McTiernan, Fullagar and Kitto JJ said in *R v Kirby; Ex parte Boilermakers' Society of Australia*:

> The position and Constitution of the judicature could not be considered accidental to the institution of federalism: for upon the judicature rested the ultimate responsibility for the maintenance and enforcement of the boundaries within which government power might be exercised and upon that the whole system was constructed.[23]

Under the conception of the state as a force for the common good, judicial review need not have any traction outside this federalism rubric.

As for constitutional 'rights',[24] to the extent that they can be explained and applied as provisions central to the federal architecture, then they have little to say about the relationship between the individual and the state outside that federal context. Section 80 of the Constitution may be taken as an example. It provides that '[t]he trial on indictment of any offence against any law of the Commonwealth shall be by jury'. Echoing the constitutional jury provisions in the United States Constitution, it is easy to slide into assumptions about the liberty protecting function of section 80. Dixon and Evatt JJ did so in *R v The Federal Court of Bankruptcy Ex parte Lowenstein*[25] when they said that section 80 operated as a 'check[] against

[21] *Official Record of the Debates of the Debates of the Australasian Federal Convention*, Adelaide, 23 March 1897, 25 (Edmund Barton).

[22] *The Waterside Workers' Federation of Australia v J W Alexander Ltd* (1918) 25 CLR 434, 469 (Dixon and Rich JJ); *R v Kirby; Ex parte Boilermakers' Society of Australia* (1956) 94 CLR 254, 276; *Attorney-General (Cth) v The Queen* (1957) 95 CLR 529, 540–41 (PC).

[23] (1956) 94 CLR 254, 276. See also *Forge v Australian Securities and Investments Commission* (2006) 228 CLR 45, 73 (Gummow, Hayne and Crennan JJ).

[24] I put 'rights' in inverted commas only to emphasise that the character of the limitations might, in fact, be up for grabs.

[25] *R v The Federal Court of Bankruptcy Ex parte Lowenstein* (1938) 59 CLR 556, 580.

legislative encroachment on individual freedom'. However, even in the United States, the constitutional requirement for jury trials for certain offences is not so easily explained. The democratic role of juries within the constitutional system played a very large part in the adoption of the United States jury provisions.[26]

I have explained elsewhere that section 80 can be seen as a provision that is central to the federal architecture. Specifically, it can be seen as providing an institutional option for the Commonwealth Parliament to use lay persons, rather than judges, for the administration of federal justice.[27] On this view, the functional focus of the provision is less on the individual liberty of the accused and more on the choice of Parliament to involve the community in the administration of justice. The adoption of such an approach would have important consequences for various interpretive disputes arising under section 80: can a jury be waived at the election of the accused? When will a trial be on indictment for the purposes of triggering the provision? Can a jury give a majority verdict? The detail of the analysis need not be repeated here. The point is that section 80 may take on a different complexion depending on the assumptions that are made about the function it performs and the way in which it forms part of the constitutional system defining the relationship between the individual and the state. On one view, it merely forms part of the federal architecture for the exercise of federal government power with very little disruption to an understanding of the state as a vehicle for the common good, leaving it within Parliament's discretion to decide when jury trials are required.

An easier case along these lines can be made for other provisions commonly characterised as protective of individual liberty. Section 116 of the Constitution can be, and has been, seen rather routinely as intended to divide topics of regulation between the Commonwealth and the States.[28] In *Kruger v The Commonwealth*, Dawson J said:

> The appearance of s 116 in a chapter headed 'The States' has often been regarded as anomalous, but in fact the section deals with the division of legislative power between the Commonwealth and the States within the federation.[29]

Even Gaudron J, who was at the frontline of constitutional rights development, conceded:

> By its terms, s116 does no more than effect a restriction or limitation on the legislative power of the Commonwealth. It is not, 'in form, a constitutional guarantee of the rights of individuals'. It does not bind the States: they are completely free to enact laws imposing religious observances, prohibiting the free exercise of religion or otherwise intruding into the area which s116 denies to the Commonwealth. It makes no sense to speak of a constitutional right to religious freedom in a context in which the Constitution clearly postulates that the States may enact laws in derogation of that right. It follows, in my view, that s116 must be construed as no more than a limitation on Commonwealth legislative power.[30]

26 See, eg, Akhil Reed Amar, *The Bill of Rights: Creation and Reconstruction* (Yale University Press, 1998) 81–118.

27 J Stellios, 'The Constitutional Jury "A Bulwark of Liberty?"' (2005) 27 *Sydney Law Review* 113.

28 G Williams and D Hume, *Human Rights Under the Australian Constitution*, 2nd edn (Oxford University Press, 2013) 62–64.

29 *Kruger v The Commonwealth* (1997) 190 CLR 1, 60.

30 ibid 124–25.

Section 117 can be, and has been, seen primarily as directed to enhancing national cohesion in much the same way as section 92.[31] It is well known that, until *Street*, the Court gave section 117 a formalistic interpretation, denying the limitation much of its force. The *Street* Court revitalised the provision with a substantive interpretation. However, there remains, lurking below the unanimous revision in *Street*, a deep division in the Court on the operative purpose of section 117. As Simpson has said:

> [T]he major fault line is the underlying division between two alternate conceptions of the purpose and value of s 117. On the one hand, there are those judges who prefer to understand s 117 as a right to be valued, instrumentally, for its securing federal-structural objectives. On the other hand, there are the judges for whom s 117 declares a right with intrinsic value and is principally about the individuals that it protects. The decision in *Street* strikes, at best, an uneasy truce between the demands of s 117's textual focus upon individuals, and the traces of a federal-structural purpose in the provision's context and history.[32]

As will be discussed further below, the limitations protective of political communication and voting that are implied from representative and responsible government can be, and have been, justified as necessary to ensure that the system works well so that the people can exercise federal public power through the apparatus of the state.[33]

Thus, if one assumes a conception of the state as a positive force for the common good, the constitutional liberty value takes on a particular significance and constitutional provisions and implications can be attuned correspondingly to its achievement.

B. Alternate or Alternative Conceptions of the State

However, that is not the only way in which political theorists have conceived the state and its relationship to the individual. State power might be feared and viewed with suspicion, and the constitutional system might be designed to protect individual liberty from an exercise of government power.[34] This conception of the state has implications for the way in which government power is exercised and controlled.

There are different versions of this 'negative' view of the state. Again, very crudely, we might describe these as the 'liberal' view and the 'republican' view. At the risk of oversimplification, the liberal view fears *all* state power; the republican view fears *arbitrary* power.[35] Constitutions can be designed to guard against state power in various ways. State power might be divided horizontally to slow down the exercise of public power.[36] The dispersal of power in this way might also guard against arbitrary power by preventing the 'consolidation of functions in the hands of one

[31] A Simpson, 'The (Limited) Significance of the Individual in Section 117 State Residence Discrimination' (2008) 32 *Melbourne University Law Review* 639.

[32] ibid 648.

[33] I will return to the question of whether it is the court's role to ensure that the political system is working effectively.

[34] Skinner, above n 7, 11.

[35] See the way in which these conceptions have been explained in Pettit, above n 7, 17–50; Skinner, above n 7, 11–20.

[36] See NW Barber, 'Prelude to the Separation of Powers' (2001) 60 *Cambridge Law Journal* 59, 60–61.

person or group'.[37] As Jeremy Waldron has put it, the division of power minimises 'the concentration of too much political power in the hands of any one person, group or agency'.[38] The division of power vertically might be seen in the same way.[39] In addition to these *divisions* of power, *checks and balances* might be built into the constitutional system to ensure that no government actor can 'conclusively determin[e] the reach of their own powers'.[40] In this way, the judicial review of constitutional rights might be seen as operating to protect a particular individual interest from government authority.

So, have these conceptions been seen by the High Court as informing the constitutional architecture? I will leave aside for the moment Chapter III jurisprudence. Given Gageler J's treatment of it in *Magaming*, it requires separate consideration. Outside that context, the liberal view of the state has found little traction in Australian constitutional law. There were unsuccessful attempts in the 1990s to confine Commonwealth power by reference to fundamental rights.[41] There was also the suggestion by Kirby J that federalism, as a structural feature of the Constitution, was 'liberty-enhancing'[42] and a 'safeguard of limited government and of personal freedom'.[43] That view of federalism has not been endorsed.

Unsurprisingly, there has been more success in the area of constitutional rights. For example, a liberal conception of the state appears in judgments (albeit mostly dissenting) in the context of section 80 of the Constitution. It is clearly evident in the passage, set out earlier, from the judgment of Dixon and Evatt JJ in *Lowenstein*, and in Deane J's judgments. In *Kingswell v The Queen*, Deane J described the function of the jury requirement in section 80 of the Constitution in the following terms:

> The rationale and the essential function of that guarantee are the protection of the citizen against those who customarily exercise the authority of government: legislators who might seek by their laws to abolish or undermine 'the institution of "trial by jury" …'; administrators who might seek to subvert the due process of law or be, or be thought to be, corrupt or over-zealous in its enforcement; judges who might be, or be thought to be, over-remote from ordinary life, over-censorious or over-responsive to authority.[44]

The fear of the state, *in all its institutional forms*, informed his Honour's view that jury trials were required for all offences for which the accused could be sentenced to 12 months or more imprisonment,[45] and that jury trials could not be waived in favour of a judge sitting alone.[46] Kirby J's view in *Cheung v The Queen*[47] that section 80 operated to further divide government power within the judicial arm of

[37] Pettit, above n 7, 177.

[38] J Waldron, 'Separation of Powers in Thought and Practice?' (2013) 54 *Boston College Law Review* 433, 438.

[39] ibid. See the various conceptions of federalism discussed by Stephenson, above n 20, 711–15.

[40] L Claus, 'Montesquieu's Mistakes and the True Meaning of Separation' (2005) 25 *Oxford Journal of Legal Studies* 419, 420.

[41] See, eg, *Leeth v Commonwealth* (1992) 174 CLR 455, 486 (Deane and Toohey JJ); J Toohey, 'A Government of Laws, and Not of Men?' (1993) 4 *Public Law Review* 158, 169–70.

[42] *New South Wales v Commonwealth* (2006) 229 CLR 1, 229, 245 (*Work Choices Case*).

[43] *XYZ v Commonwealth* (2006) 227 CLR 532, 582. See also at 582.

[44] *Kingswell v The Queen* (1985) 159 CLR 264, 300 (*Kingswell*).

[45] *Kingswell* (1985) 159 CLR 264.

[46] *Brown v The Queen* (1986) 160 CLR 171.

[47] *Cheung v The Queen* (2001) 209 CLR 1, 44.

government also appeals to the liberal tradition of dispersing government power to minimise intrusion into individual liberty.

But, from a perspective of protecting the individual from state action, the High Court's interpretation of claimed constitutional rights has been 'disappointing'.[48] To continue the example of section 80, the Court's interpretation has robbed it of much of its protective force for the accused.[49] The Parliament can avoid the requirements of section 80 by providing that trials are not to be on indictment and can define an offence in such a way that allocates important fact-finding tasks to the trial judge and not the jury. The right to waive a jury, a necessary correlative of an individual privilege, has also been denied by the Court. Although a persistent minority of judges have considered section 80 to be protective of the accused, that view has never found the support of a High Court majority.

While the liberal view plays a marginal role in constitutional jurisprudence, the fear of *arbitrary* government is a more common undercurrent across a range of constitutional areas. This can be demonstrated briefly in eight contexts. First, responsible government can be seen as an institution for controlling arbitrary executive power. It is clear that the operational lines between positive and negative conceptions of the state are not clean. Representative and responsible government arose as institutions of government to control the exercise of public power, particularly arbitrary power of the executive arm of government.[50] Thus, not only are they embraced as the vehicles for driving the common good, they also operate as the mechanisms of accountability. Gageler J made this point in *McCloy v New South Wales*:

> The concept of electoral choice acting as a constraint on the exercise of Commonwealth legislative and executive power accords with the classic explanation given in the joint reasons for judgment in the *Engineers' Case*, that 'the extravagant use of the granted powers in the actual working of the Constitution is a matter to be guarded against by the constituencies and not by the Courts'.[51]

Secondly, the very strong defence of judicial review over executive action in cases like *Plaintiff S157/2002 v Commonwealth*[52] and *Kirk v Industrial Court (NSW)*[53] exhibits a concern about arbitrary executive action. As the joint judgment said in *Plaintiff S157/2002*:

> The reservation to this Court by the Constitution of the jurisdiction in all matters in which the named constitutional writs or an injunction are sought against an officer of the Commonwealth is a means of assuring to all people affected that officers of the Commonwealth obey the law and neither exceed nor neglect any jurisdiction which the law confers on them. The centrality, and protective purpose, of the jurisdiction of this Court in that regard places significant barriers in the way of legislative attempts (by privative clauses or otherwise) to impair judicial review of administrative action.[54]

[48] A Stone, 'Australia's Constitutional Rights and the Problem of Interpretive Disagreement' (2005) 27 *Sydney Law Review* 29, 32.

[49] See Stellios, 'The Constitutional Jury', above n 27.

[50] A Tomkins, *Our Republican Constitution* (Oxford, Hart Publishing, 2005) 46–65.

[51] *McCloy v New South Wales* (2015) 257 CLR 178, 226–27 (citation omitted).

[52] *Plaintiff S157/2002 v Commonwealth* (2003) 211 CLR 476 (*Plaintiff S157/2002*).

[53] *Kirk v Industrial Court (NSW)* (2010) 239 CLR 531 (*Kirk*).

[54] *Plaintiff S157/2002* (2003) 211 CLR 476, 513–54.

The Court went on to identify a federalism justification for this position[55] but its extension to state executive power in *Kirk* says more about the concern for arbitrary executive power— whether federal or state. The concern to avoid 'islands of power immune from supervision and restraint'[56] is a telling indication of the functional underpinning of the decision in *Kirk*.

Thirdly, there is an unclear, yet sufficiently discernible, limitation on the Commonwealth Parliament when delegating (or, perhaps more correctly, abdicating) power to the executive. The limitation was raised by Dixon J and Evatt J in *Victorian Stevedoring & General Contracting Co Pty Ltd and Meakes v Dignan*[57] in the context of statutory provisions authorising the Governor-General to make regulations, and in *Giris Pty Ltd v Federal Commissioner of Taxation*[58] in the context of legislation that permitted the tax commissioner to disapply certain provisions if he or she were of the view that their application 'would be unreasonable'.[59] In *Plaintiff S157/2002*,[60] the limitation was raised by the Court in response to an argument that the Commonwealth Parliament could, instead of enacting a privative clause insulating decisions from review, confer on the Minister a totally open-ended discretion to determine which aliens could come to Australia. While the precise basis and scope of this limitation remains opaque,[61] it seems reasonably clear that the Court is concerned with the arbitrary exercise of power by the executive.

This concern also is quite plain in Hayne J's judgment in *Plaintiff M79/2012 v Minister for Immigration and Citizenship*. In response to an argument that the discretionary power to detain unlawful non-citizens was confined solely by public interest considerations, his Honour said that such a construction would raise 'fundamental questions about the relationship between the Parliament and the Executive', in particular

> the present significance of the protest recorded in The Bill of Rights (1 Will & Mar Sess 2 c 2) against the assumed 'Power of Dispensing with and Suspending of Lawes and the Execution of Lawes without Consent of Parlyament' and the provisions of that Act declaring 'That the pretended Power of Suspending of Laws or the Execution of Laws by Regall Authority without Consent of Parlyament is illegall' and 'That the pretended Power of Dispensing with Laws or the Execution of Laws by Regall Authoritie as it hath beene assumed and exercised of late is illegall'.[62]

Fourthly, the executive power of the Commonwealth has been subjected to increasing constraints in the *Williams* cases.[63] At least in relation to the executive power in

[55] 'Such jurisdiction exists to maintain the federal compact': ibid 514.

[56] *Kirk* (2010) 239 CLR 531, 581. For a broader discussion of a concern for arbitrary power in the development of administrative law principles, see W Bateman, 'The Constitution and the Substantive Principles of Judicial Review: The Full Scope of the Entrenched Minimum Provision of Judicial Review' (2011) 39 *Federal Law Review* 463.

[57] *Victorian Stevedoring & General Contracting Co Pty Ltd and Meakes v Dignan* (1931) 46 CLR 73.

[58] *Giris Pty Ltd v Federal Commissioner of Taxation* (1969) 119 CLR 365.

[59] See also *Attorney-General (NT) v Emmerson* (2014) 253 CLR 393, 429.

[60] *Plaintiff S157/2002* (2003) 211 CLR 476.

[61] See J Stellios, *Zines's the High Court and the Constitution*, 6th edn (Federation Press, 2015) 200–11.

[62] *Plaintiff M79/2012 v Minister for Immigration and Citizenship* (2013) 252 CLR 336, 366–67.

[63] *Williams v Commonwealth* (2012) 248 CLR 156 (*Williams [No 1]*); *Williams v Commonwealth* (2014) 252 CLR 416 (*Williams [No 2]*).

section 61 to contract and spend, prior legislative approval, in addition to a valid appropriation, is required for much contracting and spending to be valid. In *Williams [No 1]*, Crennan J supported her conclusions in the following way:

> Prior to Federation, it was appreciated that the sharing of political power was an important mechanism for avoiding arbitrary government and thereby maintaining civil order. That appreciation underpinned the principle of responsible government and the idea that a democratic representative assembly would give qualified persons a 'stake' in government, both of which are sourced in the constitutional history of Britain and Australia in the nineteenth century. The same appreciation also underpinned the doctrine of the separation of powers, sourced in the constitutional history of America in the eighteenth century.

In rejecting the assimilation of the government's power to contract and spend with that of the individual, her Honour continued:

> [U]nlike the capacities of a non-governmental juristic entity to contract and to spend, the Commonwealth's capacities to do so are capable of being utilised to regulate activity in the community in the course of implementing government policy. This consideration highlights the importance of the mechanisms for responsible government designed to protect the community from arbitrary government action.[64]

Fifthly, the judgment of Crennan J from *Williams [No 1]* shows how the limitations protective of political communication, derived from representative and responsible government, can be rationalised as an attempt at 'avoiding arbitrary government'. Her Honour referred to her earlier judgment in *Rowe v Electoral Commissioner*,[65] where her discussion of John Locke's *The Second Treatise of Government*[66] reveals a concern about arbitrary government.

Sixthly, at least for Gageler J, section 51(xxxi) is designed to prevent *arbitrary* acquisitions of property. As his Honour said in his dissenting judgment in *Attorney-General (NT) v Emmerson*[67] about the character of the guarantee set out in that provision:

> The particular legislative power—to make laws 'with respect to ... the acquisition of property'—'was introduced ... not ... for the purpose of protecting the subject or citizen, but primarily to make certain that the Commonwealth possessed a power compulsorily to acquire property'. The condition—'on just terms'—was 'included to prevent arbitrary exercises of the power at the expense of a State or the subject'. The condition operates to prevent an 'acquisition of property' within the meaning of the power from occurring otherwise than 'on terms' which are provided by law and which can be characterised as 'just'.[68]

Seventhly, it has been recently emphasised in *Alqudsi v The Queen*,[69] particularly by Gageler J, that the function of section 80 is to guarantee 'democratic participation in the administration of Commonwealth criminal law'.[70] This is a different function

[64] *Williams [No 1]* (2012) 248 CLR 156, 350, 352 (footnotes omitted).
[65] *Rowe v Electoral Commissioner* (2010) 243 CLR 1, 107, 108–12.
[66] ibid 110–11.
[67] *Attorney-General (NT) v Emmerson* (2014) 253 CLR 393, 446 (footnotes omitted).
[68] See R Dixon, 'Overriding Guarantee of Just Terms or Supplementary Source of Power?: Rethinking s 51(xxi) of the Constitution' (2005) 27 *Sydney Law Review* 639.
[69] *Alqudsi v The Queen* (2016) 258 CLR 203.
[70] ibid 256–59.

for section 80 from others already noted. If accepted, section 80 is more than just a structural federal provision facilitating the involvement of juries in the administration of justice. However, on this view, its primary function is not to protect the individual liberty of the accused by limiting or dispersing government power. Its function is to guarantee the involvement of the community in the exercise of government power, echoing republican understandings of liberty to avoid the exercise of arbitrary government power.[71]

Finally, section 109 of the Constitution has been seen as 'of great importance for the ordinary citizen, who is entitled to know which of two inconsistent laws he is required to observe'.[72] This is not a protection within the liberal tradition. On no plausible reading could section 109 be viewed as protective of the individual from state action: it is a mechanism for deciding which state action is to apply. The way in which the Court has conceived its operation owes more to the reluctance of the Court to endorse an arbitrary application of public power on the people.

Thus, there are multiple threads in the High Court's jurisprudence demonstrating that fear of *arbitrary* government drives the design of constitutional principles.

IV. THE JUDICIARY AND JUDICIAL POWER

I have left for separate treatment the context addressed by Gageler J in *Magaming*: the judiciary and judicial power. The separation of judicial power is often presented, as it was by Gageler J, as a safeguard of liberty. A classic statement of that position can be found in Kitto J's judgment in *R v Davison* that 'it is necessary for the protection of the individual liberty of the citizen that th[e] three functions should be to some extent dispersed rather than concentrated in one set of hands'.[73] But, it is not always clear what that means. As already explained, the conception that the state is to be feared in its entirety has not generally been accepted. The constitutional 'rights' have not been embraced by the High Court, so the protection of individual interests through judicial review is not indicative of a negative conception of the state. The institutions of representative and responsible government have been accepted as the primary drivers of the common good and the mechanism through which arbitrary power is controlled. So, what can the courts or judicial power bring to the liberty table (in addition to the role of judicial review of arbitrary executive action)?

The principles of judicial separation have been seen primarily as serving the instrumental purpose of protecting the intermediate values of judicial independence and impartiality. This instrumental role can be, and has been, justified entirely on federalism grounds: the seminal cases certainly explain it in that way.[74] However,

[71] Pettit, above n 7, 179, 192–93.

[72] *University of Wollongong v Metwally* (1984) 158 CLR 447, 457–58 (Gibbs J). See also *Dickson v The Queen* (2010) 241 CLR 491, 503–04 (French CJ, Gummow, Hayne, Heydon, Crennan, Kiefel and Bell JJ).

[73] *R v Davison* (1954) 90 CLR 353, 380, cited in *Wilson v Minister for Aboriginal and Torres Strait Islander Affairs* (1996) 189 CLR 1, 11 (Brennan CJ, Dawson, Toohey, McHugh, Gummow JJ).

[74] See above n 22.

the statements on the separation of power and judicial independence go further: independence and impartiality is needed to provide a check on 'public power'[75] and guarantee 'liberty'.[76] Controlling public power can be rationalised, at least partly, according to the federalism explanation for judicial independence.[77] To the extent that it cannot, it is referable to concerns about the exercise of arbitrary executive power.

But, what about the statements that judicial independence protects liberty? What conceptions of the state and liberty are presupposed? Certainly, it might be a reference to the Blackstonian notion of 'the administration of common justice':[78] that is, determining disputes about rights and duties that arise between the state and citizens and among citizens themselves. This is probably what Jacobs J was referring to in *The Queen v Quinn; Ex parte Consolidated Food Corporation* when his Honour said that

> we have inherited and were intended by our Constitution to live under a system of law and government which has traditionally protected the rights of persons by ensuring that those rights are determined by a judiciary independent of the parliament and the executive. But the rights referred to in such an enunciation are the basic rights which traditionally, and therefore historically, are judged by that independent judiciary which is the bulwark of freedom. The governance of a trial for the determination of criminal guilt is a classic example. But there are a multitude of such instances.[79]

The example given in the penultimate sentence links us back to Gageler J's quote from *Magaming*. What are the 'deeply rooted notions of the relationship of the individual to the state going to the character of the national polity created and sustained by the Constitution'? In *North Australian Aboriginal Justice Agency Ltd v Northern Territory*,[80] his Honour elaborated by saying that the foundation of *Lim* was a 'concern for the protection of personal liberty lying at the core of our inherited constitutional tradition, which includes the inheritance of the common law'.[81] 'The centrality of personal liberty to the functioning of government within our 800 year old inherited tradition' was further explained by reference to statements by Sir William Blackstone warning against despotism, tyranny and arbitrary government.[82]

Thus, Gageler J might simply be assuming a role for the courts in guarding against *arbitrary* power by the state in punishing criminal guilt. There must be a breach of legislative norms of conduct and an adjudication by a fair, open and impartial judicial process, before criminal punishment is exacted by the executive on an individual.[83]

[75] *TCL Air Conditioner (Zhongshan) Co Ltd v Judges of the Federal Court of Australia* (2013) 251 CLR 533, 574 (Hayne, Crennan, Kiefel and Bell JJ). See also *Wilson v Minister for Aboriginal and Torres Strait Islander Affairs* (1996) 189 CLR 1, 11 (Brennan CJ, Dawson, Toohey, McHugh, Gummow JJ).

[76] *Wilson v Minister for Aboriginal and Torres Strait Islander Affairs* (1996) 189 CLR 1, 11 (Brennan CJ, Dawson, Toohey, McHugh, Gummow JJ).

[77] ibid 12.

[78] William Blackstone, *Commentaries on the Laws* (1765) book 1, ch 7.

[79] *The Queen v Quinn; Ex parte Consolidated Food Corporation* (1977) 138 CLR 1, 11.

[80] *North Australian Aboriginal Justice Agency Ltd v Northern Territory* (2015) 256 CLR 569.

[81] ibid 610.

[82] ibid 610–11.

[83] *Magaming* (2013) 252 CLR 382, 400–01 (Gageler J).

In this sense, the imposition of punishment by the state must be mediated by a court through a dispute between the state and the individual in relation to a contravention of existing norms of conduct. In *Lim*, this had been elevated by Brennan, Toohey and Dawson JJ to the level of a 'constitutional immunity from being imprisoned by Commonwealth authority except pursuant to an order by a court in the exercise of the judicial power of the Commonwealth',[84] and in *Fardon v Attorney-General (Qld)* Gummow J had emphasised that the 'concern' of the principle from *Lim* 'is with the deprivation of liberty without adjudication of guilt'.[85] This version of the separation of judicial power is centred on the exercise of state power against an individual's liberty interest (in the sense of freedom from detention in the custody of the state).

By contrast, Jacobs J's version does not seem to be defined by a concern for the exercise of state power. Under that view, the court's protection of rights is not limited to disputes between a citizen and the state, even though the adjudgement of criminal guilt might be a leading example. There is something about the character of the function of determining a dispute between parties (involving the state or not) that appears central to Jacob J's conception of the judiciary protecting liberty. It might in fact be a conception of the separation of powers that places government functions with decision-makers who are best equipped to perform the task.[86] When seen alongside a positive conception of state action as contributing to the common good, then courts administer common justice because they are well placed because of their skills and habits to make the best decisions, thereby maximising individual liberty. In the words of Nicholas Barber, when describing Locke's conception of the separation of powers, 'the legislature ought not pass judgment on particular cases because it was structurally ill equipped to undertake this task: even if it acted in good faith it was unlikely to adjudicate as fairly or as impartiality as a court'.[87]

For the most part, it is unnecessary to take the functional analysis of Chapter III this far: it is usually enough to focus on the intermediate constitutional value of judicial independence. However, these differing conceptions are not unimportant,[88] and there are at least two areas where pressing the functional role further is necessary to resolve some difficult questions. First, where the legislature, with or without executive decision-making, acts directly on the liberty of the individual outside the context of the resolution of a dispute about existing rights and duties; and secondly, where the judiciary is called upon to act directly on the liberty of the individual without an adjudgement and punishment of criminal guilt. In the first area, we might place the detention of aliens or preventative detention by the executive. In the second, we might place the *Kable*-type of preventative or continuing detention regimes that involve a court in the decision-making process.

At least in the first area, there is an argument that the non-judicial arms of government are structurally equipped to make better judgements about the exercise of the powers in question. This is perhaps what McHugh J had in mind

84 *Lim* (1992) 176 CLR 1, 28.
85 *Fardon v Attorney-General (Qld)* (2004) 223 CLR 575, 613–14 (*Fardon*).
86 Barber, above n 36, 65.
87 ibid 64.
88 See Dixon, 'The Functional Constitution', above n 3, 464.

in *Re Woolley; Ex parte M276/2000*[89] when rejecting statements from *Lim* that individuals enjoy a constitutional immunity. In his Honour's view, detention for non-punitive purposes need not be assigned to the judicial category. Equally difficult questions arise where a court is authorised to order preventative or continuing detention 'detached'[90] from a determination of criminal guilt. For McHugh J in *Fardon*,[91] such a function was judicial in character and could be conferred by the Commonwealth Parliament on a court. For Gummow J it could not.[92] Whether it can be done remains unclear,[93] but the answer will require a closer functional lens being applied to the separation of judicial power.

I do not propose to resolve these dilemmas. The point for present purposes is that the answers to these questions will depend upon differing conceptions of 'the relationship of the individual to the state'. A functional analysis assists to expose the presuppositions underlying the various views.

V. A CONCEPTION OF THE JUDICIAL ROLE: 'WHO OUGHT TO PURSUE THESE AIMS'?[94]

In his insightful contribution to separation of powers constitutional and political theory, Nicholas Barber reminds us that, in a system of horizontally separated powers, an important set of questions to be asked relates to the appropriate mechanisms in a state to achieve its objectives. It is one thing to identify the aims of a state as the protection of liberty; it is another to allocate functions across the arms of government to give effect to those objectives.

If the sole aim of the Constitution were to establish a federal polity, we might say that the role of the judiciary was limited to determining federalism questions. But, on the assumption that the establishment of the Commonwealth Government was intended to create a wider 'national polity' that was designed, at least in part, to enhance individual liberty in one way or another, which institution of government should pursue these aims? And, would it matter whether the liberty interest is to be protected from state intervention or, alternatively, is to participate in, or engage with, the new polity? These are important questions. When liberty is at stake, it may be assumed too readily that the judiciary is to play a role in protecting liberty interests. It might be a safe assumption in relation to the role of the judiciary, outlined in the previous section, appropriately distilled from the separation of judicial power. But, beyond that, it is less clear. Take for example the arbitrary exercise of *executive* or *legislative* power. How is it to be guarded against?

Writing in 1902, Professor Harrison Moore said that '[t]he great underlying principle [of the Constitution] is, that the rights of individuals are sufficiently secured

[89] *Re Woolley; Ex parte M276/2000* (2004) 225 CLR 1.
[90] ibid 613 (Gummow J).
[91] *Fardon* (2004) 223 CLR 575, 597.
[92] ibid 613–14
[93] See J Stellios, 'The Masking of Judicial Power Values: Historical Analogies and Double Function Provisions' (2017) 28 *Public Law Review* 138, 151–52.
[94] Barber, above n 36, 66.

by ensuring, as far as possible, to each a share, and an equal share, in political power'.[95] Provided that there is an equal share of political power, it is the institutions of representative and responsible government (that is, the political process) that protect the liberties of the individual from government power, including arbitrary government power.

So, what justifies the Court's role in controlling the delegation of legislative power; policing government spending; and protecting political communication and voting rights? Why is the political process not the forum for addressing and remedying any excesses of legislative and executive power? There is a tendency here to focus on backward-looking federalism justifications to avoid answering these questions head on. In a 2009 article,[96] Gageler J linked the constitutional protections for political communication and the franchise to control of *federal* power. That position has been adopted by his Honour in *McCloy*.[97]

A similar proposition was put by Gummow, Kirby and Crennan JJ in *Roach v Electoral Commissioner*:

> [I]n the federal system established and maintained by the Constitution, the exercise of the franchise is the means by which those living under that system of government participate in the selection of both legislative chambers, as one of the people of the relevant State and as one of the people of the Commonwealth. In this way, the existence and exercise of the franchise reflects notions of citizenship and membership of the Australian federal body politic.[98]

Federalism justifications also abound in the *Williams* cases[99] for explaining why the Commonwealth could not have an unlimited power under section 61 to contract and spend.

However, despite these efforts (including my own),[100] the development of these principles present a challenge to the role of the democratic process in controlling public power. The principles seek to respond to a perceived 'deficit in the system of representative government'[101] and constitute a shift in our understanding of the place and role of the democratic process within the constitutional system. Of course, a forward-looking conception of the judicial role might more easily explain these shifts.[102] My own view is that a backward-looking conception is necessary to arrest a slide from functionalism to pragmatism or policy-oriented reasoning.[103] In any event, a functional analysis of the 'relationship of the individual to the state' must grapple with these questions as well.

[95] WH Moore, *The Constitution of the Commonwealth of Australia* (London, John Murray, 1902) 329.

[96] S Gageler, 'Beyond the Text: A Vision of the Structure and Function of the Constitution' (2009) 32 *Australian Bar Review* 138, 154–55.

[97] (2015) 257 CLR 178, 226–30. See also *Tajjour v New South Wales* (2014) 254 CLR 508, 577 (Gageler J).

[98] *Roach v Electoral Commissioner* (2007) 233 CLR 162, 199.

[99] See Stellios, Zines's the High Court and the Constitution, above n 61, 396–97.

[100] J Stellios, 'Using Federalism to Protect Political Communication: Implications from Federal Representative Government' (2005) 31 *Melbourne University Law Review* 239.

[101] *Williams [No 1]* (2012) 248 CLR 156, 234 (Gummow and Bell JJ).

[102] R Dixon, 'Response to Commentators' (2015) 43 *Federal Law Review* 517, 519, fn 14.

[103] J Stellios, 'Conceptions of the Judicial Review: Commentary on Dixon' (2015) 43 *Federal Law Review* 511, 512.

VI. CONCLUSION: THE VALUE OF FUNCTIONALISM

As conceived by Rosalind Dixon, functionalism does not, necessarily, provide determinative solutions to uncertain constitutional meaning. Instead, it provides a lens through which constitutional values might inform the interpretive process. Its value lies in its insistence on a transparent process of analysis that exposes the values (and biases) that inform the determination of constitutional meaning. It presses us to think more precisely about the function performed by constitutional provisions, structures and implications.

As I have said, there is some danger if functionalism is left uncontained. The track record of liberty as a constitutional value bears that out. One needs to look no further than the disagreements on the function of section 80 or the separation of judicial power within the constitutional system. I have expressed the view that functionalism requires a conception of the judicial role within the constitutional system,[104] and this is particularly important where the constitutional liberty value is at stake. I accept that such a conception would be required for any approach to constitutional interpretation—whether the interpretive exercise presents an easy or hard case.[105] However, it becomes particularly important in hard cases where there is greater scope, in a forward-looking way, to take liberties with the constitutional value in question. I do not discount the potential for functionalism to provide valuable insights on constitutional meaning in a forward-looking way. For example, I have mentioned the value of pressing further conceptions of judicial power and the democratic-enhancing conception of federalism. However, I think that potential must be confined within a backward-looking understanding of the judicial role.

Justice Gageler's reference in *Magaming* to 'deeply rooted notions of the relationship of the individual to the state' is a refreshing acknowledgment of underlying assumptions that inform the search for constitutional meaning.[106] It provides a platform for a more nuanced, functionalist understanding of the character of our constitutional arrangement. However, it is also question-begging as to the nature of the relationship between the individual and the state that is embedded within the constitutional system.

[104] ibid 514–15.

[105] Dixon, 'Response to Commentators', above n 102, 519.

[106] See also his Honour's consideration of Chapter III values in *Palmer v Ayres* [2017] HCA 5; (2017) 91 ALJR 325, [93].

11

Equal Treatment and Non-Discrimination through the Functionalist Lens

AMELIA SIMPSON

I. INTRODUCTION

THE AUSTRALIAN CONSTITUTION invokes the ideas of equal treatment and discrimination in a number of places, as a direct textual feature of some provisions and also at times as an element of implications drawn from constitutional text and structure. This chapter will explore these instances through a functionalist lens and assess whether, and when, the High Court has produced doctrine that is broadly consistent with the dictates of a functionalist interpretative approach.

Equality and discrimination are notoriously elusive concepts. At their most abstract these concepts have been described as 'empty', serving as mere placeholders for other values that do the real work of framing comparisons.[1] Academic debate has, at any rate, moved on and now centres on what those underlying, more substantive, values are and how they can ground and discipline legal invocations of the slippery abstract terms.[2] Searches for symmetry and unity in the constitutional deployment of the concepts of equality and discrimination are often fraught. The bare concepts are so elastic that they can denote both deontic and utilitarian aspirations, in parallel, within the one constitutional document. Given these complexities, this chapter will forego abstract consideration of whether 'equality' and 'non-discrimination' are attractive or morally defensible constitutional objectives. It will focus instead on the meaning that the Australian High Court has fashioned out the bare words of the Constitution.

The chapter proceeds upon the premise that a functionalist interpretative methodology offers a sound—defensible and workable—framework within which

[1] P Westen, 'The Empty Idea of Equality' (1982) 95 *Harvard Law Review* 537; P Westen, 'The Meaning of Equality in Law, Science, Maths and Morals' (1983) 81 *Michigan Law Review* 604.

[2] See, eg, S Fredman, 'Substantive Equality Revisited' (2016) 14(3) *International Journal of Constitutional Law* 712; CA MacKinnon, 'Substantive Equality: A Perspective' (2012) 96 *Minnesota Law Review* 1; H Collins, 'Discrimination, Equality and Social Inclusion' (2003) 66 *Modern Law Review* 16.

the Australian Constitution can be interpreted and applied. It is defensible because it respects and upholds the philosophical foundations of Australia's constitutional model and, in particular, the circumscribed form of judicial review assumed therein.[3] It is workable because it endorses a range of potential sources of interpretative guidance, rather than any rigid or exclusive hierarchy, and thus rests comfortably with the eclectic approach that the High Court has favoured in recent times.[4] In terms of its understanding of functionalism this chapter adopts the conceptual content provided by Rosalind Dixon in chapter one of this volume and elsewhere.[5] Dixon in turn acknowledges the significant and much earlier contribution made by Professor Leslie Zines in this area.[6]

It will be seen that the Mason High Court was, in line with its reputation, the standard-setter in the use of functionalist analysis to navigate this terrain. More recently, though, the High Court's fidelity to functionalism in this domain has wavered. The Court's perspective has narrowed as a consequence of its enthusiasm for a particular doctrinal test and it has, consequently, been inattentive to how well that test serves relevant constitutional values. In sum, this corner of the Court's constitutional jurisprudence keenly illustrates the importance of focusing on those values as the starting point for interpretation. Losing sight of those values has, in this area, yielded confusing and unstable doctrine.

The analysis in this chapter will adopt the shorthand 'constitutional non-discrimination principles' to describe, collectively, all the Constitution's invocations of discrimination, equal treatment and related concepts like uniformity and preference.[7] The chapter first identifies a series of alternative values that compete for explanatory power in the context of the Constitution's non-discrimination principles. Some of those principles have been consistently aligned with only one of the identified values, while others have been more fluid in their associations. The chapter then describes the different kinds of doctrinal test that have been invoked in these contexts, noting that these do not map consistently onto the different categories of value. The remainder of this chapter is then devoted to an exploration of the High Court's reasoning in several constitutional contexts where non-discrimination principles have been in play. Particular attention is paid, here, to how faithfully the Court has aligned its reasons with the objectives and methods of functionalism.

[3] See especially the explanation offered by Gageler J in *McCloy v New South Wales* (2015) 257 CLR 178, 223–30 [102]–[123]. See also his earlier scholarly treatments: S Gageler, 'Beyond the Text: A Vision of the Structure and Function of the Constitution' (2009) 32 *Australian Bar Review* 138; S Gageler, 'Foundations of Australian Federalism and the Role of Judicial Review' (1987) 17 *Federal Law Review* 162.

[4] Most recently, see *Commonwealth v Australian Capital Territory* (2013) 250 CLR 441, 455 (French CJ, Hayne, Crennan, Kiefel, Bell and Keane JJ) (*Marriage Equality Act Case*), citing *SGH Ltd v Federal Commissioner of Taxation* (2002) 210 CLR 51, 75 (Gummow J).

[5] See ch 1 by Rosalind Dixon in this collection. See also R Dixon, 'The Functional Constitution: Re-reading the 2014 High Court Constitutional Term' (2015) 43 *Federal Law Review* 455.

[6] L Zines, *The High Court and the Constitution*, 5th edn (Sydney, Federation Press, 2008) ch 17.

[7] For an attempt to list such provisions, see A Simpson, 'The High Court's Conception of Discrimination: Origins, Applications, and Implications' (2007) 29 *Sydney Law Review* 263, 264–66.

II. THE VALUES UNDERLYING CONSTITUTIONAL NON-DISCRIMINATION PRINCIPLES

Functionalism is an interpretative methodology that encourages a focus upon constitutional values.[8] An enquiry into values offers a natural starting point in any quest to attribute a 'function' to a particular provision or principle, around which its interpretation would then revolve. As other chapters in this volume reveal, the search for an animating value for a given provision or principle can at times be a challenging undertaking.[9] It should come as no surprise, then, that seeking to tease out and particularise constitutional values of the 'equality' or 'non-discrimination' variety presents a unique set of complications.

In investigating whether a constitution shows any degree of commitment to non-discrimination as a value, one cannot get far without realising that there are, in fact, several possible values which might lay claim to that term. In a constitutional setting, there are at least four quite distinct kinds of value that might be found to underlie any particular non-discrimination principle:

(a) Formal equality of persons (ie, as per the 'rule of law').[10]
(b) Substantive equality of persons.[11]
(c) Formal equality of component polities within the federal system.[12]
(d) Substantive equality of polities and/or citizens within the federal system.[13]

The various non-discrimination principles housed within the Australian Constitution are distributed across these four possible categories of underlying value. Of the Constitution's three explicit prohibitions of 'discrimination', two have been universally assumed to exist in the service of 'federal-structural' goals—that is, goals directed to the preservation of the federal system of government, for instance through the fostering of goodwill among the component polities of the Australian federation. Section 102 empowers the Commonwealth to forbid discrimination by States in granting access to their railway infrastructure, but has received scant attention in the case law.[14] The proviso to the section 51(ii) taxation power forbids the

[8] See ch 1 by Rosalind Dixon in this collection.

[9] See, eg, the ch 5 by Lisa Burton Crawford and ch 6 by Janina Boughey and Greg Weeks in this collection.

[10] The original expression of this idea is widely credited to Aristotle, *The Nichomachean Ethics* (eds) JL Ackrill and JO Urmson, trans W Ross (Oxford, Oxford University Press 1980) 112–17, 1131a–1131b (trans of: *Ethica Nichomachea*). Echoes of this outlook persist to this day in prominent constitutional equality law contexts. See, eg, the United States Supreme Court's cautious and qualified endorsement of race as a criterion in university admissions decisions: *Fisher v University of Texas at Austin*, 133 S Ct 2411 (2016).

[11] This is well explained in the leading Canadian decision adopting a substantive conception of equality of individuals: *Andrews v The Law Society of British Columbia* [1989] 1 SCR 143. For scholarly treatment see: Fredman, above n 2; MacKinnon, above n 2.

[12] For a judicial treatment of this position, and an explanation of its historical significance in Australia, see: *Permanent Trustee Australia Ltd v Commissioner of State Revenue* (2004) 220 CLR 388, 446–48 (McHugh J), 464–65 (Kirby J) (*Permanent Trustee*).

[13] This is arguably the value substrate of the contemporary understanding of s 117 of the Australian Constitution, forged in *Street v Queensland Bar Association* (1989) 168 CLR 461 (*Street*) and discussed later in this chapter. See also A Simpson, 'The (Limited) Significance of the Individual in Section 117 State Residence Discrimination' (2008) 32 *Melbourne University Law Review* 639.

[14] Railways were a particular preoccupation of the Constitution's framers, reflecting the late 19th-century context as well as the distances to be overcome in trading.

Commonwealth to, in that context, 'discriminate between States or parts of States'. As to which kind of equality value—formal or substantive—that prohibition serves, the recent case law reveals some indecision, to be discussed later in this chapter. A third express mention of discrimination, in the section 117 prohibition of discrimination based on State residence, has been the subject of greater values contestation and this will also be discussed later in this chapter.

Other constitutional provisions invoke conceptual equivalents of discrimination—'uniformity' in sections 51(iii) and 88 and 'preference' in section 99. These have been consistently viewed as provisions underpinned by federal-structural objectives, although in the context of section 99, to be discussed later, there has been some uncertainty as to whether the goal is formal or substantive equal treatment. The section 92 exhortation to 'absolutely free' trade among the States has been understood to import a non-discrimination principle. More detailed discussion to come will explain that this is firmly settled as a protection of substantive equality within a federal-structural framework.

The High Court has also been invited, at times, to protect equality values via implication-based reasoning. Where the suggestion has been that the Constitution could support a substantive guarantee of the equality of individuals, that possibility has been firmly rejected. The cases in which this stance was taken will be discussed in more detail below. Where, on the other hand, the Court has been invited to identify constitutional support for a principle of formal equality as between individuals—for example, as subjects of judicial power and as participants in the electoral system—it has shown greater willingness to ascribe such values to the Constitution.

On the subject of electoral systems there is one provision that warrants mention here. The Constitution invokes the idea of equality directly in relation to the composition of the Senate, with section 7 mandating the 'equal representation of the ... Original States'. In terms of the typology of values outlined above, this provision embodies scenario (c): formal equality of component polities within the federal system. The potential for the section 7 requirement to come into direct conflict with a type (a) constitutional value—an expectation of individual voter equality arising from the Constitution's commitment to representative government—was long ago realised in the litigation concerning Territory Senators.[15] While this chapter will delve no further into that controversy, the *Territory Senators Cases* do underline the importance of differentiating the possible variants of equality and discrimination in any discussion of constitutional values.

Importantly, the linkages between specific provisions and types of equality value can shift, so that, for example, a provision once aligned with a value of formal equality among polities might be reimagined instead as a guarantee of the substantive equality of persons. The fact that these different values compete for dominance across time in different corners of jurisprudence makes this a fruitful setting in which to unpack the High Court's fluctuating commitment to functionalist reasoning. While it cannot be said that judgments in this domain are *always* attentive to underlying values, it is nonetheless true that structurally and historically based values analysis

[15] *Western Australia v Commonwealth* (1974) 134 CLR 201; *Queensland v Commonwealth* (1977) 139 CLR 585 (collectively referred to as the *Territory Senators Cases*).

has become commonplace in this context over recent decades. Key examples will be explored in the discussion to follow.

III. TESTS FOR IDENTIFYING UNEQUAL TREATMENT OR DISCRIMINATION

A different, crosscutting, distinction that is often central to discussions of non-discrimination jurisprudence concerns the tests employed to identify instances of discrimination. Much of the literature on constitutional and statutory non-discrimination law employs a dichotomous distinction between so-called 'form-based' doctrinal tests and 'substance-based' tests. A parallel distinction is sometimes drawn between the legal rules which are understood in these respective ways. So, a 'formal' guarantee of non-discrimination means simply one that is applied by reference to a form-based test, whereas 'substantive' guarantees of non-discrimination are those which are instead understood and applied by reference to substance-based tests. While there are likely to be, across contexts, some minor differences in the way these tests are formulated, it is still useful to describe them here in prototypical terms, as follows.

When a non-discrimination principle is applied according to a form-based test (commonly described in Australian constitutional jurisprudence as a 'criterion of operation' or 'criterion of liability' test)[16] a single abstract rule or standard is applied to all legal subjects, without regard to context; in other words, if a law treats subjects equally 'on its face' it will not be found to discriminate. For example, if a rule prohibiting sex-based discrimination were to be applied according to a form-based test, the different treatment of people according to their sex would have to be evident in the very terms of an impugned law before it would be vulnerable to invalidation. A law discriminating on the basis of a criterion that might function as a proxy for sex (such as stature, availability for full-time work, carer responsibilities, etc) would be protected from scrutiny.

Substantive tests of discrimination, on the other hand, involve probing more deeply into the impact of legal classifications. Where a non-discrimination principle is applied by reference to a substantive test, the decision-maker may look behind the rule's facial classification to assess what effect the rule has within the context in which it operates. In principle, this substance-based approach to assessing a law's validity would seem a good fit with the priorities and teachings of a functionalist approach. Presumably, in the ordinary course of things, evidence-based testing of a law's congruence with relevant values is easier where a broader range of inputs is permitted.

Many modern incarnations of substance-focused tests have a further important dimension—they may invite, or require, courts to consider whether the distinctions drawn and outcomes generated are 'reasonable'. Often this will involve an enquiry into whether particular distinctions or criteria are 'appropriate' in a particular context, making it possible to conclude, for example, that facially equal treatment yields

[16] For a detailed discussion of these tests, see J Stellios, *Zines's The High Court and the Constitution*, 6th edn (Annandale, N.S.W., Federation Press, 2015) 651–54.

patterns in outcome that amount to discrimination. On this approach, a law denying some privilege or opportunity to a class of legal subjects by reference to a criterion operating, in practice, as a proxy for another, prohibited, criterion (like sex) would be vulnerable to invalidation—though often subject to a saving test of reasonableness. Such saving tests, where they are employed, in effect render a constitutional guarantee defeasible—that is, vulnerable to being overridden—by reference to their criterion of reasonableness or proportionality.[17]

While these prototypes are helpful for appreciating the alternatives available to judges in crafting discrimination doctrine, it may be more realistic, at least in the Australian constitutional context, to think of these distinct approaches as situated at opposing ends of a spectrum, along which various other positions—or gradations of interest in substantive criteria—could be taken. The notion of a spectrum is likely more illuminating in, for instance, looking at the Court's section 117 jurisprudence.[18] Doctrine in this area will be explored more fully below. Also considered below are the most recent decisions applying the non-discrimination proviso to the section 51(ii) taxation power. Here, again, the Court's approach is difficult to locate within a binary form versus substance schema and might be more easily understood by reference to a spectrum.

The key challenge facing Australian judges when navigating the concepts of equality and discrimination in constitutional settings has been to make good matches between the available tests, on one axis, and the underlying values, on another. The possible permutations are many, especially where the doctrinal tests are understood to fall along a spectrum of subjectivity rather than present a binary choice. This chapter contends that the jurisprudence in this area is at its most clear and compelling when it prioritises the exploration of values—and when those values guide the selection of a doctrinal test. Conversely, most if not all the unsatisfying decisions in this area have come about through judicial attachment to a doctrinal test that is not well matched to the values animating the relevant equality or discrimination principle.

IV. EQUALITY AND NON-DISCRIMINATION REASONING IN THE HIGH COURT

This section will explore and evaluate the construction of identified (or suggested) constitutional non-discrimination principles in a number of contexts. It will be seen that the Court has generally been successful in aligning its doctrine with a functionalism-inspired assessment of constitutional values. There are, however, gradations of success in this enterprise and at least one area is identified as scoring poorly on functionalist criteria.

[17] This is, for example, the orthodox understanding of how considerations of reasonableness work within the s 92 prohibition of protectionist discrimination in trade and commerce: see further below; see also Simpson, 'The High Court's Conception of Discrimination', above n 7, 281–83.

[18] On the question of gradations of commitment to substance-focused discrimination analysis, see A Simpson, '*Sweedman v Transport Accident Commission*: State Residence Discrimination and the High Court's Retreat into Characterisation' (2006) 34 *Federal Law Review* 363, 371–73.

A. The Lack of a Broad Equality Principle

Before proceeding to discussion of the areas where the High Court has recognised non-discrimination as an operative value, something must be said of one important context in which it has refused to do so. Consistently with the teachings of functionalism, the Court has refused to countenance for Australia a broad constitutional guarantee of equality for individuals. This has been despite a series of opportunities to infer such a protection and thereby align Australian constitutional law, in this respect, with that found in the rest of the liberal democratic world. In choosing this course, the Court's reasons have been tethered firmly to the text, structure and history of the Constitution.

The framers of the Australian Constitution debated, but ultimately rejected, the inclusion of a provision to guarantee equality of treatment of individuals under the law.[19] While the language they considered had borne a clear resemblance to the United States Constitution's 'Equal Protection' clause,[20] it is not clear from the Australian debates that the framers had a full appreciation of the significance, in its country of origin, of the language they were debating.[21] In any case, what is clear from the Convention Debates is that many delegates' objections were grounded in an attachment to parliamentary supremacy and a related discomfort with judicial involvement in the resolution of social disagreement. The debates also reveal a concern among some delegates to protect the capacity for States to discriminate on racial grounds against, for instance, migrant workers.

Given the prominence of equality guarantees in other liberal democratic constitutions, it is unsurprising that there has been scholarly debate in Australia about whether our position is satisfactory. In particular, there has been discussion about whether the High Court could, or should, employ the logic of implied limitations on power to identify an equality protection for individuals. This idea appears in scholarship, and sporadically in judicial reasoning, going back many decades.[22] For proponents of the idea, it channels a longing for constitutional recognition of the value of individuals and a commitment to protecting them from discrimination. In the schema of values outlined above, this would likely fit within the second category—'substantive equality of persons'.

The ante was raised on this issue from the late 1980s—a time during which the Mason High Court was innovating in a number of areas of constitutional law

[19] JA La Nauze, *The Making of the Australian Constitution* (Melbourne, Melbourne University Press, 1972) 230–32.

[20] United States Constitution amend XIV.

[21] See, eg, JM Williams, *The Australian Constitution: A Documentary History* (Carlton, Vic., Melbourne University Press, 2005) 798–801, 846–48; WG Buss, 'The Lion in the Path and the Eagle Overhead: The Influence of the American Constitution in the Making of the Australian Constitution' (unpublished manuscript).

[22] For scholarly considerations see especially: J Kirk, 'Constitutional Implications (II): Doctrines of Equality and Democracy' (Pt II) (2001) 25 *Melbourne University Law Review* 24; MJ Detmold, 'The New Constitutional Law' (1994) 16 *Sydney Law Review* 228; AR Blackshield, 'The Implied Freedom of Communication' in G Lindell (ed), *Future Directions in Australian Constitutional Law: Essays in Honour of Professor Leslie Zines* (Sydney, Federation Press, 1994). For judicial contemplations, see: *Leeth v Commonwealth* (1992) 174 CLR 455, 486 (Deane and Toohey JJ) (*Leeth*); *R v Director-General of Social Welfare (Vic); Ex parte Henry* (1975) 133 CLR 369, 388 (Murphy J).

including an expansion of the domain of implied limitations upon legislative power. Against this background, scholars and lawyers speculated as to whether the Court might be prepared to discern within the Australian Constitution, either from the document as a whole or from one or more provisions, an implicit equality principle. Such a principle—of, for instance, equal treatment of individuals under the law—might then justify courts in striking down legislative or executive action deemed inconsistent with it.

In two test cases brought during the 1990s—*Leeth v Commonwealth* (*Leeth*)[23] and *Kruger v The Commonwealth* (*Kruger*)[24]—the High Court refused to find that the Constitution contains an implicit guarantee of equality in any broad-ranging sense. *Leeth* involved a challenge to the rules governing grants of parole to Commonwealth prisoners. The rules pegged parole eligibility and expectations to the standards applying in the State prisons in which federal prisoners were housed. The plaintiff argued that this infringed an implied constitutional requirement of substantive equality of treatment, in that federal prisoners convicted of the same federal offence in different parts of Australia were left with greatly divergent parole expectations. In *Kruger*, the plaintiffs had argued that Commonwealth laws providing for the removal of Indigenous children from their families and communities singled those children out for unequal treatment that was constitutionally impermissible.

While neither of those arguments inspired a High Court majority to recognise substantive legal equality as a constitutional imperative, there may yet be a much narrower principle to be salvaged from the decisions, one enjoying clearer synergies with other established areas of Australian constitutional doctrine. Much of the reasoning contained in the majority judgments in *Leeth* and *Kruger* appears consistent with a narrowly confined implied guarantee of equal treatment within the context of exercises of judicial power (or in short form, 'equal justice').[25] All things considered, if this narrowly delimited equal justice principle were to be cemented this would most likely be as one strand of the limitations derived from the separation of judicial power rather than as a freestanding implied limitation.[26]

In considering and rejecting the feasibility of an implied guarantee of equality, the High Court in *Leeth* and *Kruger* displayed solid functionalist credentials. Given the power of the case assembled, when measured against the criteria of functionalism, it would take a radical shift in accepted methodology for these decisions to be revisited. This likely means that any future Australian constitutional guarantee of equality would have to come about by way of textual amendment following a referendum.

[23] *Leeth v Commonwealth* (1992) 174 CLR 455.
[24] *Kruger v The Commonwealth* (1997) 190 CLR 1.
[25] See Stellios, above n 16, 308–09; see also F Wheeler, 'Due Process' in C Saunders and A Stone (eds), *The Oxford Handbook of the Australian Constitution* (Oxford University Press, 2018, forthcoming); D Meyerson, 'Equality' in C Saunders and A Stone (eds), *The Oxford Handbook of the Australian Constitution* (Oxford University Press, 2018, forthcoming).
[26] Stellios, above n 16, 308–09; Wheeler, above n 25.

B. 'Absolutely Free' Trade, Commerce and Intercourse: Section 92

Given a choice among the various equality and discrimination principles within the Australian Constitution, the most straightforward context in which to examine the utility of functionalist interpretation may be that of the section 92 exhortation to 'absolutely free' trade.[27] The notoriously succinct expression of this provision[28] leaves it amenable to a variety of different interpretations. Having laboured for many decades in the absence of a clear vision of section 92's purpose the High Court finally, under the leadership of Mason CJ, invoked a functionalist methodology to justify a fresh start for doctrine in this area. The authoritative reinterpretation of section 92 that was achieved in the unanimous seven-member joint judgment in *Cole v Whitfield* provides a prime illustration of the potential benefits that can flow from fidelity to this methodology.

The resolution of the doctrinal mess which preceded *Cole v Whitfield* was made possible only by the Court's decision in that case to allow itself recourse to the Convention Debates to find reason to, finally and conclusively, prefer one set of suggested animating values over rival suggestions.[29] The Court in and since *Cole v Whitfield* has been insistent that section 92 is not concerned with individual rights and must, in line with the clear intentions of its framers, be accorded a solely federalism-reinforcing role.[30] Its purpose, in other words, is to discourage protectionist policies that would fuel interstate rivalry and antagonism and in turn undermine a sense of national unity.[31] Previous decisions which had turned on an 'individual rights' understanding of section 92 were disapproved; they were found to have generated unsatisfactory outcomes and created perverse incentives, by immunising interstate trade from sensible non-protectionist regulation to which local trade had remained subject.[32]

Aside from clarifying section 92's animating purpose, the Court in *Cole v Whitfield* also nominated a preferred doctrinal test. The unanimous judgment insisted that section 92 should be applied by reference to a substantive test of discrimination, as only a substance-focused test could secure fully the objectives of section 92 as revealed in the historical record.[33] A form-focused test would, it was reasoned, catch only a narrow subset of State protectionist initiatives and would be easily evaded.[34] While it was acknowledged that a substance-focused approach would throw up, in

[27] The 'intercourse limb' of s 92 will not be considered here, as it is not understood to incorporate a non-discrimination principle: *APLA Ltd v Legal Services Commissioner (NSW)* (2005) 224 CLR 322, 353 (Gleeson CJ and Heydon J), 393 (Gummow J), 462 (Hayne J).

[28] Discussed in *Cole v Whitfield* (1988) 165 CLR 360, 385.

[29] See ch 3 by Jeffrey Goldsworthy in this collection.

[30] *Cole v Whitfield* (1988) 165 CLR 360, 391, 402–03; *Betfair Pty Ltd v Racing New South Wales* (2012) 249 CLR 217, 266–68 (French CJ, Gummow, Hayne, Crennan and Bell JJ).

[31] This theme is explored in A Simpson, 'Grounding the High Court's Modern Section 92 Jurisprudence: The Case for Improper Purpose as the Touchstone' (2005) 33 *Federal Law Review* 445.

[32] *Cole v Whitfield* (1988) 165 CLR 360, 402–03; *Betfair Pty Ltd* (2012) 249 CLR 217, 266–68 (French CJ, Gummow, Hayne, Crennan and Bell JJ).

[33] *Cole v Whitfield* (1988) 165 CLR 360, 399, 408.

[34] ibid 401–02.

many cases, difficult questions of fact requiring engagement with non-legal policy considerations, this did not deter the Court from its course.[35] These 'questions of fact and degree on which minds might legitimately differ' were considered unavoidable and entirely within the remit of courts presented with section 92 arguments.[36]

While no other reasons were proffered in *Cole v Whitfield* for the choice of a substance-focused test, it could readily be inferred that other considerations were also in play. Textually, the provision's enigmatic and sparse language, which makes no mention of equal treatment or discrimination, offers no clear anchor for a form-based test. As for policy, given the general statements, mentioned above, confirming the Court's willingness to grapple with non-legal policy considerations in this field, it is a reasonable assumption that these were in the mix as the *Cole v Whitfield* decision was crystallising. Had there been any notable policy reason for *not* adopting a substantive test in applying section 92 (as is arguably the case in some other contexts, as discussed below) this would likely have prevented the attainment of a single unanimous judgment.

The landmark decision in *Cole v Whitfield* was followed quickly by another, setting out an essential refinement to the Court's new approach to section 92. In *Castlemaine Tooheys Ltd v South Australia* (*Castlemaine*),[37] the Court was unanimous in holding that the section 92 rule should be tempered with a proportionality-based savings test. Specifically, both judgments held that a law which gave rise to protectionist discrimination would escape invalidity where that discrimination was only incidental, and suitably adapted, to a non-protectionist policy goal.[38] The incorporation of this proviso at the heart of section 92 doctrine provides one of the clearest illustrations of the Mason Court's commitment to functionalist reasoning, in line with the latter's inherent interest in causality. The strong preference expressed in *Castlemaine* for evidence-based testing—of the compatibility of impugned laws with relevant constitutional values—makes this case one of the Court's benchmark applications of a functionalist methodology.[39]

In more recent times the High Court has made some subtle modifications to section 92 doctrine, none of which undermine its functionalist credentials as established in *Cole v Whitfield* and *Castlemaine*. In terms of the values ascribed to section 92, recent cases could be read as de-emphasising the interstate nature of trade as an ingredient within the concept of protectionist discrimination. In *Betfair v Western Australia* the plurality expressed the purpose of the trade and commerce limb of section 92 in terms of the 'creation and fostering of national markets', taking the view that the provision's reference to 'trade … among the States' should, in the twenty-first century, mean simply trade within the nation.[40] It is unclear at this stage whether this shift in emphasis will prove to be transient or, perhaps, more enduring.[41] Even if this

[35] ibid 408–09.

[36] ibid 409.

[37] *Castlemaine Tooheys Ltd v South Australia* (1990) 169 CLR 436.

[38] ibid 472–73 (Mason CJ, Brennan, Deane, Dawson and Toohey JJ), 478 (Gaudron and McHugh JJ).

[39] Dixon, 'The Functional Constitution', above n 5, 459, 483.

[40] *Betfair v Western Australia* (2008) 234 CLR 418, 452 (Gleeson CJ, Gummow, Kirby, Hayne, Crennan and Kiefel JJ).

[41] See D Meagher, A Simpson, J Stellios and F Wheeler, *Hanks Australian Constitutional Law: Materials and Commentary*, 10th edn (Chatswood, N.S.W., Australia, LexisNexis, 2016) [9.4.36].

attempted updating sticks, it still seems broadly consistent with the spirit in which section 92 was drafted and so cannot easily be cast as regressive against the criteria of functionalist analysis.

There have also been some important markers of continuity in the Court's understanding of the values animating section 92. Most importantly, in a subsequent case brought by Betfair Pty Ltd, the plurality reaffirmed its conviction that protectionism is the mischief to which section 92 is directed and insisted that that concept must remain the centrepiece of the doctrinal test applied in this area.[42] In that same case, the Court both reaffirmed its commitment to the proportionality-based proviso and was at pains to emphasise that 'the subject of s 92 is interstate trade, not traders' (meaning the Court remains unmoved by arguments channelling earlier 'individual rights' understandings of section 92).[43]

A further recent modification to the Mason Court's section 92 jurisprudence—as laid out in *Cole v Whitfield* and *Castlemaine*—concerns the way in which the substance-focused test of discrimination is to be applied. In *Sportsbet v Racing New South Wales* (*Sportsbet*)[44] the plurality insisted that, in assessing whether a law discriminates in a protectionist sense, only the law's practical effect is relevant and no significance at all should be placed on its legal operation. The plurality suggested that one decision from the Mason Court era—*Bath v Alston Holdings Pty Ltd*—had broken faith with this aspect of the *Cole v Whitfield* test by attaching some weight to considerations of legal form.[45] If that charge is accepted, then *Sportsbet* should be viewed as a heightening of the Court's attachment to a substance-focused doctrinal test.

The plurality in *Sportsbet* refined the substance-focused test for section 92 in one further respect. It insisted that no weight should here be attached to possible inferences about legislative purpose; rather, a finding of protectionist discrimination should be based purely on the substantive effects to which the law gives rise.[46] While I have argued elsewhere that there is a meaningful difference between these alternate emphases,[47] it remains the case that both variants fit comfortably within the concept of a substance-focused test. In short, the elimination since *Sportsbet* of legislative purpose as a possible touchstone does not undermine the good fit in this area between the federal-structural (or, since *Betfair*, perhaps nation-building) values underpinning the provision and the substance-focused test through which those values are secured.

In its interpretation of section 92's trade and commerce limb, then, the High Court has over a 25-year period remained committed to grounding its doctrine in an historically derived constitutional value and executing it by means of an evidence-based, substance-focused test. The identified values have, appropriately, informed

[42] *Betfair Pty Ltd* (2012) 249 CLR 217, 265 (French CJ, Gummow, Hayne, Crennan and Bell JJ); see also at 271 (Heydon J) and, more equivocally, at 293 (Kiefel J).

[43] ibid 266, 268 (French CJ, Gummow, Hayne, Crennan and Bell JJ); see also at 272 (Heydon J), 286 (Kiefel J).

[44] *Sportsbet v Racing New South Wales* (2012) 249 CLR 298, 318–20 (French CJ, Gummow, Hayne, Crennan, Kiefel and Bell JJ).

[45] ibid 319 (French CJ, Gummow, Hayne, Crennan, Kiefel and Bell JJ).

[46] ibid 320 (French CJ, Gummow, Hayne, Crennan, Kiefel and Bell JJ).

[47] Simpson, 'Grounding the High Court's Modern Section 92 Jurisprudence', above n 31.

the selection of a doctrinal test. Doctrine in this area can, broadly speaking, be regarded as a model of good judicial practice from the perspective of a functionalist interpretative methodology.

C. Discrimination on the Basis of State Residence: Section 117

Many within the Australian legal fraternity would likely nominate *Street v Queensland Bar Association* (*Street*) as the High Court's signature foray into constitutional discrimination analysis. That case turned on the meaning to be given to section 117 of the Constitution, which prohibits discrimination based on State of residence. Specifically, section 117 provides that

> [a] subject of the Queen, resident in any State, shall not be subject in any other State to any disability or discrimination which would not be equally applicable to him if he were a subject of the Queen resident in such other State.

Prior to the Court's decision in *Street* the provision had been applied narrowly, by reference to a formal test for discrimination. State laws would only be found to fall foul of the section 117 prohibition if they explicitly singled out non-residents for some burden.[48]

Street involved a challenge to one State's efforts to maintain regulatory barriers to impede barristers resident outside that State from working within it. The plaintiff, Alexander Whistler Street,[49] was a New South Wales-based barrister whose desire to work also in Queensland was frustrated by regulations in place in that State. The impugned Queensland law did not, however, discriminate on its face—rather, it imposed a uniform requirement upon all aspirants to the bar, but one which would be easily satisfied by existing residents while being burdensome for others. The plaintiff's case, then, invited a significant departure from preceding doctrine under which uniform rules were unassailable.

The decision in *Street* swept aside the previously dominant form-based test for discrimination and replaced it with a robust test focused on substantive effect. While all judges agreed that a substantive test should be favoured, there was nonetheless significant underlying disagreement about the rationale to be attributed to the section 117 principle.[50] It is to the Court's credit, though, that the disagreement was laid out openly.

Consistently with functionalist methodology, each of the seven separate judgments delivered in *Street* gave explicit attention to the question of which values should inform the interpretation of section 117. There were two distinct themes vying for ascendancy: on one hand, the view that section 117 protected individuals from discrimination because this was intrinsically just or desirable; on the other, the view that this protection was important for instrumental reasons tied to the pursuit

[48] See, eg, *Davies and Jones v Western Australia* (1904) 2 CLR 29, 47 (Barton J), 49 (O'Connor J); *Henry v Boehm* (1973) 128 CLR 482, 489 (Barwick CJ), 497–98 (Gibbs J).

[49] Now Street J of the Federal Circuit Court.

[50] Simpson, 'The (Limited) Significance of the Individual', above n 13, 644–48.

of harmonious federal relations at a polity level. While all seven judgments pay at least some lip service to both perspectives, many imply a clear rank order as between the two.

Some judges placed greater emphasis on the federal-structural rationale for the inclusion of section 117 in the Constitution, insisting that the end goal of the framers had here been to sustain a harmonious federal union. Mason CJ, Dawson J and McHugh J each reasoned primarily along these lines, emphasising that the 'rights' conferred by section 117 were intended, by the Constitution's framers, to have as their principal benefit the promotion of harmonious relations among the component polities of the federation.[51] Each insisted, in turn, that any judicially crafted limitations on the reach of the section 117 non-discrimination principle would need to rest comfortably with that federal-structural objective. While it would overstate things to suggest that these three judges attached no intrinsic value to protecting individuals from discrimination, their judgments nonetheless prioritise the federal-structural consequentialist rationale for section 117.

The remaining members of the *Street* Court placed greater emphasis on section 117's potential as an individual rights-protective provision, providing a more deontological kind of justification for expanding the ambit of this limitation. Toohey J contested the idea, developed most fully in McHugh J's judgment, that the historical record revealed only federal-structural motivations for section 117.[52] Others chose instead to downplay the importance of that drafting history. Gaudron J contended that the text of section 117—in particular, the pivotal term 'discrimination'—should be read consistently with the contemporary legal value of equality and non-discrimination, within which the interests of the individual are central.[53] For Deane J, the wider constitutional context was the key to justifying an individual rights-focused interpretation of section 117. He contended that the Constitution contains other provisions which 'serve the function of advancing or protecting the liberty, the dignity or the equality of the citizen', and those other provisions lent weight to a similar construction of section 117. This reasoning was bolstered with references to comparative law.[54]

Subsequent cases raising section 117 have yielded no greater level of agreement as to the provision's underlying values. I have explained elsewhere that in both *Goryl v Greyhound Australia Pty Ltd*[55] and *Sweedman v Transport Accident Commission*[56] the High Court glossed over the question of which values should inform section 117's interpretation and, in addition, retreated somewhat from the robust application of a substantive test of discrimination. Both manoeuvres could be understood as risk-averse responses to discomfort with the values contestation left unresolved in *Street*.[57] This retreat may reflect, in other words, a desire to remove significant internal disagreement from the public eye.

[51] *Street* (1989) 168 CLR 461, 491 (Mason CJ), 541 (Dawson J), 583 (McHugh J).
[52] ibid 553–54.
[53] ibid 570.
[54] ibid 522, 527.
[55] *Goryl v Greyhound Australia Pty Ltd* (1994) 179 CLR 463.
[56] *Sweedman v Transport Accident Commission* (2006) 226 CLR 362.
[57] Simpson, 'The (Limited) Significance of the Individual', above n 13, 649–51; Simpson, 'State Residence Discrimination and the High Court's Retreat into Characterisation', above n 18, 370–74.

How does the reasoning in *Street* and subsequent cases measure up against Rosalind Dixon's functionalist model? In short, these cases would yield a mixed report card. On the one hand, the judgments in *Street* provide some good illustrations of functionalist modes of reasoning. Many embark on an explicit search for the values undergirding section 117 and acknowledge that those values—whatever they may be—should be an important factor guiding interpretation. On the other hand, the *Street* judgments illustrate the potential for divergent conclusions about the values properly to be attributed to a single constitutional provision or rule. Even where judges have been focused on the same sources, the result may be disagreement as to what values those sources yield. In *Street*, this is particularly evident in the different conclusions drawn from the historical drafting record by Deane J and Toohey J, on the one hand, and Mason CJ, Dawson J and McHugh J on the other.[58] *Street* makes clear that whatever reasons might exist for urging functionalist interpretative method upon judges, to hold out the promise of concrete outcomes would be disingenuous.

The judgment of Gaudron J in *Street* is interesting for many reasons. When viewed by reference to the criteria of functionalist analysis it points up a potential loophole, of sorts, in that methodology. Depending on how it is defined, a functionalist approach may enable a superficial commitment to be maintained which then provides cover for what is, in substance, a more controversial interpretive approach.

If functionalist interpretive methodology is understood to demand attention to constitutional values as discerned, first and foremost, from the Constitution's text *and* history, then it leaves scope for various sleights of hand under its name. Gaudron J demonstrated one such possibility in *Street*, by seizing upon the word discrimination in the text of section 117 and insisting that, as a well-known legal concept, it could be understood and applied without any excursion into the provision's drafting history.[59] This was superficially compliant with the demands of a functionalist approach—a key value was distilled from constitutional text. Yet to end the enquiry there meant overlooking important insights to be found in the structure and history of the Constitution, both of which point strongly to an interpretation of section 117 tethered to a constitutional value of national unity.[60]

So, any version of a functionalist methodology that permitted recourse to constitutional text to be conclusive of relevant underpinning values—that is, without demanding cross-checking against constitutional structure and history—has the potential to offer a Trojan horse for other methodologies. Jeffrey Goldsworthy describes this scenario as one of functionalism collapsing into pragmatism and Gaudron J's judgment in *Street* offers a ready example of that suggested phenomenon.

As Gaudron J skilfully demonstrated, recourse to text, without more, can amount to identification of an empty vessel into which a variety of content could be poured—including pragmatic or progressivist content. Thus the particular genius of

[58] *Street* (1989) 168 CLR 461, 485–86 (Mason CJ), 521–22, 528 (Deane J), 537–38 (Dawson J), 553–54 (Toohey J), 583–84 (McHugh J).

[59] ibid 570 (Gaudron J).

[60] This point is discussed in greater detail in Simpson, 'The (Limited) Significance of the Individual', above n 13, 651–61.

Gaudron J's approach to equality and discrimination principles was her insistence that that language, when found in the Constitution, represents a shell to be filled with contemporary legal content. And, while Gaudron J was explicit in eschewing the historical record in *Street*,[61] the variety of crosscutting themes and opinions evident in the debates on section 117 would nonetheless have enabled her to mount a more cautious circumvention; she could simply have insisted that her 'empty vessel' approach to the meaning of discrimination was an appropriate response to the framers' multiple and diverse intentions.

Do the judgments in *Street* display an equal degree of fidelity to functionalist interpretative methodology? An answer might depend on whether it is possible—and desirable—to define that methodology in such a way as to de-legitimise certain readings of the historical record; that is, to permit recourse only to 'sensible' or 'objective' readings. In other contexts, bearing on other doctrinal puzzles, it may indeed be feasible to distil a single 'best' historical reading by reference to which alternative readings could be branded disingenuous. That might, for instance, be a viable way of viewing the historical record as to section 92's exhortation to 'absolutely free' trade (as to which, see above). But many enquiries into the historical record would not yield such a decisive result.[62] Whether any of the divergent conclusions drawn from section 117's historical record in *Street* should be regarded as disingenuous is a question likely to provoke such disagreement.

If pragmatic reasoning can, in various ways, be dressed up as functionalist reasoning to cloak it with greater legitimacy, then this might suggest either that functionalism is of more rhetorical than practical significance or, alternatively, that its expectations need to be further particularised in order to distinguish true believers from pretenders. Another angle on the significance of *Street* is that it illustrates the potential for gradations of fidelity to functionalist methodology. Specifically, the judgments in *Street* seem to offer a useful lens through which to explore the difference between purist functionalist reasoning—as represented by Mason CJ, Dawson J and McHugh J—and a much looser, or perhaps even pseudo-, kind of functionalist reasoning as undertaken by several other members of the Court.[63]

D. Fiscal Discrimination and Preference among States: Sections 51(ii) and 99

The most recent area of constitutional non-discrimination doctrine to be upended and reset by the High Court is that of the related restrictions contained in sections 51(ii) and 99 of the Constitution. Section 51(ii) confers upon the Commonwealth a power to make laws with respect to 'taxation; but so as not to discriminate between States or parts of States'. Section 99 provides that '[t]he Commonwealth shall not, by any law or regulation of trade, commerce or revenue, give preference to one State or any part thereof over another State or any part thereof'. Either through a poor matching of doctrinal test to underlying values or, alternatively, a problematic

[61] *Street* (1989) 168 CLR 461, 570.
[62] See ch 3 by Jeffrey Goldsworthy in this collection.
[63] See generally Simpson, 'The (Limited) Significance of the Individual', above n 13.

re-conceptualisation of those values, the Court's jurisprudence in this area has become unstable. As becomes apparent when considering the single most persuasive judgment on offer here—that of French CJ in *Fortescue Metals Group Limited v Commonwealth* (*Fortescue*)[64]—functionalist insights provide a roadmap that could greatly assist the Court in rehabilitating doctrine in this area.

As an interesting aside, the Constitution nowhere insists that disbursements to States, via the section 96 'grants power' or any other means, must conform to any standard of equality or non-discrimination. It was established early on that grants to States made under section 96 are not subject to the limitations contained in sections 51(ii) and 99.[65] The Commonwealth distributes a large portion of its tax revenue to the States via a formula that is based on a complex assessment of States' need, rather than their respective populations alone.[66] That distribution framework is the product of intergovernmental agreements, rather than any constitutional mandate, and could be understood as pursuing a value of substantive equality among polities within the federation. Whether or not the fact of these arrangements has influenced the High Court's interpretation of sections 51(ii) and 99 is impossible to discern from the decided cases and so will not be considered further in this chapter.

The values underpinning section 99 and the proviso to section 51(ii) have always been understood to be federal-structural in nature.[67] At least until recently it has been universally accepted that the constitutional value animating these limitations is, in terms of the typology set out above, the securing of formal equality among the component polities of the federation. For many decades the case law on section 99 and the section 51(ii) proviso applied those limitations by way of familiar form-based tests pivoting on a legal criterion. In other words, these concepts of discrimination and preference were understood in a way that required different treatment to be manifest on the face of the law—with no scope for consideration of the context in which that law would operate nor the law's attractiveness in policy terms.

Scholarly attention to the viability in these settings of substituting a substance-based doctrinal test (where context and policy objectives might impact validity) has yielded the following reasons to resist such a shift:

— A form-based test would be most faithful to the framers' reasons for including these provisions in the Constitution—being that a bright line rule would do most to maintain an appearance of even-handedness in this aspect of federal fiscal relations, in the interests of rapid and enduring national economic integration.

[64] *Fortescue Metals Group Limited v Commonwealth* (2013) (2013) 250 CLR 548.

[65] *Victoria v Commonwealth* (1926) 38 CLR 399, 406 (Knox CJ, Isaacs, Higgins, Duffy, Powers, Rich and Starke JJ) (*Federal Roads Case*); *Deputy Federal Commissioner of Taxation (NSW) v WR Moran Pty Ltd* (1939) 61 CLR 735, 763 (Latham CJ), 775 (Starke J); *WR Moran Pty Ltd v Deputy Federal Commissioner of Taxation (NSW)* (1940) 63 CLR 338, 346–47 (Privy Council).

[66] For an explanation of these arrangements, see A Fenna, 'Commonwealth Fiscal Power and Australian Federalism' (2008) 31 *UNSW Law Journal* 509, 516; C Saunders, 'Federal Fiscal Reform and the GST' (2000) 11 *Public Law Review* 99.

[67] See, eg, WH Moore, *The Constitution of the Commonwealth of Australia* (London, John Murray, 1902) 184; R Garran, *Prosper the Commonwealth* (Sydney, Angus & Robertson, 1959) 99, 118–19.

— On a form-based test, these constitutional limitations would have a very limited sphere of operation, in turn ensuring to the Commonwealth maximal freedom to manipulate economic levers as it sees fit, in the national interest.
— A form-based doctrinal test, with its simple focus on uniformity of treatment as a matter of legal operation, would protect judges from the expectation that they adjudge a law's 'reasonableness' in the politically sensitive context of economic policy, where they may perceive themselves (and/or be perceived by others) as having neither expertise nor legitimacy.[68]

i. Radical Change

In 2004 in *Permanent Trustee Australia Ltd v Commissioner of State Revenue* (*Permanent Trustee*)[69] the High Court was presented with an opportunity to revisit the choice of a form-based doctrinal test for section 99. It was invited to find that a law which framed a single rule to be applied in all parts of Australia—that tax on certain transactions connected with 'Commonwealth places' would 'mirror' the rates applying in the surrounding State or Territory[70]—in fact worked a preference among States because of the contextual fact that the rates thus mirrored differed greatly as between jurisdictions. This was for a few reasons a complicated scenario. There was room for argument as to whether the Commonwealth law, given its mirroring nature, could properly be characterised as applying a uniform rule. In addition, the States themselves were not greatly affected as polities. Rather, most of the tax collected by the Commonwealth under this regime came from individuals and corporations.[71]

Perhaps in part because of these distractions, the plurality judgment muddied the waters of section 99 doctrine. Its reasoning is so truncated that it is difficult to be sure whether the plurality consciously chose to anoint a new constitutional value at the heart of the section 99 limitation or, alternatively, merely lost sight of the value identified in earlier cases out of abstract enthusiasm for a new type of doctrinal test. Either way, the reasoning is impoverished and unconvincing in ways that could have been largely remedied if the insights of functionalist analysis had been harnessed here.

Even if some of those insights were contemplated behind the scenes, the plurality's judgment was steadfastly focused on a different task. That task was to defend and further consolidate a unified understanding of the nature and reach the concept of non-discrimination, wherever found in Australian constitutional law.[72]

[68] L Zines and G Lindell, 'Form and Substance: "Discrimination" in Modern Constitutional Law' (1992) 21 *Federal Law Review* 136; Simpson, 'The High Court's Conception of Discrimination', above n 7, 280–81, 294; A Simpson '*Fortescue Metals Group Limited v Commonwealth*: Discrimination and Fiscal Federalism' (2014) 24 *Public Law Review* 93.
[69] *Permanent Trustee* (2004) 220 CLR 388.
[70] Commonwealth Places (Mirror Taxes) Act 1998 (Cth) ss 3–9.
[71] The significance of this in the resolution of *Permanent Trustee* is discussed in Simpson, 'The High Court's Conception of Discrimination', above n 7, 291.
[72] This contention is developed in ibid 273–77.

To emphasise the utility of a particular test in the abstract, without consideration of its suitability in a specific context by reference to relevant constitutional values, is to adopt a decidedly non-functionalist mode of analysis.

The substance-focused doctrinal test that the plurality adopted was notable in a further respect, one growing from its roots in other areas of constitutional jurisprudence. The test made the section 99 limitation a defeasible one, by introduction of a criterion of 'reasonableness'. Accordingly, even if the impugned legislation was best understood as applying different tax rates by reference to geographic locale, that would still be constitutionally permissible if accompanied by a compelling policy rationale. Even though this worked a fundamental change in the operation of section 99, the plurality did not seek to justify the transformation by reference to the structure or drafting history of the Constitution. Rather, it seems that the justification was founded entirely on Gaudron J's analysis in *Street*, and subsequent cases relying upon it[73]—an analysis identified as problematic earlier in this chapter.

Confronting then its newly minted decisive question—ie, the reasonableness of the impugned measure—the plurality found that there was indeed a defensible objective underlying the differential tax rates. That objective was a desire to tax Commonwealth places at the same rate as other places in the surrounding State. Again, there was no attempt to defend this as an outcome consistent with the framers' concern to promote harmonious relations among the federation's component polities and their constituents.[74] Hence there was not even a veneer of functionalist methodology informing this judgment. The considerations that would be prioritised on a functionalist approach—those finding support in the text, structure and history of the relevant provisions and/or the Constitution as a whole—were deftly sidestepped in the plurality judgment.

Those conclusions were rejected emphatically in the separate dissenting judgments of McHugh J and Kirby J in *Permanent Trustee*. Both dismissed the suggestion that section 99 could be read so that a Commonwealth law meting out different treatment, as between States, in the hope of equalising some baseline disparities in their positions might be spared. It was, they insisted, a bright line rule, indefeasible and indifferent to the policy rationales motivating impugned Commonwealth laws.[75] In reaching that position, Kirby J emphasised considerations of constitutional structure and history while McHugh J focused on the interpretations given to section 99 in earlier decisions of the Court.[76] Kirby J' stance is particularly striking, given that he has often been cast as a stubborn progressivist inclined to discount the value of the text, structure and history in interpreting the Constitution.

ii. In Search of a Unifying Principle

The suggested deficiencies in the position adopted in *Permanent Trustee* have, in more recent cases, come home to roost. The High Court seems now to be retreating

[73] *Permanent Trustee* (2004) 220 CLR 388, 424 (Gleeson CJ, Gummow, Hayne, Callinan and Heydon JJ).
[74] ibid 424–25 (Gleeson CJ, Gummow, Hayne, Callinan and Heydon JJ).
[75] ibid 428 (McHugh J), 461–62 (Kirby J).
[76] ibid 427–28, 446–48 (McHugh J), 462–67 (Kirby J).

rapidly to a pre-*Permanent Trustee* conception of section 99, and certainly has resisted the extension of the latter's reasoning into the domain of the section 51(ii) proviso. Unfortunately, though, the deficiencies in methodology that were on show in *Permanent Trustee* also feature in most judgments in the two follow up cases of *Fortescue*[77] and *Queensland Nickel Pty Ltd v Commonwealth* (*Queensland Nickel*).[78]

The leading judgments in these recent cases, to be explored here, do not do much better on a functionalist evaluation than does *Permanent Trustee*. In disregard of the key interpretative goals of clarity and transparency, the Court's apparent change of heart has mostly been buried under layers of obfuscating doctrinal exegesis. While both *Fortescue* and *Queensland Nickel* seem to have worked a reversion to a doctrinal test much closer to the form-based tests of old, both decisions are nonetheless satisfying only in the result. The methodology remains problematic.

In *Fortescue* the plaintiff challenged the Commonwealth's mining tax legislation that had, like the legislation upheld in *Permanent Trustee*, attempted a kind of equalisation as between States. In keeping with its avowed nature as a tax on economic rents, the Commonwealth law—the Minerals Resource Rent Tax Act 2012 (Cth) and related provisions[79]—imposed a higher effective tax rate in States with lower rates of State-imposed mining royalties. The plaintiff company challenged the tax on several constitutional bases, including by reference to section 99 and the section 51(ii) proviso. The plurality of Hayne, Bell and Keane JJ applied a form-focused test to find that the provisions did not engage in prohibited discrimination or preference.[80]

While this approach was consistent with existing case law on the section 51(ii) proviso, which had insisted that a uniform Commonwealth law could never amount to discrimination in this context, it did not engage with the significant developments in interpretation of the proviso's close relative, section 99. Those doctrinal developments (ie, the adoption of a defeasible substance-focused view of 'preference' in *Permanent Trustee*) would, if extended to the section 51(ii) context and to this case, have opened the possibility that the mining tax regime did not in fact treat miners equally irrespective of their States of operation. The plurality judgment was unconvincing as to why the new approach adopted for section 99 was not to be extended to the section 51(ii) proviso. Specifically, it attempted to distinguish section 99 from the section 51(ii) proviso on tenuous semantic grounds, focusing on the latter's terminology of 'discrimination between' and insisting that this connotes a form-based test.[81]

This attempt to isolate the section 51(ii) proviso from developments in related doctrinal areas did not, however, come entirely out of left field. In *Austin v Commonwealth* (*Austin*),[82] where there was some discussion of substance-focused

[77] *Fortescue* (2013) 250 CLR 548.

[78] *Queensland Nickel Pty Ltd v Commonwealth* (2015) 255 CLR 252.

[79] Minerals Resource Rent Tax Act 2012 (Cth) div 10. See also Minerals Resource Rent Tax (Imposition—Customs) Act 2012 (Cth); Minerals Resource Rent Tax (Imposition—Excise) Act 2012 (Cth); Minerals Resource Rent Tax (Imposition—General) Act 2012 (Cth).

[80] *Fortescue* (2013) 250 CLR 548, 601–05.

[81] Simpson, 'Discrimination and Fiscal Federalism', above n 68, 96.

[82] *Austin v Commonwealth* (2003) 215 CLR 185.

tests of discrimination, there was explicit mention—albeit fleetingly and in obiter—of the possibility that the section 51(ii) proviso was exceptional among the Constitution's non-discrimination principles on account of its dealing with taxation laws.[83] The plurality in *Austin* did not go further and explain why this characteristic might suggest a different interpretative approach. In *Fortescue*, only French CJ took up that challenge, giving explicit consideration to the possible merits of protecting section 51(ii) from the march of substance-based analysis.[84]

French CJ's judgment in *Fortescue* was without doubt the most candid and considered of any in this area for many decades. His methodology was solidly functionalist and his reasons provide not only a comprehensive roadmap by which the Court might make sense of section 99 and the section 51(ii) proviso, but also an important illustration of the virtues of the functionalist method in navigating difficult constitutional terrain. Taking as his starting point the indisputable federal-structural purposes for which these provisions were included in the Constitution[85] French CJ deftly constructed a post-hoc rationalisation for the outcome in *Permanent Trustee* that manages to reconcile it with earlier decisions—an achievement that eluded the plurality in that case.

His analysis advanced, in effect, a tripartite classification of Commonwealth laws. Indisputably valid, he said, are laws which apply a single uniform rule to States but which, through contextual factors, might operate to the advantage of some States or their residents more so than others.[86] Indisputably invalid, on the other hand, will be laws which explicitly apply different rules to different States.[87] The novel feature of French CJ's reasoning was his description of a third category, situated between the other two. In this category he placed laws which are harder to categorise—which have some features of a uniform law but also in other respects resemble different treatment.[88] He included in this category laws which attempt to *create* uniformity of treatment by setting out to equalise the positions of States in spite of their different baselines. Also in the middle category, French CJ suggested, will be laws like that considered in *Permanent Trustee*, which work synergistically with State laws to produce a result that could be cast as either equal or unequal treatment.[89] Here, he contended, the text of section 99 and the section 51(ii) proviso are inconclusive and so the Constitution's structure and drafting history could play a part in deciding how to approach such cases.[90]

In this third category of case, prompting the most delicate and difficult questions of interpretation, French CJ found a home for a criterion of reasonableness. Here, he said, and only here—where the insights of text, structure and history run out—judges can properly have regard to the extra-constitutional policy considerations

[83] ibid 247 (Gaudron, Gummow and Hayne JJ).
[84] *Fortescue* (2013) 250 CLR 548, 576, 578 (French CJ).
[85] ibid 563, 572.
[86] ibid 574.
[87] ibid 572.
[88] ibid 578, 583.
[89] ibid 572, 574.
[90] ibid 583.

that often inform a criterion of reasonableness in constitutional doctrine.[91] In this analysis French CJ displayed the functionalist preference for carefully delimiting the zone in which those pragmatic considerations can have influence.[92] Such careful tailoring was not present in *Permanent Trustee*, however, where the plurality said nothing to suggest that their substance-focused test, with a criterion of reasonableness at its heart, might be applicable only to a subset of possible section 99 challenges.

Via this nuanced and policy-sensitive treatment of the issues, French CJ arrived in *Fortescue* at the same conclusion as was reached in the other judgments—ie, that the mining tax legislation infringed neither section 99 nor the proviso to section 51(ii).[93] That legislation fell, he reasoned, into the intermediate category of laws, in that there was room for real debate as to whether it laid down a uniform rule or not. Once the criterion of reasonableness was in play, French CJ was able to consider the law's aims against, initially, the constitutional values motivating these non-discrimination rules and, secondarily, broader policy considerations. The admirably clear and careful way in which this analysis proceeded confirms French CJ as the standard-bearer of functionalist methodology in this corner of constitutional jurisprudence.

In the most recent case of *Queensland Nickel*[94] the retreat from a substance-based test for section 99 has seemingly continued, though with no further clarity being provided regarding the reasons for it. The High Court rejected unanimously a section 99 challenge to Commonwealth regulations governing the granting of tax credits to heavy greenhouse gas emitters. The novel claim in the plaintiff's case, unventilated in previous cases, was that the claimed section 99 breach here flowed from the Commonwealth law's uniform application to taxpayers who were differently situated in their 'natural, business or other circumstances' (so as not to be 'relevantly alike' for purposes of discrimination analysis).[95] It is a measure of the confusion that followed *Permanent Trustee* that this case was ever commenced. The scenario it presented was of the first category identified by French CJ in *Fortescue*—a uniform rule that would, prior to *Permanent Trustee*, have been universally assumed to fall outside section 99's remit. But the threadbare reasoning provided by the plurality in *Permanent Trustee* left open the possibility that this type of case, too, should now be resolved by application of a substance-based test pivoting on a criterion of reasonableness.

The leading judgment in the case was delivered by Nettle J, with whom all other members of the Court agreed. He sidestepped the crucial question of whether a uniform rule could ever infringe the section 99 prohibition, on the basis that the plaintiff had failed to demonstrate a connection between its disadvantaged status under Commonwealth law and its geographical location.[96] The curious thing about this reasoning is that it gives only the briefest of mentions to the idea of a substance-focused

[91] ibid 585.
[92] See ch 1 by Rosalind Dixon in this collection.
[93] *Fortescue* (2013) 250 CLR 548, 585–86.
[94] *Queensland Nickel* (2015) 255 CLR 252.
[95] ibid 265 (Nettle J).
[96] ibid 268.

test for section 99 preference[97] and neglects entirely to mention *Permanent Trustee*, despite it being the most recent High Court authority on section 99.

Rather than confront the holding and implications of *Permanent Trustee*, Nettle J's reasons took refuge in the taxing character of the impugned scheme, insisting that 'the view consistently taken in relation to taxation laws has been that it is not enough, in order to demonstrate discrimination in the relevant sense, to show only that a taxation law may have different effects in different States'.[98] In this, he echoed the view of the plurality in *Fortescue*. But what this analysis does not resolve is whether and when the criteria informing a substance-focused test—in particular, an assessment of the reasonableness of treating legal subjects identically or differently—will have any bearing on the application of section 99. Nettle J quoted French CJ in *Fortescue* but only alongside the plurality, with nothing to suggest that he found French CJ's judgment the more enlightening.

The Court's approach going forward in relation to section 99 and the section 51(ii) proviso is, then, genuinely hard to predict. *Permanent Trustee* introduced into section 99 a substance-focused test, imported from other corners of constitutional jurisprudence, which would render that limitation defeasible by reference to a reasonableness standard in at least some, but possibly not all, types of case. The deficiencies in the judgment are ones that tie back to its authors' failure to engage with the methods and tools of functionalist analysis; in particular, their apparent selection of a doctrinal test ahead of any analysis of relevant constitutional values. Those reasons exist in stark contrast to the illuminating and compelling position that French CJ was able to craft, in the subsequent case of *Fortescue*, by calling in aid those very tools and methods.

If indeed there is a retreat underway from the apparently radical change worked by *Permanent Trustee*, this might perhaps seem a good thing by reference to some of the policy considerations raised in the scholarship over the years and referenced above. Even so, the approach to executing the rewind is unfortunate, if it is to be characterised by simply pretending that key cases were never decided, and taking shelter in decades-old authorities as though there had been no conscious break with them. While any retreat from *Permanent Trustee* may be defensible by reference to the values that reveal themselves on a functionalist analysis, most of the reasoning to date has shown little fidelity to the procedural demands of a functionalist approach.

V. CONCLUSIONS

This chapter set out to illuminate the multiplicity of values that might sensibly be attributed to particular equality and discrimination principles in the Australian constitutional setting. Significant variation exists even within the four value groupings set out above. Hence there can be no reliable mapping, in the abstract, of doctrinal tests onto these values groupings. Each equality or discrimination rule must be

97 ibid 265–66 (Nettle J).

98 ibid 266.

assessed individually to determine its animating values and then, with the benefit of clarity around values, matched to a doctrinal test.

This methodological tour of the High Court's equality and discrimination jurisprudence, incomplete though it has been, tells a tale of fluctuating commitment to the goals and methods of functionalist analysis. In some contexts the Court's reasoning has been consistent with—and at times even a model of—functionalist methodology. At other times, however, majorities have neglected the insights of functionalism and have, in direct consequence of this, produced confused and unsatisfying doctrine. Where reasoning does not proceed in the optimal order—that is, with values being identified first and doctrinal tests contemplated only as a second-order consideration—the resulting principles have been unstable.

In contexts—for example, the current impasse over section 99 and the section 51(ii) proviso—where the Court has strayed from the functionalist path of transparent and evidence-based engagement with text, structure and history, the explanations for this may be as much sociological as doctrinal. Such commonplace human motivations as solidarity with peers and face-saving, along with a desire to avoid any reputational damage that might follow from a perception of successive changes of mind, are able at times to prevail over deeper commitments to process. Even then, functionalist methodology, as an enduring presence, can be expected to surface again when wrong turns eventually are acknowledged and rebuilding work commences.

Part V

Federalism and Constitutional Identity

12

Democratic Experimentalism

GABRIELLE APPLEBY AND BRENDAN LIM*

I. INTRODUCTION

WHILE THE AUSTRALIAN Constitution was making its way out of the Federal Conventions in the 1890s, the American philosopher John Dewey and his wife Alice were establishing their Laboratory School at the newly founded University of Chicago. Dewey imagined this pioneering elementary school 'as a scientific laboratory staffed with college trained teachers and devoted to research, experiment, and educational innovation'.[1] Passive transmission of abstract knowledge was disfavoured. Instead, 'learning came most importantly from the [students' own] experience of devising and trying out different responses' to practical problems, while students were also 'taught to move beyond immediate experience by subjecting it to speculative and analytical generalization'.[2] This was not merely a pedagogical commitment, but fundamentally a philosophical one. Indeed, it would not be inapt to describe it as a *constitutional* commitment for Dewey, who saw in the microcosm of his classroom 'the possibility of a broadened role for collaboration in the political realm'.[3]

By this time, the scientific achievements of the seventeenth and eighteenth centuries had demonstrated compellingly the power of enquiry that prioritised observed phenomena over first principles—the triumph of empiricism over belief. 'A hypothesis', William Whewell explained in 1847, 'should be close to the facts, and not connected with them by other arbitrary and untried facts; and … the philosopher should be ready to resign it as soon as the facts refuse to confirm it'.[4] Dewey believed that human thought itself, and not only scientific knowledge, was a 'continual collision of acquired belief and new experience'.[5] He sought to extend the

* We would like to thank Professor Andrew Lynch for his helpful comments on an earlier draft of this chapter, and Tom Allchurch for his research assistance in finalising it.

1 M Knoll, 'Laboratory School, University of Chicago' in DC Phillips (ed), *Encyclopedia of Educational Theory and Philosophy* (Los Angeles, London, New Delhi, Singapore and Washington DC, Sage, 2014) vol 2, 455–58.

2 WH Simon, 'The Institutional Configuration of Deweyan Democracy' in BE Butler (ed), *Democratic Experimentalism* (Amsterdam and New York, NY, Rodopi, 2013), 9–10.

3 ibid 10.

4 W Whewell, *The Philosophy of the Inductive Sciences Founded upon their History* (London, John W Parker, 1847) vol 2, 276.

5 Simon, above n 2, 9.

scientific commitments of the time to the ethical sphere, 'making ethical values, as well as empirical facts, the subject of on-going inquiry'.[6]

The form of 'on-going inquiry' that Dewey articulated was not only '*provisional*', in the scientific sense of its results being always falsifiable by experience, but also '*dynamic*' (involving 'feeling, observation, analysis, hypothesis, and experimental action'), '*self-correcting*' (its techniques and assumptions remaining always 'open to correction, modification or deletion'), and '*social*' (involving 'collaboration and communication among people navigating a problematic situation together').[7] Just as Dewey's pupils at the Laboratory School were confronted with practical classroom problems calling for the application of this very kind of enquiry, so the public, as Dewey saw it, was confronted with practical social problems calling for much the same. The enquiries to be conducted by the students and by the public differed in their scale but not in their essentially pragmatic or experimentalist character.

Dewey's constitutional vision called forth a conception of democracy that would nurture the provisional, dynamic, self-correcting and social enquiry that he envisaged for the public in tackling the problems of the day. That conception required that 'policies and proposals for social action be treated as working hypotheses'; that they be regarded as 'experimental in the sense that they will be entertained subject to constant and well-equipped observation of the consequences … and subject to ready and flexible revision'.[8] The very 'legitimacy of decision making', in Dewey's thinking, 'hing[ed] on the extent to which citizens [would] not feel permanently bound by [their] decisions in the face of new and different political changes'.[9] Dewey's vision also required serious information deficits to be addressed through a genuinely collaborative and deliberative enterprise between the public and their elected representatives: on the one hand, those in power, even if knowledgeable, do not by themselves have sufficient information to regulate effectively; on the other hand, the citizens may not have sufficient knowledge or coordination to address the problems they experience.[10] Between these deficits, Dewey saw 'the mutual constitution of the individual and society, struggling together to extend the limits of their knowledge in response to surprising failures of what they thought they already knew'.[11]

Australia's constitutional framers probably knew little, if anything, of Dewey's contemporaneous educational experiments in Chicago. Dewey's influence on the Australian teaching profession appears not to have arrived until just after the turn of the century.[12] The framers probably knew even less of Dewey's constitutional thinking.

[6] C Ansell, 'What is a "Democratic Experiment"?' (2012) 9 *Contemporary Pragmatism* 159, 165.

[7] DL Hildebrand 'Pragmatic Democracy: Inquiry, Objectivity, and Experience' (2011) 42 *Metaphilosophy* 589, 592–93, quoted in Ansell, above n 6, 166.

[8] J Dewey, *The Public and its Problems: An Essay in Political Inquiry* (University Park, PA, The Pennsylvania State University Press, first published 1927, 2012 edn) 152. See also ML Rogers, 'Dewey and His Vision of Democracy' (2010) 7(1) *Contemporary Pragmatism* 69, 84.

[9] Rogers, above n 8, 84.

[10] See Dewey, *The Public and its Problems*, above n 8, 154 quoted in Rogers, above n 8, 80–81. See also Simon, above n 2, 10.

[11] C Sabel, 'Dewey, Democracy, and Democratic Experimentalism' (2012) 9(2) *Contemporary Pragmatism* 35, 35.

[12] L Dunt, *Speaking Worlds: The Australian Educators and John Dewey 1890–1940* (Parkville, Vic., University of Melbourne History Department, 1993) 9.

Although laid out in a nascent form as early as 1888,[13] Dewey's ideas about democracy continued to mature well into the twentieth century. But the framers did know of James Bryce,[14] who had taught the young Dewey in his doctoral studies at Johns Hopkins University.[15] And the framers undoubtedly shared Dewey's pragmatist instincts.[16] They were steeped in a legal tradition that consciously eschewed reasoning from abstract principles: the case-by-case technique of the common law produces rules only by generalisation from the resolution of specific factual controversies; moreover, those generalised rules are only ever provisional, in the sense that they must, if the need arises, yield to the demands of new facts. The framers were steeped in a political tradition that was dependent upon its own internal malleability and therefore instilled deep suspicion towards any absolutist claim. So while Dewey, in his radical Chicago classroom, was developing, testing and refining the intellectual apparatus for his modern, normative vision of democratic experimentalism, the constitutional framers in Australia were designing an inherently pragmatist system of government that would prove over time to be capable of realising that emerging vision.

Our objective in this chapter is exploratory rather than prescriptive. We survey broadly the features of the Australian constitutional structure that can be seen to embody a commitment to democratic experimentalism or at least to enable pursuit of such a commitment. Constitutionalism itself, which on one view functions as a form of pre-commitment designed precisely to put certain matters beyond revision,[17] may inevitably be in tension with the premises of democratic experimentalism, which insist that *nothing* be beyond the revisions that experience may prove to be necessary. There are two reasons to think that this apparent tension is more illusory than real. First, constitutions not only constrain but also enable,[18] and it is in the enabling functions that the value of democratic experimentalism is most likely to find expression. Secondly, there are structural preconditions to the kind of enquiry which Dewey had in mind, and to the kind of relationship between the government and the governed that is necessary to sustain an experimental democracy. Constitutional entrenchment may be one way to protect these preconditions.

We examine two structural features of the Australian constitutional system. The first is the *political constitutionalism* that infuses the relatively spare legal constraints that the Australian Constitution imposes. This is an enabling feature in the sense that it permits relatively wide latitude for law-making, both legislative and bureaucratic, and therefore maximises flexibility to revise experimental laws and

[13] J Dewey, 'The Ethics of Democracy' (first published 1888) in JA Boydston (ed), *The Early Works of John Dewey 1882–1898, Volume 1* (Carbondale and Edwardsville, Ill Feffer & Simons Inc, London and Amsterdam, Southern Illinois University Press, 1969).

[14] S Gageler, 'James Bryce and the Australian Constitution' (2015) 43 *Federal Law Review* 177; N Aroney, *The Constitution of a Federal Commonwealth: The Making and Meaning of the Australian Constitution* (Cambridge, UK, Cambridge University Press, 2009) 78.

[15] E Ions, *James Bryce and American Democracy 1870–1922* (New York, Humanities Press, 1970) 118.

[16] *cf* FE Johns, 'Human Rights in the High Court of Australia, 1976–2003: The Righting of Australian Law?' (2005) 33 *Federal Law Review* 287, 304 (referring to evidence of a late 20th-century 'jurisprudential instinct of pragmatic derivation' even in the absence of a 'direct evocation' of Dewey's views).

[17] See, eg, S Freeman, 'Constitutional Democracy and the Legitimacy of Judicial Review' (1990) 9 *Law and Philosophy* 327; A Scalia, 'Common-Law Courts in a Civil-Law System: The Role of United States Federal Courts in Interpreting the Constitution and Laws' in A Gutmann (ed), *A Matter of Interpretation: Federal Courts and the Law* (Princeton, New Jersey, Princeton University Press, 1997), 40.

[18] See especially J Balkin, *Living Originalism* (Cambridge, Massachusetts, Harvard University Press, 2011); B Lim 'An Australian Reads *Living Originalism*' (2012) 34 *Sydney Law Review* 809.

policies in light of experience. The second is *federalism*, which is an enabling feature in a somewhat different sense: its creation and maintenance of smaller and multiple decision-making centres permits a greater density of experience against which to test competing or evolving policies and programmes.

We take up political constitutionalism in section II. We call the form of experimentalism enabled by this structural commitment *longitudinal* experimentalism, because the experience against which iterative policy hypotheses are tested is generated over time and not necessarily over different jurisdictions. We take up federalism in section III. Federalism specifically enables policies to be tested against experience that is generated simultaneously in multiple jurisdictions, thereby giving rise to what we call *horizontal* (as between coordinate sub-national units) and *vertical* (as between the national and sub-national units) experimentalism. In each of sections II and III, our objectives are three-fold: first, to identify for each of these varieties of democratic experimentalism the constitutional and other sources which render it a candidate for recognition as a 'constitutional value' (*Locating Democratic Experimentalism*); secondly, to identify the legal protections given to Dewey's structural preconditions for democratic experimentalism (*Protecting Minimum Requirements*); and thirdly, to explore the ways in which the constitutional arrangements leave room for choice in favour of or against democratic experimentalism (*Room for Choice*). In section IV we consider the interaction between political constitutionalism and federalism: the centralisation of power that has been facilitated at the national level by limited constitutionalism directly undermines the extent to which federalised experiments can occur. This interaction prompts a consideration of three further constitutional structures: section 109 inconsistency; fiscal federalism; and localism against the backdrop of constitutional prohibitions against discrimination and preference. We examine the role that each of these can play in managing Commonwealth supremacy consistently with the value of democratic experimentalism. Section V concludes with some reflections upon the nature of constitutional values in light of our enquiries.

II. POLITICAL CONSTITUTIONALISM

A. Locating Democratic Experimentalism

Democratic experimentalism, to the extent it demands that law be *provisional* and *self-correcting*, favours forms of law-making that are above all flexible: laws that are readily amenable to change by procedures with relatively low transaction costs. To the extent it demands that law be amenable to such change according to a form of enquiry that is both *dynamic* and *social*, it favours forms of law-making that are responsive to inputs from the broadest possible range of sources. Clearly enough, legislative and administrative decision-making, rather than judicial decision-making, better meet these prescriptions.[19] But the precise allocation of responsibility for controlling the exercise of governmental power between *political* and *legal* institutions

[19] *State Government Insurance Commission v Trigwell* (1979) 142 CLR 617, 633–34 (Mason J).

can vary, with many if not most constitutional systems utilising a mixture of both political and legal constraints. The Australian system presents a particularly acute accommodation of the two, owing to the self-conscious amalgamation of the British and American constitutional models.[20]

The British constitutional model, at least as it was prior to its recent reforms, largely if not completely eschewed legal constraints on the power of the sovereign legislature. The constraints on a Westminster-style Parliament are *political* constraints, rather than constraints derived from any *legal* conception of fundamental law. They include the practical limits, such as they may be, that derive from the legislature's periodic accountability to the electors voting in regular elections.[21]

The Americans, on the other hand, perceived their rejection of the British model and the codification of fundamental law as 'the greatest improvement on political institutions'.[22] Given legal and not merely political protection by constitutional entrenchment, fundamental law puts the matters it deals with beyond ready self-correction and may give a greater allocation of power to the courts (if the courts, as is usually if not necessarily the case,[23] be given power to enforce the fundamental law). Federalism, for example, will usually 'mean[] legalism' and 'the predominance of the judiciary in the constitution'.[24] The same may be said of other matters that might be selected for rigid legal protection in a constitution, such as individual rights.

The Australian framers 'admired and respected British institutions, including parliamentary sovereignty' and the Constitution they wrote 'was not the product of a legal and political culture, or of historical circumstances, that created expectations of extensive limitations upon legislative power for the purpose of protecting the rights of individuals'.[25] Although the framers, confronted with the practical need to make a workable federation, had to look beyond the British model with which they had the closest experience, their attachment to political constitutionalism nonetheless pervades the document that they produced. Much of the Constitution was settled only provisionally, 'until the Parliament otherwise provides'. This provisional formulation applied even to some very important structural features such as the creation of electoral subdivisions (sections 7 and 29), the federal franchise (sections 8 and 30), the applicable methods of voting (sections 9 and 31), and the mechanism for resolving disputed elections (section 47). Other important features were settled only minimally and supplemented with a conferral of legislative power to enable further provision in

[20] See generally L Burton Crawford, *The Rule of Law and the Australian Constitution* (Sydney, NSW, Federation Press, 2017) ch 4; J Goldsworthy and L Burton Crawford, 'Constitutionalism' in C Saunders and A Stone (eds), *The Oxford Handbook of the Australian Constitution* (Oxford, UK, Oxford University Press, 2018).

[21] AV Dicey, *Introduction to the Study of the Law of the Constitution* (London, Macmillan, first published 1885, 1959 edn) 27–28.

[22] *Marbury v Madison*, 5 US (1 Cranch) 137, 178 (1803) (Marshall CJ). See also GS Wood, *The Creation of the American Republic 1776–1787* (Chapel Hill, North Carolina, University of North Carolina Press, first published 1969, 1998 edn) 265–68; RS Kay, 'American Constitutionalism' in L Alexander (ed), *Constitutionalism: Philosophical Foundations* (Cambridge, UK, Cambridge University Press, 1998), 27.

[23] See J Bryce, *The American Commonwealth*, 1st edn (London, Macmillan and Co, 1888) vol I, 346, referred to in Gageler, 'James Bryce and the Australian Constitution', above n 14, 190.

[24] Dicey, above n 21, 100.

[25] *Roach v Electoral Commissioner* (2007) 233 CLR 162, 172 [1] (Gleeson CJ).

the future. The conferral of federal jurisdiction is of this character, settled minimally by provision for a High Court with some entrenched jurisdiction (section 75), and supplemented by legislative power to confer additional jurisdiction (section 76), and to create lower federal courts and confer federal jurisdiction on State courts (section 77). Legislative power (albeit limited by subject matter) was conferred upon the Commonwealth Parliament in the broadest language of power to make laws 'for the peace, order and good government of the Commonwealth' (section 51). Some heads of power selected for conferral upon the Commonwealth legislature were subjectively understood to have authorised 'legislative experimentation'.[26] Similarly, the legislative powers of the States, rather than being defined and thereby potentially limited, were simply 'continue[d]' in their plenary form (section 107). The executive power of the Commonwealth was vested largely without legal constraint (section 61).

Political constitutionalism may also be discerned by a negative implication from matters not dealt with in the Australian Constitution, such as individual rights. One of the reasons for not dealing with individual rights at a constitutional level was the thinking of the era, grounded in political constitutionalism, that 'the protections ... provided by the traditions of acting as honourable men were quite sufficient for a civilised society'.[27]

While the High Court might have steered the Australian Constitution in a more rigid direction, as indeed it did in its first two decades, the prevailing approach has given primacy to political over legal constraints. In that way, the Constitution has come to reflect a commitment that the courts should generally leave space for legislative policy experimentation in which mistakes and excesses are identified from the experience of the law and self-corrected through the democratic process. Thus, the subject matters with respect to which the Commonwealth has legislative power are to be construed 'with all the generality which the words used admit'.[28] If there exists a sufficient connection between a law and a head of power, then 'the justice and wisdom of the law, and the degree to which the means it adopts are necessary or desirable, are matters of legislative choice'.[29] The possibility of 'extravagant use' of legislative power is no reason to limit the interpretation of the power, that possibility being 'a matter to be guarded against by the constituencies and not by the Courts'.[30] Indeed, Higgins J, who with Isaacs J first advanced this approach against the authority of the Griffith Court, defended it explicitly by reference to 'experiment':

> The legislatures, not this Court, are responsible for the wisdom of the legislation. Our attitude should not be that of either approval or disapproval. Great social experiments are being tried; and they should get a fair trial—whatever we may think of their merits.[31]

[26] *New South Wales v Commonwealth* (2006) 229 CLR 1, 131–32 [230]–[232] (Gleeson CJ, Gummow, Hayne, Heydon and Crennan JJ) (*Work Choices Case*).

[27] RCL Moffatt, 'Philosophical Foundations of the Australian Constitutional Tradition' (1965) 5 *Sydney Law Review* 59, 85–86.

[28] *The Grain Pool of Western Australia v Commonwealth* (2000) 202 CLR 479, 492 [16], quoting *R v Public Vehicles Licensing Appeal Tribunal (Tas); Ex parte Australian National Airways Pty Ltd* (1964) 113 CLR 207, 225–26.

[29] *The Grain Pool of Western Australia v Commonwealth* (2000) 202 CLR 479, 492 [16] (Gleeson CJ, Gaudron, McHugh, Gummow, Hayne and Callinan JJ).

[30] *Amalgamated Society of Engineers v Adelaide Steamship Co Ltd* (1920) 28 CLR 129, 151 (*Engineers' Case*). See also *South Australia v Commonwealth* (1942) 65 CLR 373, 429 (Latham CJ).

[31] *Federated Saw Mill etc Employees' Association v James Moore & Sons Pty Ltd* (1909) 8 CLR 465, 539.

In this way, even the dictates of the constitutionally entrenched federal structure (a topic we return to in the next section) are seen to be controlled more by the ordinary political process than by judicial intervention.[32]

Codified limits on legislative power that do exist have been construed with a judicial scepticism, often historically informed, of arguments that the Constitution entrenches more than in truth it does. A predisposition to see the scope of the entrenched Constitution in narrow compass is the flipside of seeing expansively the scope for the very flexibility that democratic experimentalism demands. There is, Gageler J recently said, 'no difficulty in accepting that a constitutional prescription which is expressed in unqualified mandatory terms might be shown in light of its purpose or purposes to have a more confined operation than might be apparent from its language'.[33] His Honour referred to section 41 of the Constitution, which appears to guarantee federal voting rights for State electors, but which is construed only to have preserved those rights existing before the enactment of a statutory franchise.[34] The general proposition may explain other constructions of the fundamental law. Perhaps most strikingly, the guarantee that interstate trade 'be absolutely free' is subjected, understatedly, to 'some gloss':[35] in fact, it is understood to permit regulation of interstate trade provided, broadly speaking, that it is not protectionist or, if it is protectionist, that it is reasonably appropriate and adapted to a legitimate end.[36] Similar concessions are made in relation to the guarantee of free exercise of religion.[37] The bias towards narrow constructions might also explain in part the prevailing view of section 80 of the Constitution, according to which a trial on indictment of a Commonwealth offence must be by jury but by which, crucially, there is said to be 'nothing to compel procedure by indictment'.[38] That view of section 80 has been explained by one judge as being protective of 'the freedom of the Parliament to choose' which offences should be tried by jury.[39]

If legislation is a mode of law-making more suitable than adjudication to achieving the aspirations of democratic experimentalism, then broadly speaking it might be thought that administrative law-making is even more suitable than legislation. An administrative decision-making body: need not be subject to procedural requirements as onerous as those governing the Parliament; can be

[32] See especially S Gageler, 'Beyond the Text: A Vision of the Structure and Function of the Constitution' (2009) 32 *Australian Bar Review* 138, 152; S Gageler, 'Foundations of Australian Federalism and the Role of Judicial Review' (1987) 17 *Federal Law Review* 162. See also P Partridge, 'The Politics of Federalism' in G Sawer (ed), *Federalism: An Australian Jubilee Study* (Melbourne, FW Cheshire, 1952); H Wechsler, 'The Political Safeguards of Federalism: The Role of the States in the Composition and Selection of the National Government' (1954) 54 *Columbia Law Review* 543.

[33] *Alqudsi v The Queen* (2016) 258 CLR 203, 253 [125].

[34] *R v Pearson; Ex parte Sipka* (1983) 152 CLR 254.

[35] *Betfair Pty Ltd v Western Australia* (2008) 234 CLR 418, 474 [91].

[36] *Cole v Whitfield* (1988) 165 CLR 360; *Castlemaine Tooheys Ltd v South Australia* (1990) 169 CLR 436; *Betfair Pty Ltd v Western Australia* (2008) 234 CLR 418.

[37] See further *Adelaide Company of Jehovah's Witnesses Inc v Commonwealth* (1943) 67 CLR 116, 132 (Latham CJ); *Kruger v Commonwealth* (1997) 190 CLR 1, 134 (Gaudron J).

[38] *R v Archdall & Roskruge; Ex parte Carrigan and Brown* (1928) 41 CLR 128, 139–40 (Higgins J). See also *R v Bernasconi* (1915) 19 CLR 629, 637 (Isaacs J); *Cheng v The Queen* (2000) 203 CLR 248, 268–70 [49]–[58] (Gleeson CJ, Gummow and Hayne JJ), 299 [152] (McHugh J), 344–45 [283] (Callinan J); V Bell, 'Section 80—The Great Constitutional Tautology' (2014) 40 *Monash University Law Review* 7.

[39] *Cheng v The Queen* (2000) 203 CLR 248, 295 [141] (McHugh J).

expected to be smaller and less diverse; and can be expected to have a more limited agenda and therefore greater capacity for ongoing and sustained attention to the one set of problems. In these ways, the administrative sphere more readily fosters the aspiration for truly 'responsive regulation', or 'creative implementation and refinement',[40] because the regulator can, in a way that legislatures and certainly courts cannot, listen to the responses of those being regulated, and adapt and modify its regulatory choices according to those responses and other contextual factors.[41] There has generally not been perceived in Australia, either at the State or federal level, any constitutional difficulty with a legislature delegating to the executive the authority to make subordinate legislation.[42] It is a pervasive feature of the modern Australian administrative state that regulatory bodies, often expert in a complex field of human endeavour, promulgate and frequently revise the law by way of rule-making, or even by less formal exercises of regulatory discretion.[43] Supervision by way of judicial review will not 'go beyond the declaration and enforcing of the law which determines the limits and governs the exercise' of executive power'.[44] Further, it seems that Parliament (at least in theory) can legislate to exclude judicial review otherwise than for errors of a jurisdictional kind.[45]

B. Protecting Minimum Requirements

Some constitutional limitations, in addition to being inherently accommodating of legislative intrusion, serve the ends of democratic experimentalism in other ways. As Dewey recognised, experimentalism requires more than simply provisionality and a capacity for self-correction. In addition, the means by which self-correction is to be achieved must be informed by enquiry that is both dynamic and social—that is, responsive to the consequences of the provisional law, as experienced by the subjects of law, and assessed by reference to wide-ranging inputs. This requires among other things, as we mentioned previously, that informational asymmetries between the governors and the governed be corrected. The right to vote,[46] and the freedom of political communication that has been implied from the Constitution's prescription of representative and responsible government, go some way to this end. The Court

[40] J Braithwaite, 'The Essence of Responsive Regulation: The Fasken Lecture' (2011) 44 *University of British Columbia Law Review* 476, 476.

[41] I Ayres and J Braithwaite, *Responsive Regulation: Transcending the Deregulation Debate* (New York, Oxford University Press, 1992). See also, on responsive law, P Nonet and P Selznick, *Law and Society in Transition: Toward Responsive Law* (New York, Harper and Row, 1978).

[42] *Powell v Apollo Candle Co* (1885) 10 App Cas 282; *Commonwealth v New South Wales* (1928) 42 CLR 69; *Victorian Stevedoring & General Contracting Co Pty Ltd and Meakes v Dignan* (1931) 46 CLR 73.

[43] See, eg, S Bottomley, 'The Notional Legislator: The Australian Securities and Investments Commission's Role as a Law-Maker' (2011) 39 *Federal Law Review* 1.

[44] *Attorney-General (NSW) v Quin* (1990) 170 CLR 1, 35–36 (Brennan J).

[45] *Plaintiff S157/2002 v Commonwealth* (2003) 211 CLR 476, 507 [81]; *Kirk v Industrial Court (NSW)* (2010) 239 CLR 531, 581 [100] (French CJ, Gummow, Hayne, Crennan, Kiefel and Bell JJ).

[46] *See Roach v Electoral Commissioner* (2007) 233 CLR 162; *Rowe v Electoral Commissioner* (2010) 243 CLR 1.

has settled upon an understanding of the freedom as a systemic protection of the 'free flow' of communication between 'all interested persons' in order that electors can form judgements.[47] No doubt this baseline protection is not sufficient to correct informational asymmetries at a level that would truly foster Deweyan experimentalism, but it is a necessary condition. Other structural features which can be seen to be directed towards correcting the asymmetries include Parliament's powers to scrutinise executive action, which can bring into the public domain information that would otherwise remain secret, and quasi-constitutional freedom of information statutes and the more recent introduction of protections for whistleblowers.

C. Room for Choice

While the structure of political constitutionalism can be seen to *enable* an approach to law-making that can fulfil the vision of democratic experimentalism in which regulation is provisional, self-correcting, dynamic and social, it surely does not *mandate* such an approach. There remains room for choice. Indeed, it may be thought to be inherent in the notion of a constitutional 'value' (as distinct from a constitutional rule, standard or even principle) that it may coexist with competing values and require that there be room for choice.

The Deweyan vision of law that is provisional and self-correcting in response to experience presupposes what might be thought to be a rather idealistic conception of the lawmaker's desire to enact policies that are successful in the sense of achieving the social objectives at which they are directed. Perhaps lawmakers more often desire to enact policies that are successful in the quite different sense of achieving partisan gains: re-election, a boost in the polls, the wedging of an opponent, or similar. The difference is between *efficacious* laws, and merely *popular* laws, the latter being a distortion of democratic experimentalism. We review below the uptake of anti-bikie laws in several States as an example of law-making based not on any experience of the law but only of the popularity of it.

The strength of competing incentives to pursue efficacious or merely popular laws is affected by constitutional structures such as the parliamentary term. The prevailing view is that longer terms would be more likely to induce longer-term policy planning, and reduce the frequency of political campaigning: 'governments in short-term systems are accused of focusing on making politically expedient decisions during their term, rather than pursuing policy that is in the national interest'.[48] At the federal level, a three-year term for the House of Representatives is constitutionally entrenched. The three-year term had been an Australian colonial experiment, introduced into most of the colonies through the lobbying of the

[47] *Unions NSW v New South Wales* (2013) 252 CLR 530, 551 [27]–[29] (French CJ, Hayne, Crennan, Kiefel and Bell JJ), 578 [135]–[137] (Keane J).

[48] Joint Standing Committee on Electoral Matters, Parliament of Australia, *The 2004 Federal Election: Inquiry into the Conduct of the 2004 Federal Election and Matters Related Thereto* (2005) 166 [7.48]. See also S Bennett, 'Four-year Terms for the House of Representatives?' (Research Paper No 4, Parliamentary Library, Parliament of Australia, 2000–01).

nineteenth-century Chartist movement to guarantee effective representation of and accountability to the people.[49] All Australian States have since moved to four-year terms. Other parliamentary systems adopt four or even five-year terms.[50] Longer federal terms have been agitated almost since federation, were supported by the 1929 Royal Commission on the Constitution, and proposed unsuccessfully in the 1988 referendum. Australia remains 'in a clear minority' on the point.[51]

III. FEDERALISM

A. Locating Democratic Experimentalism

The potential for federalism to deliver something like democratic experimentalism was perceived, if dimly, as early as the United States Constitutional Convention in 1787. James Madison proposed that Congress ought to have the power to 'negative' any State legislation. This veto would, Madison thought, properly protect against the risk that States might legislate in ways that harmed other States or the Union as a whole. The proposal was rejected in favour of Jefferson's alternative solution to the same problem, which came to be reflected in the Supremacy Clause of article VI and ensured *judicial* review of State legislation for conformity with federal law. Jefferson thought that Madison's proposal for a congressional veto 'in all cases whatsoever' was overkill and, 'in order to give [Congress] 1 Degree of power which they ought to have, [gave] them 99 more which they ought not to have'.[52] To the same effect, but with an eye more keenly on the experimental promise of a less centralised federation, Elbridge Gerry objected that it 'may prevent the encouragements which particular States may be disposed to give to particular manufactures'—in other words, that it would have 'a potentially chilling effect on the states' ... creativity'.[53]

Federalism can enable democratic experimentalism in two main ways. First, by creating smaller governmental units, it lowers the cost of experimentation because it permits new policies to be tested in the first instance on a smaller subset of the national population. Secondly, by creating multiple decision-making centres, it enables simultaneous experimentation which 'generates a density of experience that produces information quickly', whether between sub-national units (horizontal experimentalism) or between the national and sub-national units (vertical experimentalism).[54]

The first notion—smaller units—is perhaps most recognisably captured in Holmes' and Brandeis' early twentieth-century statements of laboratory federalism.

[49] M Sawer and N Kelly, 'Parliamentary Terms' in *Democratic Audit of Australia* (Report, February 2005).

[50] *The 2004 Federal Election*, above n 48 (2005) 161–63 [7.28]–[7.34].

[51] Bennett, above n 48.

[52] AL LaCroix, 'What if Madison Had Won? Imagining a Constitutional World of Legislative Supremacy' (2011) 45 *Indiana Law Review* 41, 43–45, quoting a letter from Thomas Jefferson to James Madison (20 June 1787).

[53] AL LaCroix, *The Ideological Origins of American Federalism* (Cambridge, Massachusetts, Harvard University Press, 2010) 157.

[54] RM Cover, 'The Uses of Jurisdictional Redundancy: Interest, Ideology and Innovation' (1981) 22 *William & Mary Law Review* 639, 678.

In 1921, Holmes J said that he 'deprecated' nothing more than 'to prevent the making of social experiments that an important part of the community desires, in the insulated chambers afforded by the several states'.[55] In 1932, Brandeis J extended the metaphor, describing as a 'happy incident' of a federal system that 'a single courageous State may, if its citizens choose, serve as a laboratory; and try novel social and economic experiments without risk to the rest of the country'.[56] But the notion appears to have been understood by the Australian framers even prior to federation. For example, in the course of opposing constitutional definition of State legislative powers, Dr Cockburn opined that 'it is very much to the advantage of evolution that as much ground as possible should be left available to the states in which to make experiments in legislation' because 'it is much easier to work out a problem on a small scale, where it is possible to make an experiment on a small scale, than it is to work it out on a large scale'.[57] This insight was echoed by Kingston, who warned in a paper he wrote following the 1895 Hobart Conference that a larger federal parliament, as compared to the smaller legislative assemblies of the colonies, would 'materially increase the difficulty of experimental legislation'.[58]

The second notion—multiple units—also appears to have been comprehended. In debating section 51(xxiii), the power to make laws with respect to invalid and old-age pensions, Higgins, although ultimately voting in favour of its inclusion, explained why he had initially been inclined to oppose it: not because he did not support pensions, but because he 'wanted to see an experiment ... made by the states'. He continued:

> It seems to me that these Australian colonies are a grand field for experiments in such matters. I was hoping sincerely that we should have experiments here and there, and that we should learn by our mistakes, one colony from the other.[59]

The framers' appreciation of the opportunities that federalism presented for experimentation is perhaps not surprising. Bryce had explained the benefit of both smaller and multiple units in *The American Commonwealth*:

> Federalism enables a people to try experiments in legislation and administration which could not be safely tried in a large centralized country. A comparatively small commonwealth like an American State easily makes and unmakes its laws; mistakes are not serious, for they are soon corrected; other States profit by the experience of a law or a method which has worked well or ill in the State that has tried it.[60]

Despite this evidence of an early appreciation of democratic experimentalism within the federal structure, it does not appear to have been particularly influential in

[55] *Truax v Corrigan*, 257 US 312, 344 (1921).

[56] *New State Ice Co v Liebmann*, 285 US 262, 311 (1932).

[57] *Official Record of the Debates of the Australasian Federal Convention*, Sydney, 10 March 1891, 201. See also *Official Record of the Debates of the Australasian Federal Convention*, Melbourne, 14 February 1898, 915 (John Cockburn).

[58] Charles Cameron Kingston, *The Democratic Element in Australian Federation* (JL Bonython & Co, 1897, reprinted from the 'Review of Reviews', February 1896).

[59] *Official Record of the Debates of the Australasian Federal Convention*, Melbourne, 7 March 1898, 1994. See also *Official Record of the Debates of the Australasian Federal Convention*, Melbourne, 15 February 1898, 952–53.

[60] Bryce, above n 23, 353.

the subsequent interpretation or implementation of the Constitution. Prominent invocations of the notion in recent cases have been in dissenting judgments. Those judgments, with respect to their authors, have the flavour of protestation against the relentless centralisation of power, rather than of any appeal to an established federal principle. In the *Work Choices Case*, Kirby J described an 'important advantage' of the federal structure illustrated in the industrial relations sphere by 'occasional diversity of approach, inventiveness in standards and entitlements and appropriate innovation ... by which industrial standards determined in one jurisdiction of Australia are tested and sometimes copied in another'.[61] In *South Australia v Totani*, Heydon J referred to 'the role of the States as jurisdictions in which experiment may be conducted and variety may be observed' as a reason not to restrict State legislative power by 'somewhat general implications',[62] a theme his Honour repeated a couple of years later, once again in dissent.[63]

Striking practical examples of cross-jurisdictional convergence, which illustrate both the vertical and horizontal possibilities of experimentalism, can be seen in the modern 'protective' or 'preventative' law and order agendas. Criminal law is a field in which both the Commonwealth and the States legislate and in which the Commonwealth generally does not seek to pre-empt State law: in 2005, an Explanatory Memorandum said that a provision of the Criminal Code designed to allow 'overlapping federal, State and Territory offences' in relation to controlled drugs was 'consistent with Parliament's approach with other serious crimes, such as terrorism, serious harm, fraud, money laundering and sexual servitude offences'.[64] It is the field that Dr Cockburn seized upon in the Convention Debates as illustrating the virtues of democratic experimentalism.[65]

Terrorists in the federal sphere, and bikie gangs and serious sex and other violent offenders in the State spheres, have been seen to present broadly analogous problems for governments focused on protective or preventative measures. The evolution of policy in these spaces has flowed in both directions. On the one hand, the federal preventative control-order regime, enacted in response to the threat of terrorism, was adopted and adapted by several States and Territories in service of their efforts to combat serious organised crime.[66] On the other hand, a recent federal law authorising post-sentence detention for high-risk terrorist offenders was 'modelled closely'[67] on the States' post-sentence detention regimes for high-risk sex and other

[61] *Work Choices Case* (2006) 229 CLR 1, 222 [534]. See also at 190 [446], 222–23 [535].

[62] *South Australia v Totani* (2010) 242 CLR 1, 96 [246].

[63] *Public Service Association and Professional Officers' Association Amalgamated of NSW v Director of Public Employment* (2012) 250 CLR 343, 369 [61].

[64] Explanatory Memorandum, Law and Justice Legislation Amendment (Serious Drug Offences and Other Measures) Bill 2005 (Cth) 13, considered in *Momcilovic v The Queen* (2011) 245 CLR 1, 239 [656] (Crennan and Kiefel JJ).

[65] *Official Record of the Debates of the Australasian Federal Convention*, Sydney, 10 March 1891, 201–02.

[66] See, eg, G Appleby and J Williams, 'The Anti-Terror Creep: Law and Order, the States and the High Court of Australia' in N McGarrity, A Lynch and G Williams (eds), *Counter-Terrorism and Beyond: The Culture of Law and Justice after 9/11* (New York, Routledge, 2010); R Ananian-Welsh and G Williams, 'The New Terrorists: The Normalisation and Spread of Anti-Terror Laws in Australia' (2014) 38 *Melbourne University Law Review* 362.

[67] Commonwealth, *Parliamentary Debates*, Senate, 15 September 2016, 1035 (George Brandis).

violent offenders.[68] As we explain in greater detail below, the development of the control order laws fell short of the aspirations of democratic experimentalism, because they were not adopted or developed in light of any significant experience with the operation of the law. They nonetheless illustrate the potential for cross-jurisdictional learning.

B. Protecting Minimum Requirements

Experimental federalism requires more than just the two key notions of *smaller* and *multiple* decision-making units. Those two notions enable the generation of experience against which competing policies can be evaluated. But the evaluation itself can occur only if other basic conditions are satisfied.[69] What is presupposed is that there be an opportunity for *comparison* of competing policies. The dynamic and social enquiry underpinning democratic experimentalism in the Deweyan sense requires that the consequences of a law be experienced, communicated to lawmakers, evaluated against wide-ranging inputs, and adjusted appropriately in an iterative fashion. Without at least 'yard-stick comparisons of outcomes' there is no reason to think that policy will evolve responsively to the diverse experience generated throughout the federation.[70] This in turn depends on certain structural protections: clear lines of political accountability for the promulgation and revision of the law; the free flow of information about the law and its practical operation; and the capacity of citizens to express their evaluations by 'exit' (the ability to relocate to a better-performing jurisdiction) and 'voice' (the ability to seek to influence the political branches through protest and political communication and at the ballot box).[71] Michael Dorf and Charles Sabel argue that a constitution based on a system of democratic experimentalism will necessarily require what they refer to as 'benchmarking':[72] the surveying of policy experimentation in other jurisdictions and the pooling of knowledge and information so that the best possible solutions can be identified for the particular circumstances of a given jurisdiction.

We explained above that the right to vote and the implied freedom of political communication, supplemented by parliamentary scrutiny of executive action and freedom of information and whistleblower protection legislation, can be seen in the context of political constitutionalism to protect the free flow of information that is

[68] Criminal Code Amendment (High Risk Terrorist Offenders) Act 2016 (Cth). For a critical analysis of the effectiveness of such regimes, see Tamara Tulich, 'Will Post-sentence Detention of Convicted Terrorists Make Australia Any Safer?' (*The Conversation*, 26 July 2016): theconversation.com/will-post-sentence-detention-of-convicted-terrorists-make-australia-any-safer-62980.

[69] The matters addressed in this paragraph are explored more fully in B Lim, 'Laboratory Federalism and the *Kable* Principle' (2014) 42 *Federal Law Review* 519, 526–28.

[70] See C Walsh, 'The Economics of Federalism and Federal Reform' (2008) 31 *UNSW Law Journal* 553, 562.

[71] AO Hirschmann, *Exit, Voice, and Loyalty: Responses to Decline in Firms, Organizations, and States* (Cambridge, Massachusetts, Harvard University Press, 1970). See also H Gerken, 'Exit, Voice and Disloyalty' (2013) 62 *Duke Law Journal* 1349; HK Gerken, 'Federalism All the Way Down' (2010) 124 *Harvard Law Review* 4.

[72] MC Dorf and CF Sabel, 'A Constitution of Democratic Experimentalism' (1998) 98 *Columbia Law Review* 267, 286–87, 345–47.

necessary for responsive law-making. In the context of experimental federalism, we might add the freedom of movement (both of persons and of capital) between the States that is guaranteed by section 92.[73] The 'competition for a mobile citizenry',[74] which underpins the notion of 'exit', may be somewhat dampened by section 117, which prohibits discrimination on the basis of residence. It is therefore significant for the maintenance of experimental federalism that the Court has construed section 117 to permit certain kinds of differential treatment for State residents. The kind of differential treatment that is permissible has been described in different ways. It is perhaps best encapsulated in Mason CJ's formulation of discrimination in relation to 'rights naturally and exclusively associated with residence in a State'.[75] Brennan J, similarly, considered that differential treatment would not be discrimination within the meaning of section 117 where it was necessary 'precisely because [the person] is not an in-State resident'.[76]

There may be other constitutional structures that operate to protect the requisite conditions of experimental federalism, although views differ in this respect. In particular, the two of us have taken opposing views about the relationship between experimental federalism and the *Kable* principle.[77] One of us has argued that *Kable* has a harmonising effect across the federation and that it pre-empts the democratic choices of State legislatures, particularly in their law and order policies.[78] The other has argued, in contrast, that by preventing State legislatures from conscripting the courts to enact political designs, the *Kable* principle ensures that State legislatures cannot 'cloak' political choices with the imprimatur of the independent courts. This, so the argument goes, ensures clear lines of political accountability for experimental legislation, which is one of the preconditions of effective evaluation and comparison by the subjects of the law.[79]

C. Room for Choice

Even with the necessary preconditions for experimentalism given constitutional protection, federalism (like political constitutionalism) only *enables* experimentalism and does not necessarily *mandate* or even *encourage* it. Inherent in a federal structure are also barriers to experimentalism. There is a 'free-rider' problem: if information about a pioneering policy is readily accessible in all jurisdictions and

[73] See *Cunliffe v Commonwealth* (1994) 182 CLR 272; *AMS v AIF* (1999) 199 CLR 160.

[74] *Gregory v Ashcroft*, 501 US 452, 458 (1991).

[75] *Street v Queensland Bar Association* (1989) 168 CLR 461, 462.

[76] ibid 514. See also at 528 (Deane J) (referring to incapacities or disadvantages that 'flow naturally from the structure of the particular State'); 548 (Dawson J) (referring to discrimination based on 'the ordinary and proper administration of the affairs of [the] State'); 560 (Toohey J) (referring to differential treatment that 'is a natural consequence of legislation aimed at protecting the legitimate interests of the "State community"'); 583 (McHugh J) (referring to 'matters which are the concern only of a State and its people').

[77] *Kable v Director of Public Prosecutions (NSW)* (1996) 189 CLR 51.

[78] G Appleby, 'The High Court and *Kable*: A Study in Federalism and Rights Protection' (2014) 40 *Monash University Law Review* 673. See also E Campbell, 'Constitutional Protection of State Courts and Judges' (1997) 23 *Monash University Law Review* 397, 421; R Orr, '*Kable v DPP*: Taking Judicial Protection Too Far?' (1996) 11 *AIAL Forum* 11, 15–17.

[79] Lim, 'Laboratory Federalism', above n 69. See also B Lim 'Attributes and Attribution of State Courts—Federalism and the *Kable* Principle' (2012) 40 *Federal Law Review* 31.

relatively costless to copy without taking the risk of its failure, then there may be insufficient incentive to move first with a risky legislative venture.[80] Poorly resourced States especially might be expected to copy legislative innovation in better-resourced States. That said, there is likely to be sufficient internal political incentive to address a social problem to ensure that there will be a first mover. There is also a 'premature convergence' problem: States may tend to be risk-averse, may tend to rely on information or experience generated in first-moving States rather than information or experience generated independently in their own State, and may therefore tend to adopt policies rather than test policies.[81]

The anti-bikie measures, to which we referred above, may illustrate premature convergence.[82] The first iteration of the measures was introduced in South Australia in 2007, just weeks after the High Court had upheld the federal anti-terrorism control order regime on which the anti-bikie measures were modelled.[83] At the time, only Jack Thomas had been subjected to a control order under the federal regime and that control order had in any event been lifted and replaced with a negotiated undertaking. The South Australian law was challenged at the first opportunity and magistrates did not apply it pending the outcome of that challenge. In those circumstances, there was *no* evidence of whether the regime was effective to address what were said to be pernicious features of organised crime difficult to target using ordinary law enforcement methods. Despite the lack of experience with the novel law, the New South Wales government introduced its own version of the regime in 2009, at which time only one further control order had been issued under the federal law. A political imperative, rather than responsiveness to the South Australian experience, motivated the New South Wales government to act quickly after bikie-related violence at Sydney Airport. Jim McGinty, a former Attorney-General of Western Australia, commented that: '[t]oughening the law is fine at a political, rhetorical level … [but] [o]ur experience in Western Australia has shown that … [the laws] haven't been used and therefore have not been effective'.[84]

Overcoming these inherent barriers is a matter of political choice for participants in the federation. Experimental federalism is often associated with a competitive or coordinate approach to federalism, which can pit governments against each other in securing funding and popularity. In contemporary Australia, however, federalism is more often *cooperative* than competitive. Cooperative federalism values collective action and collaborative problem-solving to achieve a universal standard in promotion of the common good. Cooperative federalism, it is thought, might overcome negative characteristics of divided government, in that it might 'manage the conflict, duplication, costs and inefficiencies that can arise in the operation of a federation'.[85] It allows national and sub-national governments to collaborate to achieve outcomes

[80] See S Rose-Ackerman, 'Risk Taking and Reelection: Does Federalism Promote Innovation?' (1980) 9 *Journal of Legal Studies* 593; D Gewirtzman, 'Complex Experimental Federalism' (2015) 83 *Buffalo Law Review* 241, 265–69.

[81] Gewirtzman, above n 80, 269–73.

[82] See further Appleby, above n 78, 676–80.

[83] *Thomas v Mowbray* (2007) 223 CLR 307.

[84] Michael Edwards, 'Hit Bikies' Hip Pockets in Gang Crackdown: McGinty' *ABC News* (1 April 2009): <www.abc.net.au/news/2009-04-01/hit-bikies-hip-pockets-in-gang-crackdownmcginty/1637242>.

[85] R French, 'Co-operative Federalism—A Constitutional Reality or a Political Slogan' (FCA) [2004] *Federal Judicial Scholarship* 21.

that, because of the constitutional division of power, they might not achieve alone. The choice to pursue a cooperative approach to federalism might cohere with the aspirations of democratic experimentalism in the following ways. First, self-correction by dynamic and social enquiry requires 'benchmarking' (in the sense used by Dorf and Sabel as discussed above).[86] Secondly, cooperation may be necessary or desirable to implement a policy at a national level, once experimentation has demonstrated its benefit.

While cooperation may facilitate the collection and sharing of information about the design, implementation and consequences of policy trials, it can do so effectively only if the forums of cooperation are themselves open to scrutiny by the subjects of the law. The major forum for intergovernmental cooperation, the Council of Australian Governments, was said in 2006 by the then Secretary of the Attorney-General's Department, to 'sidestep[], more or less completely, any sort of democratic scrutiny'.[87] The same might be said of other Ministerial Councils. Although most issue a brief 'communique' after a meeting, other documents are generally unavailable and are often exempt from release under freedom of information laws if non-disclosure would be in the public interest.[88] There can be, therefore: a lack of transparency and information about intergovernmental processes; a marginalisation of Parliament and resultant undermining of responsible government; and a lack of public participation in the relevant processes.[89] All this might well serve other values, but along the dimension of democratic experimentalism tends to deprive the evolution of the law of its self-correcting, dynamic and social aspects.

IV. COMMONWEALTH SUPREMACY

Political constitutionalism and federalism, as discussed in sections II and III, can enable democratic experimentalism in different ways. But the two structural features are in considerable tension with each other. The entrenchment of a rigid federalism would reduce the flexibility inherent in political constitutionalism, while the prioritisation of political constitutionalism (at least at the federal level) would reduce the rigidity of the federal structure and could lead, depending upon the prevailing political climate, to an erosion of some of the federalist features that might otherwise enable experimentalism.

In Australia, priority has been given to political constitutionalism over rigid federalism: the maintenance of any 'federal balance' lies primarily in the realm of ordinary politics. The rigid limits, speaking generally, are reflected in the baseline

[86] Dorf and Sabel, above n 72, 286–87, 345–47; see also RB Ahdieh, 'Dialectical Regulation' (2006) 38 *Connecticut Law Review* 863, 893; RA Schapiro, 'Toward a Theory of Interactive Federalism' (2005) 91 *Iowa Law Review* 243, 288.

[87] R Wilkins, 'A New Era in Commonwealth–State Relations?' (2006) 7 *Public Administration Today* 8, 12. See also C Saunders, 'Constitutional and Legal Aspects of Intergovernmental Relations in Australia' in B Galligan, O Hughes and C Walsh (eds), *Intergovernmental Relations and Public Policy* (North Sydney, NSW, Allen & Unwin, 1991) 39.

[88] See, eg, Freedom of Information Act 1982 (Cth) ss 11A(5), 11B, 26A and 47B.

[89] P Kildea, 'Making Room for Democracy in Intergovernmental Relations' in P Kildea, A Lynch and G Williams (eds), *Tomorrow's Federation: Reforming Australian Government* (Sydney, NSW, Federation Press 2012), 76.

mandate that the States continue to exist as bodies politic endowed with the continuing capacities to function as 'separately organized' governments.[90] This means that the constitutional value of democratic experimentalism enjoys minimal legal protection and is a value committed primarily to the political branches. Political forces in each jurisdiction will determine the extent to which law-making is pursued in a provisional, self-correcting, dynamic and social way. Furthermore, political forces at the Commonwealth level will largely determine the areas in which, and the extent to which, the States and Territories are not excluded from engaging in simultaneous experimentation.

A. Section 109

The exclusion of the States from a field of regulation depends critically upon the operation of section 109 of the Constitution, which is therefore an important provision in the mediation of the balance between political constitutionalism and federalism. The provision turns upon the notion of 'inconsistency'. Inconsistency between a State law and a Commonwealth law is both the trigger for the operation of section 109 ('[w]hen a law of a State is *inconsistent* with a law of the Commonwealth'), and marks the extent of the work the provision does ('the latter shall prevail, and the former shall, *to the extent of the inconsistency*, be invalid').

In the early years of the Constitution, 'inconsistency' was understood to be engaged only by duties incapable of simultaneous obedience (although this tended to emerge from cases about industrial awards rather than any true section 109 issue).[91] It was probably 'more than a coincidence' that this narrow approach cohered with the reserved State powers doctrine in limiting federal power and enhancing State autonomy.[92] Contemporaneously with the *Engineers' Case*, the High Court embraced a wider notion of inconsistency, which encompassed the circumstance in which a State law, although capable of simultaneous obedience with federal law, nonetheless took away a right conferred by federal law or otherwise intruded upon a field intended to have been regulated exclusively by federal law.[93] This wider notion was re-expressed by Dixon J in language which endures today: inconsistency will subsist if the State law 'would alter, impair or detract from the operation of a [federal] law' or if 'it appears from the terms, the nature or the subject matter of a Federal enactment that it was intended as a complete statement of the law governing a particular matter or set of rights and duties'.[94]

[90] *Melbourne Corporation v Commonwealth* (1947) 74 CLR 31, 82 (Dixon J).

[91] See, eg, *Federated Saw Mill v James Moore & Sons Pty Ltd* (1909) 8 CLR 465; *Australian Boot Trade Employees Federation v Whybrow & Co* (1910) 10 CLR 266.

[92] P Hanks, 'Inconsistent Commonwealth and State Laws: Centralising Government Powers in the Australian Federation' (1986) 16 *Federal Law Review* 107, 111.

[93] *Clyde Engineering Co Ltd v Cowburn* (1926) 37 CLR 466.

[94] *Victoria v Commonwealth* (1937) 58 CLR 618, 630 *(The Kakariki)*, quoted in *Telstra Corporation v Worthing* (1997) 197 CLR 61, 76 (Gleeson CJ, Gaudron, McHugh, Gummow, Kirby, Hayne and Callinan JJ) and in *Dickson v The Queen* (2010) 241 CLR 491, 502 [13] (French CJ, Gummow, Hayne, Heydon, Crennan, Kiefel and Bell JJ) and in *Jemena Asset Management (3) Pty Ltd v Coinvest Ltd* (2011) 244 CLR 508, 524 [39] (French CJ, Gummow, Heydon, Crennan, Kiefel and Bell JJ).

The contemporary approach permits significantly more scope for the Commonwealth Parliament to assume an exclusive regulatory role in the fields of its otherwise concurrent legislative competence. Not only that, it fixes on Commonwealth legislative 'intention' as the determinant of whether the Commonwealth Parliament has assumed an exclusive regulatory role. This underscores that it is principally a *political* question whether democratic experimentalism (in its federalist dimension) is to be pursued in a given field or not.

The determinative status of legislative 'intention' is not to be equated with any determinative status accorded to legislative *statements* of intention. The Court has generally placed significant weight on legislative statements to the effect that a law is or is not intended 'to make exhaustive or exclusive provision on the subject with which it deals' or otherwise displace State law.[95] But in *Momcilovic v The Queen*,[96] the Court rejected a joint submission by seven governments that 'an express statement of Commonwealth legislative intention is an effective statement of Commonwealth legislative intention for the purpose of s 109' (provided only that it be supported by a head of power and capable of being supported by the substantive provisions of the law).[97] That was, essentially, because legislative 'intention' is an objective construct which depends not only on what the legislature says, but also on the application by the Court of accepted rules of interpretation.[98]

The Court has marked out other sources of latitude for ultimate control over the engagement and operation of section 109. In particular, there has consistently been recognised what Dixon J called in 1948 a 'debatable area', albeit one that has never been applied, whether a federal law that is 'aimed at preventing the exercise of State legislative power' is invalid or not a 'law of the Commonwealth' for the purposes of section 109.[99] It may be that this 'debatable area' is simply a particular example of the *Melbourne Corporation* doctrine, which was also articulated by Dixon J just one year earlier in 1947.

Section 109 can thus be seen to be sufficiently malleable to afford greater or lesser significance to the apparent or stated intention of a Commonwealth law to pre-empt concurrent State regulation. That malleability may reflect in greater or lesser degrees any constitutional value that might be placed upon democratic experimentalism. Experimentation would be enhanced by a greater tolerance for concurrent laws. In the *First* and *Second Airlines Cases*,[100] which concerned highly contested regulation by both the Commonwealth and the State of intrastate airline routes in New South Wales,

[95] See *R v Credit Tribunal; Ex parte General Motors Acceptance Corporation* (1977) 137 CLR 545, 563 (Mason J), quoted in *John Holland Pty Ltd v Victorian Workcover Authority* (2009) 239 CLR 518, 527–28 [21] (French CJ, Gummow, Hayne, Heydon, Crennan, Kiefel and Bell JJ).

[96] (2011) 245 CLR 1, 74 [111] (French CJ), 120 [269] (Gummow J), 124 [285], 131 [307], 142 [344] (Hayne J, dissenting in the result), 235 [638], 238–39 [654] (Crennan and Kiefel JJ), 240–41 [660] (Bell JJ).

[97] Attorney-General (Vic), 'Written Submissions of the Second Respondent and of the Attorneys-General of the Commonwealth, New South Wales, Western Australia, South Australia, Tasmania and the Australian Capital Territory (intervening) on Questions 1–3 of the High Court's Letter Dated 1 March 2011', submission in *Momcilovic v The Queen*, no M134 of 2010, 28 March 2011 [9].

[98] *Dickson v The Queen* (2010) 241 CLR 491, 507 [32], quoting *Zheng v Cai* (2009) 239 CLR 446, 455–56 [28] (French CJ, Gummow, Crennan, Kiefel and Bell JJ).

[99] *Bayside City Council v Telstra Corporation Ltd* (2004) 216 CLR 595, 628–29 [36]–[37] (Gleeson CJ, Gummow, Kirby, Hayne and Heydon JJ), referring to *Wenn v Attorney-General (Vic)* (1948) 77 CLR 84, 120 (Dixon J). See also *West v Commissioner of Taxation (NSW)* (1937) 56 CLR 657, 707 (Evatt J).

[100] *Airlines of New South Wales Pty Ltd v New South Wales* (1965) 113 CLR 1 (*First Airlines Case*); *Airlines of New South Wales Pty Ltd v New South Wales [No 2]* (1965) 113 CLR 54 (*Second Airlines Case*).

the concurrent operation of the two licensing regimes led to 'a situation of stalemate or deadlock' when no one operator held both requisite licences. It was said that '[t]he answer to stalemate or deadlock ... is co-operation'.[101] One could imagine, for example, something like an interpretive presumption or at least a thumb on the scales against pre-emption in fields where regulation is highly contested and might benefit from continued horizontal or vertical experimentation. Such a presumption would, in effect, require the Commonwealth Parliament to state its intention clearly: this would not only tend to support federalist experimentation but would also tend to enhance the electoral accountability of Commonwealth decisions to pre-empt State law.

B. Fiscal Federalism

Commonwealth financial supremacy also has the capacity to stifle experimentation in the States. Different solutions are possible to the 'vicious principle of one authority raising taxation for another authority to spend'.[102] To prioritise federalism might involve apportioning the taxation yield to the States, so that they received a 'permanent share of income tax'.[103] On the other hand, to prioritise responsible government might involve correcting not the distribution of income to reflect a federal balance of spending responsibilities, but rather to correct the spending responsibilities themselves, to reflect the unequal distribution of income. Such an enlargement of Commonwealth spending responsibilities has been achieved by, among other things, the Commonwealth's expansive use of conditional grants under section 96, by which it is able to influence considerably the spending priorities of the States. The almost unrestricted power to make conditional grants would, however, carry with it the power to structure those grants in ways that promoted horizontal or vertical experimentalism. Targeted grant design might, for example, ensure that State recipients share information about the trialling and development of innovative policies; or it might be structured to incentivise experimental reform in difficult policy areas.[104]

C. Localism, Discrimination and Preference

It is generally assumed that any virtues of small-scale experimentation are achievable by sub-national units, but not directly by the national unit. This is not obviously true, because there is likely to be at least some scope for the Commonwealth to trial policies in the first instance on subsets of the national population and, in that way, achieve at least a simulacrum of experimental federalism.

101 *Second Airlines Case* (1965) 113 CLR 54, 144 (Menzies J).

102 Commonwealth, *Parliamentary Debates*, House of Representatives, 4 June 1926, 2682 (Earle Page).

103 Liberal and National Country Parties, *Federalism Policy* (Policy Paper, September 1975) 2. See also R Menzies, *Central Power in the Australian Commonwealth: An Examination of the Growth of Commonwealth Power in the Australian Federation* (London, Cassell, 1968) 89; PH Lane, 'Economic Federalism, Excise Duty and Receipt Duty' (1969) 43 *Australian Law Journal* 614, 623.

104 For a more detailed analysis of how this might be achieved, see N Warren, 'Designing Intergovernmental Grants to Facilitate Policy Reform' in P Kildea, A Lynch and G Williams (eds), *Tomorrow's Federation: Reforming Australian Government* (Sydney, NSW, Federation Press, 2012).

One recent illustration of the Commonwealth's apparent power to regulate in a localised manner is the National Disability Insurance Scheme, which was first implemented in targeted 'launch areas' and continues to be rolled out progressively across the country. This approach is seen to enable the detail of the scheme to be recalibrated in light of experience generated in trial sites.[105] The localised and progressive implementation was and is being achieved through 'residence requirements' imposed on eligibility to participate in the scheme.[106] It is significant that those residence requirements are effected by rules made by the Commonwealth Minister only with the concurrence of each 'host jurisdiction' (being a State or Territory specified by the Minister with that State or Territory's agreement).[107] It is significant because it illustrates the practical or political necessity, and perhaps perceived constitutional necessity or at least prudence, for localised Commonwealth regulation to be supported by sub-national cooperation and consent.

Without sub-national cooperation, and perhaps even with it,[108] there may be difficulty with certain kinds of localised Commonwealth regulation arising from section 99 of the Constitution, which prohibits the Commonwealth from giving 'preference' to a State or part of a State over another State or part of a State by any law or regulation 'of trade, commerce, or revenue'. The meaning of this provision 'cannot be regarded as settled',[109] the Court not having had occasion to 'disentangle the reasoning in all the disparate authorities in the first 50 years of the court'.[110] Two things may, however, be regarded as tolerably settled. First, section 99 applies only to laws 'of trade, commerce, or revenue'. Secondly, a Commonwealth law does not give a 'preference' within the meaning of section 99 unless it 'discriminates' between States or parts of States,[111] and discrimination relevantly connotes not merely differential treatment or unequal outcome but differential treatment or unequal outcome that is not 'the product of a distinction which is appropriate and adapted to the attainment of a proper objective'.[112]

In relation to the first point, that section 99 applies only to laws 'of trade, commerce, or revenue' means that section 99 is no barrier to discriminatory Commonwealth laws that are not laws 'of trade, commerce, or revenue'. On the present authority of

[105] See, eg, Council of Australian Governments, *Principles to Determine the Responsibilities of the NDIS and Other Service Systems* (Policy Paper, 27 November 2015); NSW Government, 'NDIS: NSW Roll Out' (Participant Information Pack, September 2015).

[106] National Disability Insurance Scheme Act 2013 (Cth) ss 21(1), 23(1)(c).

[107] ibid ss 10, 209(1), 209(4), 209(8) (item 1(b)).

[108] *cf Re Wakim; Ex parte McNally* (1999) 27 CLR 511, 540 [2] (Gleeson CJ), 546 [26] (Gaudron J), 556–57 [54]–[56] (McHugh J), 576–82 [113]–[127] (Gummow and Hayne JJ), 625 [256], 626 [265] (Callinan J).

[109] *Permanent Trustee Australia Ltd v Commissioner of State Revenue* (2004) 220 CLR 388, 433 [126] (McHugh J) (*Permanent Trustee*).

[110] *Fortescue Metals Group Ltd v Commonwealth* (2013) 250 CLR 548, 607 [124] (Hayne, Bell and Keane JJ), quoting *Permanent Trustee* (2004) 220 CLR 388, 423 [86] (Gleeson CJ, Gummow, Hayne, Callinan and Heydon JJ).

[111] *Queensland Nickel Pty Ltd v Commonwealth* (2015) 255 CLR 252, 265 [52] (Nettle J, with whom French CJ, Hayne, Kiefel, Bell, Gageler and Keane JJ agreed), referring to *Elliott v Commonwealth* (1936) 54 CLR 657, 668 (Latham CJ), 683 (Dixon J); *Fortescue* (2013) 250 CLR 548, 575 [30] (French CJ), 607 [124] (Hayne, Bell and Keane JJ).

[112] *Permanent Trustee* (2004) 220 CLR 388, 424 [89], 424–25 [91] (Gleeson CJ, Gummow, Hayne, Callinan and Heydon JJ).

Morgan v Commonwealth, this is a significant limitation on the reach of section 99 because laws 'of trade [or] commerce' are said to be *only* those that could be enacted pursuant to section 51(i).[113] However, a law 'of ... revenue' has more recently been held *not* to be limited to a law that could be made under section 51(ii),[114] and it may be doubted whether *Morgan* would survive reconsideration by the High Court. In that event, section 99 may be given a wider operation upon all laws that answer the description of laws 'of trade, commerce, or revenue' whether supported by section 51(i) or some other head of power such as section 51(xx). Any wider operation would come at the expense of some of the Commonwealth's power to engage in localised experimentation.

In relation to the second point, concerning discrimination, the High Court has yet to develop a contemporary jurisprudence on what 'proper objectives' may be pursued conformably with section 99. One imagines that that is likely to be as contested as the related body of law on section 92. The modest point we make for present purposes is that there may be scope for it to be accepted that it is a 'proper objective' to conduct a trial of an experimental policy in a defined locality, at least for a defined period of time and in anticipation of nationwide implementation. This would facilitate forms of localism that underpin democratic experimentalism. Small-scale trials in a Territory, rather than in a State, might be on safer constitutional ground, unless it were to be held that a law for the government of a Territory under section 122 may contravene section 99 (as, for example, such a law may contravene section 51(xxxi)).[115] The question of which is the superior and which is the subordinate provision remains to be answered authoritatively.[116]

V. CONCLUSION

Constitutional values are said to have salience 'in resolving areas of formal legal indeterminacy' and in bringing into focus 'the potential consequences of various legal choices' that implicate those values.[117] Values, then, go hand-in-hand with indeterminacy and choice. They will inevitably coexist with other values, even competing or contrary values, and need to be adjusted accordingly. If they had mandatory content they would cease to be values, and would crystallise as rules, standards or principles with more determinate legal contours.

This sounds a note of caution for those (like us) writing and those (like you) reading about constitutional law from the perspective of just one value. Comprehending the constitutional structure raises not only the question of 'what values underlie the structure?' but also, and perhaps more importantly, 'how far does the structure go in

[113] *Morgan v Commonwealth* (1947) 74 CLR 421, followed by three judges in *Commonwealth v Tasmania* (1983) 158 CLR 1, 153 (Mason J), 182 (Murphy J), 248–49 (Brennan J); see also at 251 (Deane J not deciding) (*Tasmanian Dam Case*).

[114] *Permanent Trustee* (2004) 220 CLR 388.

[115] *Wurridjal v Commonwealth* (2009) 237 CLR 309.

[116] But see *Capital Duplicators Pty Ltd v Australian Capital Territory [No 1]* (1992) 177 CLR 248, 277 (Brennan, Deane and Toohey JJ).

[117] R Dixon, 'The Functional Constitution: Re-reading the 2014 High Court Constitutional Term' (2015) 43 *Federal Law Review* 455, 459.

pursuit of those values?'[118] We have focused in this chapter on identifying ways in which one particular value—democratic experimentalism—is or might be pursued. But it is well to remember that choosing to pursue one value may come at the cost of pursuing other values.

To take just one example, we considered above whether a greater degree of tolerance for concurrent federal and State laws in the application of section 109 might further the aims of democratic experimentalism. Be it so, such greater tolerance might simultaneously undermine other important values. Hayne J, dissenting on the point in *Momcilovic v The Queen*, expounded in strong language the 'fundamental constitutional principles' (his Honour might equally have said 'values') that section 109 implicates:

> The law does not admit of contradiction. The law may say many different things. In a federation there may be more than one legislative voice. But in the end there is and can be only one body of law. There cannot be contrariety; there cannot be contradiction. The rules that make up the law, regardless of their origin as federal, State or Territorial, must speak as a single and coherent whole to those to whom they are addressed.[119]

The system obviously cannot pursue all relevant values at all times in equal measure. The indeterminate pockets of the constitutional structure call for judgement informed but not controlled by those values.

We do not think it entirely coincidental that this strong statement of constitutional values is found in a dissenting opinion. We referred above to separate dissenting opinions of Kirby J and Heydon J, in which there can be found strong statements in favour of experimental federalism. Precisely because values are more amorphous and less tangible than rules, standards or principles, they are apt to go unnoticed until they are under threat or have been lost. For that reason, dissenting opinions are likely to be rich resources for identifying expressions of constitutional values.

This leads to another point. The aptness for constitutional values to go unnoticed until they are under threat or have been lost may be especially present in a constitutional culture that does not openly acknowledge the normative force or even existence of those values. Openly acknowledging our constitutional values, and openly debating their relative importance in guiding the application of legally indeterminate aspects of the system will tend to ensure that they are not inadvertently or collaterally abrogated without sufficient attention being paid to the consequences of doing so. Many of the constitutional provisions and doctrines that we have surveyed in this chapter are, as we have indicated, capable of being moulded in ways that are more or less favourable to the value of democratic experimentalism. We do not necessarily suggest that they should be moulded in any particular way. We do suggest that they should be moulded and if necessary remoulded with democratic experimentalism—*together with all other relevant constitutional values*—consciously in mind.

John Dewey, whose vision of democratic experimentalism lives on in the pragmatic, political, and federal constitution of James Bryce's *other* student, would have asked for nothing less.

[118] *cf Construction Forestry Mining and Energy Union v Mammoet Australia Pty Ltd* (2013) 248 CLR 619, 632–33 [40]–[41] (Crennan, Kiefel, Bell, Gageler and Keane JJ), quoting *Carr v Western Australia* (2007) 232 CLR 138, 142–43 [5]–[7] (Gleeson CJ).

[119] (2011) 245 CLR 1, 124 [283].

13

Indigenous Recognition

DYLAN LINO

I. INTRODUCTION

THERE IS AN uneasy fit between the project of advancing a more values-based approach to interpreting the Australian Constitution and the project of recognising Aboriginal and Torres Strait Islander peoples within the Australian constitutional order. The former is based on the insight that there are certain values embedded in the Constitution's text, structure and history, which can and ought to be used to flesh out constitutional meaning. The latter project, by contrast, is widely premised on an understanding that, when it comes to respecting the claims of Aboriginal and Torres Strait Islander peoples, the Constitution presently contains no such values: it does not recognise Indigenous peoples at all. The cause of functionalist constitutional interpretation, if it is to get off the ground, is emphatically one to be undertaken in the courts—by judges and the lawyers arguing before them, and indirectly by academics promoting the same cause in their scholarship and teaching. Contrarily, Indigenous constitutional recognition is generally understood to require not so much the development of new, values-oriented constitutional doctrine as it requires formal change to the Constitution itself.

To many people, then, it will seem that to contemplate advancing the cause of Indigenous recognition through functionalist constitutional interpretation is to put the cart before the horse. For courts to be able to interpret the Constitution in accordance with the value of Indigenous recognition, that value first needs to be officially incorporated into the Constitution through new constitutional provisions: explicit statements acknowledging Indigenous peoples' histories, cultures and connections to their traditional territories, protections against racial discrimination, Indigenous parliamentary representation, machinery for the negotiation of treaties, and so on. Only then (and, on some accounts of Indigenous constitutional recognition, not even then) might the courts—and functionalist constitutional interpretation—come into play.

There is a great deal of truth in that view. Indeed, standard accounts of Indigenous peoples' exclusion from the Constitution's drafting, ratification and original language fail to adequately appreciate the depth of Indigenous non-recognition. For the Constitution was drafted as a colonising instrument designed to further entrench and expand settler society, economy and government across the Australian landmass, with Indigenous dispossession and displacement the inevitable if implicit corollary. It was an endeavour premised on values of progress and civilisation that took European ways of life as their apogee and Indigenous ways of life as a doomed atavism. Contemporary projects of Indigenous recognition can never entirely transcend the legacies of settler colonialism, even as they nonetheless present the best option for addressing those legacies in the here and now.

Despite its dark history, the Constitution contains some underappreciated possibilities for advancing Indigenous recognition through the courts. Certainly, absent more fundamental constitutional changes, there are major limits to how far the cause of Indigenous constitutional recognition can be progressed through the courts alone. But contrary to widespread assumptions about Indigenous recognition, opportunities for advancing that value through functionalist constitutional interpretation do exist—ironically enough, within the 'race power' (section 51(xxvi)), a much-maligned hangover from Australia's racially discriminatory founding. Pursuing those opportunities, despite their limitations, could well be a worthwhile political strategy for proponents of Indigenous recognition.

Even if successful, though, such doctrinal shifts would not by themselves satisfy all contemporary Indigenous demands for constitutional recognition. Meeting those demands requires political action and institutional reform beyond what might be achieved through the courts via the existing Constitution. Nonetheless, I will argue that, while the Constitution presently provides only limited resources for Indigenous-recognition-by-litigation, it does provide resources that advocates can draw upon in advancing Indigenous recognition as a political project of constitutional reform. In particular, the constitutional values underpinning Australian political constitutionalism as well as Australian federalism can support Aboriginal and Torres Strait Islander peoples' aspirations to be better recognised as first peoples. Throughout, I will also emphasise that in thinking about the 'constitutional' side of Indigenous constitutional recognition, we should be willing to think outside the Constitution (and outside the courts).[1] When it comes to the constitutional recognition of Indigenous peoples, changing the basic distribution of public power as it affects Indigenous peoples is what matters most, and there are many ways to achieve that redistribution—including but by no means limited to formal amendment of the Constitution's text and the empowerment of the judiciary.

II. THE SETTLER-COLONIAL FUNCTIONS OF THE ORIGINAL CONSTITUTION

There is a relatively well-known story about how the original Australian Constitution excluded Aboriginal and Torres Strait Islander peoples. They were not involved in any of the negotiations and debates over the Constitution's drafting that occurred throughout the 1890s.[2] By dint of existing colonial law and administrative practice,

[1] See also D Lino, 'Thinking Outside the *Constitution* on Indigenous Constitutional Recognition: Entrenching the *Racial Discrimination Act*' (2017) 91 *Australian Law Journal* 381.

[2] See generally JA La Nauze, *The Making of the Australian Constitution* (Melbourne, Melbourne University Press, 1972).

very few Indigenous people would have been eligible to vote (and far fewer still would have actually voted) in elections for the delegates to the constitutional conventions or in the referendums that approved the product of those conventions.[3] The white male framers of the Constitution had a near-total disregard for the status and circumstances of the continent's first peoples in their deliberations, proceeding almost on the basis that Indigenous people did not exist.[4] In fact it was widely believed at the time that, by the 'inexorable forces of nature', Aboriginal people would indeed soon cease to exist.[5]

The very terms of the Constitution made Indigenous peoples' exclusion explicit. Since Indigenous peoples did not present such a threat—whether military, economic or racial—that their governance would necessitate concerted national action by the new federal government, matters of Indigenous rule could be confidently left with the colonies-cum-States.[6] Accordingly, while the Commonwealth Parliament would acquire a 'race power' (section 51(xxvi)) to regulate the affairs of 'coloured' migrants menacing the white settler populations, that power would explicitly exclude 'the aboriginal race in any State'.[7] Another exclusion was contained in section 127. Its effect was that when constitutional machinery relied on population figures for their operation—as in allocating representation to the States in the Commonwealth Parliament—'aboriginal natives' were to be excluded from the population figures.[8] As Quick and Garran said in their canonical 1901 constitutional commentaries, section 127 was a symbolic exclusion of Indigenous people from 'membership of the Federal community', a discursive border implicitly delineating the bounds of Australian citizenship.[9]

While that story of Indigenous constitutional exclusion is a vitally important one to remember, it does not properly capture just how profoundly the original 1901 Constitution failed to recognise Indigenous peoples. This lack of recognition was not simply a problem of excluding Aboriginal and Torres Strait Islander peoples from participating in the Constitution's drafting and ratification, or of the Constitution's explicit textual exclusions of the 'aboriginal race' and 'aboriginal natives'. The larger problem was that the Constitution as a whole was about the consolidation of settler-colonial rule and an alien form of government, and the consequent displacement of Indigenous societies and their modes of social, political and economic organisation.

[3] P Stretton and C Finnimore, 'Black Fellow Citizens: Aborigines and the Commonwealth Franchise' 25 (1993) *Australian Historical Studies* 521; M Goot, 'The Aboriginal Franchise and its Consequences' (2006) 52 *Australian Journal of Politics and History* 517, 518–21.

[4] G Sawer, 'The Australian Constitution and the Australian Aborigine' (1966–67) 2 *Federal Law Review* 17, 17–18; B Galligan and J Chesterman, 'Aborigines, Citizenship and the Australian Constitution: Did the Constitution Exclude Aboriginal People from Citizenship?' (1997) 8 *Public Law Review* 45, 46–48.

[5] R McGregor, *Indifferent Inclusion: Aboriginal People and the Australian Nation* (Canberra, Aboriginal Studies Press, 2011) xx.

[6] ibid xi–xxi; Galligan and Chesterman, above n 4, 46–47.

[7] Sawer, above n 4, 18–24; J Williams and J Bradsen, 'The Perils of Inclusion: The Constitution and the Race Power' (1997) 19 *Adelaide Law Review* 95, 106–10.

[8] Sawer, above n 4, 25–26; E Arcioni, 'Excluding Indigenous Australians from "The People": A Reconsideration of Sections 25 and 127 of the *Constitution*' (2012) 40 *Federal Law Review* 287, 296–301.

[9] J Quick and R Garran, *The Annotated Constitution of the Australian Commonwealth* (Sydney, Angus & Robertson, 1901) 957. See further Arcioni, above n 8, 301–03.

In this respect, the Australian Constitution continued a process set in train during the second half of the nineteenth century, when the Australian colonies' attainment of their own constitutions and responsible government went hand-in-hand with the overthrow of autonomous Indigenous political and social orders.[10] The Constitution was a colonising instrument.

To put it in the language of constitutional functionalism: consolidating Indigenous dispossession through the establishment of foreign forms of government, society and economy—a well-advanced but patchy and far from complete settler project at the *fin de siecle*—was one of the Constitution's basic functions, supposedly in the service of values of progress and civilisation.[11] The colonies-cum-States, retaining virtually unfettered power over Indigenous peoples and their lands, could continue making inroads into the vast tracts of largely uncolonised space in the centre and north of the continent and build on their existing settlements without any need to respect Indigenous ways of life and practices of government.[12] The new federal government could exercise unrestrained power over any Territories it acquired—a possibility contemplated and soon realised for the Northern Territory, which might at last be 'developed' through settler expansion on Commonwealth initiative.[13] Not unrelatedly, the Constitution was also premised on the prospect of more wide-ranging Australian colonial expansion throughout the Pacific Islands, which would come to fruition in the early decades after federation via Australian rule over Papua, New Guinea and Nauru.[14]

The project of settler expansion was embedded in the most mundane powers of the Commonwealth Parliament: powers over postal and telecommunications services, railways, census and statistics, meteorological observations, even lighthouses.[15] In the first instance, the Commonwealth's use of its powers to support the construction of basic material infrastructure, from railway tracks to weather stations,

[10] A Curthoys and J Mitchell, 'The Advent of Self-Government, 1840s–90' in A Bashford and S Macintyre (eds), *The Cambridge History of Australia* (Melbourne, Cambridge University Press, 2013) vol 1.

[11] See, for instance, the encomium to colonisation—both its ancient and modern European varieties—that commences Quick and Garran, above n 9, parts I–II. Quick and Garran's comments on modern European colonisation begin (at 6) with a paean to Columbus: '[b]old mariner was he ... to gaze across the wild waves of the Atlantic, and, beyond its primeval darkness, to see the light of promise with its glimmering rays leading on to modern civilization'. See more generally R McGregor, *Imagined Destinies: Aboriginal Australians and the Doomed Race Theory, 1880–1939* (Carlton, Melbourne University Press, 1997) especially ch 1.

[12] Constitution ss 51(xxvi) 107. On the patchiness of colonisation in Australia's centre and north, see T Rowse, 'Indigenous Heterogeneity' (2014) 45 *Australian Historical Studies* 297, 303–04.

[13] PF Donovan, *A Land Full of Possibilities: A History of South Australia's Northern Territory* (St Lucia, University of Queensland Press, 1981) especially 202–05, ch 10; PF Donovan, *At the Other End of Australia: The Commonwealth and the Northern Territory 1911–1978* (St Lucia, University of Queensland Press, 1984); R McGregor, *Environment, Race and Nationhood in Australia: Revisiting the Empty North* (New York, Palgrave Macmillan, 2016).

[14] Commonwealth of Australia Constitution Act 1900 (Imp) Preamble ('whereas it is expedient to provide for the admission into the Commonwealth of other Australasian Colonies and possessions of the Queen'); Constitution s 51(xxx) ('the relations of the Commonwealth with the islands of the Pacific'), s 122 ('[t]he Parliament may make laws for the government ... of any territory placed by the Queen under the authority of and accepted by the Commonwealth, or otherwise acquired by the Commonwealth'). See further M Lake, 'The Australian Dream of an Island Empire: Race, Reputation and Resistance' (2015) 46 *Australian Historical Studies* 410.

[15] Constitution ss 51(v), (vii), (viii), (xi), (xxxiii), (xxxiv).

could have a direct dispossessory effect on Aboriginal peoples.[16] But technological developments such as these also had far broader cumulative significance in enabling colonial settlement and broadening the reach of settler rule. For it was through the state-sponsored development of material infrastructure, as well as the often associated generation of scientific knowledge and the extension of administrative capacity and coverage, that the spread of settler society, economy and authority over Indigenous territories and populations could be advanced.[17]

From this perspective, section 127 of the Constitution—which exempted 'aboriginal natives' from the population counts on which various constitutional machinery depended—appears less as an invidious exclusion of Indigenous peoples from the Australian political community and more as a concession to the incompleteness of settler expansion. The category of 'aboriginal native' was for the most part concerned with the many Aboriginal peoples still living partly or wholly beyond the reach of settler society, institutions and technology, including census administrators.[18] While the provision symbolically excluded Aboriginal people from the new Commonwealth polity, in doing so it also implicitly acknowledged the continued existence of relatively independent Aboriginal political communities in certain parts of the country.[19] It was not until the 1960s that the Commonwealth was sure of its capacity to completely enumerate the Aboriginal population of Australia, an indication of the earlier limits of settler administrative reach.[20] That being said, section 127 did nothing to arrest the colonisation of Indigenous territories and the subsequent incorporation—or, as was widely assumed, the extinction—of those tens of thousands of Aboriginal people who had hitherto remained relatively autonomous from settler society.

This exceedingly bleak picture of the Constitution's settler-colonial functions and values would seem to bode ill for efforts to use the Constitution as a vehicle for Indigenous liberation today. Indeed, this history suggests that the injustice embedded within the Constitution stems not so much from its failure to properly recognise Indigenous peoples but from its very existence. On this view, turning to the settler Constitution for Indigenous recognition would seem to simply entrench the underlying injustice rather than transcend it.[21] This powerful critique goes beyond the

[16] See, eg, F Paisley, 'No Back Streets in the Bush: 1920s and 1930s Pro-Aboriginal White Women's Activism and the Trans-Australia Railway' (1997) 12 *Australian Feminist Studies* 119; L Dousset, 'Politics and Demography in a Contact Situation: The Establishment of the Giles Meteorological Station in the Rawlinson Ranges, West Australia' (2002) 26 *Aboriginal History* 1.

[17] See generally D Headrick, *The Tools of Empire: Technology and European Imperialism in the Nineteenth Century* (New York, Oxford University Press, 1981); BS Cohn, *Colonialism and its Forms of Knowledge: The British in India* (Princeton, Princeton University Press, 1996) ch 1; RA Butlin, *Geographies of Empire: European Empires and Colonies c1880–1960* (Cambridge, Cambridge University Press, 2009); JC Scott, *Seeing Like a State: How Certain Schemes to Improve the Human Condition Have Failed* (New Haven, Yale University Press, 1998).

[18] Arcioni, above n 8, 295–96; G Taylor, 'A History of Section 127 of the *Commonwealth Constitution*' (2016) 42 *Monash University Law Review* 206. For the earlier experience in Western Australia, see T Shellam, '"Our Natives" and "Wild Blacks": Enumeration as a Statistical Dimension of Sovereignty in Colonial Western Australia' (2012) 13 *Journal of Colonialism and Colonial History* 1.

[19] Cf on this front the United States Constitution, which still contains provisions excluding 'Indians not taxed' from constitutionally required population counts: art I § 2 cl 3; 14th Am § 2.

[20] T Rowse and L Smith, 'The Limits of "Elimination" in the Politics of Population' (2010) 41 *Australian Historical Studies* 90, 91.

[21] GS Coulthard, *Red Skin, White Masks: Rejecting the Colonial Politics of Recognition* (Minneapolis, University of Minnesota Press, 2014).

Australian Constitution and indeed beyond Australia: it is a dilemma that confronts all settler-colonial societies, which must grapple with similar histories of dispossession, genocide and discrimination. It would seem that the egregious past of settler societies puts the present-day structures that have emerged out of that past beyond redemption.

Powerful as that objection to an ongoing Indigenous–settler constitutional relationship is, there are three responses to it that, in combination, make resort to such a constitutional relationship a defensible undertaking. First, the alternative—dissolving that constitutional relationship and, if one is serious about returning to the *status quo ante*, dissolving the settler state altogether—is politically unfeasible. Maintaining an Indigenous–settler constitutional relationship, albeit in a way that seeks to transform its terms, is a pragmatic response in circumstances where there is no realistic alternative.

Second, abandoning an Indigenous–settler constitutional relationship would create new forms of injustice, both for Indigenous and non-Indigenous peoples. That is not to accept that the historical injustices of settler colonialism have been 'superseded'.[22] But it is to acknowledge that, as a result of the drastic changes in circumstances brought about by settler colonialism, those historical claims now compete and must be reconciled with more recent justice claims, both historical and distributive.[23] Importantly, those more recent justice claims belong not only to non-Indigenous people but to Indigenous peoples as well, whose lives—which are now to varying degrees interwoven with the social, cultural, political and economic fabric of broader Australia—would be seriously disrupted by an effort to wholly restore the pre-invasion *status quo*.[24]

Third, dissolving the Indigenous–settler constitutional relationship does not seem to be what Aboriginal and Torres Strait Islander peoples want.[25] Indigenous self-determination necessarily involves choice, including the option to accept rather than reject a constitutional relationship with the settler state, and Indigenous peoples overwhelmingly appear to prefer the former. These three considerations—the political unfeasibility of the alternative, competing justice claims and Indigenous choice—render the maintenance of an Indigenous–settler constitutional relationship a justifiable response to the long and deep history of settler-colonial injustice visited upon Aboriginal and Torres Strait Islander peoples.

There remains, nonetheless, the challenge of trying to use *this particular constitution*, with its original settler-colonial values, as an instrument of Indigenous emancipation. Certainly, it would seem a hopeless task to attempt such constitutional redemption through the courts without radically reforming the Constitution first. But that task of pursuing Indigenous recognition through the courts, I will

[22] J Waldron, 'Superseding Historic Injustice' (1992) 103 *Ethics* 4.

[23] D Sanderson, 'Against Supersession' (2011) 24 *Canadian Journal of Law & Jurisprudence* 155, 177, 180–82; J Thompson, 'Historical Obligations' (2000) 78 *Australasian Journal of Philosophy* 334, 343–44.

[24] D Lino, 'Replacing the Race Power: A Reply to Pritchard' (2011) 15(2) *Australian Indigenous Law Review* 58, 59.

[25] See, eg, L Behrendt, *Achieving Social Justice: Indigenous Rights and Australia's Future* (Annandale, Federation Press, 2003) 174.

suggest, is not entirely hopeless, at least to the extent that the courts are willing to look beyond the Constitution's origins. I will also argue that some deeply embedded Australian constitutional values—especially those associated with Australia's traditions of political constitutionalism and federalism—offer valuable resources for those seeking to achieve Indigenous constitutional recognition through political (rather than exclusively judicial) avenues. Before making those arguments, though, it will be necessary to explain what exactly Indigenous constitutional recognition is.

III. THE MEANING OF INDIGENOUS RECOGNITION

It will be obvious by now that the phrase 'Indigenous recognition' cannot be found in the text of the Australian Constitution or the *Commonwealth Law Reports*. Rather than a constitutional turn of phrase or a judicial term of art, it is a concept that has emerged within wider Australian public discourse.[26] There is a qualification: at the State level, Indigenous recognition *has* become an explicit constitutional concept—though not a judicial one—with all States incorporating legally unenforceable Indigenous 'recognition' sections into their own constitutions since 2004.[27] These State developments have both reflected and contributed to a wider political discourse of Indigenous recognition. The language of recognition is one that Australians, Indigenous and non-Indigenous, have increasingly come to use as a way of debating the basic political relationship between Indigenous and settler peoples.

While that language has roots going back many decades in activism and public debate over Aboriginal and Torres Strait Islander peoples' political status, it has become especially prominent within mainstream political discourse in the past half-decade or so.[28] The main reason for its rising fortunes is that mainstream politicians, both State and federal, have made 'recognition' matter. They have adopted the language in support of various political projects to revise the terms of the Indigenous–settler constitutional relationship and have fed that language into a range of official inquiries and processes. At the national level, governments and oppositions have remained committed to Indigenous constitutional recognition for the better half of a decade, though for most of that time unwilling to formally commit to any particular reforms in its name. If mainstream politicians have increased the salience of recognition, Aboriginal and Torres Strait Islander people have nonetheless been central contributors to the discourse as well—inside and outside

[26] This section draws heavily on D Lino, 'What is Constitutional Recognition of Aboriginal and Torres Strait Islander Peoples?' (2016) 8(24) *Indigenous Law Bulletin* 3.

[27] Constitution (Recognition of Aboriginal People) Act 2004 (Vic); Queensland (Preamble) Amendment Act 2010 (Qld); Constitution Amendment (Recognition of Aboriginal People) Act 2010 (NSW); Constitution (Recognition of Aboriginal Peoples) Amendment Act 2013 (SA); Constitution Amendment (Recognition of Aboriginal People) Act 2015 (WA); Constitution Amendment (Constitutional Recognition of Aboriginal People) Act 2016 (Tas).

[28] For one prominent earlier iteration, see Aboriginal and Torres Strait Islander Commission, *Recognition, Rights and Reform: A Report to Government on Native Title Social Justice Measures* (Report, 1995).

official processes, and well before its relatively recent ascendance—voicing their own visions of recognition and contesting others.

A study of the contemporary discourse over Indigenous recognition reveals 'recognition' to be a contested, indeterminate and malleable language.[29] While the broad thrust of Indigenous recognition is towards a just postcolonial reconstitution of the political relationship between Indigenous and settler peoples, there is no single account of what the terms of that revised relationship should be. There are instead, as Megan Davis has put it, 'competing notions of constitutional recognition': a range of rival accounts adopted in support of various political projects.[30] The language of Indigenous recognition is capacious enough to accommodate diverse political ends—radical political transformation, Indigenous inclusion, protection and empowerment, settler nation-building, cautious symbolism, conservative resistance, and combinations of those. Indigenous recognition is, to quote Davis once more, 'an inchoate Australian project', but this is inchoateness born not so much of recognition's underdevelopment as its conceptual multiplicity.[31]

According to one of the most dominant conceptions of Indigenous constitutional recognition in Australian political debate, constitutionally recognising Indigenous peoples involves the insertion of an explicit symbolic acknowledgement of Indigenous peoples within a written constitution, whether State or federal. The model was popularised by Prime Minister John Howard, who put it to an ultimately unsuccessful constitutional referendum in 1999 as part of a new preamble for the Australian Constitution, and then revived the idea shortly before he lost office in 2007.[32] This has also been the model adopted by the States, which have over the past decade inserted unenforceable Indigenous recognition provisions into their constitutions, either by way of a new preamble or standalone section.[33]

Situating settler constitutions as important cultural symbols of the polity, this model of Indigenous recognition is an attempted exercise in Indigenous inclusion, reconciliation and settler nation-building. It has largely been promoted and advanced by non-Indigenous politicians, with some notable exceptions.[34] While this vision of Indigenous recognition has been supported by some Indigenous people, it is fair to say that few Aboriginal and Torres Strait Islander peoples see it as adequate in itself as a form of recognition, because it does little of substance to revise the terms of the Indigenous–settler relationship.[35] In this sense, this project of Indigenous constitutional recognition is relatively conservative.

[29] Lino, 'What is Constitutional Recognition?', above n 26, 3–5.

[30] M Davis, 'Competing Notions of Constitutional "Recognition": Truth and Justice or Living "Off the Crumbs that Fall Off the White Australian Tables"' in P Waring (ed), 'Lectures in the Senate Occasional Lecture Series, and Other Papers' (Papers on Parliament No 62, Department of the Senate, 2014).

[31] M Davis, 'Seeking A Settlement' *The Monthly* (Melbourne, July 2016) 8.

[32] M McKenna, A Simpson and G Williams, 'With Hope in God, the Prime Minister and the Poet: Lessons from the 1999 Referendum on the Preamble' (2001) 24 *UNSW Law Journal* 401; Prime Minister John Howard, 'The Right Time: Constitutional Recognition for Indigenous Australians' (speech delivered at the Sydney Institute, Sydney, 11 October 2007) 5: <parlinfo.aph.gov.au/parlInfo/download/media/pressrel/L41P6/upload_binary/l41p62.pdf;fileType=application%2Fpdf#search=%22media/pressrel/L41P6%22>.

[33] See above n 27.

[34] Lino, 'What is Constitutional Recognition?', above n 26, 3.

[35] ibid.

If this vision of Indigenous recognition once dominated mainstream political debate on the issue, it does no longer—at least not at the federal level. A major reason is because of the intervention of the Expert Panel on Constitutional Recognition of Indigenous Australians, a Gillard Government initiative which undertook a national inquiry throughout 2011.[36] With roughly equal Indigenous and non-Indigenous representation, the Expert Panel consisted of 22 members who were broadly sympathetic to legally substantive constitutional reform—a position further urged upon them, especially by Indigenous communities, in their national consultations.[37] The Expert Panel was, however, also committed to the pragmatically achievable.[38]

In its 2012 report, the Expert Panel accordingly articulated a vision of Indigenous recognition aimed at redeeming a dark history of racially exclusionary settler nationalism, as embodied in the Australian Constitution, through a more inclusive and non-discriminatory constitutional settlement. In addition to advancing symbolic reforms aimed at explicitly acknowledging Aboriginal and Torres Strait Islander peoples' histories, cultures and languages within the Constitution, the Expert Panel made recommendations to expunge 'race' from the Constitution and to ensure that settler rule of Indigenous peoples could no longer be racially discriminatory.[39] In the Expert Panel's elaboration of Indigenous recognition, then, to a nation-building and reconciliatory symbolism it added a component of Indigenous protection from the depredations of government mistreatment—the all-too-well-known experience of Indigenous peoples in the past. While this element of the Expert Panel's recommendations has occasioned conservative resistance for threatening to empower the courts at the political branches' expense, the Expert Panel's proposals have nonetheless worked to broaden mainstream political conversations over Indigenous recognition away from the purely symbolic to the more legally substantive.[40] And certainly, the Expert Panel's proposal for a constitutional ban on racial discrimination has not been without supporters, including a parliamentary Joint Select Committee on Constitutional Recognition of Aboriginal and Torres Strait Islander Peoples.[41]

As the mainstream debate over constitutional recognition has evolved in the years since the Expert Panel, visions of collective Indigenous political empowerment have emerged to increasing prominence in the debate. These ideas have been principally put forward by Aboriginal and Torres Strait Islander thinkers and activists, often using the language of self-determination and sovereignty.[42] One idea, first developed by influential Aboriginal policy intellectual Noel Pearson, would involve creating

[36] Expert Panel on Constitutional Recognition of Indigenous Australians, *Recognising Aboriginal and Torres Strait Islander Peoples in the Constitution* (Final Report, Department of Prime Minister and Cabinet, 2012).

[37] ibid 112–15.

[38] ibid 3–4.

[39] ibid xviii.

[40] On conservative objections, see S Morris, 'Undemocratic, Uncertain and Politically Unviable? An Analysis of and Response to Objections to a Proposed Racial Non-Discrimination Clause as Part of Constitutional Reforms for Indigenous Recognition' (2014) 40 *Monash University Law Review* 488, 495–503.

[41] Joint Select Committee on Constitutional Recognition of Aboriginal and Torres Strait Islander Peoples, Parliament of Australia, *Final Report* (June 2015) ch 5.

[42] D Lino, 'Towards Indigenous–Settler Federalism' (2017) 28 *Public Law Review* 118, 120–22.

a constitutionally protected First Nations representative body to advise the federal Parliament in matters of Indigenous governance.[43] Another idea that has gained considerable political traction, and one that is a long-time aspiration of many Aboriginal and Torres Strait Islander people, is for a treaty or treaties between First Nations and the Australian state.[44] Significantly, following Aboriginal activism for treaty, the Victorian Government commenced treaty negotiations with Victorian First Nations in early 2016, and the South Australian Government followed suit towards the end of 2016.[45]

These two ideas for collective Indigenous political empowerment—a constitutionally entrenched First Nations body and treaty—were put at the centre of the constitutional recognition debate nationally in mid-2017 by the Uluru Statement from the Heart.[46] At an unprecedented First Nations Constitutional Convention held at Uluru in May 2017, the Uluru Statement was proclaimed by over 250 Aboriginal and Torres Strait Islander delegates. The Uluru Convention followed in the wake of 13 First Nations Regional Dialogues held around the country from late 2016. This deliberative process had been designed and overseen by the Aboriginal and Torres Strait Islander members of the Referendum Council, a body established by the federal government to make recommendations about Indigenous recognition. Powerfully asserting an 'ancient sovereignty' that endures to this day, the Uluru Statement sought to make that sovereignty tangible by creating a First Nations Voice enshrined in the Constitution, as well as a Makarrata Commission to oversee treaty negotiations and a process of truth-telling.[47]

Such proposals for collective Indigenous empowerment, though sometimes framed as rejections of Indigenous constitutional recognition, are better seen instead as counter-proposals for Indigenous recognition.[48] For one thing, while their proponents sometimes repudiate 'constitutional recognition' for its perceived conservative minimalism and apparent inhospitality to Indigenous demands for sovereignty, self-determination and treaty, they often rely on the concept of recognition in making their own demands. To quote Yolngu leader and treaty advocate Yingiya Mark Guyula: '[w]e want our own sovereignty recognised … Recognise our power, recognise who we are, recognise that we were here before any law that came and ruled all over us'.[49] Although demands for sovereignty, self-determination and treaty have a decidedly internationalist bent—they are to some extent demands for

[43] N Pearson, 'A Rightful Place: Race, Recognition and a More Complete Commonwealth' (2014) 55 *Quarterly Essay* 1, 62–67.

[44] Davis, 'Seeking A Settlement', above n 31, 8; Lino, 'Towards Indigenous–Settler Federalism', above n 42, 130–31.

[45] See Lino, 'Towards Indigenous–Settler Federalism', above n 42, 130.

[46] See further D Lino, 'The Uluru Statement: Towards Federalism with First Nations' on *AUSPUBLAW* (13 June 2017): auspublaw.org/2017/06/towards-federalism-with-first-nations.

[47] 'Uluru Statement from the Heart' (26 May 2017): www.referendumcouncil.org.au/sites/default/files/2017-05/Uluru_Statement_From_The_Heart_0.PDF.

[48] Lino, 'What is Constitutional Recognition?', above n 26, 4.

[49] Calla Wahlquist, 'Treaty Push Should Replace Recognise Campaign, Says Yolngu Leader' *The Guardian Australia* (11 March 2016): www.theguardian.com/australia-news/2016/mar/11/treaty-push-should-replace-indigenous-recognise-campaign-says-yolngu-leader.

international recognition of Indigenous peoples as peoples—they are overwhelmingly not secessionist. They instead seek forms of Indigenous autonomy that revise rather than dissolve the constitutional relationships between Indigenous and settler peoples, along the lines of treaty relationships in other common law settler societies.[50] As Davis has perceptively emphasised, notwithstanding a publicly constructed dichotomy between treaty and Indigenous recognition, '[t]reaty *is* recognition'.[51]

The connection between Indigenous constitutional recognition and treaty becomes even clearer when 'the constitutional' is understood to encompass more than simply the contents of written constitutions. Australians, like our common law counterparts elsewhere, are well accustomed to thinking about the constitutional domain in this broader, less formalistic fashion. For instance, some of the most important constitutional norms, such as those surrounding responsible government, can be found not in the text of Australia's State and federal constitutions but in unwritten political conventions.[52] The most fundamental of all constitutional matters—the rules governing the acquisition of British sovereignty in Australia, which, as *Mabo [No 2]* recognised, intimately concern Indigenous peoples—find their basis in British common law, not the Australian Constitution.[53] These and many other norms, principles and structures, found variously in statute, the common law and political custom rather than a 'big-C' Constitution, are 'small-c' constitutional: they concern the basic distribution and exercise of public power.[54] With this understanding of the constitutional domain in view, it becomes plain that questions of Indigenous sovereignty, self-determination and treaty are constitutional matters of the highest order, even if they do not directly implicate the contents of a written constitution.

There remains the problem, though, that there are competing visions of Indigenous constitutional recognition: is there a way of making better collective sense of these alternatives, of finding some common thread and unifying value among them? Recourse to political theory on the 'politics of recognition' can help.[55] That body of theory first emerged in the early 1990s as a way of understanding the post-war rise of political mobilisation based not on class but on identity: the shift from a politics of redistribution to a politics of recognition. These identity-based political struggles take in diverse claimants, including nationalist groups, women, religious minorities, LGBTI people and, of course, Indigenous peoples. Despite the supposed shift away from questions of distributive justice entailed by identity-based politics, they also frequently involve demands for the redistribution of social and material resources and economic and political power.[56]

[50] See, eg, T McAvoy, 'Building Our House' in M Davis and M Langton (eds), *It's Our Country: Indigenous Arguments for Meaningful Constitutional Recognition and Reform* (Carlton, Melbourne University Press, 2016).

[51] Davis, 'Seeking A Settlement', above n 31, 8.

[52] Albeit with some textual hints: G Winterton, *Parliament, the Executive and the Governor-General: A Constitutional Analysis* (Melbourne, Melbourne University Press, 1983) 1–5.

[53] *Mabo v Queensland (No 2)* (1992) 175 CLR 1.

[54] Lino, 'What is Constitutional Recognition?', above n 26, 6–7.

[55] The phrase comes from C Taylor, 'The Politics of Recognition' in A Gutmann (ed), *Multiculturalism and 'the Politics of Recognition'* (Princeton, Princeton University Press, 1992) 25.

[56] Lino, 'What is Constitutional Recognition?', above n 26, 6–7.

To unduly condense a rich and sophisticated theoretical literature studying recognition politics, those politics involve the struggles by particular groups to have their identities respected within public norms, institutions and symbols.[57] The value underlying Indigenous recognition is respect for Indigenous identity. Demands for *constitutional* recognition involve claims that prevailing constitutional norms, structures or practices be altered to better respect the identities of the groups seeking recognition. For Indigenous peoples, constitutional recognition involves altering the settler constitutional order in ways that better respect their identities.

While this definition of Indigenous recognition is broad and abstract, and dictates no particular reforms in and of itself, it can help in making sense of the various positions different actors have adopted in the debate.[58] Those positions involve alternative, though not always mutually exclusive, visions of Indigenous identity—of who Indigenous peoples are—and what is required to respect that identity. First, the minimalist, purely symbolic model of recognition sees Aboriginal and Torres Strait Islander peoples more or less as ordinary Australian citizens, albeit citizens with distinct cultures and histories that ought to be acknowledged within public symbols like written constitutions in order to be respected. While this approach implicitly builds upon pre-existing, more legally substantive recognitions of Indigeneity (such as Indigenous rights to land), it does not see the need for substantive constitutional change to strengthen such pre-existing recognition.

By contrast, proponents of the other major positions—and, overwhelmingly, Aboriginal and Torres Strait Islander people themselves—claim that such purely symbolic forms of constitutional recognition, which leave the existing distribution of public power undisturbed, fail to respect who they are. Thus, a second vision of Indigenous recognition, that of the Expert Panel, conceives of Indigenous people as fundamentally aggrieved by a history of settler discrimination against them as citizens and peoples, and argues that respecting this identity based in historical grievance demands judicially enforceable constitutional protection against that history's recurrence. In a third account of Indigenous recognition, proponents of collective Indigenous political empowerment argue in different ways that Aboriginal and Torres Strait Islander people collectively constitute a people or peoples, and that respecting Indigenous peoplehood demands redistributions of power in ways that secure Indigenous self-determination.[59]

IV. INDIGENOUS RECOGNITION THROUGH CONSTITUTIONAL INTERPRETATION

Can any of these three different visions of Indigenous recognition be advanced through the courts' adoption of a functionalist, values-oriented approach to interpreting the Australian Constitution? The short answer is a heavily qualified 'yes': some visions of Indigenous recognition can be advanced through judicial interpretation,

[57] ibid.
[58] ibid 7–8.
[59] Lino, 'Towards Indigenous–Settler Federalism', above n 42, 120–24.

but only (very) partially. In particular, the courts' interpretation of the race power might secure a degree of protection for Indigenous peoples against governmental discrimination and might ensure Indigenous peoples a degree of collective political power when it comes to determining who is Indigenous.

The first vision of Indigenous recognition—explicitly and symbolically acknowledging Indigenous peoples within the constitutional text—cannot be achieved by judicial fiat. The Constitution's text has not contained explicit references to Indigenous people since 1967, and addressing that textual absence today can only come about by formal constitutional amendment. Certainly, much in the way of constitutional change can and does occur by informal methods such as revised judicial interpretations of constitutional provisions.[60] But while courts engaging in acts of interpretation can radically transform the meaning of words in a constitution or go far beyond a constitution's explicit terms, courts cannot actually add words into a constitution's written text. Only formal amendment can do that. The same holds for the removal of words from a constitution—notably, the Expert Panel's largely symbolic vision of a Constitution cleansed of its references to 'race'. Judicial interpretation can reshape the constitutional language of race in a way that advances other visions of Indigenous recognition, as I will emphasise below, but it cannot rid the Constitution's text of that language.

Holding somewhat more promise is for judicial realisation of the second vision of Indigenous recognition: placing judicially enforceable limits on the state's power to discriminate against Aboriginal and Torres Strait Islander peoples. That vision of recognition is about respect for Indigenous people as citizens and collectives aggrieved by past and present discrimination. Ironically, the major potential for advancing this goal is embedded in the race power, the very provision that proponents of a constitutional ban on racial discrimination most vehemently criticise.[61] Such criticism is by no means unwarranted, since the race power equally harbours 'dangerous potentialities of adverse discriminatory treatment', as Geoffrey Sawer warned on the eve of the 1967 referendum.[62] But the High Court has not definitively resolved the issue, which it last directly considered and left hanging some two decades ago in the notorious *Kartinyeri* case.[63] It is worth noting that *Kartinyeri* was handed down at a time with a differently composed High Court and when a range of post-1967 Indigenous rights achievements—including the *Mabo* and *Wik* judgments of the High Court itself—were under unprecedented attack from a hostile federal government.[64] Today, with different judges and a different political climate, it is possible the High

[60] For a classic account, see KC Wheare, *Modern Constitutions*, 2nd edn (London, Oxford University Press, 1966) chs 7–8. More recently, see D Oliver and C Fusaro (eds), *How Constitutions Change: A Comparative Study* (Oxford, Hart Publishing, 2011).

[61] See, eg, Expert Panel on Constitutional Recognition of Indigenous Australians, *Recognising Aboriginal and Torres Strait Islander Peoples in the Constitution* (Final Report, Department of Prime Minister and Cabinet, 2012) 14–19, ch 5.

[62] Sawer, above n 4, 35.

[63] *Kartinyeri v Commonwealth* (1998) 195 CLR 337 (*Kartinyeri*).

[64] See, eg, C Fletcher, 'From Consensus to Conflict: ATSIC and the Howard Government' in G Singleton (ed), *The Howard Government* (Sydney, UNSW Press, 2000); W Sanders, 'Never Even Adequate: Reconciliation and Indigenous Affairs' in C Aulich and R Wettenhall (eds), *Howard's Second and Third Governments* (Sydney, UNSW Press, 2005).

Court might see things differently. Certainly, in a context where creating an express constitutional ban on racial discrimination appears too politically controversial to succeed in a referendum, the potential to curb governmental discrimination through a reinterpreted race power may well be worth revisiting in litigation.

One avenue would be for courts to incorporate into the race power the egalitarian values that underpinned the power's extension to Indigenous peoples in the 1967 referendum.[65] As Brennan J in *Tasmanian Dam* interpreted it, the referendum's amendment of the race power was 'an affirmation of the will of the Australian people that the odious policies of oppression and neglect of Aboriginal citizens were to be at an end, and that the primary object of the power is beneficial'.[66] Murphy J insisted that the referendum was 'manifestly done so that Parliament could legislate for the maintenance, protection and advancement of the Aboriginal people'.[67] According to Deane J in the same case, the 1967 referendum was designed to enable the enactment of 'acceptable laws ... to mitigate the effects of past barbarism', and to thereby redeem Australia's standing as a nation.[68] While in general the race power supported laws both adverse and beneficial for particular racial groups, said Deane J, when it came to Indigenous peoples the power was confined to beneficial laws because of the 1967 referendum's egalitarian intentions.[69]

Going furthest along this track was Kirby J's dissent in *Kartinyeri*. Kirby J drew extensively on primary sources from the referendum campaign demonstrating that elite and popular motivations behind the amendments were to end discrimination against Indigenous people and ensure their advancement.[70] Interpreting the race power to support laws discriminating against Indigenous people

> would be a complete denial of the clear and unanimous object of the Parliament in proposing the [1967] amendment ... [and] would amount to a refusal to acknowledge the unprecedented support for the change, evident in the vote of the electors of Australia.[71]

It was partly on this basis that Kirby J, alone among the court, would have invalidated the Hindmarsh Island Bridge Act 1997 (Cth).

Even without relying on the 1967 referendum as an egalitarian refounding of the race power, some of the jurisprudence suggests that values of equality and non-discrimination might nonetheless find their way into its interpretation. There was, in the first place, the suggestion by six judges in the *Native Title Act Case* that the courts could police any 'manifest abuse' of the race power by Parliament—a concept which, if strongly informed by egalitarian values, might provide a substantial constitutional check.[72] Notable on this score was Gaudron J's judgment in *Kartinyeri*,

[65] See generally B Attwood and A Markus, *The 1967 Referendum: Race, Power and the Constitution*, 2nd edn (Canberra, Aboriginal Studies Press, 2007).

[66] *Commonwealth v Tasmania* (1983) 158 CLR 1, 242 (*Tasmanian Dam*).

[67] ibid 180.

[68] ibid 272–73.

[69] ibid 273. Michael Detmold refers to this reading of the race power as 'bivocal': MJ Detmold, 'Original Intentions and the Race Power' (1997) 8 *Public Law Review* 244, 251–52.

[70] *Kartinyeri* (1998) 195 CLR 337, 404–09, 413, 416, 417.

[71] ibid 413.

[72] *Western Australia v Commonwealth* (1995) 183 CLR 373, 460 (Mason CJ, Brennan, Deane, Toohey, Gaudron and McHugh JJ). For criticism of the manifest abuse test's workability, see *Kartinyeri* (1998) 195 CLR 337, 414–17 (Kirby J).

which her Honour glossed as the 'manifest abuse' test in practice.[73] Refusing recourse to the egalitarian intentions of the race power's 1967 amendment, Gaudron J took a seeming textualist line on the provision.[74] But Gaudron J emphasised that the text, with its requirement that laws passed under it must be 'deemed necessary', imported a limitation: laws affecting a particular racial group could only be deemed necessary where there was 'a real and relevant difference' between them and other racial groups.[75] Given that the contemporary circumstances of Indigenous people reflected 'serious disadvantage' both material and cultural, concluded Gaudron J, it was exceedingly difficult to conceive of a scenario in which such differences could authorise anything other than laws remedying that disadvantage.[76] Textualist on its surface but functionalist at its core, this reasoning was implicitly based in an egalitarian, anti-subordination rationale.[77]

Promising as these possibilities are for a values-based interpretation of the race power, such a reinterpreted race power holds some significant limitations as an advancement of an anti-discrimination vision of Indigenous recognition. To begin with, unlike the Expert Panel's proposal, a non-discriminatory race power would not directly constrain the executive branch of government, nor would it constrain the racially discriminatory powers of the States or Territories.[78] While the Racial Discrimination Act 1975 (Cth) does effectively limit executive power and State and Territory power on this score, there would be nothing in a non-discriminatory race power to prevent the federal Parliament winding back such protection. Moreover, unlike a broad constitutional ban on racial discrimination, a non-discriminatory race power would likely not constrain the Parliament's other constitutional powers.[79] That is a serious problem, given that the most spectacular federal incursion into Indigenous rights in recent years, the Northern Territory Intervention, drew constitutional validity not from the race power but from the Commonwealth's 'Territories power'.[80] Finally, it is likely that the degree of judicial scrutiny of legislation passed under a non-discriminatory race power would be less searching than judicial scrutiny under an express constitutional prohibition on racial discrimination.[81]

Turning to the third vision of Indigenous recognition—the allocation of collective forms of political power to Indigenous peoples—constitutional interpretation would appear to offer little hope. Aboriginal and Torres Strait Islander peoples do not number among the agents and institutions to which the Constitution formally distributes public power: chiefly the Commonwealth government, its core branches

[73] *Kartinyeri* (1998) 195 CLR 337, 366–67.

[74] ibid 361–64.

[75] ibid 367; see further ibid 365.

[76] ibid 367.

[77] J Morgan, 'Equality and Discrimination: Understanding Context' (2004) 15 *Public Law Review* 314, 316–17.

[78] Expert Panel on Constitutional Recognition of Indigenous Australians, *Recognising Aboriginal and Torres Strait Islander Peoples in the Constitution* (Final Report, Department of Prime Minister and Cabinet, 2012) 167–73.

[79] D Lino, Submission to the Expert Panel on Constitutional Recognition of Indigenous Australians, Parliament of Australia, *Recognising Aboriginal and Torres Strait Islander Peoples in the Constitution*, 30 September 2011: <papers.ssrn.com/sol3/papers.cfm?abstract_id=2202024, 15>.

[80] Constitution s 122.

[81] Lino, Submission to Expert Panel, above n 79, 23.

and the States. For this reason alone, it is difficult to envision possibilities for collective Indigenous political empowerment coming about through interpretation of the Constitution's terms. A contrast can be drawn with the United States Constitution, which implicitly affirms Native American political autonomy in its conferral of power on Congress '[t]o regulate Commerce with foreign Nations, and among the several States, and with the Indian Tribes'.[82] If this provision distinguishes 'Indian Tribes' from foreign powers and American States, it also recognises a kindred sort of collective authority in Native American tribes—a status as 'domestic dependent nations' with whom the United States government may treat, as Chief Justice John Marshall famously put it in 1831.[83] The main prospects for interpreting the Australian Constitution along these lines, dim as they may have been, were removed in the 1967 referendum.

There is, however, a small but important exception that has emerged out of the jurisprudence of the race power. In interpreting what constitutes a 'race' of Indigenous people, at least some judges have recognised the power of Indigenous communities to determine the bounds of their membership. Most notably, Deane J in *Tasmanian Dam* elaborated a now familiar tripartite test for determining who is Indigenous: first, a degree of descent from the peoples inhabiting the continent before British colonisation; second, self-identification as Indigenous; and third, recognition by the Indigenous community.[84] This definition has been taken up in the broader jurisprudence and administrative practice surrounding Indigeneity.[85] Within this definition, it is the community recognition element that distributes political power to Indigenous collectivities—in practice, the institutions of the 'Indigenous sector', such as land councils—who are afforded a decisive say on Indigenous membership boundaries.[86] If adopted as an authoritative interpretation of the Indigenous 'race' under the race power, this approach would ensure that in determining the beneficiaries or subjects of Indigenous-specific laws passed under the race power, the collective power of Indigenous peoples on such matters would be constitutionally protected.

As Mick Dodson observed some two decades ago, the value implicit in this interpretation of 'race' is Indigenous self-determination, a core incident of which is the power of collective self-definition.[87] Put in terms of Indigenous recognition, it partly instantiates the value of respect for Indigenous peoples *as peoples*. This gloss on 'race' is a major departure from the way the term was commonly understood when

[82] United States Constitution art I §8 cl 3.

[83] *Cherokee Nation v Georgia*, 10 US (5 Peters) 1, 17 (1831).

[84] *Commonwealth v Tasmania* (1983) 158 CLR 1, 273–74. See also *Mabo v Queensland [No 2]* (1992) 175 CLR 1, 70 (Brennan J).

[85] Indeed, it had already begun to emerge before Deane J's judgment. See further J Gardiner-Garden, 'Defining Aboriginality in Australia' (Current Issues Brief No 10, Parliamentary Library, Parliament of Australia, 2003) 4–8; K Gover, *Tribal Constitutionalism: States, Tribes, and the Governance of Membership* (Oxford, Oxford University Press, 2010) 56–59.

[86] ibid. On the Indigenous sector, see T Rowse, *Indigenous Futures: Choice and Development for Aboriginal Australia* (Sydney, UNSW Press, 2002) especially 1–25.

[87] M Dodson, 'The End in the Beginning: Re(de)finding Aboriginality' [1994] *Australian Aboriginal Studies* 2, 5. Dodson referred approvingly to the High Court's interpretation of the race power as a manifestation of Indigenous self-definition: at 6. See now also United Nations Declaration on the Rights of Indigenous Peoples, GA Res 61/295, UN GAOR, 61st sess, 107th plen mtg, Supp No 49, UN Doc A/RES/61/296 (13 September 2007) art 33.

the Constitution was adopted, where one's membership of 'the Aboriginal race' was determined by a settler-imposed test of blood quantum—a test based in contemporaneous scientific understandings of human difference that were themselves deeply entangled with values of white superiority and disrespect for Indigenous communal life.[88] To the extent that the older definition of race has been replaced by one that guarantees Indigenous peoples greater control over their communal boundaries, this represents a small and partial but still significant advancement of Indigenous recognition in one of its guises: the collective political empowerment of Indigenous peoples themselves.[89]

Nevertheless, this interpretation of the race power, valuable though it is, represents only a very partial fulfilment of the collective political empowerment underpinning the third vision of Indigenous recognition. It provides a degree of Indigenous communal control over Indigenous community membership. But those advocating collective political autonomy as the means of constitutionally recognising Indigenous peoples envision a much more extensive and wide-ranging distribution of power to Indigenous peoples. They envision Aboriginal and Torres Strait Islander peoples having a standing voice in the settler institutions that rule them as well as Indigenous powers of self-government. Such political empowerment would concern all matters affecting the governance of Indigenous peoples, not just their communal membership.

In summary, the prospects for advancing Indigenous recognition (at least in three of its prominent forms) through a values-based approach to constitutional interpretation are real but limited. In a deep irony, it is the race power—*bête noire* of much contemporary advocacy for Indigenous recognition—that holds the greatest interpretive promise. Construed according to egalitarian values sourced from the 1967 referendum or from Australian society and traditions more generally, the race power might work to constrain Parliament's power to discriminate against Aboriginal and Torres Strait Islander peoples. But this would be a weaker substitute for the anti-discrimination vision of Indigenous recognition put forward by the Expert Panel and others. Construed according to the value of self-determination, the race power can also secure Indigenous peoples a degree of collective authority over their communal membership, at least under federal laws made for the Indigenous 'race'. But again, this represents a very small step towards the sort of collective political autonomy many see as necessary for Indigenous recognition. And for those proponents of Indigenous recognition concerned to turn the Constitution into an Indigenous-inclusive cultural symbol of the Australian polity, they will find little succour, and perhaps serious cognitive dissonance, in relying on the race power of all things to instantiate greater respect for Indigenous peoples within a constitutional text that does not formally acknowledge Indigenous existence.

[88] Dodson, above n 87, 2–4; Gardiner-Garden, above n 85, 3. See more generally R McGregor, *Imagined Destinies*, above n 11, especially ch 1; W Anderson, *The Cultivation of Whiteness: Science, Health, and Racial Destiny in Australia* (New York, Basic Books, 2003) especially ch 7.

[89] Worryingly, it is possible that the tripartite definition of the Indigenous 'race' still permits Parliament, under the descent limb of the definition, to determine the degree of Indigenous descent required for a person to legally qualify as Indigenous. If so, Parliament could revive the much maligned blood quantum tests of Indigeneity, albeit supplemented with self-identification and community recognition.

V. AUSTRALIAN CONSTITUTIONAL VALUES AND THE FUTURE OF INDIGENOUS RECOGNITION

If resort to values is vital for any court-focused effort to advance Indigenous recognition, so too are constitutional values a necessary resource in political projects of Indigenous recognition. As Duncan Bell has emphasised, achieving (non-violent) political transformation is a task rooted 'in "rhetorical re-inscription" of the existing modes of political discourse that shape the normative architecture of a society, in the ways in which political vocabularies can be remodelled to meet or accommodate specific goals'.[90] It is only by working creatively with existing constitutional languages and the values underpinning them that proponents of Indigenous recognition can hope to muster political support for their projects of institutional reform. These discourses and values form part of the relatively stable structures that proponents of Indigenous recognition are compelled to work within, even as they seek to transform them in ways both small and large and entrench new values in the process.

Before suggesting some possibilities on this score, I want to emphasise the value of thinking beyond Australia's State and national constitutions as the exclusive means to Indigenous constitutional recognition.[91] It is worth also considering 'small-c' constitutional possibilities. As I argued earlier, a central motivation for many proponents of recognition—and especially Aboriginal and Torres Strait Islander advocates—is to change the way public power can be exercised over and by Indigenous peoples in Australia. While Australia's written constitutions are central instruments in the distribution and regulation of public power, they do not have a monopoly on it, and there are numerous possibilities outside them for achieving the reorganisation of public power in the name of Indigenous recognition. Looking to small-c constitutional reforms is valuable partly for the pragmatic reason that redistributing public power by amending Australia's constitutions, especially the strongly entrenched national document, is an extremely difficult political task. But another reason to embrace small-c constitutional thinking is that it reflects what a growing number of Aboriginal and Torres Strait Islander people want, which is a move away from settler constitutions to the small-c constitutional instrument of a treaty as the vehicle for recognition.

There is also value in thinking beyond the courts as the sole guarantors of Indigenous constitutional recognition. Again, this is partly on pragmatic grounds: proposals to create strong, judicially enforceable forms of Indigenous recognition, such as a constitutional ban on racial discrimination or entrenched protections of distinct Indigenous rights, encounter vehement resistance, especially from conservatives.[92] But beyond the question of political feasibility, it is also clear that the courts may not be particularly progressive when it comes to upholding new forms of Indigenous recognition, as the experience with native title and the recent jurisprudence of the

[90] D Bell, *The Idea of Greater Britain: Empire and the Future of World Order, 1860–1900* (Princeton, Princeton University Press, 2007) 120.

[91] See also Lino, 'Thinking Outside the *Constitution*', above n 1.

[92] Pearson, above n 43, especially 62–67; S Morris, 'The Argument for a Constitutional Procedure for Parliament to Consult with Indigenous Peoples When Making Laws for Indigenous Affairs' (2015) 26 *Public Law Review* 166, 168–69.

Racial Discrimination Act 1975 (Cth) suggest.[93] Finally, Aboriginal and Torres Strait Islander people are increasingly demanding that public power should not simply be redistributed to the courts; it should be redistributed to Aboriginal and Torres Strait Islander peoples themselves. The point of these arguments is not to abandon judicial review as an institutional guarantee of new forms of Indigenous recognition, but rather to demonstrate that it is worth thinking about other possibilities as well.

Bringing all of this together, advocates of Indigenous recognition can draw support from Australia's tradition of political constitutionalism and the cluster of values underpinning it. That strand of political constitutionalism is most pronounced when it comes to rights protection.[94] Its underlying values include political accountability, representation, political equality and democratic deliberation. To some extent, appeals to these values and political constitutionalism more generally have already been taking place, in particular with the proposal for a First Nations representative body to advise governments at the national level.[95] That model could be expanded into the States and Territories as well. In all cases, it might be achieved through ordinary legislation, without the need to go through a constitutional referendum. Indigenous seats in Australia's parliaments are another possibility, though almost certainly at the national level and probably also at the State level the creation of such seats could not be achieved without formal constitutional amendment (and having to satisfy onerous amendment procedures).[96] Within the compass of Australia's political constitutionalism, another possibility for Indigenous recognition would be to catalyse new constitutional conventions and customs governing the relationship between Indigenous peoples and settler governments. A treaty or treaties would be one obvious way to create such conventions, as in New Zealand, where the principles of the Tiriti o Waitangi/Treaty of Waitangi have formed the substance of constitutional conventions.[97]

Australia's tradition of federalism and its associated values—especially self-rule and shared rule, and respect for diversity—can likewise be used in support of political projects of Indigenous recognition.[98] In particular, federalism offers a conceptual and normative framework supportive of Indigenous demands to be recognised as self-determining, sovereign political communities—exercising, like the Australian

[93] On native title, see L Strelein, *Compromised Jurisprudence: Native Title Cases Since Mabo* (Canberra, Aboriginal Studies Press, 2009). On the Racial Discrimination Act 1975 (Cth), see *Maloney v The Queen* (2013) 252 CLR 168.

[94] See generally T Campbell, J Goldsworthy and A Stone (eds), *Protecting Rights Without a Bill of Rights: Institutional Performance and Reform in Australia* (Farnham, Ashgate, 2006).

[95] Pearson, above n 43, 62–67.

[96] But see J Chesterman, '"Chosen by the People?": How Federal Parliamentary Seats Might be Reserved for Indigenous Australians without Changing the Constitution' (2006) 34 *Federal Law Review* 261. At the State level, the creation of Indigenous seats would likely need to satisfy existing 'manner and form' requirements that protect the composition of State parliaments from alteration by ordinary legislation. See, eg, Constitution Act 1889 (WA) s 73.

[97] PG McHugh, 'What a Difference a Treaty Makes—The Pathway of Aboriginal Rights Jurisprudence in New Zealand Public Law' (2004) 15 *Public Law Review* 87, 94.

[98] Federalism as self-rule combined with shared rule is an idea popularised by Daniel Elazar: D Elazar, *Exploring Federalism* (Tuscaloosa, University of Alabama Press, 1987). On federalism as a framework for thinking about Indigenous recognition, see further Lino, 'Towards Indigenous–Settler Federalism', above n 42; Lino, 'The Uluru Statement', above n 46.

States and self-governing Territories, forms of self-rule while also participating in shared rule for Australia as a whole. One possibility would be to use the Australian Constitution's provisions permitting the creation of new States and Territories to confer recognised powers of regional self-government on Indigenous communities.[99] An idea with a surprisingly long history, Indigenous State- or Territory-hood has been proposed for many years by Torres Strait Islander activists and more recently by Aboriginal lawyer and activist Michael Mansell.[100] Remarkably enough, the creation of new Indigenous States or Territories might be pursued through ordinary legislation.[101] Another idea that can draw support from federalism is for the negotiation of a treaty or treaties as a means of institutionalising forms of Indigenous autonomy. Indeed, the very etymological and historical origins of federalism lie in the conclusion of compacts, covenants and treaties between different polities.[102] Indigenous scholars in North America have developed a discourse of 'treaty federalism' in recognition of the connections between treaty-making and federalism.[103] Finally, arrangements for Indigenous parliamentary representation (whether through reserved seats or a First Nations representative body) can be understood and justified in federal terms as a form of Indigenous–settler shared rule. In all these ways, Australia's constitutional traditions and values can be marshalled to support political projects of Indigenous recognition.

VI. CONCLUSION

Given the Australian Constitution's role in consolidating British settler colonialism over the territories of Aboriginal and Torres Strait Islander peoples, that instrument is, at first glance, a strange place to look for resources in struggles of Indigenous emancipation. However, to quote Duncan Ivison, 'we are never in a position to choose social and political norms, practices or institutions *de novo*, but instead work with the imperfect and unjust arrangements we have'.[104] It is in this spirit that Indigenous and non-Indigenous Australians have put forward an array of proposals for constitutional reform—from the relatively conservative to the more transformative—and have increasingly done so using the language of Indigenous recognition. While the visions of recognition are varied, the underlying value is about achieving respect for Indigenous identity.

[99] A Rienstra and G Williams, 'Redrawing the Federation: Creating New States from Australia's Existing States' (2015) 37 *Sydney Law Review* 357.

[100] K Blackburn, 'White Agitation for an Aboriginal State in Australia (1925–1929)' (1999) 45 *Australian Journal of Politics and History* 157; N Sharp, *Stars of Tagai: The Torres Strait Islanders* (Canberra, Aboriginal Studies Press, 1993) chs 14–15; Michael Mansell, 'Self-Determination Through an Aboriginal 7th State of Australia: An APG Model' *First Nations Telegraph* (30 October 2014) 4: issuu.com/first_nations_telegraph/docs/self-determination_through_an_abori.

[101] Rienstra and Williams, above n 99.

[102] N Aroney, *The Constitution of a Federal Commonwealth: The Making and Meaning of the Australian Constitution* (Cambridge, Cambridge University Press, 2009) 23.

[103] See, eg, J [sákéj] Youngblood Henderson, 'Empowering Treaty Federalism' (1994) 58 *Saskatchewan Law Review* 241.

[104] D Ivison, *Postcolonial Liberalism* (Cambridge, Cambridge University Press, 2002) 5.

Just as 'recognition' has proven to be a malleable concept that accommodates diverse political projects, so too are Australia's constitutional traditions and values adaptable to the ends of Indigenous recognition rather than Indigenous oppression. Indeed, even within the existing terms of the *Constitution*, there are ignored possibilities, limited though they are, for advancing some visions of Indigenous recognition by way of values-oriented constitutional interpretation. The race power, in particular, might be interpreted in a way that limits the federal Parliament's power to discriminate against Indigenous peoples and in a way that secures a degree of collective Indigenous control over Indigenous communal membership. Beyond those possibilities, though, advocates of Indigenous recognition should not overlook the potential that Australian constitutional values—especially those associated with political constitutionalism and federalism—offer their projects of political reform. And in the process they should be willing to think about what constitutional recognition outside the Constitution, and outside the courts, might look like.

Part VI

National Security and Unity

14

National Security: A Hegemonic Constitutional Value?

REBECCA ANANIAN-WELSH AND NICOLA McGARRITY

I. INTRODUCTION

NATIONAL SECURITY IS a foundational constitutional value. However, unlike many of the other values discussed in this volume, national security does not have its roots in the rule of law, human rights or democratic liberal traditions. In fact, a constitutional value of national security is likely to conflict with these notions. Furthermore, when national security has featured in constitutional interpretation, it tends to dominate—if not override—conflicting values. In this chapter, we argue that national security may be conceived of as a hegemonic constitutional value and, as such, it calls for the development of stringent guidelines that operate to restrain its role in the constitutional space.

We begin this chapter by engaging with the challenge of defining 'national security'. Section III then makes the argument that national security is a foundational constitutional value. In section IV, we consider the role that national security has played in two constitutional contexts, namely, with respect to the implied freedom of political communication and the separation of powers. These case studies demonstrate the capacity for national security to act as a trump card when played against conflicting values. We close the chapter by reflecting on how a constitutional value of national security might be constrained, as well as the lessons that can be drawn for the constitutional values project generally.

II. NATIONAL SECURITY

In 1985, Lord Denning observed that

> the words 'in the interests of national security' are not capable of legal or precise definition. The circumstances are infinite in which the national security may be imperilled, not only by spies in espionage but in all sorts of indefinite ways.[1]

[1] United Kingdom, HL Deb 6 June 1985, vol 464, col 869.

Whilst there may be 'infinite' ways in which to conceive of the security of the state and the scope of potential threats to that security, we believe it is possible to identify a 'lowest common denominator' definition. At its core, national security involves the protection of the state and its people, at least from foreign forces. As Peter Hanks surmises, the various conceptions of national security arising from Australian and foreign law and jurisprudence 'share a common objective, that of countering threats to the state'.[2] Beyond this core of meaning, however, 'national security' evades clear definition.

The idea of the state is obviously central to any conceptualisation of national security. A problem arises in that the meaning of the 'state' is not self-evident. As James Stellios argues in this volume, the state and citizens' relationships to it are disputed notions.[3] Again, Hanks provides some guidance in this regard. He suggests that there are three key aspects to the concept of the state: a physical base (meaning its population and territory); governing institutions; and a political idea of the state (an ideology which establishes the state's authority in the minds of its population).[4] Applying this reasoning to Australia, Hanks links the second and third aspects. He says:

> The dominant view of the state in Australia is the liberal democratic conception, which regards the state as embodied in its formal institutions of government—in the legislature, the courts, the executive government and the processes which link them with each other and with the population.[5]

This appropriately multifaceted conception of the state reveals the potential breadth in even the core of national security. At a minimum, the concept of national security involves the protection of Australia's population, territory, governing institutions, liberal democratic ideology and the processes that link government with the people.

Unsurprisingly, each of the formal institutions constituting the state has an interest in defining 'national security'. Whilst this concept is not explicitly mentioned, let alone defined, in the Constitution, it appears in a number of Acts of the federal Parliament. Several statutes—for example, the Intelligence Services Act 2001 (Cth)[6]—refer to 'Australia's national security' but stop short of providing any definition. Section 8 of the National Security Information (Criminal and Civil Proceedings) Act 2004 (Cth) (NSI Act), however, defines national security as 'Australia's defence, security, international relations or law enforcement interests'.

The NSI Act's broad approach is mirrored in statutes that refer to the related term, 'security'. For instance, under section 4 of the Australian Security Intelligence Organisation Act 1979 (Cth) (ASIO Act), security includes: the protection of Australia's territorial and border integrity from serious threats, and: the protection of, and of the people of, the Commonwealth and the several States and Territories from a range of activities, including espionage, politically motivated violence and acts of foreign interference, whether directed from, or committed within, Australia

[2] P Hanks, 'National Security—A Political Concept' (1988) 14 *Monash University Law Review* 114, 120.
[3] See James Stellios, ch 10 in this collection.
[4] Hanks, above n 2, 120.
[5] ibid.
[6] Intelligence Services Act 2001 (Cth) s 11.

or not. Notably, the definition also extends to the protection of a foreign country from any of the aforementioned matters.[7]

Of course, it falls to the courts to interpret and apply legislative provisions concerning national security, and in doing so to employ principles of statutory interpretation to give content to that phrase. In rare moments, the courts have taken the bold step of critiquing the Parliament's definition of national security. For instance, in *Thomas v Mowbray*—a case concerning the constitutional validity of anti-terrorism control order legislation—the High Court queried whether in section 8 of the NSI Act 'the Parliament has sought to over-reach the bounds of the understanding of "national security"'.[8] However, the reality is that neither this Court nor any other has succeeded in giving greater clarity to this important concept. This is not for lack of opportunity. The courts have engaged with the meaning of 'national security' in the course of decisions relating to the equivalent concepts of 'defence' and, to a lesser extent, 'naval and military purposes' in the Constitution.[9]

It is apparent that the courts' efforts to define national security have been coloured by their interpretations of the defence power. The scope of this power has been described as waxing and waning according to whether or not Australia is at war. For instance, Mason J has observed that national security fluctuates 'depending very much on circumstances as they exist from time to time'.[10] This elasticity renders the concept 'of indefinite extent' as it 'expands and contracts according to the dangers to the security of Australia'.[11] Given this indeterminacy, it is unsurprising that in *Australian Communist Party v Commonwealth*, two different approaches to the relationship between 'defence' and 'national security' were expressed.[12] Williams J seemed to suggest that the constitutional notions of national security and defence were synonymous.[13] On the other hand, implicit in the remarks of McTiernan J is the understanding that the scope of national security is broader than that of defence. His Honour observed that

> security, *in its application to national interests*, is capable of referring to political, social, economic, financial or military security. The constitutional power of the Commonwealth extends to security through military preparedness against an enemy and in war time to other forms of security, for then it is necessary to maintain public order, social security, industrial peace, financial and economic stability for the successful prosecution of war.[14]

[7] The complete definition in s 4 is: '(a) the protection of, and of the people of, the Commonwealth and the several States and Territories from: (i) espionage; (ii) sabotage; (iii) politically motivated violence; (iv) promotion of communal violence; (v) attacks on Australia's defence system; or (vi) acts of foreign interference; whether directed from, or committed within, Australia or not; and (aa) the protection of Australia's territorial and border integrity from serious threats; and (b) the carrying out of Australia's responsibilities to any foreign country in relation to a matter mentioned in any of the subparagraphs of paragraph (a) or the matter mentioned in paragraph (aa)'.

[8] *Thomas v Mowbray* (2007) 233 CLR 307, 358 [124] (Gummow and Crennan JJ).

[9] See, eg, *Re Colonel Aird; Ex parte Alpert* (2004) 220 CLR 308, 327–8. See generally *Thomas v Mowbray* (2007) 233 CLR 307.

[10] *Church of Scientology v Woodward* (1982) 154 CLR 25, 60. See also *Andrews v Howell* (1941) 65 CLR 255, 278 (Dixon J).

[11] *Australian Communist Party v Commonwealth* (1951) 83 CLR 1, 222 (Williams J).

[12] ibid.

[13] ibid 222 (the defence power 'is one of indefinite extent and expands and contracts according to the dangers to the security of Australia that exist from time to time').

[14] ibid 210 (emphasis added); Hanks, above n 2, 132.

On the whole, members of the federal Parliament have achieved greater success than their judicial counterparts in giving concrete meaning to the concept of national security. This may be due, as Hanks suggests, to the 'narrower focus' of the legislature 'on the terms of reference of security intelligence organisations'.[15] A different task has been given to the courts. They have been asked to define 'national security' in such a way that it may be applied to 'the diversity of the issues presented to them for resolution'.[16]

One might contrast, however, Parliament's relative success in defining national security in legislation against the much broader *political* usage of the term. The language of national security features, for example, in discussions of natural disasters and emergency management, and it pervades debates on immigration, particularly in respect of asylum seekers. In this latter context, national security has been harnessed to support controversial anti-immigration policies, and features in the legislative process of visa application and review (adopting the definition of security in section 4 of the ASIO Act, discussed above).[17] The flexible and evolving role that national security plays in political discourse warns against reliance on these less formal sources in attempting to understand the meaning of the concept.

There is, however, a third source to which we might turn for guidance on the meaning of 'national security'. Like the federal Parliament, the international community has sought to give meaning to this complex concept for a specific purpose (albeit a different one from that occupying the attention of the federal Parliament). That is, to set boundaries on the extent to which nation states may have recourse to national security as a ground for derogating from fundamental human rights. This has long been one of the preferred legal tools by which governments around the world—even democratic ones—attempt to suppress the free flow of information and ideas. Both the 'Siracusa Principles on the Limitation and Derogation Provisions in the International Covenant on Civil and Political Rights' (Siracusa Principles)[18] and the 'Johannesberg Principles on National Security, Freedom of Expression and Access to Information' (Johannesberg Principles)[19] focus their definitions of national security on the core aim of protecting the existence of the state. The former, for example, provides that '[n]ational security may be invoked to justify measures limiting certain rights only when they are taken to protect the existence of the nation

[15] Hanks, above n 2, 132.

[16] ibid.

[17] See, eg, Australian Security Intelligence Organisation Act 1979 (Cth) ss 116(1)(g), 116(3).

[18] United Nations, 'Siracusa Principles on the Limitation and Derogation Provisions in the International Covenant on Civil and Political Rights' (1984) UN Doc E/CN.4/1984/4 (28 September 1984) annex [29]–[30]: 'National security may be invoked to justify measures limiting certain rights only when they are taken to protect the existence of the nation or its territorial integrity or political independence against force or threat of force. National security cannot be invoked as a reason for imposing limitations to prevent merely local or relatively isolated threats to law and order' ('Siracusa Principles').

[19] United Nations, 'Johannesburg Principles on National Security, Freedom of Expression and Access to Information, Freedom of Expression and Access to Information' (1 October 1995) UN Doc E/CN.4/1996/39. See principle 2: 'to protect a country's existence or its territorial integrity against the use or threat of force, or its capacity to respond to the use or threat of force, whether from an external source, such as a military threat, or an international source, such as incitement to violent overthrow of the government'.

or its territorial integrity or political independence against force or threat of force'.[20] This may be contrasted with 'merely local or relatively isolated threats to law and order'.[21]

In light of these varied attempts to engage with and define a constitutional concept of national security, we agree with James Renwick's conclusion that the concept of national security is ultimately 'hard to define much beyond the deceptively simple notion that it involves the safety of a country and its people, particularly from, but not only from, foreign domination'.[22] The nature and extent of threats to the state fluctuate and evolve and, it follows, the meaning of 'national security' will also necessarily change. This is a significant, but not insurmountable, obstacle in identifying national security as a value capable of informing constitutional interpretation.

III. A FOUNDATIONAL VALUE

Insofar as it involves the continued existence of the state (in both its tangible and intangible manifestations), national security is a precondition to the preservation and maintenance of the Constitution. The real issue, however, is whether this is the same thing as a constitutional value. Konrad Lachmayer, for example, argues that the status of national security as a precondition

> does not transform security to the foundational status of the constitution, but rather refers to the minimum standard of security which must be acquired to establish a functioning legal system. When this minimum standard has been reached, security has to be understood as one of many different state objectives, which can only be fulfilled within the constitutional framework, which restricts the means of reaching these state functions.[23]

In some jurisdictions, especially those with a strong tradition of human rights protection, it may be possible to draw a distinction between a precondition and a constitutional value. The former, according to Lachmayer, are objectives of the state which—beyond a certain minimum point—may only be fulfilled *within* the constitutional framework. By way of contrast, constitutional values have a role to play in defining the boundaries and operation of that framework. Our argument in this chapter is that, at least in the Australian context, there is no concrete foundation for such a distinction. In fact, all evidence points to the characterisation of national security as *both* a precondition and a constitutional value.

As discussed by Jeffery Goldsworthy and Nicholas Aroney in this collection, one pathway to the identification of constitutional values is through originalist reasoning.[24] It is significant that the framers of the Constitution expressly acknowledged national

[20] 'Siracusa Principles', UN Doc E/CN.4/1984/4, [30].

[21] ibid.

[22] J Renwick, 'The War against Terrorism: National Security and the Constitution' (2002–03) (Summer) *Bar News* 45, 45.

[23] K Lachmayer, 'Constitutional Limits to Security—An Introduction' in H Eberhard et al (eds), *Constitutional Limits to Security: Proceedings of the 4th Vienna Workshop on International Constitutional Law* (Baden-Baden, Nomos, 2009) 18.

[24] See ch 3 by Jeffrey Goldsworthy and ch 2 by Nicholas Aroney in this collection.

security as a key factor motivating the movement to federation. George Reid went so far as to describe the 'defence of the integrity of every acre of Australasian soil' as the 'central point' of federation.[25] Joseph Abbott similarly observed that 'the primary objects of federation must be for defence purposes'.[26] James Howe 'care[d] more about this federation for defence purposes than … for any other purpose you can name'.[27] In other words, federation was conceived of as crucial in order to ensure the security of the various colonies from foreign forces. This was because—in the words of Josiah Symon—federation would be 'a bulwark against aggression and a perpetual security for the peace, freedom, and progress of the people of Australia'.[28]

Reflecting the framers' prioritisation of national security, this concept was built into the text and structure of the Constitution. The most obvious manifestation of this is section 51(vi), vesting Parliament with the power to legislate with respect to 'the naval and military defence of the Commonwealth and of the several States, and the control of the forces to execute and maintain the laws of the Commonwealth'. The framers were aware that a strong collective response was essential in order to protect national security. With that in mind, the framers referred to the defence of the nation as one of the primary reasons for giving a range of other legislative powers to the federal Parliament. These included: section 51(xxxi), allowing for the state acquisition of property on just terms; sections 51(xxxii) and (xxxiv), concerning railways; sections 51(xxvii) and (xxviii), concerning immigration, emigration and 'the influx of criminals'; and section 51(ii), the taxation power.

Even without looking to the Convention Debates, the significance of national security as a force behind the move to federation is clear on the face of the Constitution. This document appoints the Governor-General as commander-in-chief of the naval and military forces,[29] prohibits States from raising naval or military forces without national consent,[30] obliges the Commonwealth to 'protect every State against invasion and, on the application of the Executive Government of the State, against domestic violence',[31] and disqualifies those who owe allegiance to a foreign power from becoming a member of Parliament.[32]

Thus, national security finds support for its status as a constitutional value in both originalist and textual readings of the Constitution. It was identified by the framers as one of the key aims of the federation and, as such, it is woven into the text and structure of the Constitution in both obvious and subtle ways.

[25] *Official Report of the National Australasian Convention Debates*, Adelaide, 30 March 1897, 278 (George Reid).

[26] *Official Report of the National Australasian Convention Debates*, Adelaide, 13 April 1897, 495 (Sir Joseph Abbott).

[27] *Official Record of the Debates of the Australasian Federal Convention*, Sydney, 15 September 1897, 613–14 (James Howe). Howe went on to say that 'pure, real defence, as far as Australia is concerned, can only be obtained by united action and by federation for that purpose'.

[28] *Official Record of the Debates of the Australasian Federal Convention*, Melbourne, 17 March 1898, 2509 (Josiah Symon). See also *Official Report of the National Australasian Convention Debates*, Adelaide, 20 April 1897, 957 (Sir William Zeal).

[29] Australian Constitution s 68.

[30] ibid s 114.

[31] ibid s 119.

[32] ibid s 44(i).

Another means of identifying a constitutional value, as discussed by Sarah Murray in this volume, is to consider the status of the Constitution in the *absence* of that concept.[33] A constitutional value will be identified by its necessity to the effective functioning of the constitutional system and its integral role in the constitutional fabric, thus revealed. This approach counters Lachmayer's claim that a constitutional precondition is not necessarily also a constitutional value. As noted above, by preserving the very existence of the state, national security is an absolute precondition to the constitutional system. This foundational status—whereby the state must exist before even basic rule of law concerns may be considered—goes some way to explaining how and why national security must be acknowledged as a constitutional value. Protecting national security is regarded throughout the world as one of the central objectives of the state. The United States Supreme Court, for example, has stated that 'it is "obvious and unarguable" that no governmental interest is more compelling than the security of the Nation'.[34] It is for this reason that international human rights instruments consider the protection of national security to be one of the legitimate aims justifying restrictions on the exercise of human rights.

Strictly speaking, the only consequence of recognising national security as a constitutional value is that it should influence the courts when interpreting the Constitution. Thus, conceptualising national security as a value, rather than as a simple state objective, echoes what Cass Sunstein describes as 'National Security Fundamentalism' in the United States.[35] According to this approach, the courts should adopt a strong presumption in favour of allowing the President to do what is necessary to safeguard national security. Although a majority of the United States Supreme Court has not accepted this approach, it has nevertheless been supported by a number of judges. For example, Thomas J, in *Hamdi v Rumsfeld*, stated that the United States Constitution accords to the President the 'primary responsibility ... to protect the national security and to conduct the Nation's foreign relations'[36] and he supported an interpretive principle whereby any constitutional judgment should consider 'basic principles of the constitutional structure as it relates to national security and foreign affairs'.[37]

For these reasons, there is a powerful basis on which to conclude that national security is a core constitutional value. Once national security is identified as such, and therefore is capable of playing a real part in judicial interpretations of the Constitution, a number of issues arise. We have already discussed the difficulties courts have faced in defining what is meant by national security. However, further problems arise at the point that national security is weighed against other values in the course of judicial reasoning.

[33] See ch 7 by Sarah Murray in this collection.

[34] *Haig v Agee*, 453 US 280, 307 (1981), quoting *Aptheker v Secretary of State*, 378 US 500, 509 (1964).

[35] C Sunstein, 'National Security, Liberty and the DC Circuit' (2005) 73 *George Washington Law Review* 693.

[36] *Hamdi v Rumsfeld*, 542 US 507, 580 (2004).

[37] ibid 579.

IV. THE NATIONAL SECURITY TRUMP CARD

Existing jurisprudence demonstrates that when national security is introduced as a consideration in constitutional interpretation, the judiciary has adopted a position of deference. In other words, it has been reluctant to challenge assessments made by the executive branch of government regarding the nature of the threat to Australia or the necessity of adopting specific national security measures. This builds, in part, upon judicial acknowledgment that national security is an elastic concept, the scope of which depends upon matters that lie particularly within the expertise of the executive branch. This judicial deference exists, not only because of the perception of the distinct roles of the respective institutions, but also the procedural and evidentiary constraints upon the courts.

Assuming that this reluctance to interrogate and ultimately challenge executive assessments of national security continues, there will be considerable difficulties for the courts in attempting to impose limits upon this constitutional value. Thus, when the subject of national security is introduced into a constitutional analysis, it has the potential to subvert the usual checks and balances and operate as a trump card, overriding any other constitutional value that it is weighed against. This is not merely a hypothetical possibility. It is demonstrated in two streams of constitutional jurisprudence—those concerning the implied freedom of political communication and the separation of judicial power.

A. The Implied Freedom of Political Communication

The High Court has interpreted sections 7 and 24 of the Constitution as giving rise to an implied freedom of political communication. This is not an absolute freedom; rather, it is governed by the test set out in *Lange v Australian Broadcasting Corporation* (*Lange*).[38] This test originally involved two steps. The first was to ask whether the impugned law effectively burdened the freedom of communication about government or political matters. If this was answered in the affirmative, the Court then moved onto the second step, concerning purpose and proportionality of the burden.

In the 2015 case of *McCloy v New South Wales* (*McCloy*), the joint judgment of French CJ, Kiefel, Bell and Keane JJ endorsed the *Lange* test.[39] They noted that the 'only question' for the High Court is 'what is required by the *Lange* test'.[40] What the joint judgment did identify, however, is that the second step actually involves two discrete questions which build upon one another. In short, the judgment redefined the *Lange* test as a *three*-step test. The second step in the analysis post-*McCloy* is to ask whether the purpose of the law, and the means adopted to achieve that purpose, are legitimate in the sense that they are compatible with the prescribed system of representative government (compatibility testing).[41] It is only if this is answered in

[38] *Lange v Australian Broadcasting Corporation* (1997) 189 CLR 520.
[39] *McCloy v New South Wales* (2015) 257 CLR 178.
[40] ibid 200–01 (French CJ, Kiefel, Bell and Keane JJ).
[41] ibid 212–13 (French CJ, Kiefel, Bell and Keane JJ).

the affirmative that the court goes on to consider whether the law is reasonably appropriate and adapted to advance that legitimate object (proportionality testing).[42]

It is principally the second and third steps of the test that have the potential to raise national security considerations. In *R v Lodhi* (*Lodhi*),[43] the Supreme Court of New South Wales considered the constitutionality of section 31 of the NSI Act. This section required the Court to give the 'greatest weight' to any prejudice to national security—over and above, for example, the right to a fair trial—when it determined what orders to make in relation to the disclosure of information at trial. Whealy J accepted

> that the object of the legislation in question is plainly compatible with the maintenance of representative and responsible government. The object of the Act ... is to protect Australia's national security and thus to protect the system of representative and responsible government established by the Constitution.[44]

In contrast, in *Coleman v Power*, McHugh J reasoned that laws that ostensibly aim to protect national security are not necessarily for a 'legitimate object or end'.[45] His Honour stated that

> a law that sought to ban all political communications in the interest of national security would be invalid unless it could be demonstrated that at the time such a prohibition was the only way that the system of representative government could be protected. In such a case, the issue would not be whether the needs of national security require the prohibition of communication on political or governmental matters. It would be whether, at that time, the system of representative government is so threatened by an external or internal threat that prohibiting all communication on political and governmental matters is a reasonably appropriate and adapted means of maintaining the system. A total prohibition would not be reasonable unless there was no other way in which the system of representative government could be protected. *Ordinarily, the complete prohibition on, or serious interference with, political communication would itself point to the inconsistency of the objective of the law with the system of representative government.*[46]

The above deals with the second step of the *Lange* test (as reconceptualised in *McCloy*). However, national security considerations have also been taken into account as part of the analysis involved in the third step of the test. In *Lodhi*, for example, Whealy J concluded that the NSI Act was reasonably and appropriately adapted to achieving the legitimate object of protecting national security.[47] However, doubts about the excessive impact of this and other aspects of Australia's anti-terrorism legislation upon the freedom of political communication have frequently been expressed outside of the courts. For example, the Public Interest Advocacy Centre submitted to the Human Rights Commission's Freedoms Inquiry that:

> In the context of counter terrorism, the pursuit of national security is quintessentially a legitimate aim. However, a number of provisions risk burdening free speech in a disproportionate way. The chilling effect of disproportionate free speech offences should

[42] ibid 213–14 (French CJ, Kiefel, Bell and Keane JJ).
[43] *R v Lodhi* (2006) 163 A Crim R 448.
[44] ibid 473 [119].
[45] *Coleman v Power* (2004) 220 CLR 1, 209.
[46] ibid (emphasis added).
[47] *Lodhi* (2006) 163 A Crim R 448.

> not be underestimated, nor should the normalising effect of gradually limiting free speech over successive pieces of legislation.[48]

On the whole, there are very few cases which have addressed the relationship between national security and the freedom of political communication directly or in any real detail. However, the broader law and order context *has* received some attention from the courts and we believe that it is possible to reason by analogy from these cases.

The first such case is *Coleman v Power*, which was concerned with the offence of insulting language in a public place in section 7 of the Vagrants, Gaming and Other Offences Act 1931 (Qld).[49] Gleeson CJ explained that the purpose of public order offences like this was 'the preservation of order in public places in the interests of the amenity and security of citizens, and so that they may exercise, without undue disturbance, the rights and freedoms involved in the use and enjoyment of such places'.[50] Ultimately, a majority of the High Court upheld the constitutionality of this offence on the basis of a narrow reading of 'insulting'. The Chief Justice stated:

> It is impossible to state comprehensively and precisely the circumstances in which the use of defamatory language in a public place will involve such a disturbance of public order, or such an affront to contemporary standards of behaviour, as to constitute the offence of using insulting words to a person. An intention, or likelihood, of provoking violence may be one such circumstance. The deliberate inflicting of serious and public offence or humiliation may be another. Intimidation and bullying may constitute forms of disorder just as serious as the provocation of physical violence. But where there is no threat to the peace, and no victimisation, then the use of personally offensive language in the course of a public statement of opinions on political and governmental issues would not of itself contravene the statute. However, the degree of personal affront involved in the language, and the circumstances, may be significant.[51]

Another case dealing with the implied freedom of political communication in the broader law and order context is *Tajjour v New South Wales* (*Tajjour*).[52] Section 93X of the Crimes Act 1900 (NSW) made it an offence for a person to continue to 'habitually consort' with convicted offenders after receiving an official warning from a police officer. The High Court was unanimous that the section burdened political communication by restricting the ability of people to meet to discuss government and political affairs. However, a majority found that the purpose was a legitimate one,[53] namely, the prevention of crime by prohibiting association between convicted offenders, and between convicted offenders and others, thus making it more difficult to organise for them to engage in criminal activities and recruit others to participate.

Hayne, Crennan, Kiefel and Bell JJ ultimately concluded that the section was constitutional because the means chosen by the legislature were proportionate to

[48] Public Interest Advocacy Centre, Submission No 55 to Human Rights Commission, *Freedoms Inquiry*, 3 March 2015, 9.
[49] (2004) 220 CLR 1.
[50] ibid 32 [32].
[51] ibid 26 [15].
[52] *Tajjour v New South Wales* (2014) 254 CLR 508.
[53] ibid 571 (Crennan, Kiefel and Bell JJ).

achieving that legitimate purpose. The main argument put forward by the applicants to the contrary was that measures with a lesser impact on the freedom, in particular, the inclusion of a defence specifically with respect to political communication, would have been just as effective. In rejecting this argument, Crennan, Kiefel and Bell JJ stated:

> Putting aside difficulties in drafting a defence of that kind, such a defence would be easily claimed but difficult to investigate, test or challenge, both factually and legally. This would be especially so if the prosecution were required to negative the claim once raised. In reality, the defence would create a gap which is readily capable of exploitation.[54]

Although neither *Coleman v Power* nor *Tajjour* were directly concerned with issues relating to national security, there are nevertheless important lessons to be drawn from these cases as to the approach that the courts are likely to take if such issues are involved. In particular, the reality is that a court would not regard legislative measures as reasonably and appropriately adapted to dealing with 'ordinary' criminal activity and yet find them unconstitutional when adopted in response to a threat to national security. Put another way, the High Court's deference to the executive as to the requirements of law and order suggests an even more deferential approach will be taken when national security is invoked in support of legislative action.

B. The Separation of Powers

The concept of national security has been employed by the High Court to help define the scope and limits of executive and judicial powers under the Constitution. At the Commonwealth level, there exists a strict separation between the judicial and non-judicial powers of the state. This separation provides a key limit on the scope of executive power; as a general rule, judicial powers may not be granted to the executive or legislature and non-judicial powers must be withheld from federal courts.[55] National security is generally regarded as a concern of the federal Parliament and the executive branch of government, whereas the courts' role is to determine rights and liabilities in confined disputes between citizens, and between citizens and the state, by application of law to the facts at hand.[56] The broader policy aims of national peace and security are irrelevant, and indeed improper, to the latter; though an exception would arise if a law specifically made such concerns relevant to the determination of a legal dispute (for example, if a court was called upon to interpret section 31 of the NSI Act as it was in *Lodhi*).

In two sets of cases, the High Court has allowed national security concerns to subvert the traditional separation between the judicial and executive branches of

[54] ibid 573 (Crennan, Kiefel and Bell JJ).

[55] *R v Kirby; Ex parte Boilermakers' Society of Australia* (1956) 94 CLR 254. Though courts may exercise non-judicial powers that are ancillary or incidental to their judicial functions, and a general historic exception exists by which all branches of government may continue to exercise traditional functions irrespective of their identification as judicial or non-judicial.

[56] *Huddart Parker & Co v Moorehead* (1909) 8 CLR 330, 357 (Griffith CJ); *R v Trade Practices Tribunal; Ex parte Tasmanian Breweries Pty Ltd* (1970) 123 CLR 361, 374–75 (Kitto J).

government. In these cases, national security has operated to trump competing values, including individual liberty, fairness and impartial justice. In the first set of cases, administrative detention has been permitted for national security purposes. In the second, the executive has been permitted to avoid core elements of fair court process.

In *Chu Kheng Lim v Minister for Immigration, Local Government and Ethnic Affairs* (*Lim*), the High Court famously held that, exceptional cases aside, 'the involuntary detention of a citizen in custody by the state is penal or punitive in character and, under our system of government, exists only as an incident of the exclusively judicial function of adjudging and punishing criminal guilt'.[57] This gives rise to a 'constitutional immunity from being imprisoned by Commonwealth authority except pursuant to an order by a court in the exercise of the judicial power of the Commonwealth'.[58] However, in the two decades since this case was decided, the number of exceptions have multiplied to the point that the mere existence of the immunity is now in serious doubt. The reality today is that detention proportionate to a legitimate non-punitive end may be the subject of a civil or administrative order.[59]

Just as national security is a legitimate object supporting incursions on the implied freedom of political communication, it may also provide a foundation for administrative detention. Even in *Lim*—the genesis and high-point of the immunity from involuntary detention—the High Court refrained from considering how the immunity might operate in times of war, instead hinting that administrative detention for national security purposes may be permitted under the Constitution.[60]

Although as yet untested, the general view that national security detention may be imposed outside the judicial process is reflected in a number of statutes. The clearest examples arise in the anti-terrorism context. For instance, preventive detention orders (PDOs) may be issued by agencies and individuals other than the courts, including by the Australian Federal Police, and allow up to 48 hours of secret detention.[61] Australian Security Intelligence Organisation (ASIO) questioning and detention warrants are likewise issued and administered outside the courts, and allow for up to seven days of secret detention.[62] Both PDOs and ASIO warrants have national security purposes—they are directed to the prevention or effective prosecution of terrorism. Both are schemes administered entirely by the executive branch of government. Both involve severe incursions upon civil liberties, including by restricting the detainee's contact with legal representatives, family members and anyone else. And, finally, both are divorced from the usual trappings of judicial

[57] *Chu Kheng Lim v Minister for Immigration, Local Government and Ethnic Affairs* (1992) 176 CLR 1, 27 (Brennan, Deane and Dawson JJ).

[58] ibid 28–29 (Brennan, Deane and Dawson JJ).

[59] ibid 71 (McHugh J); *Kruger v Commonwealth* (1997) 190 CLR 1, 162 (Gummow J), 62 (Dawson J), 110–11 (Gaudron J); *Al-Kateb v Godwin* (2004) 219 CLR 562, 576 (Gleeson CJ), 562 (Gummow J), 650–51 (Hayne J), 659 (Callinan J), 662–63 (Heydon J).

[60] *Lim* (1992) 176 CLR 1, 27 (Brennan, Deane and Dawson JJ).

[61] Criminal Code Act 1995 (Cth) div 105.

[62] Australian Security Intelligence Organisation Legislation Amendment (Terrorism) Act 2003 (Cth).

process, such as a person's right to know and answer the case against them, as well as the traditional rules of evidence.[63]

Scholars have questioned the constitutional validity of PDOs and ASIO warrants.[64] However, there is every chance that the national security grounds for the orders would provide a solid constitutional footing for these forms of administrative detention. Based on present case law, it can be confidently surmised that extra-judicial, administrative detention is permitted under the Constitution when that detention is proportionate to a national security aim. The extent to which prolonged or widespread detention of citizens outside the judicial process might be permitted in times of war remains to be seen. The likelihood, however, is that it would pass constitutional muster if, as the High Court has indicated in the context of the defence power, the definition of national security fluctuates depending on the nature and extent of the threat facing the nation.

The second set of cases concerns the constitutional protection of procedural fairness in judicial proceedings. The Constitution has been interpreted to protect the defining features of all Australian courts.[65] One such feature is procedural fairness.[66] The integral relationship between judicial independence and procedural fairness is clear enough. However, in a number of instances the fairness of court proceedings has been undercut by national security concerns and these schemes have nonetheless survived constitutional challenge. For instance, legislation allows for information to be withheld on national security grounds—resulting in not only a closed court (undermining open justice), but also the potential withholding of information from a party and his or her representatives (undermining fair process rights such as the capacity to know and answer the case against you).[67] The withholding of information in such a manner is not unprecedented. The public interest immunity traditionally operates to allow information to be withheld from the public, a court and/or a party to the proceedings. However, the consequence of invoking this immunity is that the information may no longer be adduced and relied upon as evidence. More recent legislative developments permit the state to withhold national security information from the other party and his or her legal representatives *and* rely on that information to support its case.[68]

63 See S Tyulkina and G Williams, 'Preventative Detention Orders in Australia' (2015) 38 *UNSW Law Journal* 738, 746–47; R Ananian-Welsh, 'Preventative Detention Orders and the Separation of Judicial Power' (2015) 38 *UNSW Law Journal* 756; J McCulloch and Joo-Cheong Tham, 'Secret State, Transparent Subject: The Australian Security Intelligence Organisation in the Age of Terror' (2005) 38 *Australian and New Zealand Journal of Criminology* 400, 402.

64 R Welsh, 'Anti-terror Preventive Detention and the Independent Judiciary' in P Keyzer (ed), *Preventive Detention: Asking the Fundamental Questions* (Cambridge, Intersentia, 2013).

65 *Wainohu v New South Wales* (2011) 243 CLR 181, 208 (French CJ and Kiefel J).

66 ibid; *Leeth v Commonwealth* (1992) 174 CLR 455, 469–70 (Mason CJ, Dawson and McHugh JJ); *International Finance Trust Co Ltd v New South Wales Crime Commission* (2009) 240 CLR 319, 354–55 (French CJ), 379–80 (Heydon J).

67 National Security Information (Criminal and Civil Proceedings) Act 2004 (Cth). See, eg, *Leghaei v Director-General of Security* [2007] FCAFC 37, [56]–[60] on the operation of the ASIO Act in this respect.

68 ibid. See A Lynch, T Tulich and R Welsh, 'Secrecy and Control Orders: The Role and Vulnerability of Constitutional Values in Australia and the United Kingdom' in D Cole, F Fabrini and A Vedaschi (eds), *Secrecy, National Security, and the Vindication of Constitutional Law* (Cheltenham, Edward Elgar, 2013).

In these circumstances, it may be up to the judge to determine whether the information has been properly classified and, if it is ultimately adduced, the weight it should be given. This can be a difficult task—to say the least—for a judge when that information has not been adduced in the traditional manner. By this, we mean in open court, with full disclosure to both parties, and in accordance with our adversarial and accusatorial processes. In the migration context, in *Leghaei v Director-General of Security* (*Leghaei*) the Federal Court recognised the difficulty that judges face in forming an opinion contrary to that put forward by the state on matters of national security.[69] Despite these concerns, the High Court has upheld legislation allowing for secret evidence as compatible with separation of powers principles. As with the cases discussed in section IV.A above, these cases arose not in the national security context but rather they concerned anti-organised crime legislation and the withholding of 'criminal intelligence'.

Culminating in its decision in *Assistant Commissioner Condon v Pompano Pty Ltd*, the High Court has held that evidence may be relied upon in court but withheld from the other party and their representatives, provided that three conditions are met.[70] First, the court must have the capacity to independently determine whether the information had been properly classified. Secondly, it must not be forced to take a particular course of action with respect to the secret evidence. And, finally, the court must retain sufficient discretion to allow it to counteract any potential unfairness resulting from the secret evidence; for example, the court must retain the capacity to attribute less, or even no, weight to the evidence or order a stay of proceedings for want of fairness.[71]

The High Court's approach to resolving the tension between traditional court processes and state claims of secrecy reveals the fragility of fair process protections under the Constitution. One of the authors of this chapter has previously argued that the High Court should adopt a 'purposive formalist' approach to the constitutional separation of powers, thus focusing on the constitutional values which animate this doctrine. The effect of this would be to better protect fair process from legislative or executive erosion.[72] However, if this was coupled with an equally enhanced focus on the conflicting constitutional value of national security, it would seem likely that the court would permit secret evidence to undermine open justice and fair process at least where the state claims that this is necessary in order to protect its security and that of its citizens. Though in a different context, this echoes the Court's observation in *Leghaei* that 'it will be a rare case where the public interest in national security will yield to the public interest in the administration of justice.'[73] As national security

[69] *Leghaei* [2007] FCAFC 37, [56]–[60].

[70] *Assistant Commissioner Condon v Pompano Pty Ltd* (2013) 252 CLR 38. The earlier cases developing this point were: *Gypsy Jokers Motorcycle Club Inc v Commissioner of Police* (2008) 234 CLR 532; *K-Generation Pty Ltd v Liquor Licensing Court* (2009) 237 CLR 501.

[71] *Assistant Commissioner Condon v Pompano Pty Ltd* (2013) 252 CLR 38, 482 (French CJ), 495–96 (Hayne, Crennan, Kiefel and Bell JJ). According to Gageler J, the only effective remedy for any unfairness arising from the secret evidence would be an exercise of the court's inherent jurisdiction to order a stay of proceedings for want of fairness: at 59.

[72] R Welsh, 'A Path to Purposive Formalism: Interpreting Chapter III for Judicial Independence and Impartiality' (2013) 39 *Monash University Law Review* 66.

[73] *Leghaei* [2007] FCAFC 37, [52].

forms a legitimate basis for the curtailment of the implied freedom of political communication and the immunity from administrative detention, it would in all likelihood justify compromises to open and fair justice principles.

These problems are exacerbated in the context of the preventive, forward-looking focus of national security schemes such as PDOs and control orders.[74] In his Honour's judgment in *Thomas v Mowbray*, Hayne J highlighted the risk that this scenario poses to judicial independence from the executive government, stating:

> For the most part courts are concerned to decide between conflicting accounts of past events. When courts are required to predict the future, as they are in some cases, the prediction will usually be assisted by, and determined having regard to, expert evidence of a kind that the competing parties to the litigation can be expected to adduce if the point in issue is challenged. Intelligence information, gathered by government agencies, presents radically different problems. Rarely, if ever, would it be information about which expert evidence, independent of the relevant government agency, could be adduced. In cases where it could not be tested in that way (and such cases would be the norm rather than the exception) the court, and any party against whose interests the information was to be provided, would be left with *little practical choice except to act upon the view that was proffered by the relevant agency*.[75]

Hayne J may have been in dissent in *Thomas v Mowbray*, but this warning echoes the opinions of other judges—in Australia and elsewhere. For instance, a similar argument was expressed by Wilson and Dawson JJ in the 1984 *Hilton Bombing Case*:

> Questions of national security naturally raise issues of great importance, issues which will seldom be wholly within the competence of a court to evaluate. It goes without saying in these circumstances that very considerable weight must attach to the view of what national security requires as it expressed by the responsible Minster.[76]

In the key English case of *A & Ors v Secretary of State for the Home Department*, Lord Nicholls of Birkenhead likewise warned that:

> All courts are acutely conscious that the government alone is able to evaluate and decide what counter-terrorism steps are needed and what steps will suffice. Courts are not equipped to make such decisions, nor are they charged with that responsibility.[77]

Together, the case studies of those constitutional cases concerning the *Lim* immunity from administrative detention and procedural fairness demonstrate that, when national security has been invoked in the constitutional context it has served to enlarge executive power, supporting serious incursions on judicial powers and processes. Administrative detention is highly problematic in a constitutional system grounded on respect for individual liberty and the rule of law. National security presents a far-reaching basis on which the government may assert a capacity to detain citizens, even in secretive circumstances, lacking procedural fairness, and subjecting the individual to compulsory interrogation and searches—as may occur under some

[74] Criminal Code Act 1995 (Cth) divs 104–05.

[75] *Thomas v Mowbray* (2007) 233 CLR 307, 477 (emphasis added).

[76] *Alister v R* (1984) 154 CLR 404, 435. See also, 455 (Brennan J).

[77] *A & Ors v Secretary of State for the Home Department* [2004] UKHL 56 [79].

of Australia's anti-terrorism laws. Even when courts are involved, national security may be invoked by government to circumvent the hallmarks of the traditional accusatorial process.

V. RESTRAINING NATIONAL SECURITY

The concept of 'national security', as well as the related notions of 'defence' and 'foreign and military purposes', have a significant role in the Constitution. This is so not only explicitly but also indirectly, as seen in the above discussion of the courts' interpretation of the implied freedom of political communication and the separation of powers. Assuming that a new approach to constitutional interpretation is endorsed whereby underpinning values are identified and the Constitution is interpreted in light of these, it is difficult to dispute that national security must be regarded as one such value. This prompts our concern about the constitutional values project as a whole. The acknowledgment of national security as a foundational constitutional value would seem to serve one purpose and one purpose alone, namely, to encourage the courts to take national security into account in interpreting the Constitution. However, the cases demonstrate that national security has the capacity to undermine—if not completely override—other important constitutional values once it is introduced into the process of judicial reasoning.

National security inherently conflicts with another foundational constitutional value—the rule of law. As we have already highlighted, the procedural and evidentiary constraints imposed by judicial process have compelled the courts to grant considerable leeway to the executive branch of government in determining the nature and extent of the threat to Australia as well as what measures are necessary in order to protect national security. It is therefore difficult to see how there could be any meaningful checks and balances upon the operation of national security as a constitutional value. It has proven to be difficult for the courts to effectively interrogate, question or overrule the national security claims of government in specific constitutional contexts. Ultimately, it is very difficult for the courts to do anything other than prioritise national security. The resulting danger is that the legislative and executive branches of government may effectively rely upon the concept of national security as a justification for impinging upon express constitutional provisions or implied doctrines. The courts' understandable deference to the government's national security assertions has already supported considerable incursions upon the implied freedom of political communication, the immunity from administrative detention and traditional fair trial processes. It would be unfortunate if the most significant impact of this constitutional values project was to extend this trend to constitutional interpretation generally.

As discussed in section II, the concept of national security has to date defied definition by the courts. Even the legislature has had only limited success in this regard. It is doubtful whether the courts are even *capable* of developing such a definition. Hanks suggests that this may be due to:

> The institutional constraints under which a court operates—in particular, the demand that it resolve the dispute between the parties currently before the court by issuing one of a

> limited range of remedies—structure and confined legal discourse, inhibit the development of a politically sensitive approach to politically complex issues.[78]

It is the recognition of these difficulties which underpinned Lord Diplock's conclusion that 'the judicial process is totally inept to deal with the sort of problems [involved in the national security context]' and was thus 'par excellence a non-justiciable issue'.[79]

Rather than prompting greater engagement with this value in the course of constitutional interpretation, recognising the status of national security as a constitutional value reveals the imperative that the courts develop guidelines for *restraining* national security—determining the circumstances in which national security should, and should not, be allowed to impinge on other values. In the absence of such guidelines, the risk is that the legislative and executive branches of government will exploit the concept of national security as a carte blanche for action. The necessity of developing guidelines to ensure that national security cannot operate as a universal 'trump card' is not dependent upon the endorsement of this constitutional values project. We have *already* seen the detrimental consequences for our liberal democratic framework of the courts giving undue leeway to the executive and legislative branches of government to use national security as a mechanism for reciting themselves into power.

Developing such guidelines is crucially important, but also extremely difficult. One option might be to say that only a basic level of national security constitutes a constitutional value. This is derived from Lachmayer's statement, quoted above, that a minimum standard of national security 'necessary for the functioning of a state and the functioning of a constitutional system'[80] is simply one of the objectives of the state, to be fulfilled *within* the constitutional framework; that is, national security ought not be permitted to override or undermine the Constitution.

The problem with this approach arises from the difficulties in defining the scope of national security—at a basic level or otherwise. As existing attempts to define national security reveal, the boundaries of this concept are elusive. Even the minimum standard of national security may fluctuate over time, depending upon complex contextual factors peculiarly within the expertise and knowledge of the executive government. Ultimately, this approach may constrain national security, but its effectiveness rests on problematic assumptions regarding the courts' capacities to distinguish national security measures required to preserve the functioning of the state and constitutional system, from national security measures that are not required to meet this end. For instance, is administrative detention of suspected terrorists in the absence of criminal charge necessary to preserve the functioning of the state? In all, this approach oversimplifies the concept of national security and would be unlikely to escape the difficulties that arise when national security comes into conflict with other constitutional values in specific cases.

Another option may be to identify national security not as a foundational value as we have argued, but as an intermediate constitutional value—serving an ultimate purpose of protecting individual liberty, community welfare or the public good.

[78] Hanks, above n 2, 132.
[79] *Council of Civil Service Unions v Minister for Civil Service* [1985] AC 374, 412 (Lord Diplock).
[80] Lachmayer, above n 23, 18.

This reconceptualising of national security would assist in those instances where national security appears to conflict with these values, by granting national security the status of a constitutional value only to the extent that it *assists* in the attainment of these higher goals.

Some support for this idea might be drawn from Hanks' political definition of the Australian state as being 'the liberal democratic conception, which regards the state as embodied in its formal institutions of government … and the processes which link them with each other and with the population'.[81] In other words, national security—for constitutional purposes—refers only to the security which is necessary in order to protect the liberal democratic conception of the state.

Whilst this approach is attractive, it suffers a number of serious problems. The first is that it reflects a misreading of Hanks. The political definition is simply *one* of the definitions which he provides—in addition to those more traditional definitions which refer to the territorial boundaries of the state and its governing institutions. The task that Hanks had set himself was to explain the breadth of the various conceptions of the state. In other words, it is the opposite of our aim here, namely, to impose *limits* upon the scope of national security. It would therefore be disingenuous to use Hanks' words in support of the claim that national security as a constitutional value should be limited to that which is connected with the achievement of other goals.

A further problem with this approach is that it ignores historical and practical realities. National security animated the framers of the Constitution. It also arises in the constitutional text as a goal in its own right, linked to the preservation and defence of the nation, and not as a stepping stone to the achievement of libertarian ends. In this context at least, the distinction between intermediate and ultimate values proves unhelpful. As a precondition to the existence of the state and the maintenance of the Constitution, it can only be conceived of as an ultimate value. The concept of national security is multifaceted and evolving, and, by preserving the security of the state and its citizens, it serves a vast array of constitutional, social and political ends—both libertarian and otherwise.

Ironically, the answer to the problems that arise from identifying national security as a constitutional value may lie in embracing the major premise of the constitutional values project; that is, to adopt a functionalist embrace of other constitutional values—allowing values such as the rule of law and individual liberty to determine the limits of national security. Under such an approach, any conflict between national security and a competing value would be set up in favour of the other value, with national security treated as a secondary consideration. Thus, courts would be compelled to read down and limit national security measures so as to, insofar as possible, render them compliant with the rule of law and other values.

There is nothing inherently wrong with different values being treated differently by the courts, and indeed this may be inevitable. However, to suggest that the courts should put aside their traditional deference to the executive branch of government and regard national security as a secondary consideration ignores reality. Courts are well versed and institutionally vested with the task of upholding the rule of law and

[81] Hanks, above n 2, 170.

preserving values related to, for example, impartial justice, fairness and government accountability. On the other hand, they are not well equipped to interrogate the meaning and requirements of national security from time to time. For this reason, they will necessarily rely heavily upon executive assessments as to the nature of the threat. Courts face a distinct challenge in balancing national security against other values and perhaps the best that we can expect from them is to focus as much as possible on protecting other constitutional values from succumbing to national security.

There is a further—and more fundamental problem—with this final approach. It would, in essence, amount to cherry-picking constitutional values or adopting the premise of this volume only insofar as it is consistent with grander liberal democratic ideals. There is an important lesson here for the constitutional values project as a whole. If the only way to limit the scope of national security as a constitutional value is to rid it of any coherent or meaningful content, then perhaps we need to recognise that the risks entailed by this project outweigh any potential rewards.

VI. CONCLUSION: LESSONS FOR THE CONSTITUTIONAL VALUES PROJECT

As an integral aspect of the text and structure of the Constitution and a precondition to its continued existence, national security is a foundational constitutional value. But it is one that courts are ill-equipped to deal with. Thus, we argue that national security emerges as a hegemonic constitutional value—operating as a trump card that may support infringements to competing constitutional values and doctrines. This is demonstrated in cases concerning the implied freedom of political communication and the separation of judicial power. Clearly, guidelines are needed to restrain the role and impact of national security in constitutional interpretation. However, the development of such guidelines faces serious obstacles.

Our analysis reveals some important questions and lessons for the constitutional values project as a whole. First, it is critical that the aims of the project are clearly identified. If the project aims simply to encourage judicial engagement with constitutional values, the achievement of this aim with respect to national security might endanger liberal democratic values. Our analysis has revealed that an opposite aim—namely, the development of guidelines to *restrict* the impact of a constitutional value on judicial decisions—is more appropriate with respect to national security, despite its character as a foundational constitutional value. This contradiction proves that each value must be interrogated and considered on its own merits and may need to be treated differently. But this conclusion also invites criticisms of cherry-picking, subjectivity and the moving of personal biases for one value, or class of values, over another; unless, that is, some objective principled basis might be identified to justify embracing some values whilst constraining others.

Our analysis also reveals the issues that arise when values conflict and must be 'weighed' against each other. In this inevitable scenario, national security tends to dominate and override other values. There are unavoidable, institutional reasons for this. The courts simply are not, and arguably never will be, equipped to consider, interpret, interrogate or apply the concept of national security in the same way as they have done with respect to traditional legal rights and procedural considerations. Some constitutional values are simply peculiarly within the expertise of the executive government.

This brings us full circle to the first step in the constitutional values project. It has been observed in other chapters that specific values are difficult to define with necessary precision. This is not only important in its own right, but the boundaries of a constitutional value have a particular importance when it comes time to weigh it against other competing values. The best we can probably hope for with respect of 'national security' is a lowest common denominator approach whereby national security involves the protection of the state and its people, at least from foreign forces. However, even this definition runs the risk of investing the executive and legislature branches of government with a sword capable of being wielded against other constitutional values; in effect, undoing the many positive aims of the constitutional values project.

15

Free Trade as an Australian Constitutional Value: A Functionalist Approach to the Interpretation of the Economic Constitution of Australia

GONZALO VILLALTA PUIG

I. INTRODUCTION

ROSALIND DIXON CALLS on the High Court of Australia (High Court) to take a functionalist approach to the interpretation of the Australian Constitution.[1] Functionalism, she argues, is a 'normatively desirable'[2] compromise between formalism and pragmatism:

> [F]unctionalism, at its core, invites courts directly and openly to rely on substantive constitutional values, not simply more 'formal' legal sources. But in doing so, it insists that courts should also be able in some way to source the particular values they rely on in the text, history or structure of the relevant constitution. It thus offers a potentially attractive middle-path between the extremes of pure formalism and pragmatism or policy-oriented legal reasoning, which promises to combine the strengths of both—ie, transparency and predictability, and a strong commitment to the rule of law.[3]

The Constitution does prescribe certain values. Among those values is free trade. In the introduction to this collection of chapters, Dixon agrees that the Australian Constitution recognises free trade as a key founding value.[4]

This chapter submits that free trade is indeed an Australian constitutional value. The High Court recognises the value of free trade in section 92 of the Constitution as well as in the structure and history of those other sections of the Constitution that, together, comprise the economic constitution of the Commonwealth of Australia (Australia). It further submits that the function of free trade as an Australian constitutional value is to promote the prosperity of Australians through

[1] R Dixon, 'The Functional *Constitution*: Re-reading the 2014 High Court Constitutional Term' (2015) 43 *Federal Law Review* 455.
[2] ibid 492.
[3] ibid 456.
[4] See ch 1 by Rosalind Dixon in this collection.

the creation of a market for Australia. The performance of that function depends on the interpretation that the High Court gave to the value of free trade in *Cole v Whitfield* as a freedom of trade from discriminatory protectionism. The chapter furthermore submits that such an interpretation is born of compromise: a necessary compromise between an anti-protectionist norm and a non-discrimination norm and an equally necessary compromise between the value of free trade and other Australian constitutional values.

II. FREE TRADE AS AN AUSTRALIAN CONSTITUTIONAL VALUE

Free trade is a constitutional value. It is a value that conceives the sale and purchase of goods and services among or within customs territories as an exchange without protectionist discrimination. As such, it constitutionalises the political economy of jurisdictions. The establishment of the World Trade Organization (WTO) suggests that global systems of political economy have the constitutional value of free trade at their foundation. The European Union (EU), for example, and other regional and cross-regional systems also have that foundation. All these systems include preferential trade areas, free trade areas, customs unions, common markets and other economic unions under the domain of different preferential trade agreements and economic integration agreements. It is an implicit assumption that local systems have that foundation too. The assumption holds true for unitary states. It also holds true for federal states such as the United States, the Republic of India and, of course, Australia.

The chapter submits that free trade is an Australian constitutional value. The text, structure, and history of the Constitution recognise it as such. The text of the Constitution recognises the value of free trade. Indeed, section 92 of the Constitution states that 'trade, commerce, and intercourse among the States ... shall be absolutely free'.[5]

The structure of the Constitution also recognises the value of free trade. Section 92 is in Chapter IV of the Constitution, which is on finance and trade. Correspondingly, the sections that precede and succeed section 92 provide for such related matters as the establishment of uniform duties of customs, the payment of surplus revenue to the States, the abrogation of the power of the States to levy duties of customs and excise and to levy bounties and, most relevantly, the provision of financial assistance to the States.[6] This latter provision—section 99—states that the '[t]he Commonwealth shall not, by any law or regulation of trade, commerce, or revenue, give preference to one State or any part thereof over another State or any part thereof'.

[5] J La Nauze, 'A Little Bit of Lawyers' Language: The History of "Absolutely Free" 1890–1900' in A Martin (ed), *Essays in Australian Federation* (Melbourne, Melbourne University Press, 1969) 57; I Temby, '"In this Labyrinth There is No Golden Thread"—Section 92 and the Impressionistic Approach' (1984) 58 *Australian Law Journal* 86. See also *Betfair Pty Ltd v Western Australia* (2008) 234 CLR 418, 454 (Gleeson CJ, Gummow, Kirby, Hayne, Crennan and Kiefel JJ).

[6] L Zines, *The High Court and the Constitution*, 5th edn (Cambridge, Federation Press, 2008) 140. See also J Stellios, *Zines's the High Court and the Constitution*, 6th edn (Sydney, Federation Press, 2015) ch 8. See further Nicholas Aroney et al, *The Constitution of the Commonwealth of Australia: History, Principle and Interpretation* (Melbourne, Cambridge University Press, 2015) 324–37.

The joint judgment in *Betfair Pty Ltd v Western Australia* observed that 'the trade and commerce of which section 92 speaks is not limited to dealings in goods and this indicates that Chapter IV implemented a broader scheme of political economy',[7] one, that is, under free trade.

Outside Chapter IV, the Constitution further recognises the value free trade through s 117, which, like section 99, bans interstate discrimination:

> A subject of the Queen, resident in any State, shall not be subject in any other State to any disability or discrimination which would not be equally applicable to him if he were a subject of the Queen resident in such other State.

The provision against discrimination in section 117 implicitly recognises the value of free trade as a freedom of trade from discrimination. While its ban on discrimination may not be absolute, the interpretation of section 117 by the High Court in *Street v Queensland Bar Association* does, nonetheless, impose a ban on substantive discrimination.[8] In that case, Gaudron J spoke against 'different treatment that is not appropriate to a relevant difference'.[9] In *Castlemaine Tooheys Ltd v South Australia*, Gaudron J joined with McHugh J again to speak against discrimination:

> A law is discriminatory if it operates by reference to a distinction which some overriding law decrees to be irrelevant or by reference to a distinction which is in fact irrelevant to the object to be attained; a law is discriminatory if, although it operates by reference to a relevant distinction, the different treatment thereby assigned is not appropriate and adapted to the difference or differences which support that distinction. A law is also discriminatory if, although there is a relevant difference, it proceeds as though there is no such difference, or, in other words, if it treats equally things that are unequal.[10]

More recently,[11] in *Fortescue Metals Group Limited v Commonwealth*, French CJ spoke of non-discrimination as a federal purpose of the taxation power:

> [T]he non-discrimination requirement in s 51(ii) excludes ... laws which make distinctions between States or parts of States which are inconsistent with the economic unity of the Commonwealth and the status of the States and their people as equals inter se in the Federation.[12]

[7] *Betfair Pty Ltd v Western Australia* (2008) 234 CLR 418, 455 (Gleeson CJ, Gummow, Kirby, Hayne, Crennan and Kiefel JJ). See also M Coper, 'The Economic Framework of the Australian Federation: A Question of Balance' in G Craven (ed), *Australian Federation: Towards the Second Century* (Melbourne, Melbourne University Press, 1992) 144.

[8] *Street v Queensland Bar Association* (1989) 168 CLR 461, 489 (Mason CJ). See also L Zines and G Lindell, 'Form and Substance: "Discrimination" in Modern Constitutional Law' (1992) 21 *Federal Law Review* 136.

[9] *Street v Queensland Bar Association* (1989) 168 CLR 461, 571. See also A Simpson, 'The High Court's Conception of Discrimination: Origins, Applications, and Implications' (2007) 29 *Sydney Law Review* 263, 268, 289.

[10] *Castlemaine Tooheys Ltd v South Australia* (1990) 169 CLR 436, 478 (Gaudron and McHugh JJ).

[11] Earlier, in *Austin v Commonwealth*, the High Court said, though not in an economic context, that '[t]he essence of the notion of discrimination is said to lie in the unequal treatment of equals or the equal treatment of those who are not equals': (2003) 215 CLR 185, 247 (Gaudron, Gummow and Hayne JJ). See also *Permanent Trustee Australia Ltd v Commissioner of State Revenue* (2004) 220 CLR 388.

[12] *Fortescue Metals Group Limited v Commonwealth* (2013) 250 CLR 548, 515, 585. See also Amelia Simpson, '*Fortescue Metals Group Limited v Commonwealth*: Discrimination and Fiscal Federalism' (2014) 25 *Public Law Review* 83.

In addition to the text and structure of the Constitution, the history of the Constitution similarly recognises the value of free trade.[13] As President of the National Australasian Convention, Henry Parkes moved a resolution to propose '[t]hat the trade and intercourse between the federated colonies ... shall be absolutely free',

> that Australia, as Australia, shall be free—free on the borders, free everywhere—in its trade and intercourse between its own people; that there shall be no impediment of any kind—that there shall be no barrier of any kind between one section of the Australian people and another; but, that the trade and the general communication of these people shall flow on from one end of the continent to the other, with no one to stay in its progress or to call it to account.[14]

The Constitution unified the various separate colonial jurisdictions into a single legal, political and economic entity. Despite the prospect of federation, the framers of the Constitution knew that differences among the newly established States would persist and so the pursuit of greater integration became their paramount concern. Thus, the Constitution established structures to facilitate an ever-closer union—such as a federal parliamentary and judicial system—and sought through its various provisions to restrain the ability of government to impede integration, section 92 being a model example.

The chapter further submits that the function of free trade as an Australian constitutional value is to promote the prosperity of Australians through the creation of a market for Australia. In *Betfair Pty Ltd v Western Australia*, the joint judgment acknowledged that function: '[t]he creation and fostering of national markets would further the plan of the Constitution for the creation of a new federal nation and would be expressive of national unity'.[15]

Section 92 does create a national market.[16] It does so in combination with the rest of the economic constitution, including the trade and commerce power under section 51(i); the taxation power under section 51(ii); the bounties power under section 51(iii); the provision for uniform customs duties under section 88; the power over customs and excise under section 90;[17] and the ban on federal preferences

[13] H Irving, 'Constitutional Interpretation, the High Court, and the Discipline of History' (2013) 41 *Federal Law Review* 95, 108–12.

[14] *Official Report of the National Australasian Convention Debates*, Sydney, 4 March 1891, 24 (Sir Henry Parkes). See also La Nauze, above n 5, 70. In *Cole v Whitfield*, the High Court studied the constitutional Convention Debates and found that 'the principal goals of the movement towards the federation of the Australian colonies included ... the achievement of intercolonial free trade': (1988) 165 CLR 360, 392. The reference here to the constitutional Convention Debates does not propose to find either a formalist or pragmatic meaning to the value of free trade in the intention of the framers of the Constitution but rather to inform the federal purpose—the function—of that value: S Gageler, 'Beyond the Text: A Vision of the Structure and Function of the Constitution' (2009) 32 *Australian Bar Review* 138, 140.

[15] (2008) 234 CLR 418, 452 (Gleeson CJ, Gummow, Kirby, Hayne, Crennan and Kiefel JJ). On the theme of national unity, see P Tate, 'The High Court on Constitutional Law: The 2008 Term' (paper presented at the Gilbert + Tobin Centre of Public Law 2009 Constitutional Law Conference, Sydney, 20 February 2009).

[16] 'The purpose of the section is clear enough: to create a free trade area throughout the Commonwealth': *Cole v Whitfield* (1988) 165 CLR 360, 391. Susan Kiefel describes the functional rationale of s 92 thus '[t]he section recognises that the prosperity of individual states within a Commonwealth is dependent upon the absence of restrictions on the movement of goods and services': S Kiefel, 'Section 92: Markets, Protectionism and Proportionality: Australian and European Perspectives' (2010) 36(2) *Monash University Law Review* 1, 1.

[17] *Parton v Milk Board (Vic)* (1949) 80 CLR 229, 253–63 (Dixon J); *Hematite Petroleum Pty Ltd v Victoria* (1983) 151 CLR 599, 624–636 (Mason J).

among the States under section 99. The economic constitution establishes an economic compact, namely, 'a Commonwealth economic union, not an association of States each with its own separate economy'[18] free to trade.[19]

A national market promotes national prosperity. The value of free trade, that is, responds to the call of prosperity. Free trade facilitates economic efficiency. More particularly, it facilitates the optimal allocation of resources through the twin principles of comparative advantage and geographical specialisation, which, together, lead to trade creation and, with it, greater wealth and lesser poverty.

III. FREEDOM OF INTERSTATE TRADE

The chapter submits, furthermore, that the interpretation of section 92 and the rest of the economic constitution by the High Court is a compromise between an anti-protectionist norm and a non-discrimination norm, which is reflective of a wider compromise between the value of free trade—with its function to create a national market for national prosperity—and other Australian constitutional values. The chapter argues that such a compromise is necessary.

To interpret the value of free trade is to interpret the text of section 92, which constitutionalises this value. The value of free trade requires interpretation because the text of the section does not define it.[20] The text of section 92 does not state what interstate trade is to be 'absolutely free' from.[21] Yet, free trade is not interpretable without qualification.[22]

[18] *Capital Duplicators Pty Limited v Australian Capital Territory [No 2]* (1993) 178 CLR 561, 585 (Mason CJ, Brennan, Deane, McHugh JJ). The existence of a national economy is a constitutional fact. In *Victoria v Commonwealth* (1975) 134 CLR 338, 362 (*Australian Assistance Plan Case*), Barwick CJ said: '[t]here is but one economy of the country, not six: it could not be denied that the economy of the nation is of national concern'.

[19] The Constitution 'places particular emphasis on economic union in the form of internal free trade': C Saunders, *The Constitution of Australia: A Contextual Analysis* (Oxford, Hart Publishing, 2011) 243.

[20] M Coper, 'Freedom of Interstate Trade and Commerce' in T Blackshield, M Coper and G Williams (eds), *The Oxford Companion to the High Court of Australia* (Melbourne, Oxford University Press, 2002) 354.

[21] C Howard, *Australian Federal Constitutional Law*, 3rd edn (Sydney, Law Book Co, 1985) 294–95.

[22] ibid 294. The term 'trade' includes not only the sale and purchase of goods but also 'the pursuit of a calling or handicraft', while the term 'commerce' includes 'intangibles as well as the movement of goods': *Bank of New South Wales v Commonwealth* (1948) 76 CLR 1, 381–82. Section 92 covers not only goods but also services: *Betfair Pty Ltd v Western Australia* (2008) 234 CLR 418, 452 (Gleeson CJ, Gummow, Kirby, Hayne, Crennan and Kiefel JJ). The phrase 'among the States' makes the freedom operable in respect of trade and commerce between the States and Territories of Australia: *Sportsbet Pty Ltd v New South Wales* (2012) 249 CLR 298, 315 (French CJ, Gummow, Hayne, Crennan, Kiefel and Bell JJ). The freedom extends to any national market, that is, 'those persons who from time to time are placed on the supply side or the demand side of commerce and who are present in a given State at any particular time': *Betfair Pty Ltd v Western Australia* (2008) 234 CLR 418, 453. It also extends to the 'new economy': '[t]o focus upon the geographic dimension given by State boundaries, when considering competition in a market in internet commerce, presents practical and conceptual difficulties': *Betfair Pty Ltd v Western Australia* (2008) 234 CLR 418, 452; *Boral Besser Masonry Ltd v Australian Competition and Consumer Commission* (2003) 215 CLR 374, 269 (McHugh J). See also A Simpson, '*Betfair Pty Ltd v Western Australia*' (2008) 19 *Public Law Review* 191, 193; E Ball, 'Section 92 and the Regulation of E-Commerce: A Casenote on *Betfair Pty Ltd v Western Australia*' (2008) 36 *Federal Law Review* 265; R Posner, 'Antitrust in the New Economy' (2001) 68 *Antitrust Law Journal* 925.

That qualification, the High Court found in *Cole v Whitfield* as a test for invalidity:[23] a law or measure is invalid under section 92 if it imposes a burden on interstate trade that is *discriminatory in a protectionist sense*.[24] A burden is discriminatory in a protectionist sense if it either confers a comparative competitive advantage on intrastate traders over interstate traders or removes a comparative competitive disadvantage from intrastate traders in respect of either similar goods and services or similar consumers.[25] Members of the High Court confirmed the test in *Castlemaine Tooheys Ltd v South Australia*:

> *Cole v Whitfield* established that a law which imposes a burden on interstate trade and commerce but does not give the domestic product or the intrastate trade in that product *a competitive or market advantage over the imported product or the interstate trade in that product*, is not a law which discriminates against interstate trade and commerce on protectionist grounds.[26]

The High Court has continued to apply the *Cole v Whitfield* test ever since, heralding a period of intense federal economic integration through careful enforcement of its constitutional principles onto the state courts. In the words of the joint judgment in *Betfair Pty Ltd v Western Australia*, '*Cole v Whitfield* established that, at least in its application to trade and commerce among the States, the object of section 92 is the elimination of protection'.[27] And the judgments of the High Court in *Betfair Pty Ltd v Racing New South Wales*[28] and *Sportsbet Pty Ltd v New South Wales*,[29] which, together, comprise the most recent cases on section 92, still rule out discriminatory burdens of a protectionist kind.[30] Indeed, more than an affirmation of discriminatory protectionism, these recent cases declare protectionism to be the principal if not the sole test for invalidity under section 92. Thus, the joint judgment in *Betfair Pty Ltd v Racing New South Wales* spoke of 'the determinative importance in Australia of the characterisation of the law in question as protectionist in nature'.[31] For the High Court, '[i]t is the concept of protectionism which supplies the criterion by which discriminatory laws may be classified as rendering less than absolutely free trade and

[23] (1988) 165 CLR 360.

[24] G Carney, 'The Re-interpretation of Section 92: The Decline of Free Enterprise and the Rise of Free Trade' (1991) 3 *Bond Law Review* 149, 155–56. See also JG Starke, 'The *Cole v Whitfield* Test for Section 92 Explained and Applied: The Demise of the Theory of "Individual Rights"' (1991) 65 *Australian Law Journal* 123.

[25] T Blackshield and G Williams, *Australian Constitutional Law and Theory: Commentary and Materials*, 5th edn (Sydney, Federation Press, 2010) 1225. See also G Williams, S Brennan and A Lynch, *Blackshield and Williams Australian Constitutional Law & Theory: Commentary and Materials*, 6th edn (Sydney, Federation Press, 2014) ch 27.

[26] (1990) 169 CLR 436, 467 (Mason CJ, Brennan, Deane, Dawson and Toohey JJ) (emphasis added).

[27] (2008) 234 CLR 418, 452 (Gleeson CJ, Gummow, Kirby, Hayne, Crennan and Kiefel). Leslie Zines remarked that *Cole v Whitfield* was the most important decision of the Mason Court: L Zines, 'Most Significant Case of the Mason High Court' (1995) 30 *Australian Lawyer* 18, 18.

[28] *Betfair Pty Ltd v Racing New South Wales* (2012) 249 CLR 217.

[29] (2012) 249 CLR 298.

[30] See J Gleeson, 'What's Left of *Cole v Whitfield*?' (2013) 24 *Public Law Review* 97.

[31] (2012) 249 CLR 217, 265 (French CJ, Gummow, Hayne, Crennan and Bell JJ). See also M Coper, '*Betfair Pty Ltd v Western Australia* and the New Jurisprudence of Section 92' (2014) 88 *Australian Law Journal* 204, 210.

commerce among the States'.[32] Free trade, then, is freedom of interstate trade from discriminatory protectionism.

The High Court's interpretation of the value of free trade is a compromise: a compromise, first, between an anti-protectionist norm and a non-discrimination norm and, secondly, between the value of free trade and other Australian constitutional values. For a start, the *Cole v Whitfield* test does not totally facilitate the function of interstate trade:[33] the creation of a national market for national prosperity, equally accessible to everyone everywhere. Arguably, an anti-protectionist norm can cause the national market to function inefficiently. That is, it can validate laws and measures *that discriminate* against interstate trade *if they are not protectionist*,[34] namely, laws and measures that may not necessarily advantage local traders[35] but that, nonetheless, close off their 'part of the national market to trade from other States',[36] thereby diverting rather than creating trade. An anti-protectionist norm is, in that respect, inefficient because it allows business to divert away from low-cost producers without any federal benefit.[37] Traders in interstate imports have no other option, then, than to take the local market as they find it irrespective of any discriminatory burdens that they may encounter.[38] As Kiefel J (now the Chief Justice of the High Court) admitted in *Betfair Pty Ltd v Racing New South Wales*, '[w]hilst the discriminatory character of a measure may be regarded as indicative of protectionism, not all discriminatory measures will have a protectionist effect'.[39] To paraphrase Kirby J in the proceedings of *Betfair Pty Ltd v Western Australia*, an anti-protectionist norm 'sort of hive[s] off the little fortress'[40] of each State. Discrimination may or may not be protectionist in kind but whether protectionist in kind or not, discrimination only ever pursues unequal access to the national market.[41]

[32] (2012) 249 CLR 217, 265 (French CJ, Gummow, Hayne, Crennan and Bell JJ). See also *Betfair Pty Ltd v Western Australia* (2008) 234 CLR 418, 452 (Gleeson CJ, Gummow, Kirby, Hayne, Crennan, and Kiefel JJ). See further Ball, above n 22, 274–75; Kiefel, above n 16.

[33] A Gray, 'Compulsory Marketing Schemes and Section 92 of the Australian Constitution' (2014) 33 *University of Tasmania Law Review* 317, 332–36. Of course, before *Cole v Whitfield* came and went there were many theories for the interpretation of s 92, chief of which was the individual rights theory of Dixon J, which attempted to strike a balance between the States and Commonwealth in the exercise of their respective competences: *O Gilpin Ltd v Commissioner for Road Transport & Tramways (NSW)* (1935) 52 CLR 189, 211–12; L Zines, 'Sir Owen Dixon's Theory of Federalism' (1964) 1 *Federal Law Review* 221.

[34] M Coper, 'The Second Coming of the Fourth Arm: The Role and Functions of the Inter-State Commission' (1989) 63 *Australian Law Journal* 731, 745; M Coper, 'The Curious Case of the Callow Crayfish: The New Law Relating to Section 92 of the *Australian Constitution*' (Discussion Paper No 1, Parliamentary Library, Parliament of Australia, 1989–90) 9–10; Carney, above n 24; Coper, 'Freedom of Interstate Trade and Commerce', above n 20, 356.

[35] Coper, 'The Curious Case of the Callow Catfish', above n 34, 24–25.

[36] *Betfair Pty Ltd v Western Australia* (2008) 234 CLR 418, 459 (Gleeson CJ, Gummow, Kirby, Hayne, Crennan and Kiefel JJ). See also C Staker, 'Free Movement of Goods in the EEC and Australia: A Comparative Study' (1990) 10(1) *Yearbook of European Law* 235.

[37] D Regan, 'The Supreme Court and State Protectionism: Making Sense of the Dormant Commerce Clause' (1986) 84 *Michigan Law Review* 1091, 1118.

[38] D Rose, '*Cole v Whitfield*: "Absolutely Free" Trade?' in HP Lee and G Winterton (eds), *Australian Constitutional Landmarks* (Cambridge, Cambridge University Press, 2003) 335, 346.

[39] (2012) 249 CLR 217, 288.

[40] Transcript of Proceedings, *Betfair Pty Ltd v Western Australia* [2007] (HCA Trans 660, 9 November 2007). See also Ball, above n 22.

[41] C Staker, 'Section 92 of the Constitution and the European Court of Justice' (1990) 19 *Federal Law Review* 322, 342–43.

Of course, to make that argument is not to suggest that the value of free trade gives direct effect to an individual right to engage in trade and commerce across State lines. It is not to advocate a return to the individual rights theory, which, since *Cole v Whitfield*, the High Court has repeatedly rejected. Thus, in *Betfair Pty Ltd v Racing New South Wales*, French CJ, Gummow, Hayne, Crennan and Bell JJ declared that 'the subject of s 92 is interstate trade, not traders'.[42] Heydon J agreed, saying that 's 92 does not directly protect the individual rights of interstate traders'.[43] Kiefel J recalled that the individual rights theory of s 92 died with *Cole v Whitfield*:[44]

> It is the effects upon Betfair as an interstate trader, more particularly in its ability to compete with local traders, with which s 92 is concerned and to which the requirement of protectionism is directed. It is not enough, as Betfair's argument perhaps assumed, that it be an interstate trader.[45]

It is clear, then, that the High Court in *Betfair Pty Ltd v Racing New South Wales*[46] and, by extension, *Sportsbet Pty Ltd v New South Wales*, was concerned to block any move—real or not[47]—on the part of the appellants to resurrect the individual rights theory of section 92: the idea of free enterprise as distinct from free trade. Such concern was unnecessary. The High Court had already rejected the theory in *Cole v Whitfield*. In any case, an enquiry into the discriminatory purpose or effect of the law or measure in question does not necessarily force the analysis into a comparison between interstate traders and intrastate traders. Moreover, the perception that a non-discrimination norm is somehow tantamount to immunity for traders is not accurate. In *Betfair Pty Ltd v Racing New South Wales*, French CJ, Gummow, Hayne, Crennan and Bell JJ suggested that discrimination between interstate traders and intra-state traders does not, without more, prompt the infringement of section 92: '[n]ot every measure which has an adverse effect between competitors will attract the operation of s 92'.[48] As a statement of principle, this remark is without fault. However, a proper understanding of discrimination in trade is not dependent on the effect of a given law or measure on individual traders but on market access for those traders.

Despite these critiques, on a functionalist interpretation, discrimination need not be the sole criterion of invalidity. It should not be either. As Kiefel J said in *Betfair Pty Ltd v Racing New South Wales* 'the requirement of protectionism is both relevant and necessary'.[49] A norm based exclusively on non-discrimination would lose interpretative legitimacy in the face of the problem of circularity. The problem is that if one identifies a certain value—free trade—in a certain provision—section 92—one

[42] (2012) 249 CLR 217, 268.
[43] ibid 272.
[44] ibid 286.
[45] ibid 289.
[46] (2012) 249 CLR 217.
[47] ibid 266 (French CJ, Gummow, Hayne, Crennan and Bell JJ): '[a]t times, and despite its disclaimers, in the argument presented by Betfair to this Court, it appeared to rely upon the "individual rights" theory of s 92 which was left behind in *Cole v Whitfield*'.
[48] ibid 265.
[49] ibid 293.

then needs to use that same value to interpret the function of that same provision. The problem of circularity is especially significant if the relevant value is not found in more than one provision and is, therefore, not capable of being applied to more than one provision. That is true of the value of free trade, which, with perhaps the exceptions of sections 99 and 117, can only ever apply to section 92. The problem does not concern the value of free trade but rather its application by the High Court. To recognise free trade as an Australian constitutional value is not the same as to prescribe the amount of weight that the High Court should give to that value. The High Court is free to give the value of free trade either limited weight, through viewing it as checked by regulatory purposes (a protectionist norm) or very significant weight, through viewing it as unchecked by regulatory—for example, health and safety—purposes (a non-discrimination norm). On either approach, the High Court would be giving section 92 a functionalist interpretation.

The High Court interprets the freedom of interstate trade under section 92 to mean a freedom of interstate trade not from discrimination but from discriminatory protectionism, an invalidity test that transforms the section into, effectively, an anti-protectionist norm. On the premise that a federal market can only function efficiently and, thus, create trade and wealth—prosperity—if interstate trade is free from all regulatory discrimination, the easy argument to make would be that the interpretation of section 92 by the High Court does not align the value of free trade with its function to create a national market for national prosperity. It would be to argue that an anti-protectionist norm causes the national market to function inefficiently because it can validate laws and measures that discriminate against interstate trade if they are not protectionist. But it would be a circular argument.

Should the value of free trade mean an appropriately regulated market (anti-protectionist norm) or an absolutely free market (a non-discrimination norm)? It is a question of weight—a question of judgement—the answer to which should produce reasonable differences of opinion. It is a contestable judgement.

On a functionalist interpretation of section 92, therefore, discrimination neither needs to, nor should be, the sole criterion of invalidity. The High Court in *Cole v Whitfield* correctly recognised the value of free trade in the Constitution through section 92 and then chose to give that value a middle weight, between the one extreme of anti-protectionism and the other extreme of non-discrimination, a compromise which it named, rather uninventively, as discriminatory protectionism. Thus, the High Court's interpretation of section 92 is a compromise, a necessary compromise, between an anti-protectionist trade norm and a non-discrimination trade norm and, more importantly, between the value of free trade—with its function to create a national market for national prosperity—and other Australian constitutional values.

That twofold compromise is most evident in the saving test that the High Court developed for section 92. Discriminatory protectionism tests the invalidity of a law or measure under challenge for an alleged contravention of section 92. However, the High Court retains the discretion to save that law or measure even if, in principle, it contravenes the section. Some regulation of intrastate and interstate trade and commerce is necessary.

In *Castlemaine Tooheys Ltd v South Australia*, the High Court turned to the principle of proportionality as the criterion upon which to decide the saving test. Thus, if the purpose of the law or measure under challenge is to achieve a non-protectionist purpose and the means that it adopts—that is, the burdens that it imposes on interstate trade and commerce—are appropriate and adapted to the achievement of that purpose, then the law or measure is valid under section 92:[50]

> The freedom from discriminatory burdens of a protectionist kind postulated by s 92 does not deny to the legislature of a State power to enact legislation for the well-being of the people of that State unless the legislation is relevantly discriminatory. Accordingly, interstate trade, as well as intrastate trade, must submit to such regulation as may be necessary or appropriate and adapted either to the protection of the community from a real danger or threat to its welfare or to the enhancement of its welfare.[51]

The rationale for the saving test is the need for compromise, that is, the need for reasonable regulation of interstate trade and commerce in order to maintain the 'peace, order, and good government' of Australia, including the promotion of other Australian constitutional values:

> The exercise by a person of a right to a constitutionally guaranteed freedom can be regulated and controlled by government in order to preserve the rights and freedoms of others, without denying the individual that freedom secured by the *Constitution*. It is upon this basis that the reasonable regulation of interstate trade, commerce and intercourse is permissible under s 92.[52]

It is important to accept that 'some burdening of incoming trade is unavoidable if governments are to retain the ability to regulate effectively in the interests of health, safety, the environment, and other non-economic goals'.[53] This test of proportionality

[50] ibid 295 (Kiefel J). For the economic effect of the law or measure under challenge upon competition in the national market, see *Samuels v Readers' Digest Association Pty Ltd* (1969) 120 CLR 1 (Barwick CJ). See also *Castlemaine Tooheys v Western Australia* (1990) 169 CLR 436, 472 (Mason CJ, Brennan, Deane, Dawson and Toohey JJ); *Cole v Whitfield* (1988) 165 CLR 360, 408; *Betfair Pty Ltd v Western Australia* (2008) 234 CLR 418, 464, 477 (Gleeson CJ, Gummow, Kirby, Hayne, Crennan, and Kiefel JJ). This saving test is a kind of public interest exception to s 92. For a proposal to incorporate the public interest exception to s 92 into the interpretation of art 8 of China's anti-monopoly law, see H Makeham, 'Comparing Apples with Oranges? Drawing Lessons from the Australian Constitutional Experience with the Anti-Monopoly Law of the People's Republic of China' (2010) 40 *Hong Kong Law Journal* 129. For a comparison with art 28 of the Treaty on the Functioning of the European Union, see G Villalta Puig, 'Free Movement of Goods: The European Experience in the Australian Context' (2001) 75 *Australian Law Journal* 639; G Villalta Puig, 'A European Saving Test for Section 92 of the Australian Constitution' (2008) 13(1) *Deakin Law Review* 99; G Villalta Puig, 'The Significance of the Free Trade Jurisprudence of the Court of Justice of the European Union to the Constitutional Development of the Australian Single Market' (2009) 16(1–2) *Irish Journal of European Law* 131; G Villalta Puig, 'Section 92 of the Australian Constitution and the Court of Justice of the European Union' (paper presented at the Research Project Forum Series of the Centre for Financial Regulation and Economic Development, Chinese University of Hong Kong, 14 January 2013). See further Staker, 'Section 92 of the Constitution and the European Court of Justice', above n 41; Staker, 'Free Movement of Goods', above n 36; D Geradin and R Stewardson, 'Trade and Environment: Some Lessons from *Castlemaine Tooheys* (Australia) and *Danish Bottles* (European Community)' (1995) 44 *International & Comparative Law Quarterly* 41; P Smith, 'Free Movement of Goods within the EC and s 92 of the Australian Constitution' (1998) 72 *Australian Law Journal* 465; Kiefel, above n 16; Anthony Mason, 'European Constitutionalism: Lessons for Australia' (1998) 21 *UNSW Law Journal* 150.

[51] (1990) 169 CLR 436, 472, 473 (Mason CJ, Brennan, Deane, Dawson and Toohey JJ).

[52] B O'Brien, 'Inchoate Rights to Interstate Communications under Section 92' (1981) 13 *Melbourne University Law Review* 198, 218.

[53] A Simpson, 'Grounding the High Court's Modern Section 92 Jurisprudence: The Case for Improper Purpose as the Touchstone' (2005) 33 *Federal Law Review* 445, 464, 477.

finds support in the High Court's recent reaffirmation of legitimate purposes in *McCloy v New South Wales*.[54] In a statement that could well apply to the law of section 92 after *Cole v Whitfield*, the joint judgment of French CJ, Kiefel, Bell and Keane JJ stated:

> The freedom under the Australian Constitution ... is not an absolute freedom. It may be subject to legislative restrictions serving a legitimate purpose compatible with the system of representative government for which the Constitution provides, where the extent of the burden can be justified as suitable, necessary and adequate, having regard to the purpose of those restrictions.[55]

Is the law or measure in question suitable? Is it necessary? Is it adequate? In other words, does it have a legitimate purpose? The joint judgment helpfully defines what the High Court means by legitimate purpose:

> A legitimate purpose is one which is compatible with the system of representative government provided for by the Constitution; which is to say that the purpose does not impede the functioning of that system and all that it entails. So too must the means chosen to achieve the statutory object be compatible with that system.[56]

With the support of *McCloy v New South Wales*, the element of proportionality in the saving test for section 92 creates a gap between the normative interpretation of free trade as an absolutely free market and the alternative normative interpretation of free trade as an appropriately regulated market. That gap in the actual development of the law of section 92 acknowledges that free trade is indeed an Australian constitutional value but not one that is absolute. It is a value that the High Court wants to coexist with other Australian constitutional values, including environmental and consumer protection, health and safety, or, to give a more specific example, the integrity of the food supply. Plant or animal diseases may, to follow that example through, warrant discriminatory laws or measures. Substantive discrimination can be consistent with laws and measures that formally discriminate against interstate trade but find justification for that discriminatory purpose in alternative values. Those alternative, countervailing values, which the High Court implicitly recognises through the saving test for section 92, have equal constitutional weight to the value of free trade, be it either on a non-discrimination interpretation or an anti-protectionist one. Those values have significance in Australian constitutional law because, to some extent, they trump the value of free trade. Thus, whatever normative vision of the value of free trade one may have—free market or otherwise—ultimately, the High Court is free to decide the weight that it considers just to give that value and, in the exercise of that freedom, still operate within the boundaries of a functionalist interpretation. Free trade is, certainly, a value in the Australian Constitution but it is not an absolute value to the exclusion of all others. There are competing values, in terms of the need to regulate certain topic areas that may relate to the locality or the particular environment and so provide justifiable reasons for limiting free trade. It is a question of balance. It is, in the end, a question of weight, necessarily so.

[54] *McCloy v New South Wales* (2015) 257 CLR 178, 193–94 (French CJ, Kiefel, Bell and Keane JJ).
[55] ibid 193–95.
[56] ibid 203.

IV. TRADE AND COMMERCE POWER

This chapter calls on the High Court to take a functionalist approach to the interpretation of the value of free trade in section 92 and the rest of the economic constitution, including the trade and commerce power under section 51(i) of the Constitution. In that respect, further to the argument that this chapter made above, to acknowledge free trade as a value is not to prescribe the amount of weight that the High Court should give to that value. One may agree or disagree with the weight that the High Court gave or did not give to the value of free trade in *Cole v Whitfield*, but, irrespective of its weight allocation, the High Court's interpretative formula of discriminatory protectionism is still functionalist for it comes from the value behind section 92 itself. The same, however, is not true of section 51(i) on international trade and commerce. Its interpretation by the High Court is not functionalist and would certainly benefit from an alternative interpretation that takes account of the Australian constitutional values behind the provision. And the key value for that alternative interpretation should be free trade. There is scope for free trade, as an Australian constitutional value, to inform the scope of section 51(i), a claim which suggests that more free trade could well be possible outside section 92.

The higher the inefficiency of the national market, the lower the competitiveness of Australia in the global market.[57] The value of free trade, therefore, should extend to the national market as an external market. But it currently does not. In *Pape v Commissioner of Taxation* and earlier cases, the High Court has refused to dismantle the distinction between international (or interstate) trade and intrastate trade for the purposes of the power to regulate and, thereby, facilitate external trade under section 51(i).[58] With that refusal, the High Court refuses to acknowledge that trade and commerce in Australia is one indivisible whole. In *Pape v Commissioner of Taxation*, Heydon J said:

> Section 51(i) ... compels a distinction between trade and commerce with other countries, and among the States, on the one hand, and other forms of trade and commerce, on the other. It does not permit an argument that trade and commerce in Australia is one indivisible whole. Nor does it permit an argument that any legislation having an effect on trade and commerce in Australia must inevitably have an effect on trade and commerce with other countries, and among the States.[59]

The distinction between international (or interstate) and intrastate trade and commerce causes the national market to function inefficiently because it allows the development of multiple and sometimes contradictory regulatory frameworks: the Commonwealth can regulate those aspects of intrastate trade and commerce that are physically integrated into international (or interstate) trade and commerce but only the States can regulate the economic aspects of that integration.

The premise is that 'efficiency is understood as a "good" according to the standard economic explanation'.[60] On that premise, the efficiency of the constitutional

[57] Smith, above n 50, 477. See also Villalta Puig, 'Free Movement of Goods', above n 50, 641–44.

[58] A Gray, 'Reinvigorating the Trade and Commerce Power' (2015) 43 *Australian Business Law Review* 101.

[59] *Pape v Commissioner of Taxation* (2009) 238 CLR 1, 150, 151.

[60] Simpson, 'Grounding the High Court's Modern Section 92 Jurisprudence', above n 53.

value of free trade stems from the economic value of free trade, namely, the benefits that efficiency, as the sum of comparative advantage and geographical specialisation, brings to the process of 'economic and national integration'.[61] In *Betfair Pty Ltd v Western Australia*, the High Court mused:

> Looking at the subject of domestic protectionism and the operation of section 92, it may be suggested that the emergence of global institutions, including the International Labour Organization (1919), the General Agreement on Tariffs and Trade (1947) and the World Trade Organization (1995) ... appear to be premised on the economic value of 'free trade'.[62]

The rationale behind free trade as an Australian constitutional value is the promotion of the prosperity of the nation, both as a collective group of individual consumers and as an internal *and* external market.[63]

Much to the dismay of the Business Council of Australia (BCA),[64] it seems, efficiency is an irrelevant consideration for the free trade jurisprudence of the High Court.[65] Such an attitude is unsustainable. In this respect, David McCann observes, '[t]he High Court's narrow approach to the power is difficult to sustain theoretically and presents a technical account of commerce that is increasingly incompatible with a modern national economy'.[66]

This observation is particularly true in the age of economic globalisation. Extra-curially, Sir Anthony Mason agrees:

> With the advent of rapid transportation and communication, and the development of modern technology, trade within each state has become intricately connected with inter-state and overseas trade. And the nationalization of the economy has necessarily expanded the concept of inter-state trade to embrace activities and transactions that formerly had local significance only. These developments might conceivably justify a re-interpretation of the trade and commerce power, the existing interpretation of which may be anchored in the artifices of legal formalism.[67]

[61] *Victoria v Commonwealth* (1971) 122 CLR 353, 396 (Windeyer J) (*Payroll Tax Case*).

[62] (2008) 234 CLR 418, 459 (Gleeson CJ, Gummow, Kirby, Hayne, Crennan and Kiefel JJ). Principles of international trade law are outside the jurisprudence of the High Court but they are, nevertheless, helpful to questions of interpretation: A Simpson, 'The (Limited) Significance if the Individual in Section 117: State Residence Discrimination' (2008) 32 *Melbourne University Law Review* 639, 660, 661. To what extent should one look at international elements to understand Australian constitutional values?

[63] Simpson, 'Grounding the High Court's Modern Section 92 Jurisprudence', above n 53. See also Villalta Puig, 'Free Movement of Goods', above n 50, 648–51.

[64] Business Council of Australia, *Towards a Seamless Economy: Modernising the Regulation of Australian Business* (Report, 17 March 2008): <www.bca.com.au/docs/1DB6ED89-DBA0-4A51-BFBB-05ECD33C28C5/towardsaseamlesseconomy_final_17-3-2008.pdf>; Business Council of Australia, *Reshaping Australia's Federalism: A New Contract for Federal–State Relations* (Report, 28 October 2006): www.bca.com.au/docs/D7F56812-9AD9-4829-9192-7C94088E7CB7/combined-full-version-action-plan_28-10-2006.pdf; Business Council of Australia, *A Charter for New Federalism* (Report, 18 December 2007): www.bca.com.au/publications/a-charter-for-new-federalism.

[65] F Wheeler, 'Commonwealth Power over Infrastructure: Constitutional Tools for National Economic Regulation' (2007) 2 *Public Policy* 195, 206.

[66] D McCann, 'First Head Revisited: A Single Industrial Relations System under the Trade and Commerce Power' (2004) 26 *Sydney Law Review* 75, 78.

[67] A Mason, 'Towards 2001: Minimalism, Monarchism or Metamorphism?' (1995) 21 *Monash University Law Review* 1, 11. See also A Mason, 'The Australian Constitution 1901–1988' (1988) 62 *Australian Law Journal* 752; R French, 'The Incredible Shrinking Federation: Voyage to a Singular State?' in G Appleby, N Aroney and T John (eds), *The Future of Australian Federalism: Comparative and Interdisciplinary Perspectives* (Cambridge, Cambridge University Press, 2002).

McCann gives an example:

> If my local corner shop accepts payment for the nationally produced morning paper using an EFTPOS [Electronic Funds Transfer at Point of Sale] system maintained on a computer in India, it seems patently artificial to attempt to maintain that that paper purchase is *outside* constitutional commerce.[68]

The idea that section 51(i) does not recognise trade in Australia to be *one indivisible whole* is contrary to the value of free trade. It gives rise to a legal fiction as the High Court seeks to divide the indivisible.[69] This fiction reacts to the *Cole v Whitfield* test for invalidity under section 92, even though, at the time of judgment, 'it had become obvious that, if Australia was to maintain even its declining prosperity, it had to become a more competitive society'.[70] The internal market is an extension of the economic infrastructure of any nation and '[i]t is generally accepted that inefficient and inadequate infrastructure is impeding Australia's ... capacity to compete internationally'.[71]

The BCA has, in recent years, called for the creation of a truly national market and the 'removal of other impediments to global competition for Australian business'.[72] Thus, in its report of 2008, *Towards a Seamless Economy: Modernizing the Regulation of Australian Business*, the BCA found that 'as barriers to international trade and investment fall, the relative impact of internal trade barriers increases'.[73] Additionally, the BCA found that: 'Studies conducted in federations like the European Union and Canada highlight the importance of considering internal markets within a global context, and the importance of having well-integrated internal markets to support external trade and investment policies'.[74] The White Paper process on the Reform of the Federation corroborates the BCA's findings.[75] The Issues Paper states:

> Having multiple governments invariably leads to multiple legal and regulatory systems. This can make it harder for businesses to operate in more than one jurisdiction, can hinder

[68] D McCann, above n 66, 100.

[69] PE Nygh, 'An Analysis of Judicial Approaches to the Interpretation of the Commerce Clause in Australia and the United States' (1967) 5 *Sydney Law Review* 353, 361–65.

[70] M McHugh, 'The Constitutional Jurisprudence of the High Court: 1989–2004' (2008) 30 *Sydney Law Review* 5, 11. The former judge made the point that, while the decision in *Cole v Whitfield* was certainly radical, the rationale that the High Court followed to reach it was rather conventional.

[71] Wheeler, above n 65. See also Organisation for Economic Co-operation and Development, *Economic Surveys: Australia 2006* (Survey Report, 31 July 2016) ch 4.

[72] K Wiltshire, 'Australian Federalism: The Business Perspective' (2008) 3 *UNSW Law Journal* 583, 584.

[73] Business Council of Australia, *Towards a Seamless Economy*, above n 64: <www.bca.com.au/docs/1DB6ED89-DBA0-4A51-BFBB-05ECD33C28C5/towardsaseamlesseconomy_final_17-3-2008.pdf>, 10, 13. See also Business Council of Australia, *Reshaping Australia's Federalism: A New Contract for Federal–State Relations* (Report, 28 October 2006): www.bca.com.au/publications/reshaping-australias-federation-a-new-contract-for-federal-state-relations: 'we live in a globalizing world and increasingly, many issues require a national response ... From a business perspective, Australia could greatly benefit from completing the task begun with federation of establishing a true Australian common market': at 43; Business Council of Australia, *A Charter for New Federalism*, above n 64. See also A Gray, 'State-Based Business Licensing in Australia: The Constitution, Economics and International Perspectives' (2009) 14 *Deakin Law Review* 165, 167.

[74] Business Council of Australia, *Towards a Seamless Economy*, above n 64, 10, 13; see also C Livingstone, 'President's Address' (speech delivered at Business Council of Australia Annual Dinner, Sydney, 10 November 2011).

[75] Department of Foreign Affairs and Trade, 'Trading Our Way to More Jobs and Prosperity' (Trade Policy Statement, April 2011) 13: '[d]uring the period of high trade barriers, heavily-protected Australian

businesses' competitiveness in export markets, and can frustrate the efficient operation of national markets.[76]

A broader, functionalist free trade interpretation of section 51(i) could give the Commonwealth an equally broader head of power to enact a new competition law regime than it presently has available under the corporations power. If the Commonwealth hopes to advance competition-based principles rather than merely anti-protectionist purposes, the value of free trade could well facilitate that competency. In the end, the principle of equal opportunity of interstate competition lies at the core of the concept of a national market. Ironically, in *Cole v Whitfield*, the High Court admitted that the function of free trade is to give 'equality of trade'.[77] The reality, as Heydon J perceived in *Betfair Pty Ltd v Racing New South Wales*,[78] is that it is not only burdens that can sabotage the national market. Benefits can also have the same effect.

The development by the Council of Australian Governments (COAG) of a National Competition Policy is an intergovernmental acknowledgment of the economic value of free trade as the paradigm of competition.[79] The 'guiding principle' of that policy 'is that legislation … should not restrict competition'.[80] Two further COAG initiatives—the National Partnership Agreement to Deliver a Seamless National Economy and the White Paper on the Reform of the Federation—also acknowledge the economic value of free trade.

Similarly, a broader, functionalist free trade interpretation of section 51(xxix)—the external affairs power—could give the Commonwealth an equally broader head of power to confidently implement the kind of new generation, deep and comprehensive trade and investment agreements that Australia has, in recent years, concluded with individual countries and groups of countries in the style of the China–Australia Free Trade Agreement and the Trans-Pacific Partnership agreement. Otherwise, at that high level of bilateral and regional economic integration, a conservative free trade thesis is likely to limit the effectiveness of the High Court's policy of proportioning treaty implementation under the external affairs power, especially in the context of the incidental power under section 51(xxxix) and, possibly, the kind of proportionality

businesses sold their products and services not into a single Australian market but into a set of small, fragmented markets. As governments have gradually lowered protective barriers the Australian economy should have been making the transition to a single national market—a seamless national economy'. See also Department of Foreign Affairs and Trade, 'Winning in World Markets: Meeting the Competitive Challenge of the New Global Economy, Review of Export Policies and Programs' (Review Report, September 2008); Productivity Commission, 'Bilateral and Regional Trade Agreements' (Research Report, 13 December 2010).

[76] Department of the Prime Minister and Cabinet, 'A Federation for Our Future: Reform of the Federation White Paper' (Issues Paper No 1, 12 September 2014) 2.

[77] (1988) 165 CLR 360, 391 (Mason CJ, Wilson, Brennan, Deane, Dawson, Toohey and Gaudron JJ).

[78] (2012) 249 CLR 217, 274 (Heydon J): '[a] court faced with a section 92 challenge must assess whether an impugned law discriminates by burdening interstate trade or commerce to its competitive disadvantage or by benefiting intrastate trade or commerce to its competitive advantage'.

[79] The High Court in *Betfair Pty Ltd v Western Australia* (2008) 234 CLR 418 noted that 'the greater the degree of implementation of the National Competition Policy, the less the occasion for recourse to section 92': at 453 (Gleeson CJ, Gummow, Kirby, Hayne, Crennan and Kiefel JJ).

[80] National Competition Council, 'Competition Principles Agreement' (Policy Document, 11 April 1995) cl 5(1). See also National Competition Council, 'Compendium of National Competition Policy Agreements' (Policy Document No 2, June 1998).

test that the *Industrial Relations Act Case* established for the implementation of treaties.[81] Such a reading is well overdue in the light of the 'strongly nationalist approach to constitutional construction'[82] that informs the interpretation of the High Court since its decision in *Amalgamated Society of Engineers v Adelaide Steamship Co Ltd* and, in particular, *New South Wales v Commonwealth* (*Work Choices*).[83]

These efforts would not be so necessary if the High Court would give Australia's economic constitution a functionalist interpretation as a non-discrimination norm. Ultimately, the creation of a national market relies on 'judicial power as an extraordinary constitutional constraint' on governmental power in the interest of 'political accountability to the Australian people as a whole'.[84] Without that extraordinary constraint, the joint judgment in *Betfair Pty Ltd v Western Australia* acknowledged that 'legislators in one political subdivision, such as the States, may be susceptible to pressures which encourage decisions adverse to the commercial and other interests of those who are not their constituents and not their taxpayers'.[85] Cooperative working arrangements aside, business concerns remain and constant are calls for 'the removal of past ambiguities in constitutional wording, particularly in respect of the "free trade" provisions, thereby casting aside restrictive High Court interpretations'.[86]

V. CONCLUSION

This chapter submits that free trade is an Australian constitutional value. It further submits that the function of free trade as an Australian constitutional value is to promote the prosperity of Australians through the creation of a market for Australia. The chapter furthermore submits that such an interpretation is born of compromise: a necessary compromise between an anti-protectionist norm and a non-discrimination norm and an equally necessary compromise between the value of free trade and other Australian constitutional values.

Indeed, the judgment of Kiefel J in *Betfair Pty Ltd v Racing New South Wales* suggests that competition and consumer protection may be the ultimate value over and above free trade. Her Honour acknowledged the prospect that the test of discriminatory protectionism may, eventually, translate into constitutional invalidity for laws or measures that substantially lessen competition in the national market, irrespective of State boundaries. This translation would thus preclude any 'purely

[81] '[W]hether the law selects means which are reasonably capable of being considered appropriate and adapted to achieving the purpose or object of giving effect to the treaty, so that the law is one upon a subject which is an aspect of external affairs': *Victoria v Commonwealth* (1996) 187 CLR 416, 488 (Brennan CJ, Toohey, Gaudron, McHugh and Gummow JJ) (*Industrial Relations Act Case*).

[82] Wheeler, above n 65, 200.

[83] *Amalgamated Society of Engineers v Adelaide Steamship Co Ltd* (1920) 28 CLR 129; *New South Wales v Commonwealth* (2006) 229 CLR 1 (*Work Choices Case*).

[84] Gageler, above n 14.

[85] (2008) 234 CLR 418, 459 (Gleeson CJ, Gummow, Kirby, Hayne, Crennan and Kiefel JJ).

[86] Wiltshire, above n 72, 615.

geographical approach to the identification of a discriminatory burden on interstate trade' as the decision in *Betfair Pty Ltd v Western Australia* may suggest.[87]

Kiefel J grappled with the possibility that competition law might complement the free trade jurisprudence of the High Court in an acknowledgement of the wider economic implications of restrictive trade practices in Australia:

> [I]nsights from competition law may reveal that the practical operation of a facially neutral law discriminates against interstate trade or commerce in a way that may merit characterisation of the law as protectionist. That is because insights drawn from the economic theory of competition are useful to explain the effects of a legislative or other measure upon trade in a market. Such insights have long informed discourse on s 92. Even if it has not always been necessary to identify the effect of burdens on interstate trade in economic terms, it is evident that the focus of the courts has always been upon whether interstate trade was prevented or disadvantaged in its ability to compete within a market.[88]

Saying that 'a necessary step in establishing protectionism [is] the identification of a competitive disadvantage',[89] Kiefel J is not entirely right to insist on protectionism as a criterion of invalidity even if it is through the filter of competition law. The concern of the High Court ought to be with equal opportunity of market access and not with competitive disadvantage. In other words, market access should be the controlling criterion. This largely doctrinal point, however, may be of little consequence in practice if an anti-competitive test has the intended effect, that is, the removal of protectionism as the criterion of constitutional invalidity 'in a market which operates without reference to State boundaries'.[90]

After all, Kiefel J admitted to the possibility that a market competition norm might arise from future interpretations of section 92 to supplant the anti-protectionist norm of *Cole v Whitfield*:

> Such a principle may treat as undesirable any effect of substance lessening the ability of those in a market to compete and require, as a justification, that measures which have that effect are necessary to the achievement of their objective. If such a principle were applied in cases involving s 92, the requirement that a legislative or other measure be seen as protectionist in effect may not be essential.[91]

The development of a market competition norm for section 92 would signal the triumph of competition and consumer protection as the ultimate value of Australia's economic constitution over and above free trade. Competition and consumer protection would safeguard both the physical welfare (individual health and safety) and economic welfare (end-user surplus) of consumers of goods and services in the Australian market as a paramount criterion of constitutional interpretation.

[87] Betfair Pty Ltd, 'Appellant's Reply to Submissions of Parties and Interveners on the Court's Letter Dated 8 September 2011', Submission in *Betfair Pty Ltd v Racing New South Wales*, S116/2011, 12 October 2011, [3] (Young QC).

[88] *Betfair Pty Ltd v Racing New South Wales* (2012) 249 CLR 217, 290, 291 (Kiefel J).

[89] ibid 291 (Kiefel J).

[90] ibid 293 (Kiefel J).

[91] ibid 291, 292 (Kiefel J).

The value of competition and consumer protection would more easily delineate the interpretative boundaries of the economic constitution than the value of free trade because, unlike free trade, competition and consumer protection recognises the need, in the public interest, to regulate inefficient and inequitable market practices. And it would be in alignment with developments in economic theory since *Cole v Whitfield*.[92] Thus, on the premise that free trade can never be an absolute value to the exclusion of all others, the value of competition and consumer protection would more effectively reconcile alternative values that have equal standing and force in Australian constitutional law.

To conclude, this chapter calls on the High Court to take a functionalist approach to the interpretation of the value of free trade in section 92 and the rest of the economic constitution, including the trade and commerce power under section 51(i) of the Constitution. On a functionalist interpretation of the value of free trade in Australia's economic constitution, the High Court should understand the national market as an area for trade creation that increases welfare through choice for consumers and optimises resource allocation for producers and, thereby, promotes national prosperity. A functionalist interpretation may read in terms of a market competition norm against any law or measure that reduces sales.

[92] Kiefel, above n 16, 15.

Index

www.ingramcontent.com/pod-product-compliance
Lightning Source LLC
Chambersburg PA
CBHW081210180926
51613CB00003B/204
* 9 7 8 1 5 0 9 9 1 8 4 0 9 *